Justine Ward

AND SOLESMES

Justine Ward

AND SOLESMES

Dom Combe

The Catholic University of America Press
Washington, D.C. 20064

ACKNOWLEDGMENT

The article "Dom Mocquereau of Solesmes" taken from *Orate Fratres* (now *Worship*) March, 1930, p. 199, published by the Liturgical Press, Collegeville, MN, reprinted by permission.

Translation by Philipe de Lacoste, LL.D., and Guillemine de Lacoste, Ph.D.

Photo on jacket taken from 1953 drawing by Albert Murray.

The Catholic University of America Press
Washington, D.C. 20064

CONTENTS

FOREWORD

Justine Ward's attachment to Dom Mocquereau as a person and to his rhythmic doctrine, is known by everyone. Thus, it will not be surprising to see the Abbey of Solesmes pay homage to her in these rather brief pages. Her correspondence with Solesmes, which we will use largely, will enable the reader to know better her rich personality. This is the main objective of this essay, for we could not consider Justine Ward's entire musical activity here. Indeed, in order to discuss her pedagogical Method with competence, it would be necessary to have practiced it and to have experienced its value and fruitfulness, which are evidenced by the immense success it still knows today. And even in order to talk about her musical activity in the service of Gregorian chant, it would be necessary to have access to the archives of the different centers she supported and inspired with her tireless zeal.

Concerning the letters of Justine Ward sent to Solesmes, we must indicate that her prolonged and very frequent sojourns in Sablé, near the Abbey, deprived us of her usual correspondence with Dom Mocquereau; indeed, from 1920, the year in which Justine Ward made Dom Mocquereau's acquaintance, to 1930, the year of his death, Justine Ward spent a good part of her time in Sablé. Moreover, Dom Mocquereau destroyed many of the letters he received during Justine Ward's stays in America, and we regret this all the more since those which were preserved are most interesting. We have a few letters from 1920 to 1927, and all those from October 1928 to the end of 1929, which are quite valuable since they retrace in great detail the beginnings of the School of Liturgical Music of Catholic University in Washington. Justine Ward spent a great deal of time in America in order to follow this foundation closely, as she was very interested in its development.

On the other hand, the letters of Dom Mocquereau to Justine Ward have all been preserved since she entrusted them to the Abbey when she had to return to America in May 1941; but it is difficult to use them when we do not have the letters which they answer.

After the death of Dom Mocquereau in January 1930, Justine Ward stayed in touch with Dom Joseph Gajard, his successor. The letters to Dom Gajard are still numerous, though more occasional. It is not a regular correspondence, such as the one she had with Dom Mocquereau (as we can see in the replies). On the other hand, the letters span 40 years, with no letters, of course, during the long and frequent sojourns of Justine Ward in Sablé.

Selections from Justine Ward's journal enable us to fill in some gaps. But this journal, which begins in 1920 with Dom Mocquereau's first trip to America, ends in 1938.

This essay is in two parts: 1) The First Part deals with Justine Ward's relationship with Dom Mocquereau, 2) The Second Part deals with her relationship with Dom Gajard.

In this essay, we let the documents speak for themselves, as the Dom Mocquereau Schola Cantorum Foundation wished; this forced us, practically, to follow the chronological order very closely. It seems, however, that the story is more lively and realistic in this way.

Facts themselves have imposed the following plan:

1) Dom Mocquereau's two sojourns in America and Justine Ward's first sojourns at Quarr Abbey (Solesmes' asylum in 1901) were decisive for two reasons: on the one hand, Justine Ward discovered the rhythmic doctrine of Dom Mocquereau and, on the other hand, she discovered how the Monks' Choir interpreted it under his direction (Ch.I, *Decisive Years, 1920–1922*).

2) Certain interventions by Justine Ward revealed that she was a faithful and exacting disciple of the master (Ch.II, *Work and Discussions*).

3) The Foundation of the School of Liturgical Music in Washington and that of the Dom Mocquereau Schola Cantorum Foundation reveal her tireless zeal in the service of Gregorian chant and of the Solesmes rhythmic principles (Ch.III, *Foundation of the School of Liturgical Music in Washington*).

4) After Dom Mocquereau's death, Justine Ward recognized in Dom Gajard his faithful successor and brought him her support, especially in respect to the diffusion of the records made under his direction, whose high spiritual and artistic value she appreciated (Ch.IV to V).

Justine Ward's attachment to Solesmes, which is obvious throughout these pages, was based only on her love for Liturgy and Gregorian chant, to which she devoted her whole life in order to respond to the wishes of His Holiness Pius X, concerning sacred music.

Unless indicated otherwise, Justine Ward's letters were all addressed to Dom Mocquereau[1] and Dom Mocquereau's letters were all addressed to Justine Ward: they are dated from the Abbey (Quarr Abbey and Solesmes from 1922 on).

Dom Pierre Marie Combe, O.S.B.
Abbaye St. Pierre de Solesmes

[1]The letters of Justine Ward to D. Mocquereau are written in French. The style, sometimes incorrect, was respected in the French version of this essay in order not to distort the thought of the author.

PART ONE
JUSTINE WARD AND DOM MOCQUEREAU

Chapter I

DECISIVE YEARS 1920–1922

Dom Mocquereau in America (1920)

When Justine Ward met Dom Mocquereau, she had been a Catholic for several years and had already devoted herself to the dissemination of liturgical music and particularly of Gregorian chant. She mentions explicitly the origins of this life goal on the occasion of the 25th anniversary of the November 22, 1903 *Motu Proprio* on sacred music of His Holiness Pius X: "What memories this anniversary must bring you!" she wrote to Dom Mocquereau, "and what struggles to reach this first triumph! For me likewise! I was not a Catholic yet (she was to become a Catholic in 1904) but this papal document made a profound impression on me and I had already promised myself that when I was received into the Catholic Church I would work for this good cause" (Mora Vocis, Nov. 22, 1928). At the time of her conversion, Justine Ward was 25 years old. She was born on August 7, 1879, in Morristown, New Jersey, and had been married since 1901, to George Cabot Ward. It seems that Father John B. Young, Jesuit, of St. Francis Xavier Church in New York[1], was the spiritual guide who directed her towards the Catholic Church. He had previously initiated her to Gregorian music, of which he was the first pioneer in America (*Revue Grégorienne,* 1923, p. 32). But Father William Pardow, whose biography she wrote in 1914, could also have been at the origin of her conversion to Catholicism.[2]

However, Justine Ward did not immediately consecrate herself entirely to the propagation of an authentic religious music. She began at first, from 1905 to 1910, to write various articles for Catholic reviews and especially for the *Atlantic Monthly,* in order to promote the development of liturgical music. Indeed, she had been greatly disappointed to note that music in Catholic churches was often of inferior quality and she deplored the mediocrity of this "musiquette"—this word is often found in her letters—and the incomprehension with which the call of Pius X for a religious music worthy of the name was greeted.[3] She had learned that music does not leave one indifferent and that its educational role in the formation of souls is considerable because it acts directly on intelligence, will and sensitivity.

When Justine Ward met Father Thomas Shields in 1910, the event was decisive for her. She has related how her future was shaped definitely during a meal she had with the famous American educator who was dreaming of changing the teaching methods of primary education in the Catholic schools. He had written a remarkable set of small books, to be used sequentially over the years, in order to teach the child everything he or she could comprehend, according to a method better adapted to his or her capabilities. The subject of music had come up during the course of the meal. Since Justine Ward was visibly interested, the priest immediately showed his books to her and asked for her opinion concerning the music in them. She felt it was worthless and very frankly said so. Thereupon Father Shields asked her if she would agree to oversee the musical part of his manuals.[4] "Together—he for the pedagogy and I for the music—we prepared a practical method of music for children in Catholic schools. From the start, this method was directed toward Gregorian chant." Thus began the "Ward Method." Courses were immediately set up, whose first results were seen at Washington's Catholic University. Justine Ward thus says that her Method was, from the start, directed toward Gregorian chant. The Catholic Church revealed to her that its "liturgy is the primary and indispensable source of the true Christian spirit." Therefore, Gregorian chant, which is the Church's own liturgical chant, the chant it inherited from its oldest tradition, appeared at once to her as the ideal instrument offered by the Church itself, to make children participate actively in the sacred mysteries.

This led Justine Ward to found in 1916[5] in New York, at Manhattanville Academy run by the Sacred Heart nuns, the Pius X Institute of Liturgical Music to assist teachers in fulfilling their roles as musical and spiritual educators. Justine Ward taught at the Institute, together with Mother G. Stevens. The influence of the Institute was such that four years later, in 1920, Justine Ward was able to organize an International Congress of Gregorian Chant (the first one had taken place in Arezzo in 1882) with H.B. Gibbs, Mother Stevens and Joseph Bonnet (Paris), despite the episcopate's skepticism concerning the artistic value and popular character of this chant (Ward, S. Francis Camp, Sept. 19, 1920. *Rev. Gr.*, 1922, p. 69).

This Congress gave Justine Ward the opportunity to make another truly providential acquaintance after that of Doctor Shields, that of Dom Mocquereau, choirmaster at Solesmes. Justine Ward had already found in the rhythmic principles and in the chironomy of the *Nombre Musical Grégorien* means suitable to the achievement of her educator's dream.[6] But this meeting, this personal contact with Dom Mocquereau himself, was to give her a better understanding of his rhythmic doctrine, open new vistas in pedagogy and confirm her original objective: through the use of Gregorian chant, to encourage children to like the prayers of the Church, its liturgy and its worship, and to train cantors who would later in life become the praying and singing assembly so ardently desired by Pius X.

Had Justine Ward hesitated at first to make the choirmaster of Solesmes come from so far away? Why is it that she had at first thought of inviting Dom L. David?[7] Was the latter in America at the time? Justine Ward probably did not know the real situation, since Dom David did not follow Dom Mocquereau's principles. In any case, Justine Ward herself confirmed that, as Father

Vincent Donovan, O.P. had suggested, she asked Dom Mocquereau to direct the singing during the Congress (Mocquereau to Donovan, Jan. 28, 1920; Ward to D. Mocquereau, Mora Vocis, May 7, 1929). Dr. Harold Becket Gibbs may also have made a similar suggestion, since he was already in contact with Solesmes. (H. Gibbs to D. Mocquereau, Feb. 6 and Feb. 26, 1920.) The official invitation was sent by the archbishop of New York on February 18, 1920 (Cf. Appendix No. 1).

One month after having heard that Dom Mocquereau had accepted the invitation, Justine Ward wrote him a charming letter in which she talked about all the hopes that this visit was generating in and around her. This first letter gives the tone, so to speak, of her future relationship with Dom Mocquereau. Above all, the letter reflects the very profound religious sense which directed all the activities of Justine Ward. The call of Pius X for religious music, which coincided with her most intimate yearning, was already at that time the stimulus, the center of her whole life, which she wanted to make into "a response to the call of Pius X" (this is the title of a brochure published by Justine Ward in New York in 1922, Blanche M. Kelly, Editor).[8] The text of this letter follows:

18 East Tenth Street, March 25, 1920

Very Reverend Father,
   I have been trying for a long time to express the deep gratitude and the joy which is in all our American hearts because you are honoring us by crossing the sea to come and guide our first steps on the liturgical way and to encourage our love, very young still, for the sacred chant of the Church. But words are so cold and so commonplace—I need beautiful neums to express this to you. Because of this, I took refuge in silence—except for the few telegraphic words previously sent—but the fear that you should think I am ungrateful has given me the courage to write to you.
   You can easily imagine what joy we all share because of your great kindness to us when I say that your presence alone could make the dream of the lovers of Plain Chant in America come true by gathering all the little solitary flames into a great ardent fire.
   You will not expect perfection, will you? because I would not want you to be disillusioned—but you will find much goodwill and even some enthusiasm, especially among the nuns—and the future is in their hands. They will pass the beautiful flame on to the children—they are doing it already—and this is our promise for the future. You will perhaps see 5,000 children who will come to the Congress. These little ones will please you, I truly believe. As His Holiness Pius X said, 'Children will set a good example.' There is among them none of the personal vanity which is so obvious, unfortunately, among the older Congress members. We are suffering already lest this happen at a Congress which is dear to us—but all this suffering of the body and of the spirit is probably necessary in order to make a work of God. It is very trying, however—and it is a real excuse, Very Reverend Father, because strain and weakness did prevent me from writing to you and I left to the good Dr. Gibbs the pleasure of giving you all the details concerning the Congress.
   You are going to open a whole world of beauty for us, dear Dom Mocquereau; we have never known liturgy in America—it is ignored rather than neglected. It has to be created here. What a joy and what an honor it is that you accepted to guide our first steps—and it is the first steps that count. We shall try not to tire you too much, but rather, we shall prepare ourselves so

well ahead of time that we will be able to give you a little consolation. Furthermore, Dom Gatard will correct our mistakes—and we shall try to do well so that you will be happy with your little Americans. An old nun from the 'Middle West' wrote to me that the dream of her life has been to meet you and that she has obtained her Superior's permission to make the trip and to take part in the Congress. Then: her Nunc dimittis! You can see that you are welcome!

I hope that you will understand my poor French—but in any case, do believe, dear and Reverend Father, that although I express myself so badly, my heart is full of gratitude for this great kindness which you are bestowing on us.

Devotedly yours in Our Lord. Justine B. Ward (Cf. Appendix No. 2).

The 1920 New York Congress

Because of his great age, Dom Mocquereau had refused this invitation at first, then he accepted it with his Abbot's approval, when his request to be accompanied by Dom Gatard of the Abbey of Farnborough, who was a Solesmes veteran and one of his faithful disciples, was granted. The latter was to be his main assistant. Both arrived in New York three weeks before the Congress[9] and helped finalize the preparation of the various choirs which were to take part in the musical events, notably those of the Sacred Heart convents whose boarders were already well trained, and those of the seminaries. The general rehearsals took place in Saint Patrick's Cathedral. Dom Gatard even went to Philadelphia to prepare the students of the seminary there. (*Rev. Grég.*, 1920, Journal Mocquereau—Chronicle to his sister, cloistered nun at Sainte Cécile of Solesmes, pp. 32, 35, 52).

The Congress itself lasted only three days (June 1–3). But it was a beautiful gathering of several thousand performers and of the main leaders of the Gregorian movement in the United States. Every day there was a sung mass and vespers (except on the last day on which there were no vespers). The Proper was sung at mass by the students of a seminary, the Ordinary by the compact choir of priests, nuns, seminarians and students of colleges or schools. For vespers, the same groups sang alternately. But at mass on the first day, the Ordinary was sung by the 3,500 school children of the 47 Catholic schools of New York (Congress Program. Cf. Appendix No. 6). Generally, the cantors had a manual of chants with rhythmic signs specially edited by the Fischer Publishing House of New York. Dom Mocquereau was satisfied with the chant, and certain choirs even gave him full satisfaction, after, of course, numerous and serious rehearsals. The chant's beauty was evident and this result demonstrated that it could be used, partly at least, as a chant for the people. (Congrès International de chant Grégorien in *Rev. Grég.*, 1920; Mocquereau Journal.)

On the first day, Dom Mocquereau gave a lecture which was translated into English and published in *The Catholic Educational Review* (Sept. 1920, pp. 383–416) under the title *The Papal Attitude Toward the Restoration of Gregorian Chant*.[10] But he had to refuse the invitations to speak which were addressed to him by Boston University (FitzGerald, May 20, 1920) and by Harvard University (Mocquereau Journal, pp. 15, 46, 47). (Cf. Appendix No. 7).

After the Congress, Dom Mocquereau continued his Gregorian apostolate until June 22, notably in Albany at the Novitiate of the Religious of the Sacred Heart on June 13 and 14, and with a group of Canadian priests who came to the Congress and would have liked to take him to their country (Mocquereau Journal, pp. 45, 49). But he refused these other invitations (Cf. William McMullen of Pittsburg, Feb. 9, 1920). After Dom Mocquereau's departure, Dom Gatard stayed in America until September 15 (Gatard, card of Sept. 27. Cf. Ward, S. Francis Camp, Sept. 9, 1920) in order to continue the work that had begun so well: in Washington where 400 nuns attended his classes (Ward, S. Francis Camp, August 19, 1920) as well as in Toledo where he stayed several days (Ward S. Francis Camp, Sept. 9, 1920 Cf. Gatard to Dom Mocquereau, New York, June 28, July 15, 1920). Dom Mocquereau went back to France with Joseph Bonnet, organist at St. Eustache in Paris, who had played the organ during the various liturgical events of the Congress (Mocquereau Journal, July 4, 1920 and end).

The objective immediately attained by the Congress was solidified in the resolutions which were adopted: give back to Gregorian chant the main place to which it is entitled in the liturgy; introduce everywhere the Vatican edition of Gregorian chant (editions with rhythmic signs which were deposited at the Fischer Publishing House, as per agreement with Desclée of Tournai) (Ward, S. Francis Camp, Sept. 5, and Westbrook, Oct. 21, 1920, Jan. 26, 1921)[11]—prepare the future by creating schools of liturgy and sacred music with the goal of training teachers—and finally, the last and most important goal: progressively make all the faithful participate in the sacred chant, according to the recommendation of Piux X. In order to reach this goal, Justine Ward was counting on children. (Cf. Appendices Nos. 9, 10, 11, 12.)

"Mrs. Ward's primary goal," Dom Gajard writes,

> the goal which inspired and directed everything, the end towards which she is constantly working, is essentially religious. What she wants above all is to put the faithful, all the faithful, in the position to participate actively, as much as possible and as perfectly as possible, in the liturgy and in the chant of the Catholic Church. Her entire pedagogy is oriented only toward this ideal. To educate the people, she turns first of all to the children, I would almost say only to the children, being sure to obtain, thus, a whole singing assembly. We might even better say: she does not want to reach only certain privileged classes of children, she wants to reach all the children. (D. Gajard, Rev. Gr. 1939, p. 72, review of Mrs. Ward's book of Gregorian Chant).

Dom Mocquereau did not think differently and he very strongly encouraged Justine Ward: "These children will convert all of America to Gregorian chant," he wrote on June 3 (Mocquereau Journal, p. 44).

However, the Congress' marginal activities, so to speak, were the most important and fruitful ones. It was easier, with small groups, to reveal Gregorian chant's real character, its intrinsic beauty and its value as a prayer. Consequently, numerous rehearsals were organized, as Dom Mocquereau so greatly wished: "I would love to train, at a slow pace, during the month following the Congress, a choir which could then be a model for all the others after we are gone—Fiat, Fiat." (Mocquereau to Gibbs, March 27, 1920). These rehearsals were most appreciated. And the first person to benefit largely from them was Justine Ward, whose satisfaction and enthusiasm knew no bounds. She thought immediately not only of inviting Dom Mocquereau to come back to the United States, but also of establishing a Solesmes foundation in Washington near Catholic University (Ward, Westbrook, June 29, 1920). In the meantime, she decided to go to England where the Solesmes monks had found asylum in 1901. She wanted to ask Dom Mocquereau to review her teaching method, in order to undertake a revision of her books in the light of Gregorian chironomy which had become the basis of her rhythmic education:

> I am looking forward to seeing you during the winter at Quarr Abbey or better still, at Solesmes (the monks were indeed thinking of coming back to France). Around Holy Week, I will come and knock on the door with my manuscript under my arm. Already, I see many things which could be corrected in the first books of the Method for Children (Westbrook, June 29, 1920). (Appendix 15, paragraph 4)

A little later she says very humbly:

> Until now, neither Mother Stevens nor I pretended to be teaching Plain Chant. Dr. Gibbs, Father Donovan and Dom Gatard are the ones who gave the Gregorian lectures. Mother Stevens and I concerned ourselves only with preparatory work in the schools, with chant, with sol-fa, etc. . . . But this will not suffice any longer because the fourth year book is devoted to liturgy and to Gregorian chant. This book is already well on its way. When the MS is finished, I shall bring it to you before publishing it. As soon as the Paleography arrives, I shall carefully study the seventh volume (in which Dom Mocquereau develops his rhythmic synthesis). I have good news for you: Mr. Benedict FitzGerald is going to become one of our teachers . . . He will help us greatly. (Westbrook, October 21, 1921.)

Justine Ward at Quarr Abbey (1921–1922)

As soon as she was able to do it, Justine Ward sailed to Europe to place herself under Dom Mocquereau's educational direction. She was accompanied only by her secretary, and not by the Sacred Heart nuns Stevens and Bourke, as originally planned (Ward, Westbrook, October 21, 1920). The Solesmes monks had been forced to leave France in 1901, because of the persecution laws, and had sought asylum in the Isle of Wight, south of Portsmouth. At first, they had settled temporarily in Appuldurcombe House, on a piece of property in the vicinity of which they had built a temporary wooden chapel. Then, they had constructed a complete monastery on the site of the old Cistercian Abbey of Our Lady of Quarr, which dated from 1132, but which had been completely destroyed at the time of the Protestant Reformation. The monastery was inaugurated in 1907, and the church was consecrated in 1912. It was the work of an architect monk, Dom Paul Bellot, and the church was the best of all those he was to build later on. The monks' choir, very wide, was preceded by a nave for the faithful which was, proportionately, fairly small. A magnificent raised sanctuary, bathed in light, extended beyond the choir and enhanced the surprisingly soaring arches. The ensemble, built in beautiful pink brick, was in itself a song of praise splendidly adapted to the Gregorian cantilena. Justine Ward liked this church, of which she wrote:

> The acoustics were warm and sensitive. Those simple interior walls were not only resonant, but in their freedom from all so-called decoration, provided a sympathetic surface where the sunlight could play melodies of its own, its rays flowing in happy designs from high windows, or touching the altar tenderly in the manner of a primitive painter.[12]

The cloistered nuns of Sainte Cécile of Solesmes had also settled in the Isle of Wight near Ryde and were thus able to benefit regularly from the religious services of the monks.

Justine Ward stayed in Quarr Abbey from May 10 to February 3, 1922 (Mocquereau, May 9, 1921 and January 28, 1922). The abbess of Sainte Cécile had offered her the use of a house which faced Portsmouth, not far from the nuns' monastery. The name of this house was Barington Grange.[13] Justine Ward left the monastery only once, in order to go with Miss McKenzie, her secretary, to the Bagnères and Luchon spa in southern France from July 23 to Sept. 7, 1921, for hydrotherapy. The spa was near Lourdes and she did not fail to go there, as a fervent pilgrim, as Dom Mocquereau had recommended (Mocquereau, July 24, August 12 and 19, 1921). On the way back, Justine Ward stopped at Sablé (Saint-Martin Hotel) and went to Solesmes on September 5th or 6th. Dom Foubert, who had stayed in France to run the parish entrusted to the monks, gave her a tour of the two Abbeys which were deprived of their legitimate owners and were sadly silent. There, she met Father Norbert Rousseau, one of the founders of the *Revue Grégorienne* who was at that time at his mother's home in Précigné, near Solesmes. Justine Ward probably knew that the monks were ready to come back home, because she began at that time to look for a house which she could buy in Solesmes (Mocquereau, July 24, August 12 and 19, Sept. 27, 1921). (Appendix No. 64)

Here are some of Justine Ward's memories:

> I remember visiting the Abbey of Solesmes before the return of the monks. The property had been confiscated, and the building used as a hospital during the war. It was filthy, full of rubbish, the grounds were overgrown with thorns and thistles. The entire monastery property was squeezed into an oblong space between a road and a river. It lacked the charm of the generous lands of Quarr. The church was long, high, and narrow, with some fifteenth-century sculpture, but the whole place gave the impression of an untidy wilderness without, and suffocation within. (Cf. supra, *Solesmes and a Centenary.*)

Justine Ward returned to England on September 7th, to resume her work with Dom Mocquereau, as she mentions in her journal. In his letters, the latter mentions notably a study by his student on the Gregorian modes which he rated "excellent" (Mocquereau, Oct. 25 and 27, 1921, and another undated letter). But above all, they continued together to revise *Gregorian Chant*, the Ward series' fourth year book. They did not stop working, even during their short sojourn in Stanbrook from the 17th to the 23rd of November (Mocquereau, Travel Notes, 1921), for they set aside "several hours each day to work on this revision" (Mocquereau, no date, 1921). They were with Mother Laurentia McLachlan, a humanist, paleographer and Gregorianist cloistered nun, who was called "an English Dom Mocquereau".[14] She was the author of a book entitled *Gregorian Music* (Solesmes, Imprimerie 1897) and of a *Grammar of Plainsong*.[15] They probably also discussed with Mother Laurentia the English translation of the *Nombre Musical Grégorien* which Father Shields had considered doing himself (Ward, S. Francis Camp, Aug. 19, 1920, January 1, 1921; Shields, S. Francis Camp, Sept. 4, 1920, Cf. Appendix No. 5) and which had been entrusted for a while to Mother Laurentia after Father Shields' death in 1921. The Stanbrook journey ended with a stop in London where Dom Mocquereau and Justine Ward attended, on November 22 (feast of Sainte Cécile), the anniversary service of Dom Gatard, who had died on November 21, 1920,[16] shortly after his return from America (D. Cabrol, Oct. 16, 1921). Dom Mocquereau went alone for a quick visit to Farnborough, Dom Gatard's monastery (Mocquereau, Nov. 9, 1921. Cf. Jan. 28, 1922. Travel Notes 1921).

The Choir of Solesmes

As early as June, Justine Ward communicated her impressions on the monks' singing to Father Young in a letter written at Quarr Abbey and published soon afterwards in the *Revue Grégorienne*. It is fitting to reproduce it here despite its length and her enthusiastic praise of the monks' singing. It is not possible indeed to express better than Justine Ward herself, the richness and the depth of the experience she had at that time. Through these lines, her spirituality and her entire sensitivity as an artist are revealed. Here are the main passages of this letter dated June 30, 1921:

> One is, each day, more deeply impressed as one hears chant in all the richness and diversity of the daily offices. This impression is actually conveyed by the whole and not by the chant only: the church, so simple, which uses only the interplay of proportions and light for effect, the exquisite lines and colors of the ornaments, the gestures of the monks whose gait, full of majesty, seems to be a sort of step in perfect unison with the music and which reminds one of Fra Angelico's painting: Dancing of the Saints in Paradise. Words, gestures, music, are in perfect harmony, as if the gestures were attuned to the music or the words to the gestures; it is difficult to say which of the two, since a feeling of oneness is so profoundly felt.
>
> Yesterday was the feast of Saint Peter and of Saint Paul and a novice made his profession. It was a moving ceremony which took place during mass. Mr. Bonnet played admirable improvisations on the organ, on the various mass themes. He came here a few days ago, after his great concert in Westminster Abbey, London. He has just given a whole series of recitals throughout Europe and I did not expect to find him in such good shape. It is quite obvious that everyone loves him here, at Quarr Abbey. The Abbey's chant gives an impression of extraordinary calm and naturalness. No search for effect, but no effort to avoid it either when it is contained in the music

itself. The staccato music sometimes heard in certain Solesmes pupils in the United States is absolutely not heard here. On the contrary, what comes out above everything is the phrase in the plenitude of its development, what Dom Mocquereau calls "the great rhythm" and Dom Mocquereau's entire personal teaching tends precisely to make the phrase the supreme element and to see that the words and the parts of phrases are blended into the great ensemble of a perfect musical phrase. The division into groups of two or three notes is used only to analyze the phrase and is to the cantor what the skeleton is to the artist, the solid base upon which the great rhythm is constructed.

The schola and the community sing with an admirable *legato*, without a very considerable voice volume, but with a very firm and very good sonority, something like a cello orchestra. There is always a very alive and very sensitive melodic line, and in order to realize that the individual notes have virtually the same length—which is, of course, what they must have—it is necessary to stop and begin a real analysis; because, even though they have the same length, their value, their movement and their general character show considerable differences. The arsis notes are usually a little more hurried and tend towards *crescendo*—a mere nuance of course, almost imperceptible—while the thesis notes are rather slightly slowed down. But even here, there is no fixed rule, since each phrase has its own personal mark.

What is striking above all is this truly live undulation, in which nothing mechanical is felt, but which swells and rises to the crest of the phrase like the swelling of one wave among all the others. The monks underline in their singing the various repercussions indicated, but with such delicacy that, here again, it is hardly a perceptible nuance, a light wave of sound which is added like a new layer, having nothing of a *vibrato*.

This is perfection, a perfection one must expect to find, I suppose, in a community of monks where everybody speaks Latin and makes liturgy his daily life. Actually, their hearts are so set on singing that if one of them makes the slightest mistake, he atones for it immediately through public penance. But much of what the monks are doing could be reproduced elsewhere and it would be admirable to be able to think that, everywhere in the world, Our Lord is honored with such perfect beauty.

The scientific aspect of the work, the analysis and comparison of the manuscripts, is something extremely interesting and impressive. The extraordinary care given to the study of the smallest questions and the eager and graceful manner in which the monks explain the slightest details of their work, make a lasting impression. But even if there were no scientific element at the basis of this work, the beauty of the result would be enough to conquer the listeners, and I doubt that anyone with the slightest artistic sense could possibly stay for a while at Quarr Abbey without being converted to the method of the monks of Solesmes.

There is great art, art at its summit, but with something else which surpasses art itself so much that one has the impression of insulting the monks, it could be said, when one praises them for being great artists. It is as if, in Francis Thompson's words, one praised the seraphim for their hair's sparkling curls. It is something so holy that one is overwhelmed with fear, with faith and with adoration. If such a beauty could spread out and invade our churches, all sin would dissipate like germs under the rays of the sun.[17]

While it was in America, during Dom Mocquereau's sojourn there, that Justine Ward was conquered by his rhythmic doctrine, it was principally at Quarr Abbey that she grasped all the practical value of this rhythmic doctrine which animated Gregorian chant so well and bestowed upon it the religious character which was the choir of Solesmes' mark.

His interpretation of liturgical chant, whose very objective is to elevate souls and to lead them to God, was exactly what Justine Ward was looking for in her training of children. It may be said at this point that she appreciated it until the end of her life. She was in perfect agreement with Dom Mocquereau, who was a man of prayer and of contemplation, as those who knew him most intimately can attest. For him, science was always only a means and art was never an end in itself. "And so," he wrote, "art is not the main issue. The main issue is *prayer*, the prayer of the Church, to be precise, its solemn liturgical, official prayer, made in its name." (*Monographie Grégorienne* IV, 1923, p. 31.)

> Art then is necessary, but as I have already said, it is not sufficient in itself. To sing the chant, as it should be sung, the soul must be suitably disposed. The chant should vibrate with soul, ordered, calm, disciplined, passionless: a soul that is mistress of itself, intelligent and in possession of the light; upright in the sight of God, and overflowing with charity. To such a soul, Gentlemen, add a beautiful voice, well-trained, and the singing of those hallowed melodies, will be a finished work of beauty, the music of which Plato dreamed, a music which inspires a love of virtue: nay, more, you will have the ideal Christian prayer as St. Dennis understood it, the realization of the great Benedictine motto: *Mens nostra concordet voci nostrae.* "Let our mind concord with our voice" in the praise of God. (*L'Art Grégorien, son but, ses procédés, ses caractères*, p. 37, 1896.[18])

Thus, Justine Ward was won over immediately by the monastic spirituality which was so well adapted to what she felt deep within herself on the religious plane as well as on the aesthetic plane. She wanted to belong to the Abbey in the only way open to her, the Benedictine secular oblature which allows laypersons living in the world to participate in the life of the monks, as the Third Orders do in the Franciscan and Dominican Orders. She chose Dom Mocquereau as her spiritual director and it was he who received her into the Oblature, at first as a novice on October 11, 1921, eve of the feast of the Dedication of the Abbey Church of Solesmes (Ward Journal). She made profession as an oblate on March 21, 1923.

Joint Thought

Besides the practical lessons and especially the listening to the monks' choir, the revising of her fourth year book was of prime importance to Justine Ward. She was Dom Mocquereau's docile student during these long months spent in England. In the Introduction to her book,[19] Dom Mocquereau humbly admitted that teacher and student mutually helped each other, on the one hand, Justine Ward had perfectly assimilated a rhythmic theory which, she said, was "marvellous in its clarity and logic, so simple, indeed, that little children could grasp it and sing the praises of God devoutly" (Cf. Appendix 64.); on the other hand, Dom Mocquereau found in Justine Ward the faithful disciple who understood him well and even opened new unexpected vistas for him.

Here is the essential part of this foreword which is relevant to the point under discussion here:

> "You followed closely the liturgical offices," Dom Mocquereau writes, "you listened with attention and piety to the choir of monks as they sang the Divine Praises, and, little by little, the charm and the beauty of the Gregorian melodies captivated your soul—both as Christian and as artist. What a lesson, what an initiation in itself.
>
> "But that was not all. Merely to appreciate and enjoy the charm of those sacred melodies did not satisfy you. You wished to understand wherein lay the secret of that sweetness, that legato, that phrasing, that great rhythm— broad and undulating—which characterizes the singing at Solesmes . . . You were gladly offered every possible facility, and, in this regard, Solesmes has given you all that It has to give. All the secrets of the *Nombre Musical Grégorien* were revealed to you, with the laws that govern the plastic expression of the rhythmic flow (*chironomy*). . . . These doctrines—my own—which I explained in terms which were perhaps at times dry, scientific, and even a little obscure, you have transformed in a truly marvellous manner. Thinking always of your thousands of little children in America whom you love as a Mother, your single object in receiving these principles was to adapt them to the intellectual capacity of those little ones, and, as a matter of fact, you have so assimilated these doctrines of mine, so appropriated them, so transformed them in the laboratory of your own mind, that they appear from your pen, the same doctrines, but recast in a new form—charming, clear, simple, childlike, adapted with delicacy and skill, and with a quasi-maternal insight, to the needs of the children. The most ingenious means are used—light veils whose floating folds express the suppleness of the rhythmic movement—to instill in the imagination of your pupils a vidid sense of the graceful outline of melody and rhythm in our beautiful chants.
>
> "Again, what a happy idea are those rhythmic or chironomic games in which the children are shown the outline of a melody by the gesture of the hand and must compose a melody which conforms to that outline.
>
> "I owe you, Madame, the full expression of my thought: your 'Gregorian Chant' has enlightened me regarding the value of our *chironomy*, and in the following respect:
>
> "From a pedagogical standpoint, you have made an unexpected use of the plastic expression of the rhythmic movement. Until now, I had always looked upon this study—the science of outlining by manual gesture the undulations of the rhythm—as the culmination, the summit of all rhythmic training, as a branch of the subject which should be reserved almost exclusively for directors of music and choirmasters. You, Madame, have made it basic, the foundation of all your training. You treat it as an educational element of primary importance—and in this you are absolutely right. . . ."

In closing this introduction, Dom Mocquereau congratulated Justine Ward for never losing sight of the final goal of her musical work, which is that of the Gregorian cantilena: to enlighten the mind, to elevate the soul, and to make them participate more fully in the divine mysteries which are the source of all supernatural life.

> To bring about this result you turn to the Sacred Scriptures and to tradition, and explain carefully to your pupils the liturgical pieces which they

> are to sing . . . That these doctrines may make a deep impression, you
> have appealed to the eye by means of pictures—and what pictures!

All these facts indicate that one may apply to this fourth volume for children
the words written by Dom Joseph Gajard, Dom Mocquereau's successor,
about the volume for teachers, i.e., that it was the product of a genuine collaboration of Dom Mocquereau with Justine Ward, the former in regard to the
subject matter, and the latter in regard to the essentially personal presentation
she made of the master's doctrine (Cf. *Rev. Gr.*, 1939, p. 74).

Dom Mocquereau's Introduction to *Gregorian Chant* is dated Christmas
1921, but the book was published later. Through this first prolonged contact
with Dom Mocquereau and through the liturgical life of the monastery, Justine
Ward became fully aware of her ideal and of the means of implementing it. She
had been convinced and, to the very end, she was faithful to Dom Mocquereau's principles and never denied her attachment to Solesmes. Without a
doubt, she would have signed at that time the statement she wrote much later
in a report to the Panamerican Congress of Sacred Music which was held in
Mexico in November, 1949:

> "I offer you the fruit of my experience," she concluded. "I cannot do it
> without emphasizing that I could have done nothing without Solesmes'
> rhythmic signs or without Dom Mocquereau's rhythmic gestures."[20]

Justine Ward related, with her usual charm, how Dom Mocquereau was
training his student—none other than herself—and how she docilely accepted
some comments which were somewhat stern at times though wholly in the
style of the man whose nickname in the monastic community was 'the lion'.
Thus, after the New York Congress, he said to her:

> "One thing worries me greatly."
> "What is that?" I asked.
> "That you know nothing about Gregorian Chant."
> "Nothing? Then will you teach me?"
> "He consented and that is why I had come to Quarr Abbey—to learn."[21]

Another time, he received an exercise from Justine Ward and gave it back
to her "uncorrected because my syllables were not aligned correctly, under
the note or the neum to which each one corresponded." (Cf. Appendix
No. 64.) Nevertheless, the "respectful ultimate observations" of the master
concerning the fourth year book are only three big pages long, written in very
large handwriting, and they mention only some trifles (Mocquereau,
November 10, 1921).

While Justine Ward was working docilely under Dom Mocquereau's guidance throughout the summer of 1921, the cloistered nuns of Sainte Cécile were
able to benefit from her teaching experience, and she gave them some lessons
in vocalization which greatly improved the quality of their chant, according to
Dom Mocquereau, whose judgment was rather severe in this matter. These

lessons yielded fruit for a long time afterwards (Mocquereau, Jan. 28, Feb. 9, 1922). The nuns helped her in return, since one of them drew the chironomy of *Gregorian Chant* (Mocquereau, Jan. 28, Feb. 21, March 4, 1922). At Quarr Abbey, Dom Paul Blanchon and Dom de Subercaseaux illustrated this book (Mocquereau July 28, 1921, March 4 and May 22, 1922).

During the summer of 1921, which Justine Ward spent in England, there was a Gregorian meeting in Philadelphia on June 28, under the aegis of the archbishop, Cardinal Dougherty. Several choirs were in attendance (*Rev. Gr.*, 1921, p. 243). As for the Summer School of the Pius X Institute of New York, it was well attended by many students among which were numerous priests and organists. Lessons on Gregorian chant were given that year by Dom Eudine, a Farnborough monk and a Solesmes veteran, and were added, from then on, to the musical education courses which followed the Ward Method. Similar courses were offered in leading colleges and schools in twenty-five cities in the United States. This shows how fast the method was spreading, to the advantage of Gregorian chant (*Rev. Gr.*, 1921, p. 243; 1922, p. 151).

During the summer of 1921, a teacher from the Pius X Institute came to Quarr Abbey where he stayed for several days working with Dom Mocquereau and Dom Desrocquettes (Mocquereau, August 5 and 12, 1921). Father DesLongchamps, returning from the Pontifical Institute of Sacred Music in Rome, came there also in August, and again, it seems, in October (Mocquereau, August 19, 1921; Ward Journal, Oct. 1, 1921). Father DesLongchamps later taught at the Pius X Institute.

Finally, at the end of the year 1921, Justine Ward received a letter from Rome, from Father de Santi, S.J., director of the Pontifical Institute of Sacred Music, which brought her a blessing from the Holy Father and a diploma[22] of congratulations and encouragement (Ward Journal, Dec. 12, 1921).

Dom Mocquereau in America (1922)

Before returning to America, Justine Ward obtained from Abbot Dom G. Cozien, who succeeded Dom Paul Delatte in April 1921, permission for Dom Mocquereau to come to New York again for the upcoming Summer School (Ward Journal, Jan. 21, 1922). She left at the end of January 1922, but returned to Quarr Abbey for Holy Week (Ward Journal, Feb. 3 and March 30, 1922; Mocquereau, January 28, 1922) and stayed there from April 13th to June 16th (Ward Journal, April 13 and June 16, 1922) in order to work with Dom Mocquereau on the fourth volume of her course which was still in preparation, as her journal indicated, on May 3, "Quarr Music IV with Dom M." But Dom Mocquereau's upcoming journey to America and that of Dom J.H. Desrocquettes who was going to go along with him, had to be planned minutely since Dom Mocquereau's age required much consideration and since Justine Ward showed her master much attention. As for Dom Mocquereau, he was particularly concerned about technical preparation and he asked Justine Ward to prepare a good schola capable of leading all the singers (Mocquereau, Feb. 13, 1922).

The two Solesmians arrived in New York on July 1. Dom Desrocquettes was to monitor his companion's health, to assist him in his work, and also to give courses in Gregorian chant accompaniment, which was his specialty. Justine Ward's and Mother Stevens' courses had already begun by this time, but the two men were present when the Archbishop of New York, Monsignor Patrick Hayes, came to the College of the Sacred Heart, at the Pius X Institute of Liturgical Music, to encourage teachers and students by clearly stating that he was counting on them to restore the Gregorian melodies in America. In acknowledgment of his gratitude for the Archbishop's protection, which had already been apparent during the 1920 Congress, Dom Mocquereau read the text of the dedication to the Archbishop which was to appear at the beginning of the second volume of the Second Series of the *Paléographie Musicale* (Codex 359 de S. Gall) then at press. Dom Mocquereau's and Dom Desrocquettes' courses were to be given from July 24th to August 12th. In the meantime, Dom Mocquereau trained the choir of priests, seminarians and nuns who were to illustrate his lectures and who were ready to sing the *Salve Sancta Parens* mass satisfactorily on the 21st, after numerous fruitful efforts.

Dom Mocquereau gave a detailed account, illustrated with photographs, of Justine Ward's courses, of his own courses, and of those of Dom Desrocquettes, Father Young and Mother Stevens. (*Rev. Gr.*, 1922, 118, 151, 186, 230; 1923, 32.) When one reads what he wrote concerning Justine Ward's courses, there is no doubt that he was very pleased to see how she was applying his rhythmic principles to her own method's technique: the use of sight and of bodily gestures to understand rhythms and sound movements.

> "Some European readers may perhaps smile at these small tricks," he wrote, "and find them childish. They would be quite wrong; all means are good if they bring quick, decisive results" (*Rev. Gr.*, 1922, 186, 190; 230–238).

Dom Mocquereau's account is rich, furthermore, in lessons on the theory and practice of Gregorian chant. The Summary he made, notably of his own lectures on rhythm (pp. 231–236) and those of Dom Desrocquettes on accompaniment, should be read. The courses were followed by exercises corresponding to the subject matter taught and after the sessions, the singers often went to the chapel to prepare the final mass. Dom Mocquereau seldom had had at his disposition a large choir already so well trained. Thus, progress was fast and the crowning event, the mass sung on August 11, was one of Dom Mocquereau's greatest joys. He spoke about it in grandiloquent terms, showing how technique and art itself are surpassed when one sings for God alone.

> I cannot explain otherwise the ideal perfection reached during this mass: it surpassed the means which were used: beauty, purity of souls, in a word, divine charity made up for anything that could have been lacking on the human side (*Rev. Gr.*, 1923, pp. 32–38).

During the session, Dom Mocquereau distributed a brochure he had already published in French but which Justine Ward had wanted to have translated into English: *The Art of Gregorian Music* (Desrocquettes Journal, p. 19, August 4, 1922)[23], and Dom Desrocquettes gave a lecture illustrated with film strips on *Rhythmic Tradition in the Manuscripts*[24], prepared by Dom Mocquereau and

Dom Joseph Gajard for the next Congress of Gregorian chant and sacred music which was to be held in Paris in December 1922 (Cf. *Rev. Gr.*, 1923, p. 23. Desrocquettes Journal, p. 21. Aug. 9, 1922). (Appendix No. 8)

The final session was presided over by the Archbishop of Harrisburg, Monsignor McDevitt, who read a comforting telegram from the Holy Father giving his blessing to all. The speech of Father Young, pioneer of the Gregorian revival in America, was particularly moving, as was the speech of Dom Mocquereau, who credited Dom Guéranger, Dom Pothier and some of his other brothers at Solesmes with much of the praise bestowed upon him. Mr. Fitz-Gerald, one of the Pius X Institute supervisors, presented him with a book full of signatures.

Justine Ward took great care not to tire Dom Mocquereau too much. Two or three times a week she took him to the home of her mother, Mrs. Cutting, and nearly every evening, after classes, she took him for a long drive along the banks of the Hudson River. Nevertheless, Dom Mocquereau could not accept the numerous invitations he received, and he was represented several times by Dom Desrocquettes, notably at Albany, at the novitiate of the Religious of the Sacred Heart, and at Putnam, at the convent of the Sisters "Blanches" de Bretagne, after Summer School (Desrocquettes Journal, pp. 22, 38). There was one invitation he could not refuse, however. A large group of Canadians was in New York to attend his classes and ardently wanted him to come to Montreal. The bishop-administrator of this city sent him an official and pressing invitation. (*Rev. Gr.*, 1923, note 1—Descrocquettes Journal, p. 18, August 2, 1922.) He went there for a quick visit at the end of August, with Justine Ward and her doctor (Desrocquettes Journal, pp. 26–27) and even stopped at the Abbey of the Cistercians of Oka, where the choirmaster, Father Guillaume, had wanted him to come ever since he had arrived in America. He left Dom Desrocquettes in Montreal and this moving telegram was sent to him on September 1st from that city:

> Reverend Father Dom Mocquereau. The many members of the clergy, chapel masters, organists, religious and nuns of all the communities of Montreal, meeting at the University and learning to understand better the beauty of Gregorian chant under the superior guidance of Dom Descrocquettes, pay a most respectful homage to you, Very Reverend Father, deplore your absence and hope your health will improve. Honor to the sons of Saint Benedict and of Dom Guéranger. The National Conservatory of the University of Montreal. J. De Veaux, secretary (Dom Mocquereau to Dom Cozien).[25]

While on board ship on his way back from America, Dom Mocquereau wrote to Justine Ward:

> I want to tell you that I shall always be ready to help you most loyally in your great works of restoration. God found a surprising way to associate both of us, and we must follow his ways with love (Mocquereau, Sept. 14, 1922).

These few words accurately sum up the contents of these pages on the subject of the relationship between Justine Ward and Dom Mocquereau.

Proposed Monastic Foundation in Washington

Before we return to Dom Mocquereau in his monastery, we must say something about a project already considered by Justine Ward in 1920 (Ward, Westbrook, June 29, 1920, (Appendix No. 14)) and which was again considered prior to Dom Mocquereau's return to Europe in the middle of September 1922. Justine Ward had in mind a project concerning a Solesmes foundation near Catholic University in Washington, where some monks would take part in the teaching of Gregorian chant. She noted in her journal that she had mentioned it to Dom Mocquereau on December 10, 1921, during her first sojourn near the Abbey ("Quarr—saw Dom M. re foundation") and to the Abbot on April 27, 1922 ("Saw Abb. Cozien re American foundation"). Dom Mocquereau's second journey to America in 1922, revived the project. With this aim in mind, Justine Ward took Dom Mocquereau to Washington and to Baltimore at the beginning of September, having been encouraged to do so by Dr. Dyer, Superior of the Baltimore Seminary, who had recently been a guest at Quarr Abbey. In Washington, the proposed site for constructing the monastery was visited; in Baltimore, the conditions of this foundation were examined so that Dom Mocquereau could explain them to his Abbot. Dom Mocquereau wrote him a letter about this matter on September 12th while he was on the ship which took him back to England.

This letter to Dom Cozien summarized the situation as it was then. The site of the foundation belonged to the university; the school of music would be run by monks, possibly with the help of teachers from outside the monastery. Dom Mocquereau acknowledged that some preparatory work was necessary—especially within the episcopate—to make this idea of a monastic foundation acceptable. This could require three or four years. Above all, it was necessary to prepare for it by praying, since it was a religious work and since the "Glory of God" was at stake.[26]

On October 26, Justine Ward discussed the matter with Dr. McCormick of the University (Ward Journal, Oct. 26, 1922: "Washington discusses Solesmes foundation with Dr. McCormick"), who appeared supportive as evidenced in a letter addressed to him by Dr. Dyer on November 1. The latter was planning to discuss the matter with the rector, Monsignor Shahan, and also with the Bishop of Cleveland, Monsignor Schrembs, and with the Bishop of Harrisburg, Monsignor McDevitt. One thing was certain: financial questions would come up, and they had to be solved first (letter of Dyer to J. Ward, Baltimore, Nov. 1, 1922. (Cf. App. No. 16.) On November 23rd, Dr. Dyer met with Bishop Shahan (Ward Journal, Nov. 22, 1922: "Washington—Dr. Dyer opened question of Solesmes foundation at University with Rector D. Shahan"), and on the 25th he related to Justine Ward the rather favorable opinion of this prelate and his suggestion to have the monastery established at the University itself "in connection with the Shrine to Our Blessed Mother." The matter, however, would have to be submitted to the Board of Trustees of the University for a decision (letter of Dyer to J. Ward, Baltimore, Nov. 25, 1922, Appendix No. 17[1]).

Justine Ward transmitted this letter at once to Dom Mocquereau, with the following note:

> This arrangement would give an official character to the monks' singing and would thus be the Model given officially by the bishops of the United States to all the priests who come to the University for their graduate studies. This would have much more influence than a foundation installed independently on any site. J.W. (note of J. Ward in Dyer letter, Baltimore, Nov. 25, 1922).

On December 12, Dom Mocquereau answered:

> Dr. Dyer's letter is interesting: the matter is progressing *slowly*, but it is progressing. I still believe that it will be difficult to accept the site near The Shrine. There is not enough space for a Benedictine monastery (December 12, 1922)—yes, prayer must accomplish almost everything in a matter which goes straight to the Glory of God (Christmas Vigil, 1922). (Appendix No. 14).

It may seem surprising at first that Dom Mocquereau was able to speak so clearly about this project to his Abbot, for now, at a distance, it appears to have been quite unrealistic. But, in relation to this matter, some comments on the return of the French religious to their country at the end of the war, are in order. Having been forced to leave in 1901, they were beginning to come back to France, where they were hoping to be able to live in peace after having fought for their country. The circumstances looked favorable. First of all, since the mobilization, a ministerial order had suspended the application of the laws against religious congregations (circular Malvy, August 2, 1914); furthermore, there had been a certain period of calm during and after World War I; finally, diplomatic relations with the Vatican were reestablished, at first by sending a minister plenipotentiary on March 23, 1920 (Mr. Doulcet), then by sending an ambassador on May 18, 1921 (Mr. Jonnart). These were signs of good omen. Consequently, as soon as he was elected Abbot of Solesmes in April 1921, Dom Cozien decided to recall most of his monks to France. He came to Solesmes in June, 1921, visited the grounds and came back in September to witness the departure of the last soldiers who were occupying the Abbey which had been transformed into a military hospital. A small group of monks prepared for the return of the community which took place discreetly during the summer of 1922.

But some inveterate anti-clercial persons wanted the laws voted in 1901–1904 to be applied. The ambassador of France to the Holy See, Mr. Jonnart himself, reminded the Government that the existing laws should be observed: he suggested that the charitable and missionary congregations be readmitted, but not the teaching congregations.[27]

When Dom Cozien saw the turmoil caused in political circles by the return of the monks and of the nuns, and when he saw, notably, the reaction of a certain senator from the Sarthe Department (Mocquereau, Oct. 23, 1922), he became, it seems, more interested in Justine Ward's project, and all the more so since Quarr had become too small for the Solesmes community.

However, the project was abandoned since the French government was wise enough to look the other way and leave the religious in peace. It appears, though, that the project had been seriously considered for a while at Solesmes. Meanwhile, Justine Ward took some measures to provide for the expenses of this foundation, as evidenced in the codicil she added to her will on August 30, 1922, while Dom Mocquereau was still with her. This arrangement provided for the building and maintenance of a monastery near the University of Washington and became void if the foundation was not established 25 years after her death. The question of this monastic foundation came up again in 1923 in a letter from Dom Mocquereau, in which he noted that the Divine Providence did not want it (Mocquereau, Sept. 30, 1923). However, Justine Ward was still hoping for it, since Dom Mocquereau wrote to her on October 31 of the following year (1924): (Appendix No. 14)

> I see that you have not given up the idea of a Solesmes foundation in Washington. It will be rather difficult, I believe. It will be even more difficult if *only one monk from Solesmes* is to organize the courses.

This is indeed what Justine Ward was now proposing on this matter (cf. Appendix No. 17[2]).

Justine Ward in Sablé

When he arrived at Quarr Abbey on September 19, 1922, on his way back from America, Dom Mocquereau found a letter from his abbot who was then in France. In this letter, the abbot asked Dom Mocquereau to come to Solesmes where some monks had returned already (Mocquereau to D. Cozien, Sept. 22, 1922). He was to arrive for the first vespers of the feast of Saint Michael, that is to say, on September 28. He left on the 25th (Mocquereau, Sept. 25). Justine Ward mentioned it in her journal: "28 Sept. Dom M. arr. Solesmes after 22 years exile" (Mocquereau, Sept. 20, 23, and 25 and Oct. 1, 1922).

Justine Ward had already joined her life, so to speak, with that of the Abbey. Thus, as soon as she heard that the monks were going back to Solesmes, she asked the Father Cellarer to find a house for her near the monastery. Several dwellings were considered, the Lacombe house in Solesmes—which is now the Solesmes Town Hall—the Coudreuse house in Chantenay, a few kilometers from Solesmes, the Saint-Gilles house in Asnières, and a house near the railroad station in Sablé. In the meantime, the Father Cellarer suggested various temporary solutions. Finally, after having considered leasing the St. François Hotel in front of the Abbey (Mocquereau, Jan. 2, Feb. 17, 1923), Justine Ward chose a house near the church of Sablé (the house was offered to her on Feb. 12, 1923, and she accepted it on the 16th). This house was not ready at once, and when Justine Ward came to Solesmes in March, 1923, she had to take a room at the Saint-Martin Hotel in Sablé. She rented this house for several consecutive years, and bought it in 1929 (Ward Journal, 1929, Sept. 3 and 28, 1929).[28]

Justine Ward also wanted a companion who would, at the same time, run the house. With the help of Dom Agaësse, Dom Mocquereau found such a person: Miss Agnès Lebreton. She was, to the very end, a friend and a surrogate sister for Justine Ward. She helped in no small way to strengthen, and even at times to maintain the strong bonds which already united Justine Ward with Solesmes. Agnès Lebreton was approved of immediately and began at once to take care of the house and to prepare Justine Ward's next sojourn in France (Mocquereau, Oct. 29 and 31, 1922).

Yearning for Solesmes

Justine Ward arrived at Cherbourg for her third stay near the Abbey on March 16, 1923. Agnès Lebreton was there to welcome her. On the 17th, Justine Ward was at Sablé where she stayed at the Saint-Martin Hotel, as we just said. She had come to prepare herself to make profession as an oblate. This ceremony took place at the Abbey on March 21, which was Saint-Benedict's feast day. Then she worked with Dom Mocquereau on the fourth volume of her method. This volume was the first to be devoted to Gregorian chant and it was still in preparation. She worked until she left for America on June 13.

Before leaving, she made a donation which she wanted applied to "the renewal of the sacristy to make a beautiful Pontifical." It is now the red and gold set of pontifical vestments which still illuminates great solemnities for Pentecost and for the feast of Saint-Peter. Designed by Dom de Laborde, it shows the young King David playing the harp while King Saul is listening and perhaps already plotting his criminal project against him (Ward, Sablé, June 13, 1923). Justine Ward had already offered a lectern for the choir (Mocquereau, Dec. 12, 1922) and had made an important donation to finance the second volume of the Second Series of the *Paléographie Musicale* which contains photographic reproductions of the 359 Saint-Gall manuscript, and the Corbie antiphonary, the 115 manuscript of the Library of Amiens (Mocquereau, Oct. 5, 1922 and Sept. 24, 1923). Upon leaving Sablé, Justine Ward wrote Dom Mocquereau the following lines which contain thoughts she frequently expressed later on in a similar way:

> You know, dear Father, how heartbreaking it is for me to leave the peace of Solesmes, the source from which I draw for the future work I have to do so far away from the Master who gave so much to me (Ward, Sablé, June 13, 1923).

The 1923 Summer Session of the Pius X Institute of New York was once again very successful. Three series of practical music courses according to the Ward Method, as well as courses in harmony and in musical analysis were offered by Mother Stevens and her assistants.

> The course in Gregorian chant, the central point of the work of the Institute, was taught by Justine Ward herself. More than twenty religious orders from the United States and Canada were represented there, as well as priests and laypersons, altogether more than one hundred students—

20

men and women. There were also some 'observers' who had come to see the work being done and particularly the results being obtained. The auxiliary bishop of New York and the bishop of Hartford were among these observers and this proved that they were interested in the restoration of Church music (*Rev. Gr.,* 1923, pp. 231–232).

At the end of the session, Justine Ward sent the following telegram to Dom Mocquereau. He received it on August 11, 1923: "Teachers and Students of the Summer School, New York want to express deep gratitude and devotion to Solesmes principles. Juscutt (Justine Cutting)."

Justine Ward then went to Santa Fe, New Mexico, to have a rest. A grandiose landscape and long rides on horseback helped her to rebuild her strength. She sent many postcards to Dom Mocquereau (Ward, Santa Fe, Seite Burros, August 21, 1923). But she wrote: "I think only of returning to Solesmes. Life away from Solesmes is possible only when I am busy preparing lectures" (Ward, Santa Fe, August 21). A little later, Justine Ward gave Dom Mocquereau an account of the "last session at Manhattanville" (letter could not be found), and another time, she wrote:

> I was sure that this success would cause you much pleasure—but it is not *my* success, it is *yours*—I am only the intermediary—and it was to prove it to you that we sent the telegram to you (Ward, Santa Fe, Sept. 16, 1923).

Actually, Justine Ward was planning to have Dom Mocquereau come to America for the third time, if his health allowed it, which did not turn out to be the case (Mocquereau, Nov. 22, 1923). She pleaded again for him to come to America in a letter from Rome dated March 6, 1924:

> I pray with all my heart for this favorable decision of the Reverend Father Abbot concerning America. You know how much I desire your presence. I say no more for it shall be as God wants it. But for us, your presence would be a dream come true. I hardly dare to hope for it since I desire it so much. (Ward, Rome, March 6, 1924 in P.S.).

The matter will come up again later (Mocquereau, Feb. 29, March 2, July 25, Oct. 4, and Nov. 7, 1924).

But Americans could come to the Abbey. Thus, Father DesLongchamps came—we shall speak about him later—as well as Father Ronan (Mocquereau, August 5 and 12, 1923).

Justine Ward, 1912, starting to write her music books and the life of Father William Pardow.

1922 Summer Session students at Manhattanville College of the Sacred Heart, New York City.

A demonstration of the musical proficiency of Ward-trained children at Manhattanville College of the Sacred Heart, New York City, 1922. Standing in the background are Justine Ward, Father Young, S.J., and Mother Georgia Stevens, R.S.C.J.

Justine Ward conducting a Summer Session class at Manhattanville College of the Sacred Heart. Dom Jean Desrocquettes is seated at the harmonium.

St. Francis Camp, Little Moose Lake, Old Forge, N.Y.

Dom Mocquereau conducting a rehearsal in the chapel of Manhattanville College of the Sacred Heart, 1922.

Dom Gatard, O.S.B., and Dom Mocquereau, O.S.B., in New York, 1920.

Abbey Church, Quarr Abbey.

Chapter II

WORK AND DISCUSSIONS

Translation Problems

Justine Ward returned to Sablé on December 18, 1923, and stayed there a long time, until June 14, 1924, with only one interruption for a trip to Italy from February 26th to March 25th.

For this period, we have some very interesting information. It will be remembered that, since 1920, during Dom Mocquereau's first stay in New York, Justine Ward had been considering an English translation of the *Nombre Musical Grégorien* (Ward, St. Francis Camp, Aug. 19, 1920). (Appendix No. 3). Reverend Mother Laurentia McLachlan, Abbess of Stanbrook, with whom Dom Mocquereau had a close relationship (Cf. supra p. 8) was entrusted with this work; the matter was probably settled at the time of Dom Mocquereau's and Justine Ward's visit with her in November 1921. Dom Mocquereau did not speak English and trusted the learned Abbess entirely concerning this translation. But Justine Ward was not completely satisfied with it, as evidenced in her letters to Dom Mocquereau. The corrections she suggested and especially the annotations to be found in her journal and which are mentioned here are significant: We read effectively:

> January 20. Sablé received manuscript of English translation Nombre Musical from Mother Laurentia.
> January 26. Sablé. Diff. with Dom M. re elementary teaching—for first time.
> January 28. Sablé. Mother L. insists on her terminology.—Dom M., Wabbly.
> January 29. Solesmes. Wrote ultimatum to Stanbrook.
> January 30. Dom M. in Paris for Inst. Greg. I saw Abb. Cozien re translating Nombre Musical.
> February 4. Dom M. definit. sided with me.
> February 5. Dom M. sends firm letter to Dame Laurentia re terms.
> February 7. Dom M. wrote strong letter to Stanbrook.
> February 20. Stanbrook accepts to translate N. Mus.

As it may be seen the matter of this translation caused great concern to Justine Ward. It was the first time that she was in disagreement with Dom Mocquereau, as she herself noted; this disagreement was about a practical teaching question, a question of terminology, which was essential to her. She firmly

believed that her gratefulness and her loyalty to the Master required this in-
transigent attitude on her part. She explained this to him in a letter which
Dom Mocquereau received in Paris where he was attending a session of the
Gregorian Institute, which had just been opened in the capital city. In this letter of January 29, 1924, she alludes to a somewhat distressing discussion which
had taken place before this trip.

> Sablé, January 29, 1924
> Very Dear and Most Reverend Father,
> I want to tell you that I am extremely sorry for having spoken bluntly to
> you yesterday. Surprise and suffering made me lose my head, and I am
> afraid I hurt you. I am so sorry about this.
> However, on the matter itself, I have not changed my mind. Everything
> considered, I am confirming my first decision. If Mother Laurentia ab-
> solutely wants to keep her terms, and the errors which are found here and
> there throughout the book, I shall not insist, but I shall not accept any re-
> sponsibility—financial or otherwise—for this translation which, with re-
> spect to certain fundamental points, betrays your thought and distorts your
> teaching.
> I have only one desire: to see that you are read, understood, and approved
> by the American and English public, and for that, a genuine translation is
> needed. A translation which would be a betrayal would in no way further
> the achievement of the proposed objective, and could even be prejudicial to
> the Gregorian and Solesmian movement which has already been so suc-
> cessfully launched.
> I already wrote my ultimatum—very politely yet very firmly—to Mother
> Laurentia, without going over minute details, but I fixed the principles. I
> would like to believe that you are supporting me in this matter which—for
> me—is based on my gratefulness to you and on my duty of complete loyalty
> to your interests. I would be extremely sad if a shadow should appear be-
> tween us because of this matter, about which I only want to serve you with
> unmitigated devotion. It is the feeling that you are doubtful about me and
> that you do not trust me completely when confronted with Mother Lau-
> rentia's letter, which hurt me so much yesterday.

Another letter, again written in Sablé, followed the previous one on
February 4. Despite its length, it is interesting to quote it in its entirety. It is indeed a rousing plea which gives precious information on its author's personality
and work.

> Sablé, February 4, 1924
> Reverend Father,
> This morning I received a letter from Stanbrook—two even—which,
> even though they do not answer in any way the questions I asked, make it
> very clear that the translation was undertaken for you and not for me and
> that it is your judgment and not mine which they want. I have therefore no
> other option but to submit to you the list of terms which are to be changed
> if the translation is to be accepted by me . . .
> But I believe I should remind you of some facts which will help you to
> decide, even though it is distressing for me to speak of such things.
> 1. I have spent all my life studying music, modern as well as ancient, and
> teaching it. Thus, I may have a certain advantage over the Stanbrook nuns
> who—certainly—have had many other duties and concerns.

2. In addition to this general education, I had the pleasure of spending more than three years under your personal instruction. During that time, I did not simply try to understand and to apply your teaching by directing children and adult choirs, and by training religious and lay teachers—but in addition to this, I was able to begin a much more difficult task: to reconstruct in an entirely new form the truth of your teaching. In order to translate accurately, in order to repeat it in the original form, it is necessary to understand fully the thought of the master, and you told me I had succeeded . . . If I succeeded in the more difficult task, it is first of all because I understood you.

3. In addition to these three years of study with you, I must remind you, Father, that I am not translating you today for the first time. During the 1922 Summer School in New York, you first asked other people to translate you. They did not satisfy you. In the end, you accepted this little service from me. Among the listeners, there were some Canadians who spoke French and English equally well. They told you they were satisfied with the translation—you yourself told me this—and they even said that, at times, they understood your thought better in the English version. I am ashamed to remind you of this, but I am doing it because I think it may influence you in reaching your decision.

People have quite often told me that the *Nombre Musical* became clear and understandable after my courses, while before, no one understood anything about it. I am not saying this as if it were a phenomenal thing: in regard to matters of art and especially of this art in which there is so much light and shade, it is necessary to learn *viva voce*; later on, the books are understood—and believe me, I am not congratulating myself for this. It would be shameful if it were otherwise. I am mentioning this here simply to show that if, after my course, people understood the *Nombre Musical* better, it is because my translation did not contradict it, but rather revealed it.

I must also remind you that the terms in which I translated you in America during the summer of 1922, were reproduced daily in the mimeographed copies which were given to each of your students who—in turn—gave this same instruction in these same English equivalents to their students—religious and laypersons—in all the corners of the United States and Canada where the Solesmes principles have penetrated. One can imagine the disorder which would ensue if all this was suddenly changed. Instead of encouraging the Gregorian and Solesmian movement, this translation would throw an element of confusion and of disagreement where everything is going so well right now.

4. Finally, it is not possible for me to ask the Catholic Education Press to publish this translation if it cannot be used to develop courses at the University. For that, it must conform to the general system and to the terminology in use. For any doctorate—either in music or in science, etc. . . . certain groups of subjects are required. Among them, psychology, biology, etc. etc. . . . We cannot put at the top of our musical system a textbook which would contradict all the other books of the system. My books are at the base. Yours would be—I hope—at the top. This was Dr. Shields' desire and I have no doubt that my recommendation will be followed on this subject. If the translation were in contradiction with either the elementary books (which could perhaps be made to conform little by little), or with the scientific books—whose terminology I tried to respect and which could not be made to conform—the *Nombre Musical* could not be used in our teaching and I could not recommend this translation to the printer. Here is the matter as I see it, Reverend Father. If I have misjudged, I only ask to be made aware of it.

One last word: if you side with Stanbrook, I shall remain just as devoted to you as in the past. This will not make any difference between us, since I am devoted to you not only personally but also because I am deeply convinced that you are right. The only difference will be that I shall not accept the translation for our teaching.

If, on the contrary, you decide to support me in this matter, I am asking you to do it with conviction and in a clear manner with the Stanbrook nuns. If you do not trust me sufficiently to do that, it would be better not to do it at all . . .

This was followed by the list of "errata in the English terms of the *Nombre Musical*" (five typewritten pages) mentioned at the beginning of this letter (Appendix No. 36 Tr.).

From Santa Fe, Justine Ward had kept Dom Mocquereau informed about the book (*Gregorian Chant, Music IV*) which she was still preparing, about the drawings of Dom de Subercaseaux (Santa Fe, Aug. 21, 1923) and about the chironomy prepared by the nuns of Sainte Cécile (Santa Fe, Sept. 16, 1924). Now, before leaving for Italy, she asked him to take care of the French translation of her books, and especially of her fourth volume on Gregorian chant which she was then finishing (Journal, Jan. 21: Finished Music IV) and which was being translated at Quarr Abbey where a part of the community had remained. The foundation of the Gregorian Institute of Paris, which had taken place on December 5, 1923 (*Rev. Gr.*, 1924, p. 27) made these translations desirable, but at the same time raised some delicate problems for Justine Ward, as we are going to see. Most notably, she insisted on the necessity of her course being studied in its entirety: the fourth volume on the Gregorian chant would be useless if the three elementary preceding volumes were not studied first. Justine Ward thus wrote from Sablé on February 25, 1924:

People often asked me for these translations but when we started them it was before the formation of the Gregorian Institute of Paris. At Manhattanville, much work has already been done on the translation of the elementary books, and at Quarr Abbey the monks have been good enough to begin the translation of the fourth book (*Gregorian Chant*). If these translations cannot be used, they should be stopped as soon as possible.

On one point, I am sure: the fourth book (*Gregorian Chant*) would be above the children's capabilities if they had not previously had the musical formation of the three elementary books. The system holds together, from one end to the other. Therefore, if the elementary books cannot be used, the fourth one would not be useful at all.

I am not anxious for these translations to be done. I even hesitated for a long time and in the end I persuaded myself, almost against my own judgment, to have them done.

Furthermore, the situation has been changed completely by the formation of the Gregorian Institute. Before this event, my books would have been published like others: they would have been successful or not—it would have had no importance—but I would not want to be criticized later on. I could neither approve my books (since they would perhaps go against the teaching of the Institute) nor disapprove them since they have been so successful at home and since these principles are the only ones, in my opinion, which are capable of training children in music in such a way that they are able when they are 9 or 10 years old to read easily from the liturgical books with a well-placed voice and without hesitation. I am not pretending that there are no other ways, just as good or even better, but I do not know them and these have been successful at home, therefore I could not repudiate them.

I understand, of course, that it is too early for the Institute to make a decision about this matter. But I believe that it would be more gracious on my part to withdraw right now; to avoid additional translation expenses by stopping them as soon as possible, thus sparing the directors of the Gregorian Institute and myself a situation which would easily become very disagreeable for everyone . . . "

Goodbye, Reverend and Very Dear Father, pray for your two poor oblates (Justine Ward and Agnès Lebreton) who are going away and who will count the days until they return. Miss Lebreton will bring this letter to you. I am not coming because I have not even begun to correct the proofs.

While the letters which were just quoted reveal Justine Ward's strong personality, they do not, when taken alone, express the quality of her relationship with Dom Mocquereau and Solesmes: they are exceptions—together with one or two letters written in 1927—and even demonstrate, in a different way, Dom Mocquereau's and Justine Ward's perfect understanding about the essentials.

We could actually give an example of this now by quoting at length from the letters addressed by Justine Ward to Dom Mocquereau from Rome where she went in March, 1924, but the subject of these letters would go beyond our present subject. We shall make a quick analysis of them.

The Pius X Institute of New York

Justine Ward went to Rome because of a matter which much concerned her. A letter from Dom Mocquereau had already alluded in December, 1922, to certain difficulties concerning the Pius X School of New York: "The opposition you are talking about had to be expected," Dom Mocquereau wrote. "It is a good sign, it is a sign that it is God's work" (Mocquereau, Christmas Vigil 1922). Referring then to what he had said about Cluny in his farewell lecture given in New York in that same year, he added: "This convent of the Sacred Heart in New York is now writing one of the most glorious pages in the history of the Institute of the Sacred Heart in supporting the desires of the Holy See concerning liturgy and chant."

A little later, in January 1923, Justine Ward transmitted to Dom Mocquereau a letter from the Provincial Superior of the Convent of Albany who was refusing her consent for that year's summer session in New York, on the grounds that the Sisters needed some rest (R.M. Mary Moran, Albany, Jan. 11, 1923). Then in a telegram to Dom Mocquereau, she mentioned that, actually, "this foundation of the School of Liturgical Music was not considered to be a typical work of the Congregation" and was in danger of being suppressed (Ward, telegram of Jan. 9, 1923). Dom Mocquereau replied that this seemed impossible to him:

> The Religious of the Sacred Heart sense so well what the Lord and the Church want that they cannot consent to the suppression of the magnificent liturgical movement whose author is God himself (Mocquereau, Jan. 27, 1923).

Thus, he advised Justine Ward to approach the American bishops before getting Rome involved as she wanted (Mocquereau, July 22, 1923). Later on, the situation improved and Justine Ward, in full agreement with the Superior in Albany, considered having a large music hall constructed entirely at her own expense (Mocquereau, Oct. 16 and Nov. 8, 1923; Ward, Santa Fe, August 12, 1923; Cf. Ward to J. Bonnet, Feb. 23, 1924).

Then, another difficulty appeared and Justine Ward went to Rome in March 1924 in order to solve it: was it proper for Mother Stevens to offer courses to men, either priests or laymen?

After a brief stop in Florence where she attended the wedding of her niece (Ward, Rome, March 5, 1924), Justine Ward went at once to the Eternal City. Her first visit was to Monsignor O'Hern, Rector of the North American College,[1] who advised her to see the Superior General of the Religious of the Sacred Heart first, before discussing the matter with the Holy Father, as she was planning to do. The Superior General was quite reserved, but later said that she would bring the matter to her advisory council. This was not a categorical refusal (Ward, Rome, March 6). A little later, Justine Ward sent her the *Revue Grégorienne* articles on the Pius X School, which she had not yet seen. She then paid a visit to Dom Ferretti, who showed her the Superior School of Sacred Music,[*] promised to obtain an audience with the Pope for her, and even offered to go with her. Dom Ferretti was very helpful in this matter, for the audience was granted immediately. But he advised Justine Ward to prepare a little memo on the Pius X School before the audience, and he then introduced her to Cardinal Bisleti who was well disposed toward Solesmes (he had just sent a diploma to the Abbey on June 18, 1923—Mocquereau, July 6, 1923) but who advised against taking up Mother Stevens' case with the Holy Father (Ward, March 10, 1924). On the day of the audience—March 14th—Justine Ward went to mass at the tomb of Pius X and when the hour came, Dom Ferretti accompanied her to the Holy Father's office. He gave the Holy Father many desirable explanations concerning the work of "Pius X" before introducing Justine Ward. Pius XI came forward to greet his visitors, invited them to sit down, and the audience lasted forty-five minutes. He warmly thanked Justine Ward for her support of the School of Sacred Music in Rome and gave her the Blessing she wanted for her work in New York, while encouraging her to continue it since she was not aiming merely for beauty in the liturgical offices, but also for the sanctification of souls. The Pope then inquired about Dom Mocquereau, recalling a few memories of him. He recognized him immediately from the photographs which were presented to him (Ward, Rome, March 14, 1924).

When Justine Ward saw the Superior General again, the permission requested for Mother Stevens was granted exceptionally and temporarily, to give the Pius X School time to train a teacher of men's classes. (Ward, Rowe, March 20, 1924).

The two objectives of the journey had been reached: the Holy Father's Blessing

---

[*]Later to become the Pontifical Institute of Sacred Music. (Ed. note.)

for the "Pius X" undertaking, and the permission for Mother Stevens granted (Ward, Paris, no date). Justine Ward kept Dom Mocquereau posted on the minute details of these proceedings. What is most striking, however, is this refrain which is often found throughout her writings and which shows her deep attachment to Solesmes:

> This morning, I had the pleasure of receiving your March 7th letter. Thank you, it was a consolation for the two oblates (*Justine Ward and Agnès Lebreton*) who are feeling a little out of place so far away from Solesmes. I don't see how I could stay in Rome for so long. I am yearning for Solesmes. We are walking arm in arm all the time, if there is an accident, we will be crushed together and you will put the bones in a small box in the cemetery of Solesmes (Ward, March 10, 1924)—We will see you soon, Reverend Father, you know how we are looking forward to seeing our dear Abbey again, to telling you how we are devoted to you, and to hearing again the divine chant of Solesmes (Ward, s.d. 1924).

Justine Ward came back to Sablé on March 25, 1924. She finished her fourth year book, whose chironomy had been entrusted to a nun of Sainte Cécile E. (e.g. Santa Fe, Sept. 16, 1923). Everything was completed at the end of May. In her journal, Justine Ward mentions again a few discussions with Dom Mocquereau and Dom Gajard, who was acting-choirmaster already and who was actively working with him to write the second volume of the *Nombre Musical Grégorien*. However, we do not know what the subject of these discussions was. On May 17, Justine Ward went to Paris where she gave a lecture to the Gregorian Institute which had made her a member of its Honorary Committee (Ward, Sablé, Feb. 23, 1924). She related the story of her work in America, and talked about her Method and its results. Dom Mocquereau, who accompanied her, wrote a vibrant account of the lecture in the *Revue Grégorienne* (1924, pp. 160–164). A little later, on June 14, Justine Ward sailed again for America. (Cf. Appendix No. 37.)

In spite of the difficulties we mentioned earlier, the Pius X School of New York was expanding. The Congress of Toronto (Canada) which was held on May 7 and 8, 1924, presented an opportunity for a brilliant demonstration of the Ward Method. Organized by a diligent student of this School, Father Ronan, Music Director at the Saint Augustine Seminary, who had come to Solesmes in 1923, after having attended Dom Mocquereau's classes in 1922, this Congress was hailed as "the dawn of a whole restoration of liturgical chant in Canada." More than 2,000 young singers were noted for the sureness of their chant, the quality and ease of their voices, and Mother Stevens' choir of young women distinguished itself particularly (*Rev. Gr.*, 1925, p. 38).

At the end of 1924, on November 6th, Cardinal Patrick Hayes gave his solemn blessing to the new "Hall" of the Pius X School which had just been built at Justine Ward's expense. Built according to an archaic design, this hall was perfectly suited to its end: "creating a mystical atmosphere with a sweet and religious severity, excluding any profane thought and marvellously harmonized in advance with Gregorian rhythms." Justine Ward had a Casavant organ installed in this hall, as Master Joseph Bonnet had recommended. The Cardinal recalled the modest beginning of the Institute in 1917, the obstacles and prejudices which had to be overcome, and finally, the success of the venture: 13,000 students holding a Ward diploma, 500,000 children trained by them, the Method used in 45 states and in Canada, even in the Philippines, and adopted by more than 60 religious communities. The cardinal then transmitted the blessing of the Holy Father "expressing his hope that this blessing shall remain forever upon this Institute and upon those who are working there" (Ward, Nov. 7, 1924).

During this ceremony, 400 children representing 20 Catholic parochial schools in New York, sang psalms and Gregorian pieces, notably the *Christus vincit* and the *Te Deum*, in two choirs. After the Benediction of the Blessed Sacrament, the Cardinal, who was deeply impressed, congratulated Justine Ward and Mother Stevens and promised to appoint a priest—to be chosen by Justine Ward herself—who, upon completion of his training, would replace Mother Stevens in the men's classes. He also promised to write the Abbot of Solesmes in support of the invitation to come to America for a third time, an invitation which Justine Ward still persisted in wanting to address to Dom Mocquereau (Ward, New York, Nov., 1924).

From Lisieux, where he was at that time, Dom Mocquereau participated in this great event by sending a telegram of congratulations which was most appreciated by the addressee (Mocquereau, Nov. 9, 1924).[2] (See also Appendix No. 20.)

Sojourns in Sablé

From January, 1925 to October, 1928, very few of Justine Ward's letters were kept by Dom Mocquereau, while we have more than one hundred replies from him. And yet, Justine Ward's journal is the most useful document to consult in regard to this period, in spite of its brevity and of its lacunae. But first, we must briefly mention Justine Ward's sojourns in Sablé during this period of nearly four years, i.e.:

from December 24, 1924 to June 12, 1925 (fifth sojourn near the Abbey), with a rather short trip to Rome in March;

from April 4, 1926 to June 8, 1926, with a trip to Rome in April;

from February 22 to May 4, 1927;

from August 21 to September 17, 1927, with a very short trip to Italy in September;

from August 14 to October 9, 1928 (departure from London) with a rather short trip to Holland in August. (Cf. Appendix No. 20.)

In the following lines, we had to group certain facts concerning these years 1925–1928, for greater clarity, but each time the dates are carefully mentioned in order to respect the chronology.

Trips to Rome

The 1925 trip to Rome was made on the occasion of the Jubilee of the Holy Year, but Justine Ward wanted to take advantage of it to obtain another audience with the Holy Father and to see again the Superior General of the Sacred

Heart. It was Solesmes' procurator in residence in Rome who was to guide her in her pilgrimages. The audience with the Pope took place on March 21st (Journal) but since Justine Ward left Rome on the 23rd, we did not find any mention of it in her letters (Ward, Rome, March 8 and 15, 1925; Mocquereau, March 9th).

While she was in Rome, Justine Ward was a guest at the Superior School of Sacred Music, of which she was a distinguished benefactor. She prepared the journey of its president, Dom Ferretti, to America where he was to give lectures at the Pius X School.

> During most of the day, we work to choose and prepare the lectures of Father Ferretti for next summer in New York (Ward, Rome, March 8, 1925). We are working hard on Father Ferretti's lectures and on the preparation of the plan of all the exhibits he will need. It is necessary to arrange each lecture beforehand, with the exhibits which will illustrate it. There is much to be done . . . D. Ferretti is concerned primarily with melodic aspects and with the analysis of the pieces in terms of the melody: forms, the ancients' ways of composing. All that will be very interesting and will not deal at all with the question of rhythm, whose principles our students have mastered well (Ward, Rome, March 15, 1925).

As for the 1926 trip to Rome, we have three letters from Dom Mocquereau (April 12, 18, and 21, 1926) which give us some information. When she paid a visit to Cardinal Bisleti, Justine Ward received an "ad honorem" Master's Degree in Gregorian chant, dated March 12th and presented to her that day on the Feast of Saint Gregory the Great, "in acknowledgment of the very important artistic work which her high intelligence and her indefatigable tenacity are developing in her fatherland in order to further the noble aims of religious music" (Mocquereau, April 12, 1926, *Rev. Gr.* 1926, p. 102). Justine Ward left Rome on April 18th or 19th, returned there soon afterwards, and left again on Sunday the 25th, certainly after the audience with the Holy Father, which she had announced to Dom Mocquereau although the date had not yet been set (Mocquereau, April 18th and 21st).

We know nothing of the 1927 trip to Italy—not to Rome—which was very quick (Journal, Sept. 7, 1927: To Italy—and Sept. 10th: Return Sablé). As was the case with the preceding trip, Justine Ward probably discussed it with Dom Mocquereau but there is no recorded trace of their conversation.

Discussions and Divergences

The English translation of the *Nombre Musical Grégorien* was still causing some concern to Justine Ward. This is evident in her journal. Under the April 26, 1925 entry we read: "Working translation N.M."; and under the following day: "Saw D.M. re 'broking of ictus.' " The matter is still mentioned on May 3, and on the 16th a joint letter from Dom Mocquereau and Justine Ward to the Abbess of Stanbrook is mentioned: "Drafted letter with D.M. to Dame L. re terms"; finally on May 22nd, the abbess accepted to change her terminology: "M.L. accepts terms to vol. II N.M." It is probably in the course of these searching discussions that Dom Mocquereau confided to Justine Ward on May 1st: "It is Dom Sablayrolles (whom we shall meet again later on) and you who have understood me the best." Certainly, Mother Laurentia was a learned Gregorianist, but it is certain that she did not accept Dom Mocquereau's rhythmic system without reservations. As for the matter of the translation itself, apart from the inevitable differences in style between one side of the Atlantic and the other, the Ward Journal indicates clearly that the issue was to keep the terminology of the first volume of the *Nombre Musical* since Justine Ward was using it already (Cf. supra Ward, Sablé, Feb. 4, 1924).

Very few letters from Mother Laurentia to Dom Mocquereau have been kept, but in one of them, dated May 20, 1925, she wrote:

> I am very pleased, Father, with the way in which this episode has been concluded and with the fact that I am in agreement with you and with Mrs. Ward, whose devotion and competence I sincerely appreciate. Say this to her on my behalf and transmit my affectionate thoughts to her (20. V. 1925).

We should now say—in order not to have to take up the subject again—that in November 1929, Justine Ward, who was still concerned about this translation, obtained Dom Mocquereau's agreement that it should be entrusted to a person having a more impersonal style[3] than Mother Laurentia. She wrote to her: "a new personality has been substituted for yours." The abbess of Stanbrook was too intelligent and too virtuous to be hurt by this; she readily accepted abandoning the task that she had undertaken only to help Dom Mocquereau (M. Laurentia, Nov. 12, and 18, 1929). On this subject, see also, Ward, Mora Vocis, April 29, Oct. 26, Nov. 12, 18, and 24, and Dec. 4, 1929; S. Francis Camp, June 2nd and 10th).

A new subject of discussion came up in 1927, and caused a very lively reaction on the part of Justine Ward. The matter was nothing less than the wording of a chapter of the 2nd volume of the *Nombre Musical*, then at the printer's. The question is very complex and we shall not consider the technical details of this discussion, which seems somewhat futile today, but which should be understood in the context of the times. This little discussion will enable us to quote a very beautiful page from Dom Mocquereau.

But first, here are the annotations of the Ward Journal. After having mentioned the differences she has, for the time being, with Dom Mocquereau (Feb. 22nd), Justine Ward mentions three stormy interviews with him and Dom Joseph Gajard (Feb. 24th, 27th and 28th) and finally she mentions on March 1st Dom Mocquereau's decision to omit a page, already printed in the proofs, from Chapter XIII of the 2nd volume of the *Nombre Musical* (cf. copy and proofs of Dom Mocquereau in the Reserve of Paleography).[4]

Justine Ward thus obtained the omission of a page she deemed in opposition or at least at variance with the instruction in her fourth year book on *Gregorian Chant*, an instruction book which she claimed to have received from Dom Mocquereau himself.

Nevertheless, she wrote from Sablé, on March 5, 1927, the following letter which gives the tone of the discussion (Cf. App. No. 38):

March 5, 1927
Reverend Father,
Concern for the truth and the matter of honor with respect to my students forces me to request a categorical answer from you on the subject of the *Rythme Ondulant* taught in my book *Gregorian Chant*.
Would you be kind enough to read again in Chapter VI pages 90, 91, 92 and tell me:
1. Whether this doctrine is from you or from me?
2. Whether you taught it to me at Quarr Abbey in 1921–22?
3. Whether it is still your doctrine, or whether you believe you should change or modify it?
I am asking you also to look at the chironomy of the *Gloria Ambrosian* (p. 113–114) of the Mass responses (p. 124 –5, –6), the *Ave Regina Caelorum* (p. 209) and the *Regina Caeli* (p. 210), to mention only a few typical examples of the application of your principles (or of what I have supposed it to be in this case)—and to tell me whether this chironomy is yours or mine?
I am not offering these examples as models in terms of the drawings, rather, I am simply asking whether the doctrine is yours?
It is impossible for me to continue to teach without your written answer, Father, and I beg you not to leave me for too long in such a state of uncertainty.
I am waiting your answer, Father, and I am, Very Respectfully yours.

At the same time, Justine Ward also sent to Dom Gajard a lively letter on the same subject.

What was this about? A note from Dom Gajard explains it. It was about a detail of Gregorian chironomy, more precisely of the so-called "undulating" chironomy. According to Dom Gajard, Justine Ward herself was at the origin of this "innovation," later adopted by Dom Mocquereau. He insists on this point three times in the same note, all the more so because he himself was willing to accept this chironomy in certain cases (undulation made from a series of theses) but not in others (undulation made from a series or arses). For example, this is what he wrote:

Until 1922, at the time of the journey to America, or more precisely until Mrs. Ward's journey to Quarr Abbey in the previous winter, Dom Mocquereau practically always used loops for the ascending arsis and relied more on the melodic line than on the Latin word itself . . .

But Dom Mocquereau, having adopted the undulating chironomy even for the arsis, wrote further:

"For years I did not accept this. Why? Because I considered the undulating line as a series of theses." And he added. "If Dom Mocquereau made an 'innovation,' it was in 1922, in his conversations with Mrs. Ward."

Dom Gajard did not object any longer after Dom Mocquereau had explained to him that the undulation "is in itself written neither arsic nor thetic, that it may very well be arsic."

In her book, Justine Ward does not mention the arsic undulation rhythm, while the page in question from the *Nombre Musical* which was being prepared (Ch. XIII of Volume II) did mention it. Was it for this reason that she requested and obtained permission for its suppression in order not to appear to be in disagreement with Dom Mocquereau? It seems to be so, since a note from her proposes precisely such a clear distinction between the undulating thesis and the undulating arsis and indicates a chironomy shown above the melody—to indicate its arsis character—as the page deleted from Chapter XIII did (Appendix No. 39). But this undated note probably succeeds the discussions related above. It is an attempt to explain them. Dom Mocquereau probably deleted the indicated page in a conciliatory spirit.

In any case, on March 12, which was the Feast of Saint Gregory the Great, Dom Mocquereau sent to Justine Ward the following "Declaration" which she probably requested since she was hurt that her faithfulness to her venerated Master was questioned.

> *Declaration* (cf. Appendix No. 40)
> I have learned that some misinformed persons affirm that certain pages from *Gregorian Chant* by Mrs. J.B. Ward are at variance with the rhythmic and chironomic doctrines of the school of Solesmes. I want to protest without delay against this ridiculous assertion. I maintain absolutely everything I said in the Introduction to *Gregorian Chant*, in 1921, about the perfect conformity of the Solesmian and American teaching, in theory and practice. In the years since 1921, the complete agreement of the two Schools, Solesmes and the Pius X Institute of New York, has only been confirmed and consolidated.
> In witness thereof, I sign F. André Mocquereau, m.b.

Since Justine Ward dreaded nothing more than seeming in opposition to her venerated master, we may assume very legitimately that this declaration pleased her very much. It put an end to the discussions.

In an article in the *Revue Grégorienne* published in 1929–1930, entitled "Un perfectionnement de détail dans la chironomie grégorienne"[5] written toward the end of his life (he died in January, 1930, even before the article was published), Dom Mocquereau once again took up the subject and presented this *arsic* undulating chironomy as an *ideal* one. Dom Gajard wrote that this article "was his last work and that those who were around him knew how much effort and concern it had caused him" (*Rev. Gr.*, note of Dom Gajard at the end of Dom Mocquereau's article). Dom Mocquereau had effectively been working on it for several years and he had often announced this improvement in chironomy to Justine Ward, in writing, with much precaution, it seems, because he never indicated clearly what it was about, but he seemed assured, however, that she "would be satisfied with it" (Mocquereau, Sept. 20, May 24, Oct. 30, 1927). Here is the conclusion of this article which contains the essential part of Dom Mocquereau's thought:

It is true what I said in the N.M.G. Vol II, No. 1196–1197, (Dom Mocquereau writes,) that *contracted chironomy* is the ideal gesture of this fragment. Certainly that's true, but note that I added: "especially in terms of the conductorship, of the training of the choir": this additional remark, in my thought, hid a reservation about the perfect, complete, absolute value of this chironomy. This gesture is, truly, excellent, since it reaches its objective; and yet I hesitated to write the word "*ideal*;" I hesitated, I had scruples, afterthoughts: Is there not indeed a goal—let us repeat our adjective by transforming it into a noun: an *Ideal*, which is higher than the all external *conductorship of a choir*? Assuredly! That of the intrinsic and superior beauty of the melody itself, a supreme ideal, fully artistic, which I evoked at the beginning of this article (p. 246); an ideal which is also the ideal of chironomy in that the latter is the adequate representation of the melody and of the great rhythm.

Then, we must do better, we must aim higher. Do you want the ideal chironomic gesture? In spirit, heart, and taste, elevate yourself to the Ideal itself which is hovering over the work of art, over the melody and its text. Actually, I must confess it: often, in the quiet atmosphere of the divine office, in front of a docile, well trained choir, when presented with a fully satisfactory performance, I have caught myself suppressing, instinctively, the spirals, chironomic loops of *contracted arsis* which are not necessary for such a choir, and replacing them with a sequence of clearly ascending undulations which adequately represent the rising line of the melody and of the rhythm.

On further consideration, these *spontaneous* gestures seemed to be the perfect ideal I was dreaming of: the summit of art is then reached at the very moment one forgets it; the melody is impregnated with, soaked in prayer, supplication, joy, jubilation. The choirmaster is no longer the guide of his cantors then; he is himself influenced by them, by the cantilena he is hearing: he reproduces it in his gesture *in the same way the voices express it.*

Thus the profound impression made on the faithful, and even the unfaithful by this divine music, when it is understood, expressed, conducted on such a high plane.

This is the case of the *improvement* which we propose to study in this article; here it is, in all its simplicity: replacement of the *contracted* chironomy, in certain given circumstances, by the *continuous ascending undulating* chironomy.

This improvement should be all the more taken into consideration since it is not research, of intellectual combinations, of which we must always beware, but rather since it is the result of an *unforeseen, spontaneous* discovery; it appeared and imposed itself gently, clearly in the midst of musical activity, under exceptionally favorable conditions; it revealed, underlined the rhythm of the melody in all of its grace, truth, oneness, this time truly ideal beauty; how could we ignore it! (*Rev. Gr.*, 1929, p. 251)

As Dom Mocquereau had hoped and expected, Justine Ward was very pleased with this article, particularly with the lines which expressed Dom Mocquereau's spirituality so well. They were so much in harmony with Justine Ward's intuitive mind that she was glad to quote them later on (obituary "*Dom André Mocquereau*" in *Orate Fratres*, IV, No. 5, March 23, 1930, pp. 199–208 Cf. Appendix No. 66).

The preceding pages revealed a trait of Justine Ward's personality, her unyielding character well known by all those who approached her. Whether the

matter concerned the English translation of the *Nombre Musical*, a problem of
Gregorian rhythmics, or difficulties with the Pius X School, Justine Ward
showed her tenacious will in the pursuit of her ideas. Conscious of being a
faithful disciple of Dom Mocquereau, she defended him against himself we
could say, whenever she believed that his doctrine was at stake. She did not,
however, ignore the possible progress of science and experience or stick strictly
to her own personal point of view. She wrote Dom Gajard, during their heated
discussion:

> You see, Father, I *reserve* my judgment. I see nothing: perhaps, once the
> terms have been fixed, we shall see the light. I hope you will do the same,
> since—after all—we are only looking for the truth. I changed my mind
> enough times to do it again if the truth should require it. I am sure you will
> do it too, won't you? In this domain of ideas we must not look for personal
> preferences. But for the time being, I see only contradiction and destruc-
> tion—with one stroke of the pen—of the immense artistic work, the unique
> masterpiece which Father Mocquereau has given us . . . On a few points
> concerning details, practical application, taste, I understand that we could
> have differences without having to part with one another. But it is some-
> thing else if the question is, truly, about *principles*. Thus, I pray for light,
> either on one side or the other (Ward to D. Gajard, Feb. 24, 1927).

Such tenacity on the part of Justine Ward was thus dictated by her concern
to remain always faithful to the doctrine of the one she considered to be her
master and by her concern never to appear in disagreement with it.

The Ward Movement

We said that Justine Ward had invited Dom Ferretti to give courses in Gregorian aesthetics at the Pius X School. He gave them in June 1925, and in May
1927. Justine Ward took care of the English translation, which required much
work. These lectures were discussed at length in the *Revue Grégorienne*, but we
must mention here that in 1925, Dom Ferretti was asked by the Holy Father to
present the founder of the Pius X School with the gold medal "Pro Ecclesia et
Pontifice." In conferring this honor upon her, Pope Pius XI also intended to express his benevolence and his gratefulness to all those who were contributing to
the propagation of the Gregorian movement which had started in this School
(*Rev. Gr.*, 1925, 117, 237; 1926, 102; 1927, 197). Justine Ward notified Dom
Mocquereau at once by telegram.

> "This is a well deserved, appropriate blessing, Dom Mocquereau answered,
> and I understand "the enthusiastic hearts." I really regret that I was not there
> when you were given the award. Mother Stevens must have been delighted.
> She too deserved an award. Give her half of your medal of honor" (July 1,
> 1925).

Justine Ward seems to have attended the Gregorian Days held in Paris from
April 28 to April 30, 1925, under the chairmanship of Cardinal Dubois, because

her journal mentions this briefly. The success of the chants was attributable to the science and to the enthusiasm of Dom Gajard and of Dom Sablayrolles from the Abbey of En Calcat. It was on this occasion, it seems, that Dom Mocquereau introduced Justine Ward to this faithful disciple who was to be of great help to her in later years (cf. *Rev. Gr.*, 1925, pp. 38 and 77).

Dom Mocquereau also presented a woman organist to Justine Ward in 1926. In a letter of June 14, he writes about this organist who was a follower of the "Ward Movement": "Miss Bezançon, organist of the Schola of S. Ferdinand of Bordeaux, who already saw you at Solesmes during Pentecost, will be officially charged, this coming November, to train all the children in her parish in Gregorian chant according to the Ward Method. She would be glad to discuss her problems with you and to benefit from your experience. She already has an English copy of your Method." (Mocquereau, June 14, 1926.)

On April 19, 1927, Dom Mocquereau celebrated his fifty years of monastic profession. He had made his temporary simple profession on April 9, 1877, which was the feast of the Annunciation deferred until after Easter, and his perpetual solemn profession on April 14, 1880. On this occasion, he received a letter from Pope Pius XI who had added, in his own handwriting: "peramanter in Domino." This caused great joy to the venerated jubilarian. Justine Ward attended the ceremony. Two Dutchmen who were at Solesmes at the time, Father Henri Vullinghs and Mr. Joseph Lennards, were also in attendance. Both wanted to devote themselves to the propagation of Gregorian chant in their country and were already following Dom Mocquereau's teaching. Mr. Lennards had been coming to Solesmes since 1923, that is to say, virtually since the return of the monks to France, and Dom Mocquereau had given him his personal attention. Mr. Lennards wrote: "It is thanks to Solesmes and to Dom Mocquereau that I met Mrs. Ward and that I decided to devote my life to teaching Gregorian chant" (to D. Gajard, Dec. 14, 1953). After his jubilee, Dom Mocquereau introduced the two Dutchmen to Justine Ward. It was then decided that both of them would go to America during that year to attend Justine Ward's courses and the courses in Gregorian aesthetics which Dom Ferretti was to offer at the Pius X School. They arrived there on June 29, 1927 (Ward Journal). It was upon their return to Holland that the Ward Method was introduced in Haaver under the aegis of Father Vullinghs, and in Roermond under the aegis of Mr. Lennards. Catholic schools where Gregorian chant was taught with the Ward Method soon numbered into the hundreds. The Ward Method would shortly be adopted by many Protestant schools as well.[6]

In the following year, 1928, Justine Ward went to Holland herself. Before that, however, she came to Solesmes with two professors from the Pius X Institute, Father DesLongchamps and Father M. Breed, and with a group of seven young women from this Institute. The young women arrived on the eve of the Assumption and sang a Requiem Mass in the parish church of Solesmes on August 22 for one of their friends who had died recently. Dom Mocquereau attended the service, then the young women sang at Sainte Cécile's monastery and at Sablé where they sang for Benediction of the Blessed Sacrament (Ward Journal, Aug.

23). Justine Ward wanted Dom Mocquereau to approve the result of her Gregorian instruction before she left for Holland. We know the opinion which Dom Mocquereau transmitted immediately to Justine Ward, in an official and solemn form, in a memorable letter dated August 22, 1928, and which was published in the *Revue Grégorienne* shortly afterwards (*Rev. Gr.*, 1928, p. 238). The old master expressed there his great satisfaction, his enthusiasm, and all the hopes that this success was raising in him for the future. This letter deserves to be quoted (Translation Cf. Appendix No. 42).

Abbey Saint-Peter of Solesmes, August 22, 1928
Dear Madame,
August 22, 1928 is a date which cannot go unnoticed: all of us, you in America, we in Solesmes, must remember it: it is the first time that Gregorian melodies have been sung in Europe by voices who came from America, from New York, from the Pius X School. I want to tell you everything I think of this musical performance, quite humble outwardly, but prepared for a long time through serious studies and filled with the most precious promises for the future.

Quite humble, indeed; for a small village church is its site; but it is in the parish of Solesmes, a stone's throw from the Abbey of the Benedictines of Solesmes.

Quite humble again; for seven young American women, unknown, without fame, are simply going to sing a Requiem Mass for one of their friends, our guest last year, who died a few months ago. But these seven young women received their Gregorian and musical education from the Pius X School, they were trained in New York at first by teachers delegated by Right Reverend Dom Delatte, Abbot of Solesmes (at that time, at Quarr Abbey), then by Mrs. J.B. Ward and Reverend Mother Stevens, religious of the Sacred Heart. Today, having themselves become teachers, these children are coming to Solesmes, not to be admired for their talent, but to submit timidly to their former professor, as it is fitting for people of their age, the results obtained through more than ten years of assiduous work. In a few days, they will attend the Congress of Utrecht to plead through their singing the cause of Gregorian art; they do not dare to initiate these decisive proceedings without the encouragement and the approval of Solesmes. And in all this, dear Madame, they only obey you.

How will this Requiem Mass go? In the village, curiosity has been awakened; our guests, our foreigners, who themselves came to Solesmes to study Gregorian chant, want to attend this office, and all of them are there.

Dear Madame, you know the result; but I want to put it in writing, so that the congratulation of the entire audience will be for you, their leader, and for all your children, a reward for the steadfast zeal you exhibited during at least ten years in the intelligent, artistic and Christian implementation of the *Motu Proprio* of Pius X; this testimonial must remain in your archives for the history of your school and for the encouragement of the future students.

I am bringing up the subject of performance again. At first, the simple, collected attitude of these children makes one appreciate them and reveals that they are fully aware of the role assigned to them during Holy Mass; nothing theatrical, no attempt to pose, to exhibit their personality, to show off. As soon as the first notes are heard—no accompaniment of course—the whole audience is charmed: voice development is exquisite; purity, accuracy of the sounds, discretion in the nuances, suppleness and daintiness of the Solesmes rhythm which governs and envelops all the melody, chironomic conductorship, truly everything is perfect, from the *Requiem* Introit to the last notes of the *Libera me* responsory. A fragrance of piety, an atmosphere of calm, of peace, of artistic distinction, result from the whole and immerse the souls in prayer and contemplation. Angels sing in this manner before the Holy Trinity. Why is it surprising after all! Since their arrival, these children have received communion every day; I was told that several of them made the Stations of the Cross in our abbey church; thus, they have all the essential traits, vocal and spiritual, which, around the altar, characterize the true cantors of divine praise: beautiful voices, beautiful souls!

After that, I have nothing to add: why add praise and congratulations. They want them no more than you do, dear Madame; they came to Solesmes in order to know whether they are following the right path, whether they can present themselves, at the Congress of Utrecht, as authentic students of the School of Solesmes.

The answer is yes: they may go to Holland and elsewhere, with full confidence, they may take the most difficult tests, I can guarantee in advance that the Pius X School of New York and the School of Solesmes will be proud of their success.

One last word! I am not afraid to say it: if, though it is impossible, Gregorian rhythm happened to be lost at Solesmes or in Europe, one could then go and find it on the other side of the ocean, in New York, at the Pius X School and at Catholic University in Washington where Reverend Father DesLongchamps is solidly implanting it, with the greatest success, among the young clergy who come from all parts of the United States.

May God be praised a thousand times!

I have a duty to observe: I must thank you very much, Madame, founder and director of the Pius X School, as well as all those men and women who have contributed through their teaching to a so perfectly successful practical application of the *Motu Proprio* on sacred music of the Holy Father. Such an example is worthy of use as a model for all the schools that are eager to carry out the same program. My very special thanks are for your seven students who revealed everything we may expect from them and from their friends to us. I want to write their names here: they will remind those who will succeed them of the glorious and fruitful 1928 campaign in France and in Holland:

Miss Margaret Hurley	21 years old
Miss Marion Robinson	20 years old
Miss Julia Sampson	20 years old
Miss Margaret (Péguy) Sullivan	19 years old
Miss Mary Carroll	18 years old
Miss Catherine Carroll	18 years old
Miss Antoinette De Nigris (Denegris)	17 years old

Homage, Thanks,
  f. André Mocquereau m.b.

P.S. Since this letter, your children were heard in the parlor of the Abbey of Sainte Cécile, in front of our Benedictine nuns. The latter were delighted. I know that the perfection of the chant of your students inspired their emulation. The nuns acknowledge their inferiority, they are now eager to reach this perfection! Such is the good one single audition can make on well disposed souls! Sainte Cécile, in heaven, presided over this meeting.

This letter touched Justine Ward deeply, particularly the passage where Dom Mocquereau comforted himself by thinking that one could always find authentic Gregorian rhythm at the Pius X Institute, if it came to be lost at Solesmes.

Justine Ward thus left for Holland on August 25, but, first, she showed her students the admirable cathedral of Chartres. Two lectures by Justine Ward were scheduled at Utrecht where the Week of Sacred Music was being held. Demonstrations were to be made by the young women from New York and also by children trained by Father Vullinghs and Mr. Lennards (*Rev. Gr.*, 1928, p. 119).

In the postscript to his letter of August 22, 1928, Dom Mocquereau writes about the performance which took place in the parlor of Sainte Cécile, in front of the nuns. It was not the first time, as we may recall, that Justine Ward had given lessons there: her journal mentions that she had done it on May 27, 1925 (cf. Mocquereau, June 21, 1925). This time, the visit of Justine Ward's students resulted in the creation of courses in vocalization at Sainte Cécile (Mocquereau, Oct. 8 and Oct. 20, 1928). Justine Ward also gave courses at Précigné, not far from Solesmes, at the convent of the Marianite Sisters (Mocquereau, June 11, 1927).

Finally, this letter refers to Father DesLongchamps and to his work at the University in Washington. We will talk about him later. The Solesmes correspondence does not offer more information on the development of the Ward Movement. Up to this point, we have principally used the *Revue Grégorienne* on this subject. Moreover, we should mention the work of the "Pius X" students, to wit the work of Miss Honiss in England, then the work done in Dublin, in New Zealand, and even in China, thanks to the influence of the Religious of the Sacred Heart. Above all, we should mention the work of Miss McElligott in Serravalle, Italy. This was a foundation which generated great hopes.[7] It had been undertaken upon the request of an Italian patron of the arts, Egisto Fabbri, who gave his village a beautiful church in the purest Romanesque style (consecrated on September 8, 1927) (*Rev. Gr.*, 1928, pp. 35, 40, cf. *Rev. Gr.*, 1925, 118, 197). This foundation required much attention from Justine Ward who sent a teacher there. Soon afterwards, it caused her much concern, as the correspondence with Dom Mocquereau reveals, without enabling us to specify what the problems were. Thus, Dom Mocquereau wrote Justine Ward on September 29, 1927: "The principal news is about the state of affairs at Serravalle. Such a beautiful work *is bound* to have difficulties. It is a sign of success, which does not eliminate suffering, anxiety, and the duty to be watchful and to fight. Mr. Fabbri seems to me to be so calm and so skillful that we must trust him." Justine Ward probably went to Serravalle from September 7 to September 10, 1927 (Journal: "To Italy"). She may even have gone there from America, a little later. It seems indeed that she went to Italy in November 1927 (card from S.S. Aquitania dated Nov. 15, 1927).

In contrast, we have detailed information about Justine Ward's account to Dom Mocquereau concerning the founding of the School of Music at Catholic University in Washington. This information was transmitted to Dom

Mocquereau by Justine Ward during the course of her prolonged sojourn in America from October 1928 to August 1929. We will take up the subject in a little while. But we have already seen how her efforts to serve the noblest of all causes, that of the Sacred Liturgy, had been rewarded.

Nombre Musical Grégorien, 2nd Volume

First, we must mention that, at the end of 1927, Dom Mocquereau had the joy at last to witness the publication of the 2nd volume of the *Nombre Musical*. This book brought a letter from the Cardinal Secretary of State and a gold medal from Pius XI to its author (*Rev. Gr.,* 1928, pp. 200 and 201). He "summarized," as the Abbess of Stanbrook said to Dom Mocquereau himself, "the study and Gregorian experience of his life" (M. Laurentia, March 9, 1928). Unfortunately, we have no letter from Justine Ward on this subject, but on the other hand, we have the recension she wrote in *Catholic Choirmaster*[8] and which was partly translated and published in the August 30, 1928 issue of *La Croix*. Justine Ward expresses at the same time the great esteem she professed for her master's genius and the exceptional quality of his own intuition; indeed she saw in Dom Mocquereau the rather rare alliance of a genius with an outstanding teacher:

> These highly technical studies organized and directed by Dom Mocquereau over a period of nearly fifty years would have failed of their full object had they lacked the penetrating light of genius. For to say that Dom Mocquereau is a scholar is but a half-truth. He is an example of that rare combination of profound scholarship and flaming artistry which is given us but seldom in this imperfect world.
> The certitudes of a creative artist are the fruit of an intuitive process which seems at variance with the process of science. Based on facts, indeed, the conclusion of the artist is reached, not by logic alone, but by logic reinforced by trained intuition. The certitude reached by this process is fully convincing to the artist himself. The trouble arises when he wants his discovery to reach other minds and form them. It is then that his perception must be recast, and an equivalent found which will reach the mentality lacking the sixth sense of the artist.
> It is here that *Le Nombre Musical* has triumphed. It is one of the rare books which have translated those truths perceived instinctively by a great artist into terms which can convince the intelligent but non-intuitive reader and gradually move him toward an appreciation of high and subtle things.

Dom Mocquereau was very pleased with this article and said it with simplicity to its author:

> Splendid! I want to thank you warmly, for I sense that I have been understood and that the article has been written by a friendly and intelligent hand (Mocquereau, April 7, 1928).

Justine Ward wrote Dom Gajard at the same time, also on the subject of the 2nd volume of the *Nombre Musical* for which he had written a book review published in the *Revue Grégorienne* (1927, p. 201). This letter, dated March 7, 1928, was written at Mora Vocis. (Translation. Cf. Appendix No. 41).

> Reverend Father,
> I cannot refrain from sharing with you the immense joy which reading your article in the *Nombre Musical* caused me. I was absolutely delighted. It was so difficult, not to say impossible, to convey a real idea of the greatness of Father Mocquereau's work contained in the two volumes, but you succeeded in making this miracle, with such a beautiful general overview of the work itself, and with so much understanding toward the dear and venerable author.
> Father, may this brief letter bring you my most sincere congratulations together with my respectful thoughts.
>
> Justine Ward

In the year 1928, an article by Justine Ward published in *The Ecclesiastical Review* (May 1928, vol. 78, N.5) and entitled *Twenty-Five Years. Authority and Obedience*, was translated in the *Revue Grégorienne* (*Rev. Gr.*, 1928, p. 202). In this article, the author recalled ecclesiastic laws on religious music and attempted to dismiss the false allegations made to restrict, or even to avoid their application. (App. No. 65.)

In a postcard dated November 15, 1927, Justine Ward wrote Dom Mocquereau: "We are finally in "Mora Vocis" (Dobbs Ferry, N.Y.), but we are far from being settled there. It will still take a few weeks. It will be charming. I will send more details next week."

It was around 1926 that Justine Ward had decided to settle in a new residence in New York (Mocquereau, August 16, 1926). She had set up a *little monastery*, where she wanted to live in greater union with the Abbey. This monastery, "Mora Vocis," was built, it seems, in 1927. She had a chapel erected there, with stalls and two sides of cloister. This little monastery had its own "rules" (Ward, Mora Vocis, March 22 and Oct. 24, 1929, cf. Mocquereau, March 11 and July 14, 1928) and its residents called one another "Brother"; thus, Justine Ward always speaks of "Brother Agnès" when referring to Agnès Lebreton who was an oblate of Solesmes also. But Justine Ward did not stay in this oasis of peace very long. Later events caused her to leave New York. This happened in November 1932 (Ward Journal, Nov. 4 and Nov. 26, 1932, Jan. 28, 1933, cf. Mocquereau Nov. 26, 1932), and we shall later see that she had all the rather large furnishings of this chapel shipped from America to Solesmes.

Left to right: Justine Ward, Mother Georgia Stevens, Dom André
Mocquereau, and Dom Jean Desrocquettes, New York, 1922.

First row, left to right: Agnès Lebreton and Justine Ward. *Second row, left to
right:* a monk, Dom Ferretti, Msgr. Refice, Dom Gajard.

Dom Mocquereau and Justine Ward with a group of students from the Pius Tenth School at the entrance to the Church of St. Cecile of Solesmes, 1928. *Back row:* Margaret Hurley, Marion Robinson, Julia Sampson, Mary Carroll. *Front Row:* Antoinette De Nigris (Denegris), Mrs. Ward, Dom Mocquereau, Margaret (Péguy) Sullivan, Catherine Carroll.

Above: Justine Ward and Agnès Lebreton on their way to the Office at Solesmes—"Le char de la Sainte Liberté."

Left: The entrance gate at Solesmes through which Mrs. Ward passed many times.

The group of Americans who came to Solesmes in 1929. *Front row, left to right:*
Father Butruille, Rev. John P. Kelly, Dom Gajard, Dom Mocquereau, Dom D. Suñol,
Mr. Dennehy, Mr. Kavanaugh. *Second row:* Mss. Holden, Schumacher, McAllister,
White, Brother J. Diars, Norris, Ralph Kelly, Birmingham, McAndrews, Wert.

Above: The entrance to Mora
Vocis, Dobbs Ferry, N.Y.

Left: The chapel at Mora
Vocis, Dobbs Ferry, N.Y.

Interior of Abbey Church-St. Pierre de Solesmes

The sanctuary at Solesmes before Vatican Council II.

View of the Solesmes Abbey from across the Sarthe River.

Chapter III

FOUNDATION OF THE SCHOOL OF LITURGICAL MUSIC IN WASHINGTON

Proposed School of Religious Music

Since Dom Mocquereau kept all the letters of Justine Ward from October 1928, until his death in January 1930, we have approximately a hundred letters tracing the history of the foundation of the School of Liturgical Music at Catholic University in Washington which held Justine Ward back in America longer than usual, from October 1928 to April 1930, except for one month spent in Europe (Sablé and Italy) in August-September 1929. Her prolonged stay in America enables us to follow the details of this important foundation, the main stages of which were related by Justine Ward herself, whom we shall quote most of the time.

On October 29, 1928, soon after her return to America, Justine Ward announced to Dom Mocquereau that the new Rector of Catholic University in Washington wanted to start a School of Liturgical Music and that he was going to submit this plan to the next meeting of Bishops in November. The idea certainly came from Father DesLongchamps, a former student of the Pontifical School of Sacred Music in Rome and a professor of music at Catholic University, and this idea was welcomed by Justine Ward whose help in implementing it was certainly expected. Since Justine Ward had already desired the establishment of a Solesmes foundation devoted to the teaching of Gregorian chant (cf. supra), she eagerly welcomed this project: she thought indeed that the opportunity to advance the cause of Gregorian chant in America should not be missed, especially since Father DesLongchamps would be in charge of organizing the courses. "It would be a triumph for your ideas, Father," she said to Dom Mocquereau. The School would be open not only to the Sisters of Sisters' College, but also to the students of the University, priests, monks and seminarians, and could thus have great influence (Ward, Mora Vocis, Oct. 29, 1928). Therefore, Justine Ward went to Washington to see the Rector (Ward, no date, letter received on Nov. 5, 1928). On November 13, she gave an account of this first meeting: the Rector wanted to do something ambitious at once, but Justine Ward was able to convince him that a modest undertaking was better to begin with. Her essential concern was to guarantee a good start: "to give the genuine Solesmes tradition." Therefore, as much to help Father DesLongchamps—still the only professor, with Mr. Bernier for the organ, harmony, and counterpoint lessons, and Sister Agnèsine for elementary music in the Sisters' schools—as to guarantee the future, for, "it must be entirely according to Solesmes," Justine Ward approved Father DesLongchamps' idea to invite Dom Sablayrolles, a monk of En-Calcat and a faithful disciple of Dom Mocquereau, to Washington, since Dom Mocquereau himself could not come. Justine Ward had met Dom Sablayrolles in Paris in 1925, as we recall, and she had approved the way in which he conducted the choir. She asked Dom Mocquereau for his opinion on the matter and begged him, if he did approve of the suggestion, to support the request she was about to send to Dom Sablayrolles himself and to the Abbot of En-Calcat (Ward, Mora Vocis, Nov. 13, 1928).

On November 22, the 25th anniversary of the Motu Proprio of Pius X on sacred music, Justine Ward wrote Dom Mocquereau:

> "The Rector told Father DesLongchamps that the bishops were *enthusiastic* about the proposed school of music." But she added with caution: "We must now arrange everything in such a way that the character of the School shall not slip out of our control in the future. This foundation should not be created in haste, but after mature reflection. I shall not allow people to push me too fast. Time and even experience are needed in this milieu. We do not even know the new Rector." And she added, "We can experiment with the present Schola Cantorum and see where difficulties and oppositions are coming from" (Ward, Mora Vocis, Nov. 22, 1928).

Thus, she wanted to act prudently before committing herself fully.

A few days before, on November 20, the exhumation of the body of Father Shields, who had died in February 1921, and its inhumation in a new tomb on the grounds of the Sisters' College in Washington, had taken place. Justine Ward had her students sing for this occasion. (Program in Appendix No. 21):

> "Our 'Pius X' children will sing the mass and the sepulture on that day," she announced. "They will also sing, I hope, before the various groups of students of the University and at the Sisters' College in order to give them the idea of well rhythmed chant and legato. They need to understand that chant is truly an art and that it is not enough to sing notes and syllables to interpret the chant of the Church" (Ward, Mora Vocis, Nov. 13, 1928).

A letter of November 22nd announced to Dom Mocquereau the success of this double demonstration for Father Shields' inhumation and at the University, where there was, in the afternoon, a Gregorian chant concert in the crypt of the Basilica of the Immaculate Conception, and in the evening, another concert in Caldwell Hall chapel (Ward, Mora Vocis, Nov. 22, 1928, cf. Program in Appendix No. 22; Agnès Lebreton, Nov. 22, 1928).

On November 28, Justine Ward gave more details about the result of the bishops' meeting, in a letter sent from Mora Vocis:

> In Washington, everything is going well. The echoes of our visit with the Pius X Choir are good and their example has already entailed a change in the priests' way of singing over there: it is more relaxed and less staccato, as

Father DesLongchamps tells me. For Sunday masses, he now has a small group of boys who alternate with the priests for the Ordinary of the Mass, and everyone is satisfied with this progress.

The minutes of the Bishops' meeting indicate the decision of the Board of Trustees which charged the Executive Committee to discuss the establishment of a School of Music at the University with me. This shows that the matter has been given serious consideration. We now have to reach an agreement on courses and on many other questions. It was agreed between Father DesLongchamps and I that the hall where the courses will be given is to be called Mocquereau Hall! The whole building of the School of Music will bear your name—as the one in New York bears the name of Pius X. It is a way to assure for the future the integrity of your teaching. When Father DesLongchamps proposed this name to the Rector, the latter wanted to know more about you. Father DesLongchamps thus said: Dom Mocquereau is the Guy d'Arezzo of modern times and his name will still be alive when that of Guy d'Arezzo has long been forgotten! It was well said, was it not? The Rector was completely satisfied! And the matter is thus settled . . .

I do not want to go too fast with this matter of the School of Music. There are some very delicate points. I trust Father DesLongchamps, but what would prevent the Administration, once the building is finished, from putting in his place someone who would wreck everything. In making a foundation at the University, I cannot retain my power: therefore, we have to make sure that the conditions are understood and approved by both sides. What we have won is that the present Schola Cantorum will continue until the inauguration of the new school. Furthermore, it is the first time that the hierarchy in America gives an official consideration to liturgical music and takes my work seriously. It thus marks a new stage for me. And even if we are facing danger, we must not lose the opportunity to go ahead under the bishops' protection. Almost all those who are on the Executive Committee are rather favorable, therefore I have high hopes. I will keep you posted, Father.

You will receive the Washington programs from Brother Agnès. Next Saturday, we will demonstrate the Method in New York for an audience of musicians and music professors. There will be two groups of small girls (6 and 8 years old) and then a brief demonstration with the older ones—somewhat as in Holland—but everything must be done within one hour. Explanations, demonstrations, compositions, songs, etc. etc. . . . It is not enough time, of course, to do good work (Mora Vocis, Nov. 28, 1928).

The establishment of the New School of Liturgical Music was thus officially given the green light: Dom Mocquereau's name had been chosen for the building which Justine Ward wanted to erect and this choice thus determined the precise orientation of the teaching; in the meantime, the present Schola Cantorum of the University would continue its work—Justine Ward noted with satisfaction that the hierarchy was, for the first time, giving an official consideration to liturgical music and was paying attention to her work.

The Dom Mocquereau Foundation

A little later, on December 6, 1928, Justine Ward announced a new and important decision: she wanted to create a "Foundation" (always written with a capital F in this story) with Father DesLongchamps, Mother Stevens and herself.

This Foundation would be called the Dom Mocquereau Foundation (cf. infra) and would act in Justine Ward's name to bring financial aid to the Schools of Music in Washington and in New York and to fix the terms of this financial aid. Justine Ward especially wanted guarantees concerning control of the school of Washington:

Last Monday, I had another conversation with the Rector of Catholic University. He was in New York and asked me to come to see him. He wanted to tell me what happened at the Bishops' meeting concerning the new School of Liturgical Music proposal. It appears that the bishops spoke highly of our undertaking, beginning with the Cardinal of Boston, then the Cardinal of New York; afterwards, almost all of them showed they knew my work and had sympathy for it. Thus, all these years have not been so wasted as external results might make it appear. They approved the project with enthusiasm and they directed the Executive Committee to prepare all the details with me in order to present the project to them at their Spring meeting. I asked him several questions which seemed important to me: i.e. especially whether my Foundation would have something to say about the person to be appointed Dean of the School of Music (that's the capital point). He said: "Certainly: it is up to you to fix all the conditions which seem important to you when you present your project." He was very kind. I believe that he was perhaps reassured and that he is now more trustful since the Bishops' meeting. Tomorrow I am expecting Mr. Mason (Mrs. Ward's lawyer) to get his advice on the preparation of my conditions. It is necessary to have a better head than mine to think of everything! It is a gift in another gift. I would like to form a Foundation which would take care of everything I do financially for liturgical music: a group composed of Father DesLong-champs, Mother Stevens and myself to begin with. This Foundation would fix conditions and would provide means—for the new school at the University as well as for the Pius X School. If either one ever deviated from good principles, the Foundation could immediately withdraw its financial assistance. It seems practical to me to organize this during my lifetime and to see how it is going to work—there will thus be less trouble for everyone after my death and my works will not be jeopardized. I would like to have Mr. Mason's advice about all this and then go for the first foundation *before giving anything to the University. I* would not want to be *the one* who is giving.

No answer yet from Dom Sablayrolles! I only hope he won't say *no* to Father DesLongchamps. He needs him terribly—especially now, when the traditions have to be firmly established. You applaud this choice—I am sure. The matter of his health is not too serious because he would be well cared for and would not be made to work too hard. He would be *perfect*—even though he does not speak English! For Sunday masses, we already need two directors and two organists to train all these groups. Then, they need *art.* Dom Sablayrolles would know how to give it to them. Moreover, Father DesLongchamps obviously needs help, for, alone, he cannot cope. If it is not Dom Sablayrolles . . . who, then, would it be? No one else could give your tradition so well . . . If he could only come for six months, one year—it would already be a lot. I think that if *you,* Father, were willing to lend strong support by writing his abbot and saying that we Americans are not nasty savages, but rather, that we are beginning a major undertaking to spread the Solesmes doctrines, I believe that this would greatly influence the abbot. You know America, you made the trip twice, you too were not in very good health—and it was not bad for you! And see all the good you did on this continent. Without you, we would not have done anything good. He would not have to travel: just stay and rest in Washington. It would not be tiring for him to direct and train students since he knows how to do it effortlessly. I saw it in Paris. He has a gift for that. Yes, certainly, *we must have him*! Help us, Father. A word from you will do more than a volume from us! (Mora Vocis, Dec. 6, 1928—J. Ward, Mora Vocis, Jan. 3, 1939; to M. Lebreton, April 9, 1929).

Fidelity to Dom Mocquereau

A letter from Mora Vocis, dated December 13, 1928, gave additional information concerning instruction at the School, limited to Gregorian chant and to classical polyphony, and concerning the eventuality of a School independent of the University; it was necessary, as a matter of fact, to take precautions against any possible deviation in the future and it was also for this reason that Justine Ward so much wanted Dom Sablayrolles to come. There is also in this letter new information on the Foundation and its composition.

> Nothing from you, Father, since my last letter. I spent the week preparing the Foundation with my lawyer and Father DesLongchamps (who spent two days here). I believe everything will be arranged to our satisfaction. Once this Foundation is organized, it will be the responsibility of the Foundation and not mine alone, to deal with the University. I prefer that. I hope we can do it. But the Foundation will fix the conditions, absolutely and legally: i.e., we shall limit ourselves to teaching *Gregorian chant* and *classical polyphony* for use in churches, and within the teaching, to the subjects which will facilitate a better understanding of these two subjects. Modern music for the Church is absolutely barred (i.e. it will never receive any assistance *from our Foundation*). Gregorian chant shall be taught *according to your principles*. This binds not only our Committee, but also their successors, *forever*.
>
> Thus you see, Father, when we discuss the matter with Washington, this Committee will not have the right to be weak! Washington will have to accept our conditions or the Committee will be incapable of acting with them. In case we could not agree (which I do not expect), the Committee representing the Foundation would be free to establish a school independent of the University but which would serve the students. The essential concern is to establish this first Foundation. When you receive this letter, I believe everything will have already been done—if not, it will only be a matter of a few days—for we must wait for the arrival of the Superior from Albany, who is presently at sea, in order to obtain the formal authorization needed for Mother Stevens to serve on the Committee. This committee shall therefore be composed of:
>
> Mother Stevens
> Father DesLongchamps
> J.B.W.
>
> You can count on the complete devotion of this Committee to you and to your principles, and its successors may not deviate from them! Are you happy, Father? I believe that this will bring you joy and I want this joy to arrive in time for your December 28, 1928 anniversary. It is the offering from your overseas disciples (Anniversary of Dom Mocquereau's ordination).
>
> Dom Sablayrolles did not answer Father DesLongchamps' letter yet: I hope that this lateness is a good sign, for I am convinced that this poor

priest cannot carry the load he now has. He needs someone who is able to help him out with *chant*, and who will also truly support him, someone who knows how to encourage and advise him in difficult situations. There are only young instructors, such as Mr. Bernier and Mr. Breed; and the Faculty of the University, of whom not a single member is capable of making a judgment about a musical matter. He is marvellous—I don't believe he has made a single mistake, but how comforting it would be for him to have Dom Sablayrolles as his right hand! The delay makes me hope more and more that God will give him Dom Sablayrolles, at least for a time until he has succeeded in training assistants among the American elements. Furthermore, Dom Sablayrolles' presence would be *for you* a guarantee of the instruction given in Washington. During these years in which the permanent traditions are to be established, I believe that a *direct Solesmes representative is absolutely needed*. You remember that we had dreamed of a Solesmes Foundation at the University: well, I am now convinced that this dream could not have come true in the way we had thought because there are practical difficulties. But as far as liturgical chant is concerned, we can do everything the way we want: we have to take the opportunity to establish firmly everything in such a way that it will not be tampered with later on. Help us, Father, *as much as you can*, with Dom S. and his abbot. Your support could be decisive! (Mora Vocis, Dec. 13, 1928).

The following month, Justine Ward thanked Dom Mocquereau for his letter to Dom Sablayrolles:

Thank you so much for everything you wrote to Father Sablayrolles. If we could have him in Washington—even for one year—it would be ideal, for after that, I will be fully confident that the Solesmian principles will be unshakeable—but we must launch the venture, not only ourselves, but in such a way that everyone can clearly see that this undertaking is truly Solesmian and according to Dom Mocquereau. Oh, if only *you* could come to launch it (Mora Vocis, Jan. 3, 1929).[1]

At that time, Justine Ward went to Albany to obtain from the Provincial Superior of the Religious of the Sacred Heart all the necessary permissions concerning Mother Stevens (Mora Vocis, Jan. 3, 1929). But another question preoccupied her: how to organize regular and good courses at the University for students coming from the various religious houses surrounding the University, given the fact that music courses are often scheduled at inconvenient times? (Mora Vocis, Jan. 16, 1929). Many other problems still caused concern to Justine Ward who was more and more leaning towards total independence for her school: "I am going to try to arrange with the Rector of the University the establishment of our school of liturgical music as a school affiliated with but independent from the University. There are rather good reasons for this decision. I cannot explain them to you here" (Ward, Mora Vocis, Jan. 23, 1929).

There are also those difficulties inherent in any human undertaking. Mother Stevens had reservations about the founding of the Washington school because she wanted "everything to be concentrated at the Pius X School" (Ward, Mora Vocis, Jan. 23, 1929). Moreover, the Religious of the Sacred Heart

> want absolute control over that undertaking . . . I shall never make con-
> cessions on this point. Today, there will be a conference at the Sacred Heart
> convent with the Superior, Mother Stevens, and their lawyer on one side,
> and my lawyer, Mr. Mason, and I on the other. I do not want to break
> with the Sacred Heart; neither do I want to see the Pius X School fall, I shall
> do everything to avoid that. But if they do not accept the Dom Mocquereau
> Foundation . . . then I shall *not* make concessions on this point . . . and if
> a break is necessary, I shall interpret it as a sign from God that Pius X has
> done its work and that one must now work much more for the clergy than
> for children (Ward, Mora Vocis, Feb. 8 and March 2, 1929; cf. Ward,
> London, Oct. 9, 1928).

Moreover, Justine Ward suspected that Mother Stevens was not very faithful
to the Solesmes doctrine (Ward, Mora Vocis, Dec. 6, 1928). Later on, she
noted that Dom Ferretti himself seemed to be concerned about this American
foundation of a school which could be prejudicial to the Rome School of Sacred Music; soon afterwards, she wrote Dom Mocquereau that Dom Ferretti
"remains silent on this subject" (Ward, Mora Vocis, May 7, 1929).

For Justine Ward, however, the essential was fidelity to Dom Mocquereau's
teaching:

> With Father DesLongchamps, who is absolutely loyal, we will eventually
> obtain excellent results. He spent Sunday here. I told him that the most im-
> portant thing for me is to be able to give him *everything* which *you*, Father,
> gave me. If Dom Sablayrolles accepts, he will be able to do much for him—
> certainly better than I could myself. But if he does not, I will have to pass
> on to him everything I have learned from you (Ward, Mora Vocis, Jan. 23,
> 1929).

Referring to Dom Sablayrolles in another letter to Dom Mocquereau, she insisted:

> He should be *well* attuned to *your* ideas before coming. Otherwise, his
> coming would be a misfortune. The weeks to come will be entirely taken up
> by the arrangements for the Foundation (mine) and talks with the Rector of
> the University (Ward, Mora Vocis, Jan. 31, 1929).

For the same reason of fidelity to Dom Mocquereau, Justine Ward stuck to
her idea concerning the name to be given the School, which would be named
after Dom Mocquereau, like the Foundation.

> Concerning the matter of the school in Washington, it absolutely must be
> named after you. If there have been and still are struggles around that
> name, this will be the best way to reinforce our position. Father DesLong-
> champs is of the same opinion. Father Agaësse (from Solesmes) to whom
> Brother Agnès had written concerning this project, gave a very good reply:
> "It will be a great work based *on a great name*." "The three directors of the
> Foundation (mine) must all be persons who thoroughly know your prin-
> ciples. No other method but yours shall be supported by us or by our suc-
> cessors" (Ward, Mora Vocis, Jan. 31, 1929).

 56

Ultimate Decisions

1 — The School of Liturgical Music

Once the organization of the School of liturgical music had been decided, Justine Ward kept Dom Mocquereau posted on the latest decisions: the school shall be an integral part of the University; maximum independence is promised in organizing courses; the school will direct musical performance during the liturgical offices of the University; a site will be reserved for the school on the campus of the University; the erection of a building has been decided together with the purchase of a lot adjacent to Dr. Shields' house which will be temporarily put at the disposal of the School for the professors. A letter from Mora Vocis dated February 22, gives all these provisions:

> Since my last letter, we have spent almost one week in Washington for talks with the Rector of the University, the Dean of the Sisters' College, the Archbishop of Baltimore (who is Chancellor of the University), the architect, etc. etc. . . . Mr. Mason very skillfully conducted all the negotiations for us. The results are very satisfying—more than I had hoped for. The new school of liturgical music will form an integral part of the University—in the same sense as its Theological School, its School of Canon Law, etc. . . . It will enter into the academic system of the University itself. The professors will have to be appointed like the others—but they promised us to appoint only those recommended by our Foundation. Our school of music will always be in charge of directing music for the liturgical offices of the University. This also includes music in the large basilica of the Immaculate Conception. We retain maximum independence in the area of organization of courses, etc. . . . Finally, a beautiful site has been reserved for us on the campus, next to the basilica, but for the time being, we have received the authorization to erect a temporary building. It was my desire, because I will need other people's assistance in regard to the large building. Therefore, right now, we are going to buy the land next to Dr. Shields' house (where I already had the foundations built seven years ago) and there, we shall erect a two-story building: on the first floor, there will be three class rooms and three or four small rooms with a piano or an organ for the students; on the entire second floor, there will be a large room for rehearsals, etc. . . . it will accommodate 250 students, approximately. This will be sufficient for 5 or 10 years. Especially if they let us use Dr. Shields' house for the professors, the library, the offices. This will enable us to go ahead without wasting time. When the school expands, I will sell this building and the price will revert to the Foundation, to help build the final building on the campus. It is obvious that the first years will be tough, but we must hope that we shall be able to do some truly serious work in the end.
>
> We will carry all the costs, of course. The University does not give anything. In regard to the students, however, the school will get a prorated tuition corresponding to the hours devoted to music by these students. Consequently, a student coming *exclusively* for music courses would pay the whole tuition to our school. Those giving a minimal amount of their time to music would pay only a small prorated fee. I am afraid the first years will be very costly—but we will do the best we can. It was not an opportunity we could have turned down, was it? I must admit that everyone has been very fair and very honest. So, everything has come into place quickly and well. Of course, all of that has to be ratified by the bishops at their meeting

shortly after Easter, but once the Rector and the Chancellor are ready to give their approval, the others will say Amen. It is only a formality. Truly, I believe this was the moment chosen by God, and that he is leading us (Mora Vocis, Feb. 22, 1929).

At the end of this letter, Justine Ward announced that Dom Sablayrolles could not come immediately, but that he had agreed to come for the next school year. And she added:

I believe that it would be useful if he came, so to speak, as your *representative. You* should naturally have been here to open this school dedicated to the teaching of your principles. If your presence is impossible (?) Dom Sablayrolles should come for a while as your representative, don't you think?

2 — The "Dom Mocquereau Schola Cantorum Foundation"

In her letter of February 22, Justine Ward presented the final decisions concerning the Foundation:

Did you receive my telegram sent from Washington, which announced to you that the Foundation itself will be named after you? It will be either *"Dom Mocquereau Schola Cantorum Foundation"* or *"Mocquereau Schola Cantorum Foundation."* This Foundation is held in perpetuity to propagate Gregorian chant according to *your principles*; it will control teaching and provide financial means to the Washington School and to the Pius X School—and to others when we are able to do it, but always under these same conditions. It is for this reason that we thought it would be better if the Foundation itself was named after you, instead of naming the Washington School after you. For, the Washington School could deviate from your principles in the future; in this case, the Foundation would only have one remedy—drop this school, withdraw the funds. But the Foundation itself *can never deviate from them*. It is bound to observe them, *legally* as well as out of loyalty. I believe that this document will be signed next Monday. I was hoping for a little telegram from you but you probably thought it more prudent to write (Ward, Mora Vocis, Feb. 22, 1929).

The telegram referred to before was so written: "new Foundation called 'Dom Mocquereau Schola Cantorum Foundation,' Asking Dom Mocquereau's blessing." We cannot read the date on this telegram, but the Ward Journal indicates the date as that of February 25, 1929, and that the head office of the Foundation is in New York (Gabriel Steinschulte, *Die Ward-Bewegung,* Regensburg 1979, p. 175).

A few days later, on March 2, Justine Ward announced from Mora Vocis that the Dom Mocquereau Foundation had been established, that the documents had been signed and the Committee appointed, but that there still remained many matters to be settled with the University.

The *Dom Mocquereau Schola Cantorum Foundation* is now established! All the documents have been signed, registered, etc. . . . The first organizational meeting has been held to appoint the directors and officers. I am the President; Father DesLongchamps is Vice President and Treasurer;

Mother Stevens is the Secretary. Every year, these officers will be elected in January. If one of us is not agreeable to the others, another person may be elected instead! But I believe we will walk together in peace. Mother Stevens is not going to like this new regime very much, for until now she has been an absolute dictator—but the new regime is infinitely more secure for the future.

There still remain many matters to settle with the University. The Rector has gone on vacation for two weeks without sending me a final acceptance: he still has a few reservations but does not mention them. In the meantime, we have been in touch with the Chancellor (the Archbishop of Baltimore) who has told us to go ahead with confidence—that everything will be settled according to our proposal. Concerning the Sisters' College, everything is fine. They have agreed to sell me the land I need for the temporary building. In the meantime, the architect is drawing the plans of the building which we want to push forward as fast as possible in order to have it for the summer session which will begin in June (Mora Vocis, March 2, 1929).

But Dom Mocquereau had asked Justine Ward to name the Foundation after Dom Guéranger. She replied on March 12, which was the feast of Saint Gregory the Great, being adamant on this point:

I am answering at the same time both of your dear letters of February 23rd and 27th. You already heard the news in my previous letters that the 'DOM MOCQUEREAU SCHOLA CANTORUM FOUNDATION' has already been founded in time and almost in eternity! Nothing in the world could change it now—I can do nothing about it, and I am glad you did not reply by telegram—our good angels prevented you from doing it! We prayed to the old saints: St. Sylvestre, St. Ambrose, St. Gregory, St. Basil, St. Augustine, St. John Chrysostom—all of them felt that this Foundation should be named after Dom Mocquereau! They were stronger than little Teresa of Lisieux in this matter of liturgy and chant! Anyway, it is too late to think of something else. And when you see the bylaws of the Foundation which fix your method, your principles, as a rule for ourselves and our successors, you will understand that any other name besides yours would not have had the effect we all desired. I beg you, Father, not to be sad that this Foundation shall not be named after Dom Guéranger. Your name is known in America by all those men and women who want to sing the chant of the Church properly. You did us the honor of coming to America twice. You generously trained, for this country, a student who is infinitely grateful to you and who would like to prove it to you by guaranteeing, through this Foundation, absolute fidelity to your teaching. Anyone who does not follow your principles may not benefit from this Foundation: If Pius X or the University were someday to deviate, it would be the duty of the directors to withdraw the financial resources used for the operation of these schools. It is a great force which will act after my death, and after yours. I am very happy about that—and I hope that you, Father, will be happy too. It is not—you know this—only for you personally that I did this, but for *your principles*—for *the truth*. I beg you, Father, to accept it with simplicity, as I have offered it to you. Thus, I believe, the future is guaranteed—at least in America (Mora Vocis, March 12, 1929).

On March 21, Justine Ward further insisted on this point:

Regarding the title of the Foundation, you already know, Father, that the name of Dom Mocquereau cannot be erased. It is legal—I cannot do anything about it. This name is also indelibly written in all our hearts. It is with this name that we will triumph! It was not Dom Guéranger who found winged rhythm in the ancient manuscripts; it was not he who found chironomy. We all have much respect for Dom Guéranger, but he was not our inspiration, our model, our teacher. I am convinced that he would be the first to understand our choice! (Mora Vocis, March 21, 1929).

Teaching of Liturgy

The Foundation of the School of Liturgical Music was approved by the academic senate on March 6, 1929 (Ward Journal).[2] Father DesLongchamps was appointed dean, and the Faculty included Mister Conrad Bernier, Dom Maur Sablayrolles and Sister Agnèsine. But another question was under consideration: Justine Ward was planning to create a chair of liturgy at the School and this required the bishops' approval. On March 12, she wrote Dom Mocquereau from Mora Vocis:

> We were in Washington for the whole week. First of all, there was a special meeting of the University Academic Senate—to decide if they wanted a school of liturgical music according to our project. It was also necessary to vote on the question of the appointment of Father DesLongchamps as Dean. I was a little afraid that they might think he is too young, but fortunately, everything went well. There was hardly any opposition.
>
> After that, we were free to address a formal letter to the Rector together with the proposal made by the Dom Mocquereau Foundation to the University, for him to submit to the Executive Committee of the Board of Trustees of the University. This was done on Monday the 11th, and the answer was affirmative. We now have only to submit it to the meeting of all the Bishops after Easter. But since the matter was passed by the Senate and the Executive Committee, this approval is certain. It is only a formality. This school will do for the nuns what Pius X is doing, and for the priests, seminarians, and monks, what Pius X could never do—and what I have always desired!
>
> I hope we will be able to have Dom Sablayrolles. The death of his abbot may affect this matter. Anyway, I am patiently waiting for the matter to be settled. Until now, God seems to have arranged everything beyond my hopes. As for liturgy, no decision. I believe that Father DesLongchamps would like chant and liturgy to be taught by the same professor. But I do not see how it will be possible. I do not want to impose my ideas on him too much, since he often has better ones himself, and by insisting I could upset everything. Absolutely nothing can be done until after the Bishops' meeting (Mora Vocis, March 12, 1929).

Justine Ward had already talked about her project of creating a chair of liturgy:

> One of the things we have agreed upon with the Rector was that we, in the School of Music, would hire, at our expense, a professor of liturgy who would make students love and savour it while giving to chant its rightful place in its development (Ward, Mora Vocis, Feb. 22, 1929).

Now, Justine Ward was suggesting some names that she submitted to Dom Mocquereau for his approval and, as an alternative, she suggested sending an American priest to Europe to be trained in this field, since the best solution would be to have the same professor teach both chant and liturgy (Ward, Mora Vocis, Jan. 31, March 12, 21, April 4, 16, 29, 1929). But she always insisted that this should be done in full agreement with Solesmes, given the unavoidable repercussions of one subject upon the other:

> The question of liturgy is, for the time being, our most important problem. We need someone who is strong on the historical side, and also on the practical side—who is a good teacher and is familiar with university life. He would not have beginners only, but also priests and monks undertaking advanced studies. He should also speak English if possible. What can we do? Where can we find him? I believe this choice has a great importance at this time. Could you suggest someone? The Rector is going to Europe this summer; he is going to Rome, to France, to Germany, to Belgium. It is primarily to see certain individuals who could become professors at the University. If we had someone to propose to him, it would be appropriate to let him know that now. Let me know, Father, in your next letter, if you have someone in mind. It seems to me that we could have a professor teaching liturgy and chant. But what I am a little afraid of is getting a professor of liturgy who is not well versed in Solesmes' ideas. It would certainly be preferable for him to be Solesmian. Lastly, the Rector would prefer a professor who would be ready to spend many years here. If such a person cannot be found, we could still train an American priest for this position. It would take two years at least. We would send him to Solesmes, to Rome, etc., to study. It may possibly be the best thing to do. But, while he is being trained, we need someone. All this is confidential. The matter should not be broadly divulged, but if you have a recommendation to make, we would be infinitely grateful (Mora Vocis, S. Benoit, March 21, 1929).

Dom Mocquereau suggested two names; the first one was mentioned to him by his abbot, the second one was that of Father Donovan who, as may be recalled, had recommended Justine Ward to the Choirmaster of Solesmes in 1920.

Thus, Justine Ward's first thoughts had gradually developed and become more precise. She had dreamed first of all of a Solesmes monastery near Catholic University. Since this project was not feasible, she then undertook to found a School of Liturgical Music at the University itself. But having quickly realized the necessity of creating a structure independent of the University to organize and support this school, she came up with the idea of her "Dom Mocquereau Foundation," established to guarantee fidelity to the rhythmic principles of Solesmes. According to a note from Justine Ward to Dom Mocquereau, the capital to be used in furthering this end had been set aside as early as 1922.

The Ward Movement

A group of "Apostles"—the future apostles of Gregorian chant—to whom Justine Ward had offered a sojourn at Solesmes, arrived at the beginning of

August 1929; they stayed there from the 13th to the 31st. There was a priest, Rev. J.P. Kelly, nine seminarians, one Salvatorian brother and two lay professors from the Pius X School (Ward, S. Francis, July 12, 1929, presentation of the group).[3] Father DesLongchamps could not come since Justine Ward wanted him to stay in Washington to supervise the construction of the building of the School of Music.[4] Dom Gajard offered courses for the group, as he regularly did during the summer for guests and visitors of the monastery, priests or laypersons, who desired it. But an additional course was set up for the Americans and a young monk served as an interpreter (Dom Butruille). Justine Ward arrived shortly before her group of apostles; she still resided in Sablé, in the house near the church.

On September 17, 1929, Justine Ward made a short trip to Italy, from the 17th to the 23rd. Nothing indicates that she went to Rome, for she probably would have noted it as usual in her journal, but she certainly went to Serravalle (Appendix Nos. 71 and 74). Effectively, she soon wrote Dom Mocquereau, while on her way back to America, that there were now two professors at Serravalle (Ward, Oct. 2, from "Holland American Line"), but that there were also some serious difficulties, which she wanted to discuss with Mother Stevens:

> I have not yet spoken with Mother Stevens. She does not know that I am back . . . Then the question of Serravalle will be taken up. I would like to postpone that until my return to Washington. We need time and calm for this matter. I worked during the trip to prepare a file on each individual professor. This work is now completed. I expect a hard struggle, but it may be less difficult than I think. I will be as patient as possible but I cannot make concessions on any point.

Justine Ward alludes to an investigation she had made, with Dom Ferretti's assistance, during her short stay in Italy (Ward, Mora Vocis, Nov. 1929) which interested Mother Stevens, since the professors were from the Pius X School. Actually, there had been difficulties with the Pius X School itself for a long time already. These difficulties had resulted in a conference with the Religious of the Sacred Heart to discuss "a fundamental reorganization of the Pius X School." Since the difficulties had not been resolved, they caused a break with the School in 1931. (On this subject, cf. Ward, Jan. 23, Oct. 2 and 26, Nov. 5, 12, 18 and 24, Dec. 26, 1929.)

Upon returning from Italy, Justine Ward spent a few days in Sablé, from the 25th to the 30th of September 1929. On the day before leaving—the 29th—she noted in her journal: "Last time I ever saw Dom M."; but this entry should obviously be dated January, 1930. For the time being, not knowing what was going to happen, she wrote: "For us (Justine Ward and Agnès Lebreton), it is always uprooting to wrench ourselves away from Solesmes" (Ward, Paris, Oct. 1, 1929). In Paris, she met Dom Sablayrolles who was to sail with her and Agnès Lebreton on October 2. She was planning to come back to France only in April of 1930 (Ward, Paris, Oct. 1, 1929) because she was already quite preoccupied with her Washington school.

The School of Music Again

Everything over there seemed nevertheless to be heading toward a satisfactory conclusion in spite of a few unavoidable difficulties. Justine Ward had already written on May 28, 1929 that she had not yet obtained all the guarantees sufficient for her to decide whether to build the School on the campus of the University; she was indeed asking that this School always teach liturgical chant only under the conditions fixed by the Foundation. She had left Father DesLongchamps in Washington to attend to this matter even though he was to be part of the group which came to Solesmes in August (Ward, S. Francis, May 28, June 2, 1929). If the requested guarantees were not given, Justine Ward would then have a temporary building erected on land she owned (Ward, St. Francis, June 2, 10, 18, 1929). Finally, everything went well, but Justine Ward adopted more modest plans for the building and put her lawyer and her lawyer's brother on the Board of Directors of the Foundation to confer greater authority on it for the future (Ward, St. Francis, June 18, 1929).

At the beginning of July, the Rector of the University had a private audience with the Pope and talked about the Foundation and the new School:

> The Holy Father was very pleased with everything! He remembered me very well, the Rector said. He sent me, via the Rector, a relic of Saint Teresa, a great blessing, and the permission to keep the Blessed Sacrament in our little chapel at Mora Vocis. What a joy this is! It will truly be a small monastery from now on (Ward, St. Francis, July 12, 1929; cf. Mora Vocis, October 24, 1929).

Justine Ward explained the objectives of her Washington school in *The Catholic Choirmaster*.[5]

> It will have, I hope, a double result: first of all, it will provide a permanent organization for teaching liturgical chant and classical polyphony, as well as all related fields necessary to understand and interpret them correctly; secondly, it will unite in a single leadership those who created in this country two of the most important schools of liturgical chant and music. Both schools will work in harmony from now on, and will supplement each other in many respects.[6]

Justine Ward is alluding here to the Pius X Institute of New York and to Father DesLongchamps' Schola Cantorum which spawned the newly born Washington School.

In September 1929, the Rector Monsignor James H. Ryan sent a letter to all ordinaries in the United States to announce officially the opening of classes. "This School with its own Faculty and its independent quarters will not be a financial burden for the University. Each year, its budget shall be taken care of by the 'Dom Mocquereau Schola Cantorum Foundation, Inc.' " (Appendix No. 29). The letter announced Dom Sablayrolles' courses:

> He is coming to teach chant as it is taught and practiced in the famous Solesmes monastery whose monks have done so much for liturgy and for the restoration of Gregorian chant. (*Rev. Gr.*, 1929, pp. 273–274).

In the end, the School of Music building was constructed on the grounds of the University. According to a sketch sent to Dom Mocquereau, it consisted of three one-story buildings linked together by a small cloister (Appendix No. 28). The ceremony of the Blessing, first scheduled for November 7th (Ward, *Mora Vocis*, Oct. 24, 1929), was postponed to March 7th, 1930, Feast of Saint Thomas Aquinas, patron of the University.

Did the ceremony take place? New difficulties appeared, which we shall not mention here. While Justine Ward was very pleased with Dom Sablayrolles and his teaching, the University was not (Ward, f. ex. *Mora Vocis*, Nov. 18, Dec. 14 and 16, 1929). Justine Ward had already complained that, while serving as an interpreter for Dom Sablayrolles, Father DesLongchamps was distorting his thought (Ward, *Mora Vocis*, Dec. 14, 1929). Nevertheless, Dom Sablayrolles' success was obvious, too obvious maybe . . . "Everything would be very encouraging in Washington if Dom Sablayrolles' success pleased everybody . . . " (Ward, *Mora Vocis*, Nov. 18, 1929). The matter got to the point that Dom Sablayrolles had to look for another residence, while continuing to teach (Ward, *Mora Vocis*, Dec. 14, 1929). And on January 5, 1930, the "Dom Mocquereau Foundation notified the Rector that it would no longer support the School of Liturgical Music;[7] a little later, the Foundation requested the Abbot of Solesmes to withdraw the permission granted to the School of Music to bear Dom Mocquereau's name (Ward, Feb. 15, 1930, cf. Appendix Nos. 30, 31.). It was the rupture already noted in her journal on January 4th by Justine Ward: "Rupture with Catholic Univ. decided." She left "a beautiful building," however, to the University. In 1967, the University built a new wing which was named "Ward Hall" in honor of the founder and which was inaugurated on October 27, 1974 (J. Lennards, *Justine Bayard Ward* in *Una Voce*, March–April 1976, p. 52).

Death of Dom Mocquereau

In her last letter to Dom Mocquereau, dated January 6, 1930, Justine Ward alluded to his illness though she did not expect its fatal result; she gave many details about her difficulties with the University, details she would probably have hidden in order not to cloud over the last days of her old master. From Solesmes, she was kept informed of the evolution of the illness, which was developing rapidly, in such a way that she had time only to note the beginning of it in her journal on January 14th. On the 17th, Dom Mocquereau improved a bit, but on the 18th, a cable from Solesmes announced his death to her. At that time, airplanes were not yet used for fast traveling, and thus Justine Ward could not attend the funeral. She came back to Sablé only on April 2, with Dom Sablayrolles who had left the University in Washington.[8]

As soon as she heard that Dom Mocquereau had died, Justine Ward sent the following telegram to the Father Abbot: "Immense sorrow. United with you and Solesmes" and on January 22nd, she wrote Dom Gajard this moving letter which announces, at the same time, the final rupture with the University (Cf. Appendix No. 43):

Mora Vocis, Dobbs Ferry, New York
January 22, 1930
Reverend Father,
Faced with the anguish which has just united us in a common mourning, words are quite useless. You understand that, for me, the world has lost all that was the most beautiful, the most ideal, the most holy. I can only say a *fiat* without reservation while offering in union with Solesmes and with you, the incense of the greatest of all sacrifices.

All things considered, dear Father Mocquereau so well deserves his eternal joy after his many years of struggle and of work for divine praise, that a ray of joy is coming to us to console us. At Mora Vocis, we believe that the chant of the Seraphim will be more exquisite, better rhythmed, now that Father Mocquereau has arrived.

Allow me, Father, to save for another letter everything I would have to tell you about Washington and about my gratefulness for your good letter of January 3rd. For the time being, it is enough to tell you that the rupture is *final*.

The truth will be known in Rome at the proper time. Father Sablayrolles is staying with us, here at Mora Vocis. His presence was a great comfort to us in our sorrow. On the day of Father Mocquereau's burial, he conducted the Requiem sung by all the Faculty and students of Pius X for the master who was *everything* for them—it was sung with all their hearts and souls . . .

The three of us assure you, Father, that now and in the future, we are closely united with you for the triumph of Father Mocquereau's principles and for the beauty of the song of praise. This union shall be our strength.

Please accept my sympathy for your sorrow, Father. Together with my prayers, I wish you courage to carry the heavy burden which is yours.
— Justine Ward

The letter to which Justine Ward referred followed closely on February 15th. It actually answered a letter from Dom Gajard:

How can I tell you how much I was moved that, even in your deep sorrow, you had the delicate thought of taking the time to write me and of understanding to what extent I too am sorrowful over the death of our dear and unique Master. It was such a hard blow that, as human beings, we would be crushed by it if God were not there to fill our hearts and to heal the wounds. Our great Master is making us feel his presence and his help. More than ever, he will give to all of us, separately and together, the strength to carry our heavy burden in order to continue his work, to spread it and to consolidate it. Have no doubt, Father, about my entire devotion to this cause and to yourself who are now representing the work of Solesmes and the work of Father Mocquereau. This union among ourselves will be the token of our devotion to the Master and the token he probably deserves himself.

We are planning to come to Solesmes for Holy Week. Yes, it will truly be hard not to see alive the one who was everything for me—but it would be even harder to remain absent, and I expect always to find his spirit there, more than ever. Everything you are telling me, Father, is very moving and I warmly accept your help, which I will really need.

Tomorrow, the three of us will go to Scranton, Dom S. to see the Passionists and I the nuns. The music director at the Passionists' house in Scranton is one of my students and is very devoted. He is doing some very good work in all the houses of his order and deserves Father Sablayrolles' visit.

> There is a call, here, for articles on Father Mocquereau. I will try to send something but it is difficult and sorrowful to analyze what you love—it is as if a doctor were dissecting the body of a friend, or his own body! The wound is still bleeding. But I did what I could.

On February 20th, Justine Ward sent the Abbot a letter which was signed by Mother Stevens and by the Faculty and students of the Pius X School; in it, she expressed their gratitude to the dear deceased (Appendix No. 44). A mass had been sung at the Convent of the Sacred Heart on January 20th, in unison with the mass which was sung at the same time at Solesmes for the funeral.

In the meantime, Justine Ward had written on February 2 (Journal) an obituary which was published in the March 23, 1930 issue of the review *Orate Fratres*. She talked about the veneration she had for Dom Mocquereau. Written with exquisite tactfulness, these pages also reveal their author's spirituality. For Justine Ward indeed, all the genius of Dom Mocquereau came from his spirituality: it is because he was a real monk, gentle and humble, a man of prayer, that he was able to understand the all-spiritual beauty of the prayer of the Church.

In March, Justine Ward gave in the *Catholic Choirmaster*[9] a number of details concerning Dom Mocquereau's death, which had been related to her in letters from Solesmes. However, we prefer to quote some lines from the obituary in *Orate Fratres*, for they are so beautiful that they seem particularly fitting as an end to the first part of this study on Justine Ward's relationship with Solesmes.

First of all, here is a passage from this article, which portrays Dom Mocquereau and underlines the qualities of his ardent and generous heart, his kindness and gentleness.

> To those who knew Dom Mocquereau only through his published works, through his reputation as a scholar and a genius, it was a genuine surprise to meet him in real life. Humble, gentle, as candid as a child, he had reached that wondrous simplicity of the saints which is as truly the mark of genius as it is of holiness. He held nothing back of the riches that were his. If he accepted a pupil at all, he gave him treasure of purest gold. Who could forget who had ever seen that great man outlining with a gesture of infinite eloquence and grace (that *chironomie* of his own invention) the melodies which he sang in a voice which quavered a little but remained true to the end of his life,—softly because he was old, and sweetly because he was holy?

But what Justine Ward especially appreciated in Dom Mocquereau was the deep spirituality which enabled him to appreciate ancient melodies and which gave to the choir of Solesmes a sweetness unheard of until then, but greatly appreciated by souls at all levels of training.

> To his pupils, Dom Mocquereau was accessible, simple, kind, but always frank. "You know nothing," he remarked on his first trip to America, expecting as a matter of course the answer which he himself would have given under like circumstances: "If I know nothing, then I will take the trouble to study, and will not stop short of a full grasp of the subject."

"*Haussez-vous*" he wrote in a posthumous article which has just been published in the *Revue Grégorienne,* "Lift yourselves—your spirit, your heart and your taste to the full ideal which soars in every work of art, in its melody and its text." This alone satisfied Dom Mocquereau for his pupils as for himself. Begin again, do better, arrive at last at perfection, and when you get there, you will find there is still something beyond, which you would never have found unless you had attained that early idea of perfection. "*Haussez-vous.*" It sums up his influence and his life, and will remain with his pupils. For "The summit of the art is attained at the very moment that one ceases to be aware of it; the melody is saturated; permeated with prayer, supplication, joy, and jubilation."

True scholarship, like true art, is akin to sanctity. The same faculties of the soul come into play. I am not speaking of what too often passes for scholarship or for art where vain contact with statistics dries up the heart or mere technique fritters the soul. But I speak of the process and motivation in a life completely given to the search for truth, where the slightest deviation is intolerable, where no pains are too great, no details insignificant, where personal preconceptions must be set aside, where prejudice becomes betrayal, and compromise, a lie. Science and art, taken in this sense, use the same facilities of the soul which function in the ascent toward God. Here art and science, in God and for God, become a true form of sanctity if not its highest manifestation.

Dom Mocquereau lived, worked and directed the vast activities he had set in motion until the age of 82. When the appointed time came near, he left the earth with a swift, silent arsis. Ill for a few days, but discreetly so as to cause no undue alarm, he literally fell asleep in the Lord quite early in the morning. The infirmarian went to his cell to prepare it and to bring him Holy Communion. He knocked and received no answer; he entered and found the light burning and Dom Mocquereau as though sleeping. There was no sign of struggle or of pain. "He had finished his life like the close of a melody: lightly, softly." Thus wrote an eye witness. "He who had always taught us to lay down our voices in a final *ictus* which falls light as a snowflake touching the earth,—his ictus alighted in heaven . . . Dom Mocquereau is the glory of Solesmes. For many people Solesmes *was* Dom Mocquereau. How many were bound to him by invisible threads! . . . He had the joy on earth, not of having invented beauty but of having recognized the beauty of the Church's chants, of having given back to them their true expression. An idea of genius developed, illumined, fathomed, exalted by an entire life!" (*Orate Fratres*, vol. IV No. 5, pp. 195–208. Cf. Appendix No. 66. See also Appendix Nos. 67, 68, 69.)

These lines by Justine Ward are perfectly exact and confirm what was said before about Dom Mocquereau's musical interpretation (Cf. Ch. I—The Choir of Solesmes), which was related to his great spirituality, for he was a real monk and a man of prayer. One detail: the veterans have not forgotten the devotion with which he said Mass. We would like to emphasize here his extraordinary kindness which always impressed those who knew him and which shone through his clear and limpid eyes. His kindness was as legendary as his seemingly blunt words and his frankness, and this quality of the soul and of the heart naturally transpired in his behavior. The lion quickly became a lamb; his bluntness was quickly redeemed by a few very delicate words issued from a heart which always remained vigorous and ardent. A musicologist, Jean de Valois, alluding to the opposition Dom Mocquereau sometimes met, wrote at the time of his death:

> We personally knew and loved the *good* and dear Father Mocquereau (for he was truly a good man, as well as a saint) only too well, not to hope that the opposition will die down in the name of his venerated memory, in spite of the controversies which are necessary for the development of musical art.

We know of a gesture, although there are many, which is very expressive of his nature, when in November 1880, at the time of the first expulsion of the monks, he warmly embraced the armed guards who were evicting him from his room, leaving them quite bewildered.

> "Throughout the years," a contemporary writer said, "his kindness and fraternal charity kept increasing; his affectionate smile, even the sound of his warm, musical voice, with its gentle and deep vibrations, gave the impression of a welcoming and benevolent congeniality."[10]

The death of Dom Mocquereau did not end the relationship of Justine Ward with the Abbey. This relationship continued with Dom Gajard and with the abbots of Solesmes. Justine Ward was very attached to Dom Mocquereau, who had been a master and a spiritual guide for her; this attachment was entirely transferred to the monastery which had also brought her so much spiritual joy. There, the doctrine of the master was followed and the Choir of the monks, trained by him, revealed all its beauty and its spirituality. Justine Ward saw in Dom Gajard his master's faithful disciple and his perfect successor. Through her correspondence with Dom Gajard, which has all been kept, we shall become better acquainted with her soul, which was that of an artist and of a Christian for whom prayer was the *raison d'être* of her devotion to the Gregorian cause. Was it not indeed what she always pursued in devoting herself to training children in order to make them better participate in the liturgy of the Church?

Photograph of Dom Mocquereau made at the request of Justine Ward for the 50th anniversary of his ordination to the priesthood, December 28, 1929. Dom Mocquereau died on January 18, 1930.

Justine Ward in her library at "Interlude," Washington, D.C.

Dom Maur Sablayrolles, O.S.B.

"Interlude"—Washington, D.C.

PART TWO

JUSTINE WARD AND DOM GAJARD

Chapter IV

FIDELITY TO DOM MOCQUEREAU

We have a rather large number of letters from Justine Ward to Dom Gajard over a period of 42 years, until the death of Dom Mocquereau's successor in April 1972. We have already said that while the letters addressed to Dom Mocquereau followed one another according to a regular pattern, as may be seen from Dom Mocquereau's replies which have all been kept, the letters addressed to Dom Gajard are interspersed with long periods of silence. Moreover, it should not be forgotten that Justine Ward still resided quite often near "her" Abbey. In order to settle closer to Solesmes, she had bought, in September 1929, the house near the church of Sablé where she had already lived during her stays in France. She enlarged it later on by purchasing the house next door (Journal, June 10, 25, Sept. 28, 1929).

We can provide a few details concerning Justine Ward's sojourns in Sablé from 1930 on, since her journal, though very brief, indicates all the trips she took. This journal stops in 1938, but it can be supplemented by her correspondence on this subject.

From 1930 to 1941, when she had to return to America after her country had declared war on Germany, Justine Ward made exactly 33 trips to Italy, notably to Rome; she made 4 trips to America, 2 to Holland and one to Spain. But these trips were often very short and Sablé was her main residence.

We shall continue to use Justine Ward's letters in chronological order; this will enable us to mention certain facts which, though secondary, are quite interesting.

Recording at Solesmes in 1930

What attracted Justine Ward to Solesmes was her love of Gregorian chant and of Liturgy, as well as her deep conviction that Dom Mocquereau's interpretation of chant was the best, if not the only acceptable one. The regular subject discussed in her letters to Dom Gajard is precisely that of chant, and concerns the recordings made at the Abbey in 1930 and afterwards. It is actually in those letters that Justine Ward's explicit thinking on this point is found.

Two letters dated January 22 and February 15, 1930, addressed to Dom Gajard immediately after Dom Mocquereau's death, were quoted above, the second one only partially. In it a proposal to make Gregorian chant recordings

74

at Solesmes is also discussed, together with a recording which had just been made at the Pius X School. Here is the text of this February 15, 1930 letter, sent from Mora Vocis:

> I hope that all will go well with the recordings of the Monks of Solesmes' chant. How precious they will be for all of us. Those of the Pius X School (the Ordinary of the Mass of the Holy Virgin: Kyrie X, the rest of Mass IX, with Credo I) are finished. From a technical point of view, they are perfect. From an artistic point of view, they leave a little to be desired. The accompaniment was relatively loud. We had been told that the sound would not be loud because the organ was farther away from the recording machine than the voices. Mr. Bragers thus played louder than usual. It is too bad. Furthermore, Father Donovan's voice singing the *Preface* and the *Pater* is a little loud, a little dramatic. But, apart from these *artistic* imperfections, the records are fine. Will you tell me frankly what you think, Father, when you listen to them?
> Father Sablayrolles finds the Pius X Choir really good. He obtains magnificent nuances from these children. I would like to make a record—say, of the Requiem Mass—with him as conductor. But first, we must see what the monks of Solesmes are going to sing! (Mora Vocis, Feb. 15, 1930).

The Solesmes recordings were made during the summer. Justine Ward was informed that the records had been sent to her, but when she wrote Dom Gajard on November 5, 1930, she had not yet received them. This letter was sent from Rome (Villino Doria) where Justine Ward stayed a long time from October 4, 1930, to the middle of March 1931.

> First of all, I would like to thank you for the precious gift of records by the monks of Solesmes. I am waiting for them with great pleasure, and I am very grateful to the Most Reverend Father Abbot and to you. I hope that these records will encourage others to sing better. Here in Rome I have not yet heard Gregorian chant sung, at least not correctly, but I must say that I have visited only the Basilica of St. Peter. Let's wait and hope.
> Everything is going well for us. In Florence, we already have a beautiful choir of about forty boys, seven to eleven years old, with beautiful velvety voices. Here in Rome, we began classes this morning for young boys and even for young girls. It is a beautiful school; well organized, near St-Paul's Outside the Walls. I have high hopes that we will be successful in such a pleasant environment.
> Although we are very happy here in the Eternal City, we miss Solesmes terribly at times, but the months will pass quickly and we are still planning to be back for Passion week. I hope, Father, that there is nothing new, for one of Solesmes' greatest charms is not to change in a world where everything is in constant motion.
> Miss Lebreton joins me in sending our kindest regards to you and to everyone at Solesmes, and we beg you not to forget us, as we are not forgetting you in the sanctuaries of the Eternal City (Villino Doria, Nov. 5, 1930).

At the end of 1930, the records had not yet reached Rome:

We (Agnès Lebreton and Justine Ward) read your article on the records in the *Revue Grégorienne*, and we are longing to listen to them. Very good articles have been published in America. I will send them to you (Rome, Christmas, without date).

However, the records probably arrived shortly afterwards, since it appears that Justine Ward had already listened to them when they were played for Pope Pius XI, even though she was not present when this happened. A letter from Rome dated February 24, 1931, makes this evident. But before quoting it, we should mention the audition to which Justine Ward refers.

This audition, offered to Pius XI, took place on January 18th, the anniversary of Dom Mocquereau's death. Justine Ward was not invited to attend it, probably for reasons of protocol. The audition took place in the course of a very intimate audience in the Tronetto room. Cardinal Schuster O.S.B., two prelates from the Pontifical Court, Dom Gésnestout, Procurator of the Solesmes Congregation, and the representative of the French Gramophone Company who had offered the Holy Father a phonograph engraved with the pontifical coat of arms, were present. The Pope himself selected the five pieces which were heard: he kept saying, "Bellissimo, Bellissimo . . . " After the audience, he spoke casually with his guests and expressed all his admiration for the expressive manner in which the monks interpreted Gregorian chant and brought out its artistic value. This exceptional audience was reported in the *Osservatore Romano* of January 19–20, 1931, and on March 12, Cardinal Pacelli transmitted the Holy Father's thanks to the Abbey. On the day before the audience, a Solesmes record had been used to inaugurate the new broadcasting station of Vatican City (Cf. *Rev. Gr.*, 1930, 44 and 65–70; 1931, 41–44).

Justine Ward had thanked the Abbot for having sent her the records. Thus, she did not write Dom Gajard until February 24, 1931, apologizing for this long delay. She told him how satisfied and pleased she had been with these records, for she had recognized the beautiful chant of Solesmes, "simple and prayerful," which she appreciated so much; at the same time, she gave him diverse interesting points of information on this subject.

> I am really ashamed to send you this little letter so late—but the delay is largely due to the many things I wanted to tell you and to the hope that I would find a little more time tomorrow than today! You are truly charitable not to have sent a card similar to ours from Rome! I would have deserved it!
>
> First of all, let me tell you that the Solesmes records are our joy here—they arrived a little while ago and we have played them for many people—everyone was deeply impressed, Monsignor Refice especially. He expressed the desire to hear the chant at the monastery and he will most likely visit you next summer. He is a musician and appreciates beauty very much; I believe that such a visit could be useful in many ways. He could be received at the monastery, couldn't he?
>
> We also attended a meeting in honor of Cardinal Cerretti at the home of the Ursulines where we listened to records for more than an hour with a commentary by Father Dom Ferretti. Unfortunately, the room was cold and the phonograph did not produce the best results, but in spite of this drawback, the impression was good. There were many priests in attendance.
>
> I hear that the Holy Father gave the records that Solesmes offered him, and the phonograph, to the St. John of Lateran Chapter. They very much needed them! St. Peter too would benefit from them! Father Dom Ferretti will play them at the School for the students . . . when? Soon: "vedremo"! This is the Eternal City, indeed—time is not of the essence—but we are getting used to it!

I believe that these records are truly good—the main lines, and especially the high spirit, simple and prayerful, are marvellously present—there is absolutely no vanity. At times, the attack is somewhat brutal, the "downbeat" is too strong—but in spite of these imperfections which are perhaps unavoidable, I believe these records will help immensely. This manner of singing is so natural, its truth is so obvious, that I believe bizarre theories will collapse before the example given by these records. Father, when I see the mistakes in my French in this letter, I am tempted to tear it up. But I hope you will excuse me because I am very tired now. Things are going well in Italy, but—as is the case everywhere—one has to pay the price, don't you agree? Anyway, we are thinking of Solesmes where we hope to arrive for the feast of Saint Benedict—and where we hope to stay for Holy Week. We will tell you all the details and as we are waiting for this joy, we both send our kindest regards to you, to Father Le Corre, and to all the Fathers and Brothers (Villino Doria, February 24, 1931).

The audition at the Pontifical Institute to which Justine Ward refers in this letter took place on March 12th, on the feast of Saint Gregory the Great. Since Justine Ward returned to Sablé almost immediately afterwards, we only have this brief telegraphic evaluation she sent to Solesmes:

Room, balconies, corridors, packed. All Seminarians, students, religious, general enthusiasm. Ferretti-Ward (illegible date).

Homage to Dom Mocquereau

Recordings at Solesmes would resume only in 1953, and then Justine Ward would be even more interested by them. But before that we must mention certain facts which prove the extent to which she was attached to Solesmes and to the memory of Dom Mocquereau.

In order to unite herself in the best possible way with the prayer of the Abbey, she wanted to have a mass said there every day in her intention. This mass was entrusted first to Dom Mocquereau, then, after his death, to another priest of the monastery.

In 1932, in the wake of her difficulties with Catholic University and with the Pius X School, she closed Mora Vocis, the "little Solesmes" which she had built near New York in 1926. She then had all the furnishings of the chapel in which she had obtained the privilege of keeping the Blessed Sacrament, shipped to her beloved monastery of Solesmes.

She did more than this: desiring to honor Dom Mocquereau's memory in a permanent way, she offered an organ to the Abbey and another to the Pontifical Institute. She wanted for Solesmes "a refined and harmonious instrument, worthy of the divine melodies rediscovered by the Master" (Ward, Sept. 14, 1930). It was—for it had to be replaced in 1964—a beautiful instrument with 48 stops, which was blessed on December 24, 1932, after the Matins of Christmas and inaugurated immediately afterwards at the midnight mass which followed. Joseph Bonnet of Paris played on it for the first time, to everyone's satisfaction (Ward Journal, Dec. 24, 1932).[1]

The Rome organ, also a very beautiful instrument, was inaugurated a little later, on March 22, 1933. In order to make her intentions clear, Justine Ward had a plaque engraved dedicating the instrument to Dom Mocquereau. "Pio XI Pont. Max. A.D. MCMXXXIII Munificientia J.B. Ward. In memoriam A. Mocquereau, O.S.B." (Journal, March 22, 1933). (Photo on p. 86).

This inauguration was more formal than the one at Solesmes or, as seen in this letter written in Rome on April 1, 1933:

> I will have much to tell you upon arriving at Solesmes. You will almost be in Holy Week—will I be able to see you? I am giving you a few details anyway:
>
> Inauguration of the Great Organ of the Pontifical School: a large audience. "Cosi cosi" program, played not too brilliantly by "Maestro Manari" who had a fever! But everything went on fairly well. We were surrounded by the Solesmes Fathers, as I had asked Father Ferretti. The Pope had expressly requested that the Vatican be connected to the School by radio on this day, and His Holiness listened to the concert. We had a private audience with him on March 28th. Having talked about the organ, the Pope talked at *length* about Dom Mocquereau. First of all, he expressed his satisfaction that this beautiful instrument was given in memory of Dom Mocquereau—then, he recalled his pleasant, extended relations with Dom Mocquereau during many years in Milan; he talked about the scholarly study—very remarkable—which Dom Mocquereau had made on Cursus in Ambrosian Melodies; he talked about the correspondence he had had with him. He spoke fondly of these memories. I will tell you all that when I see you.
>
> In the evening—before the entire faculty of the School, Father Ferretti gave a magnificent speech on Father Mocquereau. I will give you the details of this speech when I come. He said that Dom Mocquereau was "the venerated Master" *of the entire School*, which has always wanted to follow literally his doctrine since its foundation, *and will always continue to do so in the future.* He said that, here, Dom Mocquereau is *at home, surrounded with sincere and devoted friends.* This speech was much more forceful than anything Father Ferretti has said until now, and it was said publicly. I will also show you the points Father Ferretti dictated to me. All the professors applauded loudly.
>
> Today, the opening of the Holy Door in the four basilicas. Rome is full of pilgrims. It is beautiful to see as a spectacle—but in terms of piety it is not on a par with Solesmes. We are leaving quickly, in order to spend Holy Week in France. Goodbye, Father. We are leaving from Rome on Wednesday—we hope to arrive at Sablé on Thursday evening (Rome, April 1, 1933).

The *Revue Grégorienne* gave more details on the audience of the Pope and on the formal session at the Pontifical Institute.

At the audience of March 28th, the fourth private audience as noted in her journal:

> the Pope took in his hands and examined attentively, with noticeable kindness and joy, a map of Italy showing the spreading and development of Mrs. Ward's undertaking to teach liturgy and music in the primary schools of the various provinces of Italy. Then, recalling the beautiful Gregorian recital given in the Vatican by the students from the diocese of Arezzo in

78

1930, His Holiness blessed this very important undertaking, the first of its kind, the faculty and the students; finally, as a mark of his special goodwill and gratefulness for the work done in Italy and in other countries, he offered Mrs. Ward the Gold Medal commemorating the restoration of the Biblioteca Pinacoteca Vaticana—a medal for art, if not for music, since are not all the arts the different rays of the Unique Beauty?

As for the reception for Justine Ward at the Pontifical Institute, the *Revue Grégorienne* contains details concerning Father Ferretti's speech:

Evoking history, Father Ferretti recalled how, since its creation, the School had been under the sign of Solesmes. Its founder, Father de Santi, a devoted friend of Dom Mocquereau, had founded the *Rassegna Gregoriana* review in Rome to defend the ideas of Solesmes and its champion, during difficult times, long before the *Motu Proprio* of Pius X came to shed light on everything. And when, in observance of the desires of Pius X, he founded the Superior School of Sacred Music, he wanted it to follow faithfully Dom Mocquereau's doctrine. Since that time, the Solesmes principles have always been and still are at the basis of the School; all the Italian and foreign students who come here to study, find no other doctrine; therefore, the Solesmes doctrine is adopted and taught in all the Rome seminaries. This doctrine, which has been at the basis of the instruction given at the Pontifical Institute of Music since its beginning, is still and shall always be in the future its most precious, most solid foundation. Therefore, if there is a place, besides the monastery of Solesmes, where this organ, a memorial to Dom Mocquereau, really belongs, it is here, in this Institute where Dom Mocquereau is truly at home, surrounded by sincere, devoted, and faithful friends. (Dom Mocquereau's portrait was at the place of honor, between those of the founder, Father de Santi, and those of three Popes: Pius X, Benedict XV and Pius XI who effectively supported the School.)
Then, Dom Ferretti congratulated Mrs. Ward for her undertaking to teach Gregorian chant to children: 'They will give us a generation of Catholics who will take an active and intelligent part in liturgical ceremonies,' the Most Reverend Father said. Finally, the Abbot gave Mrs. Ward, as a sign of gratefulness, a richly bound copy of the 'Numero Unico'[2] edited for the inauguration of the organ and signed by all the professors of the School (*Rev. Gr.*, 1933, pp. 48–49).

Concerning the Monastic Antiphonary

We remember how Justine Ward ever so carefully monitored the English translation of the *Nombre Musical Grégorien*, since she felt that the terminology of the Abbess of Stanbrook who had first been entrusted with this work, was sometimes inexact. She felt that she knew better the thought of the master and that consequently she could translate it better for the Anglo-American public (cf. supra p. 26). Later on, she had an argument with Dom Mocquereau about a page from the *Nombre Musical Grégorien*, since she wanted her teaching to be in complete harmony with his (cf. supra p. 35). After Dom Mocquereau's death, she very carefully monitored what was said or written. She was particularly upset by the opposition of a few Gregorianists or musicians, such as Dom Gregory Murray, O.S.B., and the Reverend Jean Vollaerts, S.J., and notably Dom Henri de Malherbe, Olivetan, who caused her much grief.

The *Revue Grégorienne* itself did not escape her vigilant attention. She noticed an article by Henri Potiron, professor at the Gregorian Institute of Paris. We shall add to it the discussion of an article published in *The Catholic Choirmaster* concerning Gregorian chant accompaniment. (Cf. Appendix No. 48.)

In an article published in the July-August 1934 issue of the *Revue Grégorienne*,[3] Henri Potiron had made a revision of the new Monastic Antiphonary which had just been published for the Order of Saint Benedict. This article did not please Justine Ward, who saw in it several unpleasant, even unfair, allusions to Dom Mocquereau. She mentions it in her journal on October 1, 1934: "Sablé. Wrote to Dom Gajard re Potiron's article in *Rev. Gregor.* Falsifying history re Dom Mocq. in notice on Monastic Antiphonale."

This article—or rather, a page from this article—actually retraced broadly the Gregorian work of Solesmes, and it should perhaps have been more nuanced, at least for the benefit of those who were not fully versed in the history of the Gregorian restoration. Here is the page in question:

> The second stage is famous through Dom Mocquereau's name. A faithful disciple of Dom Pothier, he founded the *Paléographie Musicale* which put at everyone's disposal, through photographs, some very important paleographic documents; and without repudiating his master's ideas, he supplemented them, codified them, made them more precise, first in his remarkable studies of Paleography itself, then in a sort of Gregorian 'Summa,' I mean the *Nombre Musical*, which represents a whole life's work (a Benedictine monk's life), and which certainly is, on the question of the very complex nature of musical rhythm, as well as on the question of Gregorian chant interpretation and many related questions, the most considerable and thorough work he ever wrote.
>
> What remained to be done then? In the domain of interpretation, probably little, except follow and comment on the *Nombre*. But in the domain of historical criticism, that is, criticism of manuscripts and scientific establishment of the text, almost everything. Generally, they agree with one another, it is true, and this made it possible to establish satisfactory, if not perfect, texts. But some apparently minor details revealed divergences; and the character of the melody was sometimes substantially modified by these. The original lesson had to be rediscovered, not by the number, but by the value of the manuscripts. This critical work was done especially by Dom Gajard, and the practical result of this research is precisely the publication of the *Antiphonale Monasticun*; this work indeed, though anonymous (*a Solesmensibus monachis restitutum*) was authored principally by Dom Gajard who directed the studies, personally decided the text to be adopted, and assumed all responsibilities. Certain ill-intentioned persons, finding their habits changed, may pretend that this antiphonary deviates from the way laid out by Dom Mocquereau (as some have attempted to oppose Dom Mocquereau to Dom Pothier): this would be a great error; we may even say that the *Antiphonale Monasticum* is the normal outcome of all the work done at Solesmes, and of Dom Mocquereau's work in particular. The work accomplished by Dom Mocquereau was sufficient to occupy him throughout his life; modal questions, historical criticism, interested him very much, but he was not able to devote special attention to these questions, despite his prodigious activity.
>
> At least, he had the great merit to begin the work and to establish the method and the plan: classification and collation of the manuscripts, methods of external and internal criticism making it possible to rediscover the authentic

version almost infallibly. The innumerable 'charts' prepared by a pleiad of monks under his direction and according to his instructions, and which were put together in the Solesmian Scriptorium, as well as the restorations made thirty years ago, show the interest he had in this question and the importance he attributed to it. But since he had other concerns, he could only lay the foundation, so to speak, and seeing in his young collaborator the proper aptitudes, he encouraged Dom Gajard to take advantage of the planned edition of the Responsorial and of the Antiphonary to follow the way he himself had opened and to complete his work. He monitored the work of his disciple with much interest and did not hide his satisfaction; and I may say, since I discussed the matter personally with him, that he shared *a priori* and without hesitation Dom Gajard's opinion on all the points about which Dom Gajard innovated . . . (very old natural signs, recitation notes, absence of 'leading tones,' etc.). Proving and definitely establishing the text had to be done, and it was not a small undertaking.

These lines are accurate, if one considers only the *melodic* restoration of the Monastic Antiphonary. The first Solesmes books of chant *prior to* the Vatican Edition (1905 and foll.) were Dom Joseph Pothier's work, primarily. Dom Mocquereau then very carefully prepared the Vatican edition of *Liber Gradualis*, but because of problems which developed within the Commission in charge of this edition,[4] his project was rejected and Dom Mocquereau then devoted himself almost exclusively to preparing the *Nombre Musical Grégorien* (Vol. I in 1907 and Vol. II in 1928), leaving to Dom Joseph Gajard the task of preparing the Monastic Antiophonary under his direction (1934). But Henri Potiron had not omitted to mention Dom Mocquereau's contribution, which was the most important one since he had "the great merit to begin the work and to establish the method and the plan; classification of the manuscripts, methods of external and internal criticism enabling to rediscover the authentic version almost infallibly."

Furthermore, it is undeniable that Dom Mocquereau always affirmed he was Dom Pothier's faithful disciple. To be convinced of it, it would be sufficient to read what he wrote in Volume VII of the Musical Paleography which, we know, is the scientific presentation and the justification of his Gregorian rhythmic synthesis.[5] Dom Pothier's *Les Mélodies Grégoriennes Selon la tradition*, establishing that the rhythm of Gregorian chant is a 'free rhythm,' is at the basis of the rhythmics of Dom Mocquereau, who only wanted to develop the melodies and make them more precise, as requested by several of his disciples. Finally, Dom Mocquereau, as an authentic scholar, never pretended to have said everything, much less discovered everything in his domain. Far from being 'satisfied' with his work, he customarily told the younger members of his team: "How much work there will still be after my death!" To a colleague who accused him of having happily suppressed many supplementary rhythmic indications in the Sangallian manuscripts, he said: "It is a reward which we did not expect. Temporarily suppressing part of them has been a real sacrifice for us; for we are well aware that such a work, thus mutilated and imposed during a storm could not last and that it would be necessary to do everything all over again one day."[6] This does not mean that he questioned what he had found through long and patient research.

Having said this, we may better understand, it seems, Justine Ward's objections, summarized in the following lines taken from a letter addressed to Dom Gajard and written in Sablé on October 1, 1934, for she wanted something other than a mere discussion in the parlor:

> Since I am full of admiration for this work in itself (*Antiphonale Monasticum*) I was all the more sadly impressed by the lead article in the Gregorian Review (July-August) signed by Mr. Potiron. This article now has *official* importance because of its publication in this Review . . .
> The *Revue Grégorienne* will never make anyone believe that:
> a) Dom Mocquereau only followed Dom Pothier's ideas without diverging from them;
> b) Dom Mocquereau has done nothing or almost nothing in the domain of historical criticism and criticism of manuscripts;
> c) Dom Mocquereau's Paléographic work was a beginning, nothing more.

Dom Gajard easily answered these questions in a long memorandum which fully satisfied Justine Ward.

Concerning Gregorian Chant Accompaniment

Much earlier, on December 13, 1928, Justine Ward had written Dom Mocquereau a long letter in which she had criticized Dom Jean H. Desrocquettes' accompaniments as well as those of Achille Bragers. We shall mention it here before discussing *The Catholic Choirmaster* article because it will give us the opportunity to present Justine Ward's and Dom Mocquereau's point of view on the question of accompaniment. The letter was written at Mora Vocis:

> Bragers' accompaniments displeased me in many ways. They gave a character which was too modern and non modal, to the melodies. My first reaction was to believe that Bragers understood nothing of the Modes. Then, I experimented myself with the chords which are characteristic of each Mode. I believe I observed the following: if one gives to each melody the chords which characterize the Mode of this melody, the melody and chords will almost fuse and there will be none of these dissonances desired by Dom D. To obtain the dissonances which will be resolved only at a member's finale, it is necessary to *distort* the accompaniment and move away from the Mode's nature. Therefore, if I am not mistaken about this, what should be done? I think that the modal character of the melodies should never be distorted—and that if, actually, we cannot get the dissonances desired by Dom D. without moving away from the Mode, then we should keep the Mode and drop Dom D.'s theory. This is what I plan to say to Bragers, but I would like to be sure that you approve. I am wondering whether Dom D. is not making a rhythmic fact out of something that is not one: he would like the great rhythm to be felt through the fact that harmonics would not be resolved until the end of the Member—the ear would stay in suspense as far as harmony goes. But is this a *true* theory? If, in order to apply it, one must contradict the modal character of the melodies, then one already has the answer, don't you think? I may be wrong to think that this contradiction exists; but if it really exists, we should conclude

that the Desrocquettes-Potiron theory is unfounded: at least this; or else that
their modal ideas—of these three harmonic modes instead of eight—must
be bizarre. Father, I would like to know whether this part of Dom D.'s
theory is really important to you. I don't think so; I believe that you never
wanted to make a decision on the grounds of harmony. One could follow
Dom D. for everything which *truly* concerns rhythm; and not follow him
when for him, resolution of chords (*harmonic fact*) is treated as *rhythmic
fact*—element in the great rhythm. This is what I propose to tell Bragers. If
you do not approve, please say so very frankly, and I will do exactly what
you desire, Father. It is certain that *if* Dom Desrocquettes' accompaniments
can use these dissonances without moving away too much from the modal
character of the melodies, it is equally certain that Bragers' accompaniments *cannot* do it. One has the impression of being in the major or minor
modern scale, which, as far as I'm concerned, is a torture for the ear (Mora
Vocis, Dec. 13, 1928).

It is appropriate to give Dom Mocquereau's thought on the matter, without
delving into the details of this delicate question. Like Justine Ward, he was not
a partisan of accompaniment for Gregorian chant, at least in principle. He
thought of it as a heavy weight, an armor which hampered and prevented the
flight of melodies, but he nevertheless considered it as indispensable, necessary
even, to support a choir and *a fortiori* a singing crowd. Consequently, without
being disinterested by it, he allowed much latitude to his faithful disciple, Dom
Desrocquettes, who had accompanied and helped him with success during his
second journey to America, as we remember. A few passages from certain letters actually explain Justine Ward's and Dom Mocquereau's common thinking.

Dom Mocquereau very briefly answered Justine Ward's long letter of December 13, 1928, to dismiss the problem. His letter is dated December 22,
1928:

Accompaniments. You know what reservations I have about them. In my
opinion, the best ones are worth nothing. I had Dom Gajard read what you
are telling me about Bragers and his dissonances. He thinks Bragers *exag-
gerates*, as Dom Desrocquettes often does himself. As far as the basics are
concerned, Dom Gajard likes their system. As for myself, I do not pay attention to it, and my head refuses to study it.

A little later, on March 2, 1929, in a letter sent from Mora Vocis, Justine
Ward commented on experiments in accompaniment by Mr. Bernier, a student
of Master Joseph Bonnet, which she appreciated:

"Mr. Bernier respects Gregorian tonality," she said, "and the *ancient spirit*
. . . harmonies are serious, sincere, unpretentious."

This time, Dom Mocquereau gave a longer reply, explaining his thought. The
letter is dated March 26, 1929:

I would gladly receive Mr. Bernier's experiments. To tell the truth,
everything that was done until now does not please me. What I appreciate
above all in accompaniment is *gentleness, moderation*. One thing displeases

me in all accompaniments: it is the *cold, dry,* mechanical repetition of the chant of the entire melody, on the organ. When this *chant* disappears to leave the voices completely free, it is a relief. It is said that voices, choirs, need this support . . . yes, some do, but your *young women*, do they need this supplementary support? And *we*, during Lent, we know how to do without it. I am dreaming of an accompaniment sustained by a sequence of gentle, linked, light chords, exactly in the mode, the melody being left to voices alone.

Justine Ward shared this view entirely, as a letter from Mora Vocis, dated April 16, 1929, shows:

Accompaniments: yes, Father, I agree entirely with you that repeating the sung melody on the organ is not only *unnecessary* for well trained choirs, but that, indeed, it bothers them. The voices which are in tune are much *more* in tune than a tempered instrument, which is not truly in tune, and this is why perfectly tuned voices always seem a little out of tune when they sing in unison with a tempered instrument. I would love to have our children sing with an accompaniment like the one you propose. *But*, there are many choirs who would need to hear the melody on the organ. I believe it will become less and less necessary in time and through good training of the cantors. But for the time being, it could only be suppressed for certain choirs.

Need we say that Justine Ward, many years later, will clearly express her thinking in Chapter XIX of her *Gregorian Chant* (Second Year), entitled precisely: "Open Questions."[7][1]

A striking detail: at Solesmes, we remember hearing Justine Ward criticize accompaniment sometimes or seeing her cover her ears, especially when the organ accompanied a soloist, which is something she could not accept.

In 1938, another article whose subject again was accompaniment, further hurt Justine Ward's sensitivity. This time, the matter was about criticisms or inexact statements concerning the work undertaken at the Abbey of Solesmes during several decades in the domain of restoration of Gregorian chant, rather than accompaniment per se. Moreover, these criticisms came from abroad. It was an article by Roland Boisvert published in the March 1938 issue of *Catholic Choirmaster* (p. 3) entitled *The Accompaniment of Gregorian Chant*. For Justine Ward, it was very important to have Solesmes' fidelity to Dom Mocquereau affirmed by a monk from the Abbey and by Dom Gajard, rather than by herself. Consequently, she sent him, from Sablé, a long questionnaire dated April 26, 1938, together with the issue she had annotated herself.[a]

Justine Ward was quite willing to admit that any art and any science can be improved, but was it necessary to begin questioning again all the discoveries already made on the scientific plane as well as on the practical plane? Notably, she asked, must we question what Dom Mocquereau established and taught concerning the relationships between melody and rhythm, the authenticity of his Gregorian rhythmics, etc. . . . Was there a transformation of the teaching of Dom Mocquereau? Was Solesmes not staying in the line of this teaching? Justine Ward requested Dom Gajard to answer Roland Boisvert's criticisms himself.

Dom Gajard did so in a long memorandum containing many details and sent his memorandum to the editor of the review. Justine Ward was satisfied with it and translated it immediately without modifications, except for two or three words whose replacement she justified.

> "As for the rest," she wrote, "I stayed as close as possible to the spirit of the French text while respecting the different characters of the two languages." (Note without date and probably personally delivered.)

Dom Gajard's reply to the editor of the *Catholic Choirmaster* review was published in the June 1938 issue under this title: *An Important Communication from Solesmes. Dom Gajard Defines Solesmes Position* (Appendix No. 49). Dom Gajard clearly affirmed that:

> it was Dom Mocquereau himself who not only laid the foundations for the work of research on all these points, but who established and organized on a scientific basis the general principles which govern the reading and interpretation of the manuscripts. That Dom Mocquereau never pretended to "have said the last word" is self evident; and we who are continuing and developing his work along the lines of his own system and direction are conscious that our task is to delve ever more deeply and to verify with ever stronger proof the reality of the conclusions at which he had arrived.
> It would be equally unfortunate should an impression be created that the technical books for practical teaching published by Solesmes are "obsolete" or even incomplete. *Le Nombre Musical* and the *Paléographie Musicale* remain today what they have been always—the base and foundation of our teaching, both theoretical and practical.

About two other points raised by Justine Ward, Dom Gajard added:

> . . . it would be rash and extremely dangerous to assert as a general rule that the form of the neums and the grouping of the notes therein has (sic) no rhythmic value *per se* and that these forms are without influence as regards the interpretation of Gregorian Chant. Such a conclusion would be inexact.
> To insinuate that Dom Mocquereau ever disapproved the accompaniments of Dom Desrocquettes is misleading. The truth is that Dom Mocquereau concentrated his attention upon the rhythmic question as distinct from the harmonic or modal treatment advanced by musicians. For this reason, he refused to take a definite stand on the modal theories of these composers of accompaniments.

The other points of Justine Ward's questionnaire could easily be answered.
Dom Gajard's conclusion summarized what was, for Justine Ward, the heart of the matter:

> These are the principal points which I felt it necessary to clarify, for the sake of precision and that there might be no misunderstanding as regards the actual teaching of Solesmes. Indeed, I welcome the opportunity thus offered to affirm once again the fact that the doctrines of Solesmes are today what they always have been and that our work is animated by a spirit of logical continuity. It is always the teaching of Dom Mocquereau that we follow with

ever increasing certitude as our publications themselves reveal. The tradition established by Dom Mocquereau continues to affirm itself effectively and increasingly not only as regards the singing of the liturgical chant at Solesmes, but also in the continuity of the scientific studies as organized by him at the *Paléographie Musicale*. Any contrary rumors that may have been circulated are utterly unfounded and are manifestly false. Today, more than ever, it is true that the two expressions—"Method of Solesmes," "Method of Dom Mocquereau"—are equivalent and synonymous. (Appendix No. 49. Trans. by J.B.W. See also under "Open Questions" Appendix No. 9, 33 and 34.)

The Rome Institute of Sacred Music

Justine Ward was also interested in the Pontifical Institute of Sacred Music in Rome. She was often in touch, particularly with Dom Ferretti. We remember that on several occasions he had given courses at the Pius X School in New York. His death in 1938, caused great sorrow to Justine Ward: "This is a terrible blow for me. And for all of us too, I believe. We cannot yet realize what gap has just been opened in our lives and in our work. We are leaving tomorrow to attend the funeral in Parma on Friday at 9:30. Father Ferretti had been a very dear friend for a long time. Solesmes also will deeply mourn his death" (Sablé, Tuesday, May 24, 1938).[8] Justine Ward remained on good terms with Dom Ferretti's successors, Dom Grégoire Suñol in 1938, and Monsignor I. Anglès in 1946. The future of the Institute and its fidelity to Dom Mocquereau's teaching was one of her preoccupations, and she intervened at various times to express all the hopes she had for this Institute; for example, in 1950, after the Rome Congress of Sacred Music whose *vota* did not satisfy her completely because she would have liked to see more clarity in the presentation of the various systems of interpretation of Gregorian chant, the only valid one for her being the system of Dom Mocquereau.

Organ given to the Pontifical Institute of Sacred Music by Justine Ward, dedicated March 22, 1933. Recital was played by Raffaele Manari.

Console of the organ
in the abbey church at
Solesmes in 1932. It
was replaced in 1964.

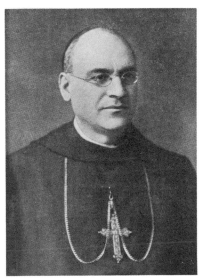

Dom Paolo M. Ferretti, O.S.B.,
President of the Pontifical Institute
of Sacred Music, from 1922 until
his death in 1938.

Chapter V

RETURN TO AMERICA

Memories of Solesmes

It is now fitting, since Justine Ward will soon return definitely to America, to say a few words concerning her relationship with the Solesmes community. Apart from Father Abbot, Dom Mocquereau and Dom Gajard, she had no relationship with anyone there, except for two or three monks and of course with the brothers at the door whom she occasionally mentioned in her letters because some of them had made a deep impression on her. About Abbot Dom Cozien, "her Abbot," she said one day that he "treated her severely, like one of his monks"; in any case, it is certain that she greatly appreciated his austere reserve and his great discretion; she knew that the Father Abbot wanted to retain his total independence and that he was not afraid at times to say words which could have entailed irremedial consequences: "I appreciate him more for this," she said one day. Justine Ward was greatly interested in the liturgical life of the monastery. She always did everything she could to be present during Holy Week and at Christmas. During her long sojourns in Sablé, she often came to the daily mass. At first, she used to come in a cabriolet; she led the animal herself, a beautiful pony with a harness decorated with bells which rang as she prodded the pony whenever she met someone she knew. Then, she came in a taxi, and the driver was expected to be right on time. Through her presence at the offices, Justine Ward was one of the most faithful habitual visitors of the monastery to which she was drawn by her love of Liturgy and of Gregorian chant. There is no other reason for her attachment to Solesmes, especially after Dom Mocquereau's death. When the record of Compline was issued, it was played every day for evening prayer and Father Abbot's blessing. We can see in the article published by Justine Ward at the time of Dom Mocquereau's death, and in the one published for the centennial of his birth, the depth of her feelings toward the Abbey (Appendix Nos. 64, 66). We quote here a few lines taken from the second of these articles. Although they refer to Justine Ward's experience at Quarr Abbey, these lines, written in 1950, apply just as well to the Liturgy of the monks now back in Solesmes, where in the well-known words spoken by a guest, "the censers really smoke." Justine Ward also liked to see the rising of incense smoke accompanying prayer and chant, and for a long time she undertook the task of supplying Solesmes with incense.

> Day by day, this liturgical splendor unfolded itself before the eyes of the few who assisted, almost as intruders. This beauty concerned them only indirectly. One alone was the object of this consecrated magnificence, this perfection of song and gesture. He who had created beauty could be adored only through the full beauty of truth, only through the *Opus Dei*, the *Work of God*, to which these monks had dedicated their lives. The sense of that Invisible Presence animated each note, each phrase, each movement, while clouds of incense rose in spiral designs and, mixing themselves with the sunbeams, entwining their mutual rhythms, executed an aerial dance that flooded the church with rays of perfume and patterns of light.

The Solesmes Abbots used to stop at Justine Ward's home when they came to visit their monasteries in Canada. When I showed Abbot Jean Prou my work on Justine Ward and Solesmes, he told me that it was he who had blessed the room occupied by the "Dom Mocquereau Foundation" for some time in Washington. He mentioned also a detail which will not surprise those who knew Justine Ward: she felt very happy after the blessing of the room and seriously thought about calling in a caterer to prepare a meal she would have liked to have there.

In 1933, Justine Ward had the Abbot of Solesmes, Dom Germain Cozien, elected a Member of the Dom Mocquereau Foundation (October 5, 1933: Meeting Foundation. Elected A. Cozien; Sept. 9, 1935: Tuesday Sablé annual meeting Dom Mocquereau Schola Cantorum Foundation. Solesmes Ab Cozien members and directors).

On April 27 and 28, 1935, the first demonstration of the Ward Method of Music and Liturgical Chant took place in Paris. It involved fifty young Dutch school children under the direction of their own teachers. The Abbott of Solesmes and Abbot Ferretti were in attendance as well as many members of the clergy, organists and chapel masters. Justine Ward gave a brief speech in which she explained the characteristics of her Method which, to reach its goal, must be taught by regular classroom instructors previously trained through courses given especially for them; must be a part of the school program on a par with sciences, and in this manner, penetrate deeply into the spirit and the soul of the child who will thus learn to sing well as he learns to read well. On the following day, the same children sang mass in the church of St. Dominic, illustrating the ultimate goal of Justine Ward's musical instruction: to make children participate in the sung prayer of the Church, in its divine liturgy. The demonstration made by these children was the most beautiful illustration of Justine Ward's words (*Rev. Gr.*, 1935, pp. 239–240, Cf. Appendix No. 46.)

The Exodus of June 1940

Justine Ward further showed her attachment to Solesmes at the time of the invasion of France by the Germans in June 1940. Her exodus was indeed somewhat linked to that of the monks.

As soon as war had been declared, she had written Dom Gajard, on September 29, 1939, a card which is worthy of being quoted:

Yes, I think that every work of beauty and civilization will have to suffer during this sad war—mine like the others. But, even if slowly, we shall try to do something. Your summer classes were the high point for all the students (a group of American students). They will benefit much from them and like me, will always be very grateful to you, Father. I wrote for them a little summary of the points on which you insisted so that the good doctrine shall not be forgotten. You must all really be very sad at Solesmes to see all your young people leave—and your greatly reduced choir—let us hope that all of them will return safely and that God will find a way to reward their sacrifices (Sablé, Sept. 29, 1939).

When, on June 10th, the French forces were ordered to retreat toward the Loire River, following the break in the front lines in the north of France, Justine Ward decided to leave for America and to sail from Bordeaux, with Agnès Lebreton. Since the French civil authorities were encouraging all the men who still had the chance of being mobilized to go south of the Loire River, Justine Ward offered the two free seats in her car to two monks of Solesmes who might go south of the Loire River with her. Father Agaësse and Father Combe were designated for the trip. They left Sablé in the afternoon of June 15th. Soon, they met much traffic on the roads, with refugees from Belgium and northern France fleeing before the German army. Cars were inching forward. The travellers had a hard time crossing the bridge at Saumur, which had already been mined. Finally, the car was able to go through, thanks to its American registration plate, which soon actually attracted someone's attention: it was followed, but the driver skillfully lost his pursuer at a crossroad.

The travellers briefly stopped at Argenton Château for a light snack in the back room of a café, and arrived in Niort at night. The monks were housed in the St. Andrew Presbytery and the ladies went to a nearby convent. During the night, they heard the humming of planes and the sinister blasts of the sirens. The Germans arrived one or two days later: a small group of soldiers took over the town where they met no opposition.

After three days spent waiting in Niort while the general situation was changing from hour to hour, Justine Ward decided to go to Bordeaux, hoping she could still find a liner bound for America or the Caribbean. As for the two monks, they were supposed to find those of their brothers who had gone south of the Loire River, but since they did not know where they were, they stayed with Justine Ward. Near Bordeaux, the car had to turn back, for the French government had decided to settle in this maritime city and forbade access to it. Justine Ward then tried to reach Royan, another port on the Atlantic, but only the French navy was there; no other boats were leaving. Since the French army had been unable to retreat toward the Loire River, the travellers decided to return to Solesmes (although they had considered going to Lourdes, from where Justine Ward and her companion could have crossed the Spanish border).

The travellers were then blocked in Niort, where they had returned to spend the night, because of a decision of the French government to forbid any movement by the refugees and forcing them to stay where they were. This happened on June 18th. To keep herself informed, Justine Ward purchased a big radio, which enabled the travellers to follow the tragedy which was developing,

92

notably the request for an armistice by Marshal Pétain, signed on June 24th
. . . Hours truly filled with anguish, which one cannot forget. Many still recall
with emotion the Marshal's many calls to be calm, prudent, and disciplined.

Father Agaësse said mass in the small chapel at the convent. The ladies attended it every day; they often returned during the day to pray before the Blessed
Sacrament, both of them leaning over the same book of prayer, like two very
close sisters. Meals were taken together. Justine Ward had found, among the
refugees, a woman who willingly accepted to cook and take care of their room.
It was a windfall for this woman who was soon going to be without a job and
without a home. Justine Ward consoled her as much as she could and gave her
enough money to enable her to go home when she could. More than once, the
ladies tried to relieve the misery of those they met.

When they were able to leave Niort, not before the 28th of June, the travellers headed for Sablé, through Nantes where Justine Ward wanted to see the
Consul of the United States. Upon leaving Niort, a crisis was barely avoided.
A German soldier who was directing traffic gave a slap to the driver, who was
about to return it to him when, fortunately, Justine Ward stopped him by taking his arm. The travellers arrived at Solesmes after the first Vespers of the
feast of the patrons of the Abbey, the Apostles Peter and Paul. The community
had been greatly reduced by the mobilization of a large part of the community
and by the exodus which had just taken place, and even though Justine Ward
brought the two monks back, the other refugees returned only later, in July.
For the demobilized monks, it was even later. And eighteen of them were prisoners in Germany for several years. Nevertheless, there were enough monks
left in the Abbey to have a very proper office. Justine Ward discussed these difficult times in an article published in *The Catholic Choirmaster* in 1941, (*Solesmes
and the War, Cath. Choir*, 1941, pp. 155–156. Cf. Appendix No. 63).

In the meantime, three monks of Solesmes, notably the Precantor Dom
Pierre Moulinet, died in action. Justine Ward could not remain indifferent. She
sent the following letter to Dom Gajard, on the occasion of Dom Moulinet's
death:

> What an affliction for Solesmes! I so often think of poor Father Moulinet.
> All that is so sad, one could even say so useless, if we did not hope that so
> much suffering by all the French people will be a great atonement for
> France's errors and her return to God (Sablé, July 26, 1940).

Return to America

Justine Ward was able to stay in Sablé until May 6, 1941. At the time that
she was forced to leave for America, she wrote Dom Gajard from Sablé:

> Needless to say, I shall always remain united with Solesmes, in spirit and
> through a deep conviction, and during my exile I shall continue to work to
> the best of my abilities to make its chant better known and appreciated. I
> hope this exile will not be too long and that I shall soon find France and
> Solesmes again (Sablé, May 6, 1941—Appendix No. 50).

Actually, Justine Ward came back to Europe only twice: The first time in 1967 for a meeting of church musicians at the Pontifical Institute of Sacred Music in Rome; the second time in 1968, when she came to Paris. She then came back to Sablé where she spent the last weekend of April (from the 27th to the 29th). Until that time, during the German occupation and during the troubled years which followed the liberation of the territory, she had not been able to come; then, the fate reserved for Marshal Pétain by the French government had made it too distressing for her to come back to France, as she admitted to Dom Gajard during one of his trips to Washington. Finally, her health no longer allowed her to travel, and when she had to do so in 1968, she had already been crippled for a long time.

She once expressed her regret to have gone back to America: "We are thinking of coming to France for a short visit. I really hope it will be possible because time seems to be dragging on—it has been twelve years since I left. If I had known that in 1941, I think I would not have left." (Washington, Dec. 30, 1952.)

We have almost no letters from Justine Ward until 1948. First of all, the situation in France until November 1942 made any correspondence within the country very difficult, since the country was divided into two zones, one zone occupied by the German army and one zone free. Correspondence between the two zones had to be done on letter-cards, written and printed in advance. Unnecessary words were crossed out, but even then censorship was very strict, since the occupying army still managed to find certain allusions and implied meanings which were questioned. As for correspondence with foreign countries, it was impossible in the occupied zone where Solesmes was located. After November 1942, when France was completely occupied, the problem remained, especially for correspondence with belligerent countries, as was the case with the United States.

Various Undertakings

Normal correspondence was slowly resumed after the liberation of the territory in 1945. A sequence of letters from Justine Ward to Dom Gajard, between 1946 and 1949, offers interesting points of information. The same yearning for Solesmes is expressed in the letters; for this reason, and also for teaching purposes, Justine Ward requested Dom Gajard to make new Gregorian recordings.

First of all, we shall quote the whole text of a letter of May 17, 1946, written in Washington, because it is particularly interesting: foundation of the *Mater Ecclesia* review by Justine Ward, preparation of her book on Dr. Shields' work at the University:

> I was so pleased to receive your two letters which are so interesting and I am sorry not to have replied more quickly. I was waiting for some free time to write in peace, but since this free time is not forthcoming, I am setting a little time aside to tell you how delicious it is for both of us to hear from Solesmes—after what has been (for me especially) a very rigorous fast.

Nevertheless, I never felt separated from Solesmes—on the contrary, I felt more united than ever to Solesmes during those very sad years.

It was great to hear that you are publishing the Gregorian Review again. Mr. Lebreton ordered a subscription for me directly from the Desclée Publishing Co., but, Father, I am very glad that you did it too because your copies will remain in Sablé to be bound and placed with the other volumes which are complete.

We started a little review here, whose ambitious title 'Mater Ecclesia' will perhaps convey the wrong idea to you. It concerns teaching and teachers especially: musical pedagogy particularly. We are beginning our fourth year. When the mail is more reliable, I will send you the whole collection for the Solesmes library—if you find them worthy of it!

I am finishing the biography of our great American educator, Dr. Shields. I have been working on it over the last three years. I must finish it before leaving America. For we are still planning on coming to Sablé-Solesmes as soon as circumstances will allow it. In the meantime, we are listening to the 'blitz-offices' which we are having here! It is not always edifying.

We are nevertheless working at the University for the priests and religious who are around the University, and also with some seminarians. The day before yesterday, our students sang Vespers at the Basilica—you would not have been ashamed of us. There were six 'great cantors'—young and somewhat shy but rather good—and a large choir of about 200—mostly religious—who alternated with our cantors. After Vespers, Benediction. Everything, without accompaniment, very sober, enthusiastic, and sufficiently nuanced. It was not perfection but it came close to it. The best thing is that the instruction we are giving all these students is spreading out—communities are beginning to take an interest in Gregorian chant—which can only happen if opportunities are offered to hear it well sung. Mr. Bernier treated us to half an hour of beautiful organ playing before vespers and at the end. The celebrant was a French bishop. Gregorian chant is being sung more and more by school children. Fine progress here also. (Cf. Appendix No. 52.)

Justine Ward has just mentioned her publication. In the same vein, we should mention here a letter written much later, in January 1948, in which she announced to Dom Gajard her intention to write a second volume on Gregorian chant in order to dispel the errors which were circulating in this domain.

In the course of the last few years, many books on Gregorian chant and its technique have been published in the English language. Most of them are full of errors or of things badly explained which create confusion . . . thinking of all these nuns who have received a good Gregorian base, I have almost made up my mind to write a second Gregorian volume. The first one had been written only to make children sing the Kyriale well. If I do not continue my work, teachers will go here or there to complete their education in any way they can. If I decide to prepare this second volume, would you give me permission to use the charts of the Little Treatise of Psalmody? The Liber Usualis would be the children's book. My book would provide the explanation of the principles and a guide for practice. It seems to me that in order to avoid dissension as well as mistakes in practice, I have to do this work. At least, I will protect my students and through them, many children (Washington, Jan. 12, 1948).

To return to the years 1946–1947, two other letters from Justine Ward should be quoted. In the first one, dated November 2, 1946, she announces

the sending of records made at the University and urges Solesmes to issue soon
a new series of records. She alludes to Father Abbot's journey to Canada where
there are two monasteries of the Benedictine Congregation of Solesmes, the
monastery of the monks of St. Benoît du Lac, and that of the cloistered nuns of
Sainte Marie des Deux Montagnes. In the second letter, dated January 10,
1947, Justine Ward thanks Dom Gajard for his comments on the University
records, while noting how his work is arduous; she thanks him also for an article for her Review and says that she has contacted the Victor Company to ac-
celerate the much wanted Solesmes records.

Both letters were written in Washington. The first one is dated November 2,
1946, as indicated previously:

> Father Abbot's visit brought great consolation to us. It was as if all of
> Solesmes was coming to us, since we could not go there . . .
>
> I thought I would send you, in Father Abbot's luggage, our *Mater Ecclesia*
> and the records made with our students from the University—but when I saw
> how much luggage Father Abbot was already carrying, I gave it up and I
> will send our reviews to you in small successive parcels through the mail.
> You will see that what we are trying to accomplish with this review is a lit-
> tle special: the first issue announces the goal. We are completing our fourth
> year and we are beginning to understand what is necessary for those who
> form our Catholic Youth (and especially the girls). We need many 'active
> projects,' ideas which can be applied in the classroom. Here, we are suc-
> ceeding, little by little, in putting the teaching of Gregorian chant in the
> *essential* program of the Catholic schools. Our goal: that all children,
> without exception, can properly sing the Ordinary of Mass in Gregorian
> chant and that the elite of the boys can sing the Propers (also in Gregorian
> chant). We are truly progressing in this direction. Children are always easy
> to train. We are aiming at the teachers (especially the teaching Sisters).
> With these little explanations, you will understand our *Mater Ecclesia*—
> sometimes a little childish!
>
> We are still planning on coming to Solesmes for Holy Week—I have not
> heard any psalmody for five years—nothing, nothing at all. Here, it is rare
> to hear even a mass properly sung. Vespers are unknown. As for the Little
> Hours, they are not just forgotten—they never existed. So, I rely on my
> memory—and I hear the chant of Solesmes inwardly. Your records are a
> pale reproduction. I think, Father, that it would be very kind of you to
> think of making a few additional records for us: especially a record of
> psalmody. Wherever one tries to psalmodize (in the religious houses), it is
> hammered in or banged in—without rhythm. I mentioned it to Father Abbot.
> He neither said yes nor no. He will think about it. I assure you that psalmodic
> records would help us very much in our classes. A beautiful antiphon fol-
> lowed by a psalm in the different Modes. Your records can provide style in
> places where a visit to Solesmes is obviously impossible. They are lessons
> spreading out into the whole world. On the other hand, *many other records*
> are being made today. All of them claim to be Solesmian and almost all of
> them are bad. Either too affected, too fast, too slow, they throw confusion in
> the mind. During the war, the Solesmes records could not be bought and the
> others were made and sold at that time. We made ours partly in order to pre-
> sent something better, but especially in order to encourage the young ec-
> clesiastical students who are being trained here at the University. There are
> about twenty seminarians, young religious from different orders, Brothers,
> etc. . . . . The records are far from being perfect—they are even full of faults
> which you will hear with displeasure—but please excuse the beginners. They

don't know what they are doing! It is a group which never sings together except in the classroom! But they will form their brothers and this is important. There is good will, enthusiasm, even too much of it some times! Young voices, not yet formed, except one which is too dominant. The pauses are all too long—yet still, I hope you will acknowledge a sincere effort in the right direction. The problem for us is that as soon as some students are half way through their training, they leave, and we have to start all over again with new people. We are always working with beginners! There is nothing else to do (Washington, Nov. 2, 1946).

The second letter, is dated January 10, 1947:

I agree completely with everything you say concerning our records. I noticed one thing though (and you probably noticed it in other records)—all the faults are exaggerated—almost like a caricature. This is not true as far as pauses are concerned—all of them are too long. I had insisted very much on this point before making the records and progress was noticeable. But when the time came to sing in front of the microphone, the old habits triumphed! What is unfortunate for us is that we can never hope to achieve something satisfying because we are putting these young religious from various houses together for three quarters of an hour per week during the winter months—they never sing together except during classes, and at home they do not sing at all. After one year (two at the most), we no longer see them—they are replaced by new students. We have to start all over again. Our task is to sow some good seeds without ever having the satisfaction of harvesting. It is a little difficult, but I do not see any other way to change little by little the bad habits and horrible taste in this country.

Working with children, if the teachers are good, is much more satisfying. There are good teachers in Holland; the one who brought the children to Paris is one of the best. Mr. Lennards is now giving a course in Paris with some students, few in number but enthusiastic. There are now more than 20 students which, at this point, is quite edifying. If we had a few schools for children in Paris, I would be very happy.

As for your article, Father, it is perhaps a little beyond the reach of the readers of *Mater Ecclesia*,[1] but I translated and shortened it a little and I believe it will be fine this way. Everyone will be pleased that you offered this gift to our little review, and we must lead them to think about rising above the average. I have a problem, however, with the presentation of the Gregorian chant examples: we have no way of printing them in this country—we do not have the proper type. If you are thinking of publishing this article in the Gregorian Review, then we could photograph the examples and make copies for *Mater Ecclesia* (provided you approve of this).

I also translated your comments on psalmody, and with your permission, I would like to publish it in *Mater Ecclesia* because the comments are very useful and will help our readers a lot.[2] Therefore, I propose to publish the article on psalmody immediately and to wait for the other article until you have published it in the Gregorian Review. I will send the article to you (keeping the translation for myself) . . .

I wrote the Victor Company recently. I no longer knew anyone in the 'Management' but I learned from Segovia that the American company is not making many records, due to scarcity of materials, but that it is not so for their London branch. Since it is probably the London branch which would be charged with the recording, I hope to get a favorable reply. There are presently many Gregorian records which are less than mediocre—those made in Canada are the least bad—the others are very bad—they are circulating and doing some harm. It is a real Penelope's task to work here—it is all the more important to have your records for counterbalance.

Miss Lebreton joins me in sending you her best wishes for a good year, with the hope to see you again in the coming months. Our souls are thirsty for the chant of Solesmes (Washington, January 10, 1947).

In her preceding letter of November 2, 1946, Justine Ward mentioned the death of Dom Grégoire Suñol, president of the Pontifical Institute of Sacred Music in Rome, which had occurred in October of 1946. Dom Suñol had succeeded Dom Ferretti who had died in May of 1938. When Dom Ferretti died, Justine Ward had written on a card dated May 24, 1938, that she had lost a very dear friend and that Solesmes would deeply mourn his death. She was equally saddened by Dom Suñol's death. Furthermore, she was concerned about the Institute, dreading that "the tradition now established would be changed," concerning Gregorian chant. She often referred to this point in her letters to Dom Gajard. But the appointment of Abbot Igini Anglès as successor of Dom Suñol reassured her entirely. At the same time, she was greatly affected by certain attacks aimed at the work of Dom Mocquereau and of Solesmes. She too was attacked; she then said, "I feel greatly honored to be so linked with Solesmes" (Washington, Jan. 10, 1947).

Project Concerning Dom Gajard

In 1949, Dom Gajard came to America for the Congress of Sacred Music held in Mexico City, but Justine Ward had already requested this trip the year before, in order to have him give courses in Washington. The Abbot approved the idea, but wondered whether Dom Gajard, who did not speak English, could do properly what was expected of him. Justine Ward believed that the difficulty was not insurmountable, since Dom Mocquereau and Dom Ferretti had done it very satisfactorily under the same conditions. She thus wrote the Abbot on July 8, 1948, from Stockbridge:

We are so happy that you are willing to consider the project concerning Dom Gajard and Catholic University. It does not seem that the question of language should worry us much. When Father Mocquereau came to America, he was very successful despite the fact that it was necessary to translate his teaching. We planned it in advance. Moreover, every afternoon we met to prepare the next day's lecture with the exact terms of the English translation. We followed the same system for Dom Ferretti's courses, and in addition we prepared (the first time) some large charts on which the stages of his instruction were shown. The second time, we printed booklets which were distributed to the students on which the main points of this course were summarized. By adopting either one of these systems we could, I believe, surmount the obstacle of the foreign language.

But I would rely essentially on an understanding (if it occurs) between Father Gajard and the young priest, Father Woollen, who will be at Solesmes for a few weeks this summer, and whom you were kind enough to invite to stay at the monastery. He speaks both languages well. He is a musician. He could perfectly assist Father Gajard in Washington, by translating for him. It is an experiment to be tried, and Father Gajard himself will be the judge. If Father Woollen seems to him to be ready for this task, I see no obstacle in terms of the language.

Justine Ward insisted:

> It would be important for us to know soon whether we may announce the coming of Dom Gajard. We have to advertise it in a dignified manner, write articles on Solesmes and on its chant in periodicals, awaken curiosity little by little (with 'follow-ups' as we say here)—and this can be done easily, but we have to be able to work on it. I am in touch with the editors of some of these periodicals, and even those who are not converts will nevertheless have to announce the *sensational* news of the visit of the Choirmaster of Solesmes. As soon as I have your permission, I will contact the Rector of the University, Monsignor McCormick, who is now on vacation but who will be back in the fall, for him to invite Dom Gajard officially.

On July 23, 1948, Justine Ward wrote Dom Gajard himself, from Stockbridge, in order to put an end to his hesitation. It was a memorandum of four long typewritten pages (Appendix No. 53) in which she answered various questions raised by Dom Gajard and in which she gave details concerning what she expected from him. She proposed a six-week stay, with 45 hours of classes altogether: an advanced course in Gregorian chant according to the Solesmes principles, to be given as an extension of her *Gregorian Chant*, with a large part devoted to practice.

But Justine Ward insisted first on the importance of the coming of the Solesmes Choirmaster.

> Thank you immensely for your letter of July 16th. I understand your anxieties and your desire for precision. As far as I am able, for I speak only for myself and not for the University, I will explain to you what the project includes — to which I am very attached, needless to tell you, for it seems to me to be the ideal moment to place the Catholic University absolutely and publicly on the side of Solesmes. All the members of the Hierarchy of the United States form the Directorship of this University that gives Pontifical diplomas and which serves as a model for the affiliated colleges. Thus the influence of this University is extensive (this aside from the question of merit). This is my thought on the project itself. If you could make this sacrifice (and it would certainly be that and not a pleasure!) I think that it would be the right moment to do it. At the moment we have a Rector who is supportive and a Dean of the Sisters' College who is also supportive and ready to help us in the spreading of liturgical Chant. (Appendix No. 53, Par. 1).

A Dom Mocquereau Centenary

Dom Gajard, however, came to America only during the following year (1949) for the Congress of Mexico City. Before we discuss it, we must mention an anniversary which Justine Ward did not let pass without associating herself

with it. On June 6, 1949, the hundredth anniversary of the birth of Dom Mocquereau was celebrated at Solesmes in the intimacy of the monastic family.
Justine Ward wanted to unite herself "with our homage, in spirit, in prayer and
in generosity," as Abbot Dom Cozien said (*Rev. Gr.*, 1949, p. 168–Appendix
No. 55). The last word refers to the commemorative marble plaque which was
inaugurated on that day in the Paleographic room created by Dom Mocquereau, and which was to remind the present and future members of the team
of the Master's program: "To investigate the thought of our Fathers; to bow
down before their authentic interpretation; and to submit humbly our artistic
judgment to theirs: this is required both by the love we must have for the whole
tradition, melodic as well as rhythmic, and by the respect of an art form,
perfect in its kind" (*Paléographie Musicale*, Vol. X).

Justine Ward had at least the satisfaction to write the article already mentioned, to mark this centenary: *Solesmes and a Centenary*. She mentioned in it
all her admiration for Dom Mocquereau and recalled, in her own charming
way, various memories of Quarr Abbey and of Solesmes, notably the experience which originated in the Gregorian vocation of her master and which Dom
Mocquereau himself had related to her (Cf. Appendix No. 64):

> In the quiet of his cell, Dom Mocquereau was preparing an Offertory for
> the feast of a martyr, *"Posuisti Domine in capite ejus coronam de lapide
> pretioso."* He hummed the melody softly. Fascinated, astonished, he ex-
> claimed, "Why this is music, real music, beautiful music." He reached for his
> cello, tuned it and played the melody, very legato. That was the moment of
> his conversion. The Offertory *Posuisti* was the blinding light which, as in the
> conversion of St. Paul, reversed the direction of his entire life. From a hater of
> Gregorian chant, Dom Mocquereau became its most distinguished apostle.

Justine Ward would have liked to have a mass celebrated at the College of
Sisters of Catholic University at the same time as this inaugural session, in
order that everyone *"unanimes, uno ore, honorificemus Deum et Patrem
Domini Nostri Jesu Christi."* But at the last minute, she had to abandon the
idea, much to her regret: "I am so glad to have received your letter together
with Father Abbot's speech for the feast of Dom Mocquereau's centenary. You
can imagine that I was with you in spirit during this feast. We could not sing
the High Mass which had been planned for that day, because the students of
the University and of the College of Sisters had already finished their courses,
taken their exams, and gone on vacation. We preferred not to do anything
rather than doing something unsatisfactory."

The Congress of Mexico City

Dom Gajard came to America for the first time when the Congress of Sacred
Music was held in Mexico City from the 10th to the 22nd of November 1949.
It was not an International Congress, but a Pan-American Congress. Never-
theless, several 'honorary invitations' were sent to the old-world, and the
Choirmaster of Solesmes was thus invited through the intermediary of the
Congregation of Seminaries and Universities (*Rev. Gr.*, 1950, p. 230).

Justine Ward was also part of the "honorary guests" from America who had been invited to participate in the Congress. However, she did not attend: "the journey, even from Washington, is too difficult and too tiring," she wrote Dom Gajard on July 24, from Stockbridge. "Do you know that demonstrations will last for 10 days and will be in various places?" But as soon as she learned that Dom Gajard was going to the Congress, she pressed him to accept an invitation to stop in Washington:

> Washington is between New York and Mexico City, and if you were willing to accept our hospitality for a few days, it would break the long trip and we would have the pleasure of seeing you and the time to discuss many things which are of interest to both of us (Justine Ward and Agnès Lebreton). You could let us know the time of your arrival and we would meet you at the Washington railroad station. It would be charming and we both hope that you will accept this proposal. It would be unfortunate if you were on this continent and we could not see you! And you will have plenty of time since the Congress will begin only on November 11th (Washington, Aug. 29, cf. Stockbridge, Sept. 24 and Nov. 9, 1949).

In September, Rt. Reverend Dom Cozien went to Canada to visit the two monasteries of the Congregation of Solesmes which are located there. Justine Ward and Agnès Lebreton came to greet him when he arrived in New York (A. Lebreton, Stockbridge, Sept. 7, 1949), but it is only at the time of his departure that the Abbot stopped in Washington for a few days. These were great moments for the two oblates. Justine Ward took advantage of his presence to organize Dom Gajard's program in the New World, which would include, before or after the Congress, a visit to Washington, to her place and to the University, and another visit to the *Regina Laudis* monastery located in Bethlehem (Connecticut) (Stockbridge, Sept. 24, 1949).

Dom Gajard was planning to stop in New York on the way to Mexico City, but Justine Ward arranged his program differently, in agreement with Monsignor Miranda, President of the Congress (Stockbridge, Oct. 11, 1949). She thus sent the following cable to Mexico: "Please inform X . . . on your Committee, that I will meet Dom Gajard at the pier in New York. Consequently, he is to cancel the arrangements for accommodation in New York . . . " (Stockbridge, Oct. 11, 1949). Justine Ward met Dom Gajard when he arrived in New York and accompanied him to the train leaving for Mexico City. He stopped in Washington on November 26th, on his way back from the Congress (Stockbridge, Oct. 11, 1949). This date was nearly postponed because of the illness and death of Mrs. Cutting, Justine Ward's mother. Justine Ward had the consolation to "prepare slowly her mother to die," so that she had "entered in her very serene eternity after having accepted the divine will, thus in a very Christian frame of mind" (A. Lebreton, Washington, Nov. 17, 1949). But Justine Ward insisted on keeping the date of November 26th to receive Dom Gajard[3] and Agnès Lebreton wrote him on November 9th:

> I immediately felt that Mrs. Ward would have been sad if you had postponed this date, because you will have very few days with us in Washington

and she has a lot of things to discuss with you—she told me this on the
telephone. And she so carefully arranged your trip to Mexico-Washing-
ton . . . (A. Lebreton, Washington, Nov. 9, 1949).

The Congress

Monsignor Miranda, Bishop of Tulancingo, President of the Congress, flew
over the immense expanse of American territory to invite personally all the
bishops and request their participation, in person or through delegates, to this
Congress. It was held in five different cities of Mexico, quite far apart from one
another: Guadalajara, Morelia, Leon, Queretaro, and finally Mexico City, in
order to reach as many people as possible. "Usually," the President said, "people are asked to come to the Congress; this time, the Congress is going to the
people."

Many archbishops and bishops participated in it (21 altogether). In addition
to the honorary guests, the delegates who had come from the various dioceses
of Canada, of the United States, and of Central and South America, numbered
approximately 80, and some of them represented several organizations. All of
them were united to work in a common spirit on a common task: the restoration or progress of sacred music in all of America according to the laws of the
Church. The objective was not to pass legislation but to apply laws which had
been promulgated a long time ago, particularly under Pius X, Pius XI and Pius
XII. A collective pastoral letter concerning sacred music had been sent by the
Mexican episcopate to all the regular and secular clergy, and to all the faithful
in this country. Beginning with the motto of Pius X, "Instaurare omnia in
Christo," this document showed how liturgy—and chant, which is an integral
part of it—is one of the best ways to re-Christianize society, and insisted on action by superior and elementary schools of sacred music to reach such a noble
end.

The main lines of the Congress, its objective, could only meet with Justine
Ward's approval. Consequently, she was very pleased to assist by sending a
paper on "The Teaching of Gregorian Chant to Children, by the Ward
Method," which was read in Morelia. In it, she showed how her teaching had
been in line with the objective of the Congress for a long time. Indeed, the objective she proposed to reach, from the beginning of her pedagogical work, was to
associate all the faithful with the prayer of the Church in which Gregorian chant
is an important element; it was to generate love for this chant which must
become the prayer of all the faithful and an efficacious means of sanctification; it
was to turn to children because any major reform in this domain can come only
through them; and, in order to foster love for Gregorian chant, it was to develop
the child's training at all levels, including that of emotive faculties on which
music has much influence. "Let us note first of all," she wrote, "that in terms of
technique, Gregorian chant is easy. It is unison, and its range is average.
Therefore, in terms of practice it does not present any difficulty. It is on the
spiritual side that one must find a way to give it all its educational value. One
must foster love for it. This is the aim of the Ward Method. Allow me to tell

you how we do it and by what means we have succeeded."[4] Justine Ward then explained the rules she proposed for *general preparation* to the study of music and especially to that of rhythm, and for *specific preparation* for teaching Gregorian chant to children. Finally, she insisted on previous training of teachers able to fulfill effectively this educational mission. In closing, she expressed her satisfaction to see that, in Mexico, the clergy was bringing its indispensable moral support to the liturgical renewal, and paid homage to Dom Mocquereau whose rhythmic principles had helped her immensely and without which she could have done nothing.

As for Dom Gajard, he presented, in Mexico City itself, the principles, ways, and rules of interpretation of the Method of Solesmes. The first part was purely technical; in the second part on practical rules of interpretation, there were new pages on style rules. Justine Ward particularly appreciated the second part, because she found in it everything which made up the beauty of the Choir of Solesmes which she appreciated so much, and especially its prayer value which was essential to her. She commented on it when the lecture was printed in a brochure in 1951 (cf. infra).[5]

Return of Dom Gajard

After the Congress, Dom Gajard came to Washington as planned, and stayed for a few days at Justine Ward's home at the Interlude. He had enough time to talk to her about the Congress which had delighted him, particularly because of its "clearly Solesmian tone." Union, or rather unity, was achieved in advance on the Gregorian question "but it was impossible for me, he wrote, not to see in everyone, from the first to the last hour, a strong sympathy for the work and ideas of Solesmes." Nothing could have pleased Justine Ward more, since she wanted Dom Gajard to come in order to discuss all the problems concerning Gregorian chant:

> You did much good in coming here. You left exquisite memories. You gave us very useful lessons. Father, you were very frank with us and we were very frank with you. I think it must have pleased dear Father Mocquereau, as it pleased us (Washington, Jan. 2, 1950).

Justine Ward alluded to the practical lessons given by Dom Gajard at the University, which were most appreciated, but since she was ill at that time, she had charged Agnès Lebreton to express her satisfaction while Dom Gajard was still on his way back; later on, she thanked him herself on January 2, and congratulated him at the same time for his book *Les Mélodies de Noël*.

> You will be happy to know now that your lessons at the University yielded good fruit. The Mass on December 8th was magnificent—may this last! For the time being, Father Woollen is well imbued with your teaching—people never sang so well at the University. The group of priests and seminarians who form the Choir of the University were very pleased—they are now enthusiastic about liturgical chant, the nuns too, but it is obviously less important to win them over—we need the clergy particularly.

I recently received *Les Mélodies de Noël* and I thank you very warmly. They are very interesting—very well made, and they will certainly help those who know little about these great works of art and piety to appreciate them and those who know them to appreciate them more. What memories are revived in me at the thought of these beauties which form all the happiness of the Christmas season! And which cannot be heard here (Washington, Jan. 2, 1950).

Dom Gajard also visited the monastery of the cloistered nuns of *Regina Laudis*, who had requested his visit through Justine Ward (Stockbridge, Sept. 24, 1949). He was very successful there too: "Mother X . . . mentioned again on the telephone how enthused *everyone* was and how grateful they are to you for your good lessons which delighted them" (Washington, December 8, 1949, May 3, 1950 in P.S.).

Dom Gajard and Justine Ward in Washington, D.C., on the occasion of her 70th birthday.

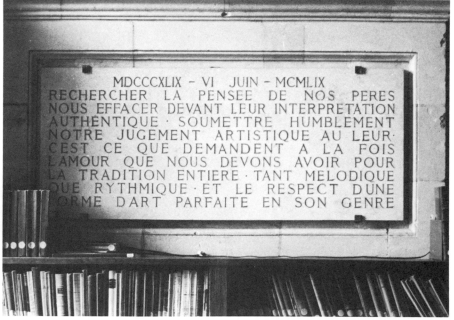

Located in the studio of paleography was plaque given to the Abbey at Solesmes by Justine Ward on June 9, 1949, to commemorate the 100th anniversary of Dom Mocquereau's birth.

105

Dom Germain Cozien, O.S.B. (1878–1960),
fourth Abbot of the Abbey of St. Peter,
Solesmes.

Justine Ward's residence in
Stockbridge, Massachusetts.

Pilgrimage by children trained in the Ward Method to sing at Lourdes, France, celebrating the centenary of the apparitions, 1958.

Chapter VI

JUSTINE WARD
AND
THE "SOLESMES MOVEMENT"

Project Concerning Gregorian Records

The following pages can be entitled: Justine Ward and the "Solesmes Movement" since she took so much interest in the diffusion of the Abbey's records and
encouraged the Gregorian tours of Dom Gajard in the United States. Since this
work is primarily documentary, one should not be surprised to find in it several
letters praising the Solesmian interpretation of Gregorian chant. These documents also enable us to understand better what Justine Ward expected from
sacred chant and the depth of her religious and artistic sense. The reader will
be kind enough to excuse us for the long quotations which will appear below.

Realizing that Dom Gajard would not come back soon to America, and wishing to obtain a new collection of Gregorian records, Justine Ward had obtained
the promise of a tape recording by the monks. She alluded to it in her letter of
January 2, 1950, quoted above, to refresh Dom Gajard's memory:

> "We are now waiting very impatiently for a tape. What a feast it will be to
> hear the voices of the Choir of Solesmes! My tape recorder, like us, is eagerly
> waiting." To be sure to receive the tape, Justine Ward even offered the tape
> recorder. A little later, she said that a little psalmody would be very useful
> to her at this time: "I hope this short letter will arrive very rapidly, so as not
> to delay the recording we are eagerly waiting for. I would like some psalm-
> ody in the first tape, if it is possible. Thank you in advance, Father.
> Remember that we are very hungry for Solesmes" (Washington, Jan. 28,
> 1950)

When the tape was played, everyone at the Interlude was in admiration.
Justine Ward immediately wrote Dom Gajard from Washington on March 21,
1950, Feast of St. Benedict, to thank him and congratulate him:

> The precious reels arrived yesterday, just in time for the first Vespers of St.
> Benedict! What a splendid gift! I will never be able to express in words the
> joy we had in listening to them—even in spite of the imperfections I will
> mention later. What a marvellous style! All these nuances, finer and more
> delicate even than when I was at Solesmes nine years ago, are so exquisitely
> natural. It is an incense of prayer—it hardly passes through the senses to
> dematerialize itself in rhythmed sounds in such a live way, without violence
> but so firm, so inevitable, and at the same time so delicate. It is great art

for God, not at all art for art's sake, but the ideal of the soul lost in God. What a marvel you accomplished! And how much good these reels will do, once they have been adjusted!

And what an exquisite surprise we found at the end of the reel: your little message, so touching, which brought tears to our eyes—and we had the feeling of being there among all of you. I will never be able to thank you enough for it—you and all those who took part in the chant on these reels. Father, you will transmit our deepest thanks to them, won't you . . .

These reels will serve as models for the students, and lead them toward greater perfection. Listening to one of these pieces is worth more than entire courses in theory . . .

Father, we had a feast for you on the 19th, but imagine, this morning, a mass in black for St. Benedict. Happily, the beautiful melodies were singing within our hearts (Washington, March 21, 1950).

After Monsignor Miranda had listened to the tape (A. Lebreton, without date), it was played at the University in Washington (J. Ward, May 3, 1950):

A few days ago, we played the tapes of your splendid chants for the students of the University. Despite the noise in some of the pieces, these chants impressed masters and students . . . Father, it is more efficient than a whole year of lessons! The Solesmes voices are now going to train an infinite number of students unknown to you! The psalmody was a revelation, the great responses of the Christmas Matins—what a splendor—and almost all the pieces, even those with which you are not completely satisfied, exude an extraordinary atmosphere of piety and of great art. As for me, you cannot imagine what a joy it was to hear your beautiful chant. It left me yearning for Solesmes. Thank you, Father, to you and to everyone (Washington, May 3, 1950).

The following year, Dom Gajard having promised to send another tape in answer to Justine Ward's request, she replied to his letter, indicating what she would like most:

The great responses of Holy Week would be marvellous. They would enable us to wait patiently for the opportunity to return to Sablé-Solesmes for the Great Week (Washington, March 3, 1951).

And when she received this second tape, she wrote this enthusiastic letter on March 31st. She felt that the Choir of Solesmes had never sung so well:

We are writing Father Abbot, but I am adding a word for you. What a marvel this tape is! How could you make such a miracle? There is no rumble—everything is clear, perfect. And what a profound, nuanced chant! One has the impression of being at Solesmes itself, and I think the chants were never before so marvellously sung! Father Mocquereau must be so happy! All his principles are there, even more perfectly expressed than during his lifetime. There are accents on the upbeat which could not be easily explained but which come alive in the chant of your schola. I am not considering the details because *everything* is so beautiful, so profound, so true. You have a magnificent schola. As for the records, would it not be a good idea to have the schola alone sing certain pieces? It is obvious that with the entire monastic choir, one cannot obtain such nuances which make Gregorian pieces enchanting. We cannot find words to tell you what joy these marvellous "sung prayers" bring to our souls. You selected all the pieces I like best—what a magnificent sequence, an abbreviated Holy Week followed by the joy of the Resurrection! The *Salve festa dies* so well played *con brio* . . .

We spent Holy Week at Regina Laudis. The nuns have improved greatly —Their offices were really well sung (Washington, March 31, 1951).

A little later, in a letter dated April 13th, Justine Ward commented again on what makes the beauty of these chants, that is to say, "style." We can see in it that her enthusiasm was not due to snobism or to fashion, because it is her artistic and deeply religious sense which, alone, could allow her to appreciate Gregorian melodies and all the spirituality in them.

This matter of 'style' shall be properly understood only through examples sung with the perfection of your present schola. Verbal explanations may be very accurate, but unless one has heard the sung example, one does not understand, unless one is a true artist—which is not often the case among those who are studying chant. This is why I am so eager to see your records being issued.

I agree entirely that these records should be made by the Schola alone. I did not dare to tell you so.[1] With the entire choir, you would have a mass effect, obviously, but that is not what people are going to look for in your records: they will look for style and the least imperfection shall be looked for and commented upon by critics of Solesmes. On the other hand, the example you will give to all the friends of Solesmes throughout the world is of capital importance. It is the most precious teaching, the most marvellous propaganda—no written article, no book could do what these records will achieve (Washington, April 13, 1951).

Thus, Justine Ward requested permission to duplicate the tapes in order to have other teaching centers benefit from them:

The tapes are superb, the nuances are marvellously expressed. It would be very useful *for Solesmes*, in my opinion, to give permission to duplicate the tapes (Washington, May 10, 1951).

Justine Ward took up the matter of style again in a letter dated October 2, 1951, written in Stockbridge, in which she acknowledged receipt of Dom Gajard's brochure on "The Solesmes Method, its constituent principles, its practical rules of interpretation" (Desclée, 1951), which recapitulated his Mexico City lecture while supplementing the important chapter on the "Rules of Style" (cf. supra 102):

Now, a few words, Father, concerning your little book. I am full of admiration. It is clear, without delving too much into details, and really pleases me because it contains advice on *style*. These remarks were never made before (except orally) and they will be so precious to choirmasters, to those men and women who cannot go to Solesmes or who have gone there but may have forgotten certain nuances of the teaching. You produced a masterpiece, Father. I am glad that this book will be translated into English. I thank you also for the charming lines of presentation you wrote (Stockbridge, Oct. 2, 1951).

Justine Ward's Insistence

From then on, Justine Ward continued to push Dom Gajard into making a new series of records. This was the subject of several letters in the months that followed. She had also written about it to the Father Cellarer (Bursar of Solesmes) during the previous year:

> "I insisted very much on the beauty of the present chant of Solesmes," she wrote Dom Gajard, even though I heard it only through the tape recorder under far from ideal conditions" (Washington, Dec. 2, 1950). And later on: "It is essential that the voice of Solesmes itself not be muffled—all those who have heard your voices on the tape recorder have been delighted—more than delighted—bewitched, despite some technical imperfections" (Washington, March 3, 1951).

Justine Ward had also given advice to Dom Gajard concerning publication and advertising of the planned records (commentaries, illustrations) offering to write the English prospectus herself.

> I am beginning to wonder whether it would not be easier for a new person who is not from the monastery to say certain things about Solesmes. What do you think? In any case, everything would be submitted to you. Again, in this matter I am completely at your disposition—to do or not to do (Washington, Feb. 18, 1951).

Justine Ward was also ready to translate into English the commentaries for the pieces. The letter in which she refers to this, as well as to a tape made for her during the recording sessions which took place in June 1951, feast of St. Peter:

> Am I allowed to give the list of the pieces which will be on these records? I do not want to be indiscreet but I am at your disposition for anything which could be useful. Naturally, I am ready to translate what you will write for the jacket and will do my best. I think that, for this country, it is preferable to be as brief as possible without doing an injustice to the subject matter. But I am asking you to send that to me as soon as possible for it is now and here that I have the time and quietude necessary to do it well. And as you know, once the translation is finished, it takes time to print and gather the pieces for this jacket . . .
>
> Once again, Father, let me tell you how touched we both are for the tactfulness with which you have kept us informed, and for the very great kindness of Father Le Corre to whom we owe this marvellous preview of the beauty of the records. Count on me for anything I can do to be helpful to you, Father. Say this to Decca also, for I want to do only that which will not hamper the projects they have in mind (Stockbridge, June 29, 1951).

The recordings were thus made in June 1951, to Justine Ward's great satisfaction, who was also pleased to learn that Solesmes had finally chosen the Decca Company as she had recommended (Washington, May 12, 1951). During the recording sessions, she had written from Washington on June 19, 1951:

> How nice of you to send me this little letter knowing how important this all is to me. And, Father, on our behalf, do thank Father Le Corre who made tapes at the same time! Tell him that we are taking our tape recorder with us to Stockbridge and that we will play the new pieces as well as the old ones! We are leaving on June 26th (June 19, 1951).

Because of technical problems, to which we shall refer, the records were slow in coming. Justine Ward took advantage of that delay to complete the work she had undertaken on the edition of a presentation brochure. Thus, she wrote on January 14, 1952:

> I received your beautiful manuscript for the records. I am going to submit very simply my opinion to you, hoping that you will pardon my frankness for, as you know, I certainly want these records to be successful.
>
> I have more than ten thousand records in my collection and there is a point which is universal concerning their presentation. If a text is in a foreign language (French, Italian, German, etc. . . .) *the translation of this text is always given.* This is the rule without exception, either for simple folk songs or for whole operas. But I do not see that you left any room for translations which, in the case of Latin, are even more important than in the case of modern languages. In my opinion, reproduction of the chants in music is very important, but translation of the texts is even more essential. Both are needed.
>
> But, if we do not want to make a whole volume to accompany the records, we will have to limit sensibly the descriptions, especially the presentations at the beginning. I know you gave me all sorts of permission; nevertheless, I do not want to substitute my conception of what is necessary for yours. This would be treason.
>
> Another point: for the public at large, would it not be desirable to say a few words about Solesmes itself—its past in the restoration of melodies and its role as an interpreter of liturgical chant? I am thinking about putting a few words on this subject at the beginning. For the rest, rhythm and accentuation rules could be much abbreviated, to the minimum necessary for finding one's bearings. We must realize that few (or none) of those listening to these records will have a Gradual—still less a Monastic Antiphonary—in their hands. The melodies printed together with the translation of the text of each piece will enable these people to appreciate fully the treasures you are offering them.
>
> This means that it will be necessary to reduce greatly the text of your project. I will do nothing without submitting my project to you, but first of all, I need to know whether you agree in principle and whether the Decca Company is ready to print these translations . . .
>
> Now, Dear Father, please be very frank with me. If you prefer to maintain your text, I am ready to translate it. It is up to you. I am only your instrument. But I believe that I must tell you what my thinking is before preparing the English manuscript. Another point: concerning the liturgical translations into English (Mass, Office), is there a copyright which would prevent me from using the translations in the Missal (Desclée), and where

could I find the English translation of the pieces of the office? I am not good enough in Latin to dare make a translation of my own!

Do believe, Father, that I am at your disposition to do my best with what you will decide (Washington, Jan. 14, 1952).

On February 14th, Justine Ward again wrote:

"I have just finished everything: translation, abbreviated commentaries, but in line with yours. Also, a brief general introduction on Solesmes and Gregorian chant" (Washington, Feb. 14, 1952). She was ready to begin again a third time, if necessary: "They returned the MS to me because the arrangement of the record does not agree with (a) your first catalogue and (b) the more recent pages which were sent to me. This means I will rewrite these pages for the *third time*" (Washington, Feb. 22, 1952).

In April, she sent the introduction she had prepared for the American public. This was a very short work, merely presenting Gregorian chant and its most general characteristics, as well as the work of Gregorian restoration undertaken at Solesmes (Washington, April 8, 1952) (Appendix No. 54[1]).

The 1953 Records

Justine Ward was greatly disappointed when she learned that the recording or rather the "re-recording" was defective, all the more so since Dom Gajard had sent her a tape made during the recording session itself, whose good quality she had been able to appreciate (Cf. Washington, June 19, 1951). It was necessary to do it over again and Justine Ward offered to intervene personally, if necessary: "If the records are bad, I will help you to the fullest extent" (Washington, Feb. 27, 1952). Then on March 8th:

"What a relief it was this morning, to receive your cable announcing that everything will be done again in May . . . It will delay the publication of the records, but it is better than publishing records which would do a disservice to Solesmes." And she added: "Tell me if you have an illustration in mind for the jackets of these records. One of your artist-monks could perhaps do something which would not be ordinary. We now have the time to plan everything well. I was asked for an illustration proposal for the covers, but I do not want to undertake anything without knowing what your plans are, and I am sure that what you do will be more beautiful than what we could do here. Let us agree on everything. We are leaving for New York on Monday to attend the meeting of the Dom Mocquereau Foundation on Tuesday. We elected Mister Bernier to the Board of Directors; he will be there. I will notify him of the Decca-Solesmes decision—he will be disappointed with the delay, but he will be happy, as we are, that the records will be perfect. Certainly, Decca *can* do good work. Their error was to overdramatize the effects (during re-recording), which is precisely detrimental to Gregorian chant, which consists entirely of delicate and subtle nuances" (Washington, March 8, 1952).

Nevertheless, Justine Ward was a little concerned: "Like you, I find that there were such beautiful pieces that I am wondering whether they can be sung so well again" (Washington, March 18, 1952, cf. May 6, 1952).

Happily, this time, everything went well, and as soon as he received the proofs, Dom Gajard sent to Washington a letter which brought great relief:

> How I rejoice with you that the records have been successfully made at last and that we will have them in February! For Christmas, we recited our Matins together, then, we listened to your Responses on the tape you made for us two years ago—and we thought we were present at Solesmes—it consoled us for the absence of music at Christmas, which is preferable, however, to the 'musiquette' often heard in our churches. We attended three low masses on Christmas morning in the chapel of the Delegation (the Abbot knows it well, for he said mass there during his stay at the Interlude). But with your tape we entered a little into the splendor of Solesmes (Washington, Dec. 30, 1952).

The records were issued only in July 1953. Their arrival in Washington was especially welcomed because Justine Ward was at the time very upset not to have yet found in the *Revue Grégorienne* a book review for the second volume of *Gregorian Chant*, which had been published four years earlier. Dom Gajard had wanted to write it himself, but the problems caused by the recordings had prevented him from finding time to do it. Being far away, Justine Ward had not realized the situation and felt much aggrieved. But the arrival of the records made her forget everything. Indeed!

> At last, we have the records—after a morning spent tracing them through three customs offices—and an evening spent listening to them. They are marvels!
>
> Truly, you gave us a treasure—and *you are pardoned for everything* because you gave us these masterpieces, which are so moving, so Solesmian in style and beauty.
>
> I hear a slight background noise especially in the Kyriale pieces, and sometimes for an instant in some other compositions—but nothing comparable to the noise of the first records you rejected. I admit that I am not used to the lengthening of pauses at the great bar. It produces a certain emphasis which is too reminiscent of modern music and gives the impression that the piece is finished before it really is. At the repeat, one has lost the guiding thread. It may be a personal impression, since I am so used to the short pause, and certainly it is a matter of taste. But what is extraordinary is that the spirit of prayer animates all these chants. They cannot be listened to simply as music—even very beautiful music—but through a kind of miracle we are able to enter the monks' life of prayer (Washington, July 24, 1953).

The Grand Prix du Disque Award

At the end of 1953, the Choir of Solesmes was awarded the Grand Prix du Disque. Justine Ward rejoiced over it, all the more so since throughout these last few years she had not ceased pushing Dom Gajard into making these recordings; she wrote to him on November 16, 1953, from Washington (only the main letters have been quoted here):

> Your letter of December 9th (sic) brings me precious news. The Grand Prix du Disque awarded your two series in such a pleasant and solemn

manner! I am as delighted as you are, if not more so, since I pushed you so much to make these recordings. I think the Decca Company must be happy to have persevered in redoing this recording until you were satisfied. Thus, we are all happy.

Mr. Farkas asked me to make the commentaries for the small record series. I am working on them. There is much less to say about them than about the large ones. All your records (large and small) are sold here in complete sets and not individually. The more I listen to the small records, the more I like them. The Mass of the Deceased is really good—one believes one is at Solesmes.

Once again, my warmest congratulations for the Grand Prix du Disque award! It is well deserved and it is truly satisfying to see the great musicians of France make such a just award! (Washington, Nov. 16, 1953).

Divergences

We noted that during the recordings, a little discussion had taken place between Justine Ward and Dom Gajard about punctuation, more precisely about pauses in musical cadence. Actually, this discussion had originated earlier in 1952. It remained peaceful and irenic, since Dom Mocquereau's principles were not questioned. Justine Ward had accepted Dom Gajard's point of view and had even considered writing a one-page explanatory flyer for the books written in French:

> You are modifying the manner of counting the pause at the great bar and at the double bar. It is a question not of principle of course, but of taste. As far as my books are concerned, the best solution, I believe, is to give the two ways (Dom Mocquereau's and yours), leaving adoption of one or the other *ad libitum*. This is what I did in sending Desclée the text of a flyer which will be inserted in my books.
>
> I have always noticed (at least in America) a tendency to prolong all pauses more than indicated. If yours is prolonged, it will result in a great gap. That is why I believe it is unnecessary, dangerous even, to allow this liberty in my English books. I will do it for the French and Dutch books. Not for Italy where Dom Mocquereau has been followed until now, and I believe there would be no advantage (quite the contrary) to show a difference between his doctrine and yours, even on a minor point.
>
> I had noticed the lengthened pause in the chant. It sounds fine, but I did not see a change of principle in it. I had attributed it to human weakness, as for triplets which unfortunately appear from time to time in the interpretation (Washington, June 9, 1952).

There is no doubt, it seems, that the interpretation of Gregorian chant offered by Dom Gajard had tempered Justine Ward's intransigence. She had accepted a compromise which she would perhaps not even have considered in earlier times. But she always expressed herself with great frankness, as revealed in this letter of July 20, 1952:

> Concerning the prolonged pause at the great bar, I would like to think the way you do, but that is impossible for me. If one wanted to do the most 'natural' thing, one would not sing with a free rhythm, but in strict time—

all the subtlety of Gregorian chant would suddenly disappear, for one is looking for the supernatural, not for the natural. As for me, I believe that this tendency to prolong cadences is not coming from a rhythmic difficulty but from simple laziness—one is resting, one is lying down for a little nap! I never found any difficulty in terms of *rhythm* in Dom Mocquereau's rule. All my students understand it well. It is when they are practicing that large groups stop in order to sleep; they don't give themselves a new impetus after a pause (even if it is minimal) and singers pause when they should not (quarter-bar, half-bar)—everything provides temptation to go to sleep! It is thus not a question of rhythm but of musical integrity. It is true that in these large groups of voices, one is not dealing with musicians; one uses what one finds—with their laziness and relaxing. But, in my opinion, it is not by recommending longer pauses that they will be provided the stimulus they are lacking. I am also thinking about the confusion which such a change will entail among those who, for many years, have been following Dom Mocquereau's principles. They will wonder why they should change (for a detail of pure personal taste).

As for the little flyer, it will appear only in my French books. It is exclusively because of Mr. Le Guennant that I am doing this, so that the groups he is directing (either Ward Method or Gregorian Institute) will be able to measure pauses at the great bars in the same manner. For America, Holland, and Italy, this sheet is not needed, since these centers follow Dom Mocquereau's doctrine completely. If, in this little flyer, I have explained the difference between Dom Mocquereau's teaching and yours on this point, it is because you did it yourself in your article (*Revue Grégorienne*) and because there was no way to allow such a change except on the basis of your authority as Choirmaster of Solesmes (Washington, July 20, 1952).

Dom Gajard in America (1959)

The Choirmaster of Solesmes went to America several times. We should mention these trips here because Justine Ward took much interest in them and invited Dom Gajard to stay in Washington. Dom Gajard had gone to Mexico in 1949. His second trip took place ten years later, in 1959. The Choirmaster of Solesmes had been invited by the Abbot of the Cistercian Abbey of Spencer (Massachusetts), who had already sent two of his monks to Solesmes for several weeks and who now wanted Dom Gajard to come, for he desired to "group around himself at Spencer some Gregorian chant specialists" disturbed as he was by the anti-Solesmes campaign led at that time by Dom Gregory Murray and the Reverend Jean Vollaerts.

Dom Gajard arrived in America on May 27, 1959, and left on June 29 (by airplane, which worried him much) due to Right Reverend Abbot Dom Cozien's resignation which forced him to shorten his stay and cancel the visit he was scheduled to make at Elmira (N.Y.), at the Benedictine monastery of Mount Saviour.

After a visit to the nuns of Regina Laudis, who very much wanted him to come (Ward, Washington, March 31, April 6 and 28, 1959), Dom Gajard stayed at the Interlude from June 7th to June 10th, where he was warmly welcomed. In the morning, he used to say mass at the Apostolic Delegation—these ladies' chapel—and in the evening, they listened to vespers and compline on

116

the record recently made at Solesmes. Finally, Dom Gajard was hoping he would have the opportunity to initiate negotiations with the purpose of bringing Justine Ward and the Pius X School of New York together again, since relations had been broken in 1931.

Dom Gajard went to Boston where he met Mr. Theodore Marier, musician and choirmaster, and then to the Abbey of Spencer where he was enthusiastically welcomed by a young and dynamic community. He stayed there ten days and met about thirty participants in addition to the members of the community. The last two days were devoted to making a Gregorian record. During his stay, Dom Gajard celebrated his fifty years of ministry, in a most cordial ceremony.

On June 13, Justine Ward wrote Dom Gajard, upon his arrival at Spencer, to express the joy his visit had brought to the Interlude:

> We are now eagerly waiting for a letter from you. It still does not seem that you have left us. You cannot imagine how these two days, so filled with complete trust and understanding, have touched us. Thank you, Father, very warmly. We are hoping you will come back next year perhaps? We are saying the best prayers we can for all that you know which is there, deep down in our souls (Washington, June 13, 1959).

She said it again in a letter of July 22nd in which she alludes to Abbot Cozien's resignation. She venerated him very much and he had immediately informed her of his decision. She also refers to a projected visit by Mr. Theodore Marier, prepared by Dom Gajard. Mr. Marier was in contact with the Nuns of the Sacred Heart in New York and Dom Gajard counted on him to reestablish the former relations with Justine Ward. Finally, she thanked Dom Gajard for the last records he had offered her:

> You can imagine how happy we were when we received both of your letters (July 7 and 17). We were concerned about your trip and we sent you a telegram (which you probably did not get) at Idlewild airport to wish you a good trip. After that, we did not want to write because of the great events happening at Solesmes. Even today, it is difficult to realize that the Abbot Dom Cozien whom we knew and loved, has resigned. It will take us a little time to adjust to this!
>
> But we cannot wait any longer to tell you how marvellous these last 45 r.p.m. records are: they are the crowning of this magnificent collection of Gregorian melodies you have given the world during these last few years. These little records are pure marvels: the pieces themselves and the beautiful style with which they are sung! Congratulations, Father. You have a monument to your memory in this series of records, which no one will ever take away from you!
>
> We cherish precious memories of your visit to the Interlude—and we hope it will happen again one of these days. It is so much easier to speak than to write. Furthermore, one hesitates to write certain things which can be said. I am expecting Mr. Marier's visit next Sunday. We will talk in the sense we agreed upon. As I told you already, I do not hold a grudge against the Sacred Heart nuns (Washington, July 22, 1959).

Later on, on October 20, 1959, Justine Ward wrote a letter in which she mentioned the reason for her decision to reach an agreement with the Pius X School:

> The reconciliation with the Sacred Heart nuns will in no way entail my involvement in the arrangements which are being prepared. What I did— you know this—was ONLY for SOLESMES. I must tell you something I am sure you will understand. I have been staying away completely from any struggle, any complication which does not directly concern my work. I am the same age (minus one year) as Dom Cozien. I want my last years to be a time of peace. In the past, I fought a lot, as Dom Mocquereau did, as you are still doing, but for me it is all over. I still have some books to write if God gives me time. Apart from this work, I do not want to enter into any complications, especially if the matter does not directly concern me. The Pius X School has been going on for thirty years without me. I am far from thinking of taking up again today a task which was too demanding even when I was young. I will, therefore, write no one. I believe that this matter concerns the monastery of Solesmes, the monastery of Spencer, and the Pius X School, and that it will be settled without my intervention . . . (Washington, Oct. 20, 1959).

Mr. Marier's approach to New York was so successful that Dom Gajard was invited to stop at the College of the Sacred Heart in 1960, when he was expected to return to the Abbey of Spencer where his work had been so much appreciated. In the meantime, two nuns from this institute were to come spend some time at Solesmes.[2]

Justine Ward was pleased with all this and the record made at Spencer gave her much satisfaction. She expressed this in a letter to Dom Gajard dated February 3, 1960, while announcing to him her intention of admitting Mr. Theodore Marier to the Dom Mocquereau Schola Cantorum Foundation, which only Dom Gajard could approve since Mr. Marier would thus be the connection between her and Solesmes:

> First of all, the Spencer record seems truly extraordinary, a real tour de force when one knows how little time you spent with these monks. The rhythm is genuinely Solesmian—and that says everything. Your visit certainly accomplished marvels and one realizes these monks did it with good will and zeal.
>
> As for Pius X: I believe you have a very good chance of being successful there too. This morning, the President of the College, Mother O'Byrne, called me on the telephone to tell me how happy she was to have received from the Right Reverend Abbot an affirmative answer to her request. Before you come to America, you will have the visit of Mother Morgan and of another nun during a period of six weeks. I know I am not announcing anything new to you since Mother O'B. told me that you had been kind enough to reserve a room for them yourself. I believe they intend to work seriously. For the United States, it will be a very necessary thing because students go to Pius X convinced that the genuine Solesmes doctrine is taught there!. I am sure you will do everything possible to help these two nuns and you will be a judge of their good will.
>
> I will now tell you something which is a most confidential matter (since it is only a project which is not accomplished yet). Thinking of the Dom

Mocquereau Foundation and of its fate after the death of its president and vice president (the Interlude residents), I realize we have no one who could make the connection between Solesmes and the directors. I have thought of nominating Mr. Theodore Marier as one of the directors. He knows Gregorian chant—and loves it—he speaks French as well as English. He is a 'persona grata' as far as you are concerned, is he not? If the other directors agree to elect him at our meeting after Easter—and I believe they will think it is a good idea—this will give us security for the future. I discussed it with Mr. Marier who is willing to serve. He will be the link between the Foundation and Solesmes (Washington, Feb. 3, 1960).

Dom Gajard in America in 1960

Dom Gajard's third journey to America took place at the beginning of June 1960. Dom Gajard arrived in New York on the 13th and was immediately taken to the Interlude by Mr. Marier (Washington, May 31, 1960). He stayed there until the 15th. After a long stay at the Abbey of Spencer, from the 16th to the 29th of June, he stopped for two days at Regina Laudis, St. Joseph in Spencer and finally, from the 1st to the 26th of July, he devoted his time to the Pius X School. Mother Morgan had come to Solesmes where she had appreciated everything that had been done for her and for her companion (quotation taken from a letter of April 30, 1960, written in Washington). What was the result of Dom Gajard's teaching in New York? We may evaluate it through the records which were made with the Pius X students. Indeed, Justine Ward wrote this on October 4th.

> You have probably received the record of the two masses sung this summer at the Pius X School under your direction, and the charming lesson for the priests. As for me, I think your work was almost miraculous. I would never have thought it possible to see such a transformation happen. Certainly, there are still improvements to be made with respect to certain details, but the ensemble is a real creation on your part. There is a life, a phrase, a Gregorian style unmistakably Solesmian! I am so happy about it and I think you too must be pleased with the good work you have done last summer at Pius X.
>
> The little lesson for the priests charmed me. You are exacting without hurting susceptibilities. This too is a most appreciable art! (Washington, Oct. 4, 1960).

There was a surprise during this Gregorian session. The new Abbot of Solesmes, Dom Jean Prou, was in America at that time visiting his houses in Martinique and Canada. He had already stopped in Washington before Dom Gajard's arrival and had brought the last records made, "a marvel," Justine Ward wrote (Washington, August 30, 1960). He also went to the College of the Sacred Heart where he was warmly welcomed.

America 1962

Dom Gajard's sojourn in America in 1962, was longer than the previous ones; it lasted from the 15th of June to the 17th of August. Dom Gajard first went to the two Canadian Solesmes monasteries, to St. Benoît du Lac, from June 21st to June 28th, then to St. Marie des Deux-Montagnes, from June 28th to July 5th; then he went to Saint Louis, to Webster College where the Ward Method was followed, from the 6th to the 20th of July, to the College of the Sacred Heart in New York and to the University from July 21st to August 10th, and finally to Regina Laudis from the 10th to the 16th of August. He went to see Mr. Marier in Boston on August 7th, and it was Mr. Marier who made arrangements for his travels. As early as January, Justine Ward had prepared Dom Gajard's program, as far as she was concerned:

> What causes me great joy is to know that the Abbot accepts that you once again visit the United States where you can do so much good for the cause of liturgical chant. Your summer 1960 students are still under the spell of your teaching and are impatiently waiting for your return.
>
> Mr. Marier says he has your permission to arrange your time in the best way possible.
>
> It is agreed that you will spend two weeks beginning on June 18 (Monday) at Webster College, Saint Louis. You will find groups of Sisters teaching in the classrooms there. The courses at Webster cover the necessary technique from the elementary classes (six-year-old children) to the end of the schooling (13- to 14-year-old children). The children will not be there—only their teachers.
>
> In addition to these classroom teachers (who must teach Gregorian chant according to the Solesmes principles), there will be other teachers—nuns and a few laypersons—who are coming only to learn liturgical chant. They represent a minority. Everyone sings mass every day at 12:00 noon. It will probably not be perfect—far from it—but these teachers will train all the new generation. It is thus important that they be on the right track.
>
> Mr. Marier will not be there to translate, but Sister Rose Vincent assures me that a very good translator will be at your disposal. Mr. Marier must give a course at Notre Dame University—which has been a center of opposition to Solesmes and which Mr. Marier is hoping to change through his teaching—then through yours, Father—into a Solesmes Center! You will thus divide your time between that University and the Pius X School in New York. I hope, Father, that this will not be too tiring for you. We will do everything possible to make your stay in the United States a pleasant one. You may be sure that you will be most welcome in my country where I hope to have the pleasure of seeing you. Mr. Marier (who handles everything) will surely manage to arrange a little stay at the Interlude! (Washington, Jan. 21, 1962)

Justine Ward expected much from this sojourn and especially from the sojourn at Webster College:

> I hope that your trip to Canada has been very good and that you are satisfied with the monastic students. As for Webster College, you will not find as much Gregorian experience there, but it is a center from which much seed is being sown. The whole community has been trained, beginning with the novitiate. In all the schools where these nuns are teaching, all the children sing and participate in the offices of the Church. Thus, it is a work which is fertilizing immense grounds. Music and chant have their

120

place in the daily instruction in all classes. This represents the future. It is for this reason that I want to link this great movement to Solesmes. Your teaching will bear fruit, even more than you may think when you are here (Washington, July 4, 1962).

She was not disappointed. This is indeed what Justine Ward wrote Dom Gajard as soon as he was back in France:

I want to thank you very warmly for everything you did for the students of Webster College who have been absolutely delighted with your teaching. I must also say that unfortunately, I will not at all be able to thank you *viva voce* since I cannot receive anyone at this time, as I explained to Mother Morgan. I hope that Father Abbot will allow you to come back to the United States in another year, and I hope that we will be able to see each other then (Washington, August 3, 1962).

It is certain that your trip to the United States did much good for the cause of Gregorian chant and the Solesmes principles. I am constantly receiving enthusiastic letters from your Saint Louis and New York students. You fulfilled perfectly the objective of your trip and the effects will be important and lasting, I am sure. Thank you once again (Washington, Sept. 29, 1962).[2]

America 1966 and 1971

Dom Gajard returned to America in 1966, for the Chicago Congress of Sacred Music, with a stop at Montreal. He had been preceded in 1965, by the Abbot who had returned to visit his houses. At the last minute, Justine Ward's health did not allow her to receive Dom Gajard, but she did not fail to encourage him strongly (Washington, August 22, 1966).

The Choirmaster of Solesmes' last journey was in 1971, from August 27th to around the 15th of November. He had to prolong his stay because of a heart condition which was to be the cause of his death in the following year. This time, in addition to a visit to Justine Ward and to Regina Laudis, Dom Gajard also went to Boston to see Mr. Marier.

As we see, we have very little information concerning these trips. But isn't the fact that they were fruitful the most important thing?

Justine Ward's Return Trips to Europe

Despite Justine Ward's strong and frequently expressed desire to return to Europe, she came back only twice and for two very brief trips. The first time was in 1967, when she went to Rome for the very important meeting of Church musicians (Washington, Sept. 28, 1967). She met Dom Jean Claire there but not Dom Gajard, who had been unable to attend. But she returned directly to America without going to France as the monks had wished. The second time was in April 1968. Since she had to come to Paris, she took advantage of the opportunity to see Sablé again, where she stayed during the last week-end of April (April 27–29). On Sunday, she came to high mass at Solesmes. The Abbot was absent, but she asked to see in parlor the monks with whom she had had direct contact, notably Dom Gajard and Dom Agaësse, as well as Dom Le Corre and Dom de Laborde, whom she had often consulted on matters of art, and Dom Combe who had accompanied her during the exodus of June 1940. She was given the gold medal she had received from Pius XI and entrusted to the Abbey in 1941. From her Sablé house, she took only Dom Mocquereau's portrait which she had commissioned in 1925, for herself and for Solesmes by a Dutch painter, Dom Henri Louwerse, monk of Oosterhout, Holland. (Mocquereau, June 12 and 21; July 1, 1925) At that time, Justine Ward was already crippled and her vision was very bad, although she had been operated on for cataracts. The handwriting in the last letters sent to Solesmes is increasingly difficult to read, lines overlap and margins are very chaotic. On certain occasions, however, Justine Ward wanted to write by herself, without assistance from her secretary—her companion, friend and confidante, Agnès Lebreton having died on February 3, 1967. When Dom Gajard had to resign as Choirmaster, she wrote him this very moving letter, whose last lines are illegible:

> Dear Father Gajard. I was extremely sad to hear from you that you will no longer be able to continue the work that you carried on for so long with such competence. It will remain your perpetual memorial: the records will be the principal memorial of all those who love Gregorian chant. Like you, Father, I have eyes which are no longer useful, therefore, please excuse, Father, this very short letter . . . Goodbye, dear Father . . . (Washington, May 21, 1971) (Appendix No. 58).

If this letter is not quite the last letter of Justine Ward to Dom Gajard, it is, however, the last one she wrote in her own handwriting, and it reveals accurately the nature of her relationship with the choirmaster of Solesmes, a relationship based only, it seems, on their common love of Gregorian chant.

Justine Ward pays a last visit to Rome, October 1967, and is greeted by His Holiness, Pope Paul VI.

Abbot Dom Prou, Justine Ward, Agnès Lebreton, and Secretary, at "Interlude," Washington, D.C., 1960.

Pius Tenth School at Purchase, N.Y., 1960. The Abbot's Secretary, Dom Gajard, Abbot Jean Prou, Mother Eleanor O'Byrne, Mother Josephine Morgan.

Dom Gajard, Theodore Marier and Mother Josephine Morgan, at Pius Tenth School, Purchase, N.Y.

Dom Joseph Gajard, O.S.B., 1885–1972, Choirmaster at Solesmes from 1914 to 1970.

Dom Gajard at the Cistercian Abbey of St. Joseph, Spencer, Massachusetts, 1959.

Justine Bayard Ward receiving a degree of Doctor of Music, *Honoris Causa*, from the Catholic University of America's President, Dr. Clarence Walton, May 15, 1971.

Mrs. Ward (center) and Joseph Lennards (right) with class of Dutch children trained
in the Ward Method, in Holland, 1928. *Back row:* Mlle. LeBreton, JBW secretary,
Marion Robinson, Mary Carroll, Margaret Hurley, C.A. Carroll, Julia Sampson. *Middle row:* Nettie De Nigris (Denegris), Margaret (Péguy) Sullivan. *Front row:* Father Henri
Vullinghs, Mrs. Ward, J. Lennards.

Dr. Joseph Lennards (Holland) and Mr. Jean Lallemand (Canada) with Dr. Justine
Ward, 1968. Photo taken in the library of her Washington home "Interlude".

126

Post conciliar redesign of the
sanctuary at Solesmes.

Photograph of a recent painting made of
Mrs. Justine Ward which now hangs at the
entrance to Ward Hall at the Catholic
University of America, Washington, D.C.

CONCLUSION

After this summary of the fifty year relationship between Justine Ward and Solesmes, we may draw a conclusion, if this word is not too pretentious, and try to sift out the essential lines.

Fidelity to the Teaching of Dom Mocquereau

In the first place, throughout this story, we saw how Justine Ward esteemed the Gregorian rhythmic doctrine of Dom Mocquereau. It is useless even to insist on this point which is so obvious, whether the matter concerns rhythmics per se or its effectiveness on a pedagogical level. On this subject, we may still quote what Justine Ward once wrote to Monsignor Igini Anglès, President of the Pontifical Institute of Sacred Music in Rome, at a time when Dom Mocquereau's rhythmic principles were being questioned after the war. This letter is dated October 29, 1950, and was probably written in Washington:

> Like you, I believe that the Solesmes principles are historically established; solidly too, as evidenced by the 15 volumes of the Musical Paleography; that the theory is not vague, imprecise like so many others, but is a live and lived theory, an acquired science, susceptible without doubt of certain enrichments on which the Solesmes Scriptorium is constantly working, in silence and in the hope of bringing them into the light some day.
>
> Against a theory so scientifically established, not only upon the theoreticians of the Middle Ages who so often contradict themselves, but upon the monuments of paleography, it is not sufficient to make vague and global affirmations, but one must also prove just as scientifically how it could be wrong. Like you, I feel that criticism must be constructive and never personal, never purely negative and destructive. It would really be too easy a task.
>
> As for those who want to return, purely and simply, to the Vatican Edition, without rhythmic signs, the pedagogical experience of my whole life, and that of many others, leads me to believe that as much for teaching children as for unity in people's chant and as for the artists themselves, it is necessary to have marks, reference marks—in this case, ictus and rhythmic signs—which affirm rhythms, locate the phrases and bring indispensable assistance in realizing rhythmic unity and correct interpretation. In an analogous domain, that of modern music, have editors and musicians ever regretted the time bars (provided they are given an exact meaning) which facilitate performance of the great polyphonic and orchestral works?

As soon as he had been appointed choirmaster in 1889, Dom Mocquereau had taken an active interest in the problem of Gregorian rhythm. His friends pushed him in this direction, since they knew from experience that the *Liber Gradualis* edition was insufficient on this point. He himself understood the importance of rhythm for choir directing. In the foreword of his *Paléographie Musicale*, he affirmed that "the manuscripts contain all we want to know about version, modality, rhythm, and the notation of ecclesiastical melodies. They are not an account of chant principles, but they substantially contain its theory and practice; they are not the old masters whose teachings we would like to hear, but they are the translation in writing of what these masters taught and executed, hence, to whoever knows how to read and understand this writing, they are the most perfect expression of liturgical cantilenas" (p. 23). Dom Mocquereau thus began working by studying the manuscripts whose composition laws he had already presented, to discover their secret on the question of rhythm. But it was choir practice also which revealed the elements of the Gregorian chant's own rhythm to him. He thus had the same experience as Dom Guéranger, but he drew all the conclusions. Finally, his very advanced musical training was very helpful to him; indeed, if the laws governing Gregorian chant are rather special, they could not, however, be in absolute contradiction with the laws of music in general. The result of his patient studies was presented in volume VII of the *Paléographie Musicale* (1901) and later in the *Nombre Musical Grégorien* (Vol. I, 1908 and Vol. II, 1927), for practical teaching purposes. This means that Dom Mocquereau devoted most of his long life to this question. We do not intend to make an analysis of Dom Mocquereau's rhythmic doctrine in these pages. But even though it is not accepted by everyone, well known musicians have recognized that it has thrown much light on music in general. For example, here is what Auguste Le Guennant wrote about this doctrine, underlining "one of the most daring aspects and at the same time one of the most fruitful hypotheses in Dom Mocquereau's thesis. Considering that live rhythm is a synthesis, composed of various elements, Dom Mocquereau wondered whether the complexity of the rhythmic problem was not coming precisely from our obstination to define rhythm in the concrete instead of defining it in the abstract. This led him to reduce the notion of essential rhythm to *pure movement*, in order to restore progressively to concrete rhythm, within the precise framework thus determined, the various qualities it has and which we perceive as one unit, without being able to separate them from one another, other than abstractly. There we find the fundamental basis of Dom Mocquereau's work. No one before him had studied the rhythmic question so thoroughly. Thus, the conclusions of the *Nombre Musical Grégorien* extend largely beyond their application to liturgical chant alone. All musicians can find in them subjects for fruitful studies, as well as draw from them renewed elements of general rhythmics." (*Le Correspondant*, 1930, p. 294)

"Not only has Gregorian chant been renewed," Justine Ward wrote, "but music in general has benefited from the light thrown in the domain of rhythm by this genial monk." Therefore, let us say, as Jean de Valois wrote in his obituary for Dom Mocquereau (cf. supra p. 67), that "Dom Mocquereau had the highest degree of artistic general culture, a concern for new and personal research, a sense of the harmony of character and beauty which, as Bourdelle says, must become the artist's second nature. Dom Mocquereau was a very great artist; and this artist was: music itself."

As for the practical results and the unquestionable benefits of Dom Mocquereau's method of chant, those who practice it properly, that is to say not materially, have experienced how its rhythm, free and precise at the same time, in which the importance of notes is not left to chance or imagination, "gives suppleness to melodies together with admirable firmness, high style, such an artistic touch and impact on the souls which is truly 'rhythming' " (Dom Gajard). Is it not there that one finds the success of the Solesmes chant? Experience also proved how this method was a factor of *unity*—Justine Ward underlined it—this unity which is indispensable to the chant and which was so essential for Dom Pothier that he did not hesitate to write: "This point is very important, for it would be a thousand times better to tolerate certain imperfections and even some real mistakes, than to break this necessary harmony, this unity in the movement which blends all the voices into one" (*Mélodies Grégoriennes selon la Tradition*, 1880, p. 266). Others have said, in this respect, that the diffusion of Gregorian chant was directly related to the development of Dom Mocquereau's method. It is first of all and primarily because of unity thus obtained, that Dom Jean Claire could write:

> If one took the time to mark on a map the countries which have adopted editions with Dom Mocquereau's rhythmic principles, one would see that one marked at the same time the countries which best preserved the practice of Gregorian chant (D.J. Claire, *L'Oeuvre rythmique de Dom Mocquereau,* in *Rev. Grég.* 1955, pp. 5–6).

But this method must be well understood. Recently, a well known musicologist, passing through Solesmes and enthused by the suppleness of the chant, said: "Your chant is admirable, but you are not following the method of Dom Mocquereau." Yes, we are! But his contradictors have not always understood it well, even if they have read certain affirmations, such as this one by Dom Mocquereau himself:

> Sometimes, the ear is made aware of the rhythmic subdivision by a sweet and discreet intensity marking the ictic note; at other times, the *legato* is more uniform, more intimate, the rhythmic subdivisions are hardly felt, as if they were veiled; still more frequently, in certain slow or fast passages, these secondary subdivisions disappear completely, blended in an uninterrupted *legato*, leaving only the feeling of the full and wide undulation of the musical phrase. The touch is then so sweet, so caressing, that it remains imponderable, more spiritual than material: interior feeling alone can notice it, if it wants to notice it, which is actually not necessary (*Nombre Musical*, I, 569).

A page from the *Revue Grégorienne* successfully explains the double characteristic of Dom Mocquereau's genius and shows how Justine Ward's teaching Method is its fruit. We do not hesitate to quote it here, despite its highly technical character:

> The real merit of Dom Mocquereau seems to us to have been double: he not only laid the foundation of neumatic semiology and found at the same time the traditional principles of *Gregorian special rhythmics*, but he also laid the foundations of *general rhythmics*, thus rendering to all music the invaluable service of bringing a little order and clarity to a question which had been hopelessly confused for centuries.
>
> The quite natural idea of applying the elementary laws of general rhythmics to Gregorian rhythm is also one of his merits. For, the data of *Gregorian positive rhythmics*—data which are indispensable and irreplaceable—are fully meaningful and reveal their full artistic value only if they are integrated into a synthesis which belongs to *natural rhythmics*. This explanatory, justificatory, interpretative context logically precedes it. It plays the role of a *general principle*, universally applied to any kind of sound movement, because it is founded on the philosophical analysis of movement per se and the study of the physiological qualities of sound. The various positive rhythmics come next, each in its own order, to determine, for each kind of music, the modalities of application of this general principle.
>
> The 'Solesmes Method' founded by Dom Mocquereau, intends to avoid two abuses, while not allowing itself to be reduced:
>
> either to *pure natural rhythmics* in the state of an abstract system separated from the positive sources of specifically Gregorian art,
>
> or to *pure positive rhythmics* whether they are strictly Gregorian, neumatic or verbal, incapable by themselves of providing a valid synthesis, or consequently, a complete musical education.
>
> And so, to come back to Dom Mocquereau, the fruit of his own teaching is perhaps indeed—among other things—the theory and practice of the so-called 'Gregorian measure' not accepted by everyone because it bothers those who do not understand it; but it is also the 'Ward Method', *a method of complete training in general music*, thanks to which thousands and thousands of children experience every day the prodigious fruitfulness of the natural rhythmic principles which he was the first to state so clearly.
>
> No one denies that there are many discoveries to be made, many points to be explicated, many details to be clarified with respect to these foundations and principles; the work now in progress at Solesmes proves it. But it would be better to leave it alone if the results were to confuse certain fundamental concepts, certain basic truths, which must—and easily can—be safeguarded (D.J. Claire—report on *Elementi di Canto Gregoriano* by Dom Luigi Agustoni, in *Rev. Gr.*, 1960, p. 39).

Needless to say, Justine Ward's faithful teaching was intimately linked with fidelity to Dom Mocquereau's teaching. All the foundations of her teaching rest on his rhythmic principles as the essential basis. We also noted that Justine Ward was fully conscious of knowing her master's exact doctrine, which occasionally she defended tenaciously and with a sometimes suspicious attention.

Sense of Liturgical Prayer

Together with Justine Ward's esteem for Dom Mocquereau's rhythmic principles, what is most striking in her is, without a doubt, her acute sense of liturgical prayer. She fully understood the spirituality of Gregorian chant, its value as prayer; she used her talent as an educator, and spared no effort to make children appreciate this, in the hope of reaching all Christians through them. We saw that this was, from the very beginning, her only objective and that she remained faithful to it. For her, liturgy was the most effective means of sanctification. In this respect, she was in the purest tradition of the Church and in the authentic line of Dom Guéranger, first Abbot of Solesmes, who described in his *Année Liturgique* the authentic spirit of Catholic Liturgy. Justine Ward nourished her faith and her piety with Dom Guéranger's great book and Dom Mocquereau often advised her to read it, particularly at the high points of the liturgical cycle (Volumes, *Holy Week, Pentecost*).

In the *General Introduction* of his work, Dom Guéranger explains how the official prayer of the church is the most agreeable to God and the most powerful, since it is inspired by the Holy Spirit who resides in the Church and whom Christ has sent to His Spouse in order that He might teach us to pray as we should. Liturgy is thus Christ's prayer continued in the Church, which renews His mysteries each year and renders them present for us. Christ is therefore the object of liturgy. He is also its means, for, by the manifestation of His mysteries in the Church and in the souls of the faithful, He transforms us increasingly, day after day, through the sanctifying action of the Holy Spirit, into an image of Himself. The liturgy, as it sings in unison with the angels, also draws us all closer together in the bonds of charity, so that "in one spirit and in one voice we might honor the God and Father of Our Lord Jesus Christ." In addition, poetry has its particular role to play during the unfolding of this great drama. First of all, it inspires the Liturgy with its most beautiful Old and New Testament Canticles. Secondly, it provides the melodies most worthy of such texts.[3]

Justine Ward appreciated this spirituality from the very moment of her conversion to Catholicism, but she found its best expression in the choir of the monks of Solesmes, and this is the deepest—if not the only—reason for her attachment to the Abbey. Love of Gregorian Chant is, in fact, identical to love of Liturgy. Chant is the Liturgy's complement, in Dom Guéranger's words (cf. *Institutions Liturgiques*, IV, 1885, p. 304), the language best suited to its proper end: the praising of God. Those who have become familiar with both the chant and the liturgy experience how the two co-operate in helping the soul to enter into a better comprehension of divine mysteries and to progress towards perfect adoration and perfect love. It is not surprising that these persons then often wish to associate themselves as closely as possible with the monastic life in order to participate in the praise of God which the monks constantly send up from the earth toward Heaven, in the name of the Church and of the whole human race. In the Benedictine Order, the Church offers Oblature to laypersons attracted by this ideal. Justine Ward had become an Oblate as early as 1921.

Dom Mocquereau quoted this maxim by Joseph de Maistre

Reason can merely speak; but love sings (*L'Art Grégorien*, 1896, p. 121).

He summarized in a word which must be correctly understood, all that he expected from Gregorian chant; it is "savour" (sweetness) or, to put it better, *unction* . . . As the product of a consummate art, it crowns the liturgical melody with an aureole which it does not share with any other musical forms and which makes it the music which the Church prefers. It is in this respect indeed that it is the truest expression of prayer, the most faithful translation of the indescribable murmurs of the Spirit which, according to the words of Saint Paul, "prays in us and for us." (*L'Art Grégorien*, p. 34). Thus, when it is said that a chant is "praying" it is not something subjective, artificially produced, but something which has a real quality, resulting naturally from its artistic and religious character (and beautiful rhythm contributes to this as we saw). "In these splendid regions," said Auguste Le Guennant writing about Dom Mocquereau, "fusion takes place between prayer and music, to form indissolubly one unique reality" (*Le Correspondant*, 1947, p. 284).

Justine Ward shared these views, and she once wrote:

I do not want to talk about Sacred Music or Liturgical Music any more. It seems to me that we should rather talk about *sung prayer* (Mora Vocis, Jan. 23, 1929).

Justine Ward appreciated this savour; she was so deeply attached to "her" Abbey that being far away was distressing for her, particularly at Christmas and during Holy Week. She found what she needed there to satisfy her artistic sense and especially her very acute sense of sung prayer. We often found vibrant testimonies of this in the letters she sent Dom Mocquereau, for example when she wrote about being "wrenched" away from Solesmes (June 13, 1923), about being "out of place" away from Solesmes (March 10, 1924), about her "yearning" for Solesmes (March 12, 1929), about "being uprooted" (October 1, 1929). The words she used with Dom Gajard to express her gratefulness for the spiritual benefits she gained from liturgy and chant were not different. It is for this reason that she so often expressed the hope to be able to return to Solesmes as soon as circumstances would allow it (May 17, 1946). It is fitting to mention a few additional examples (although there are many more):

"From now on, I shall seek refuge in the silence of low masses until we are able to find Solesmes again. You cannot imagine how much we desire it" (Jan. 10, 1947). "Excuse this hasty little letter which is bringing our best to you and to everyone at Solesmes, while we are eagerly waiting to be able to return to the dear monastery" (Feb. 3, 1947). "We still hope to spend Holy Week at Solesmes. Let us hope it will be possible. In any event, we will be at Solesmes in spirit" (Jan. 8, 1949). "Remember that we are hungry for Solesmes" (Jan. 28, 1950). "How I would love to be hearing these splendid offices for Holy Week at Solesmes! Fortunately, all this is still present in my memory and in my heart, thanks to many privileged years" (March 14,

1950). "Our best wishes, Father, for a happy Easter, after the Great Holy Week which we would have liked so much to spend in Solesmes. This will happen some day, I hope" (April 8, 1952).

We remember that she had once regretted having to return to America:

If I had known that in 1941, I think I would not have left. (Dec. 30, 1952, supra p. 93).

Justine Ward deeply appreciated the records made at the Abbey under the direction of Dom Gajard, both because of their "style," which helped to confer upon them that "prayerful" character which she rightly considered to be so essential, and because of Solesmian rhythmics. These two elements are actually indissolubly linked as Dom Gajard often demonstrated, for example, in the *Méthode de Solesmes*.

Justine Ward would certainly have given her approval to these lines written by a great choirmaster in an article discussing the "quality" of religious music:

If chant is not there to make me pray,
let the cantors be silent.

If chant is not there to appease my inner anxiety,
let the cantors leave.

If chant is not as valuable as the silence it breaks,
let me go back to silence.[4]

All this reveals the quality of Justine Ward's soul. And one understands how she always supported Solesmes' cause, sometimes by sacrificing her personal point of view: for instance, when she wrote, in this respect, that she had acted "*exclusively* for the good of SOLESMES" (word underscored by Justine Ward).

It seems unnecessary to say now that Justine Ward recognized Dom Gajard as the faithful disciple and successor of Dom Mocquereau. However, here is some additional testimony. In 1952, Dom Gajard had made a Gregorian tour in Austria where he had been invited by the highest music authorities in Vienna, and had been in contact with the various Gregorian centers in the country (seven monasteries, four seminaries). When the Abbey records were played, everyone was enthusiastic. When Dom Gajard returned, Justine Ward congratulated him:

I am so happy to hear that you had a good trip and that it was such a success. Direct contact with true Solesmian interpretation always wins over musicians and people with taste. It is the mediocre interpretations of the Solesmes theories which are disconcerting. Surely, your new records will fully enhance this interpretation which, once heard, imposes itself (Stockbridge, July 20, 1952).[5]

Justine Ward was even more explicit with an American relative who transmitted this truly laudatory appreciation she had made of Dom Gajard's records:

I feel just as you do about the almost miraculous quality of the sung offices at Solesmes. Dom Gajard has refined that choir to a point where (even technically) nothing else can touch it. Spiritually, it is absolutely unique. Dom Gajard knows how I feel about it. I have told him so very often—and the records will remain as a monument to his fidelity and competence (June 16, 1961).

She had already written Dom Gajard that the choir of Solesmes had never sung so well (cf. supra p. 108). It was the same, of course, with respect to the Solesmes Choirmaster's theoretical teaching. We already know how satisfied Justine Ward had been with Dom Gajard's brochures: his review of the *Nombre Musical Grégorien*; his *Monographies Grégoriennes*, particularly the monograph on rhythmic editions (August 8, 1935) (Cf. Appendix No. 45); his article dedicated to Dom Mocquereau for the 25th anniversary of his death, in which he had made a new synthesis of Dom Mocquereau's doctrine (*Revue Grég.*, March 4, 1955); his *Méthode de Solesmes* and his *Notions de Rythmiques Grégoriennes*, two brochures reissued in 1971 (October 19, 1971. Cf. Appendix No. 45).

And so, when Dom Gajard had to resign as choirmaster because of his great age, Justine Ward thoughtfully reminded him that his work would continue through his records, which were lasting monuments (Washington, May 23, 1971, cf. supra p. 121 and Appendix No. 58).

Justine Ward's last years were a source of great sorrow to her. The lack of appreciation for the traditional sung prayer of the Church, notably for Gregorian chant, caused her much grief. She mentioned it to Dom Gajard on several occasions, notably at the beginning of the crisis of the last decades. We quote:

"They want to lower the prayer of the Church to mud level in order to attract the most ignorant people. My opinion is completely different: I know that souls can be raised to the level of the Liturgy, by elevating the souls. Children have no preconceived ideas: if they are taught to pray in beauty, they are delighted. It is just as easy as feeding them on ugliness or poison" (Washington, Sept. 27, 1963). "We ask for ourselves your prayers while remaining always united with the beautiful prayer of Solesmes which will always last, despite the 'progressives' in all countries" (Washington, Oct. 22, 1963). "Your last records—Christmas Vigil, Matin, and Saint Stephen—are pure masterpieces. How noble these melodies are, and how well sung! How can one set Gregorian chant aside when such treasures exist! It seems to me that the choir of Solesmes has never been more nuanced, more eloquent. We are grateful to you for staying on the right path in order to prove the sublime artistic and religious quality of this music." "Give us more liturgical treasures. It is the only chant we have here . . . Only Solesmes has mercy for people who have taste" (Washington, Jan. 20, 1967).

While waiting for these difficult times to pass, she offered her suffering to hasten the return to the old melodies which had been discarded too quickly. For, as she once said, "he who had created beauty could be adored only through the full beauty of truth, only through the *Opus Dei*, the *Work of God*." (*Solesmes and a Centenary*. Cf. Appendix No. 64.)

> Thank you very much for your letter which assures us that we are in your faithful thoughts and prayers as we are ascending the *Via Crucis* as well as we can. Everything is being offered. I think the Church needs victims in these very sad times (Washington, Dec. 21, 1965). (Appendix No. 57).

The Ward Movement and its development in America and in Europe has been examined in detail in a recent book. It indicates the wide attention given to the Ward Method. The Method was officially adopted in Holland in the public schools and even in the Protestant ones. In Italy, it was considered for official adoption by the state schools. We know that Justine Ward had two audiences with the Duce in 1935, and that she had already been decorated in the preceding year by the Duchess of Aoste in the name of the King (June 19, 1933). Until the last few years, her Method was very successful in France, too. (Cf. Appendix No. 74.)

Justine Ward was a very active architect of the Gregorian restoration desired by Pius X and faithfully observed her initial program: to respond to the call of this great Pope: "A response to the call of Pius X." Pius X indeed affirmed in his *Motu Proprio* of November 22, 1903, on Sacred Music: "Public worship is the first and indispensable source of a genuine Christian spirit, and the faithful will have this spirit only in the measure in which they actively participate in the sacrosanct mysteries and in the solemn and public prayer of the Church." Justine Ward accomplished a universally recognized pedagogical task and was an ardent and tireless propagator of the authentic prayer of the Church. She put her whole artistic soul, her tireless zeal and her generosity into it. Her name will forever be associated with the great cause of the traditional sung prayer of the Church and also with the work of Dom Mocquereau, whose faithful and devoted disciple she was. For her Golden Jubilee, on January 27, 1954, a mass was celebrated at the Apostolic Delegation in Washington and the Delegate, Monsignor A.G. Cicognani, read a letter bringing to the Jubilarian the Holy Father's Blessing and his congratulations for so much devotion to the service of the Church:

> . . . conspicuous works of charity and religion performed during these fifty years, in addition to the significant stimulus you have given to Sacred Music in accordance with the wishes of Blessed Pius X, thus contributing to Divine Worship in the House of God. The remembrance of these achievements should fill you with joy, for many have benefited from them in the charity of Christ (Appendix No 56, cf. Agnes Lebreton, Washington, Jan. 30, 1954). (See also Appendix Nos. 47, 54[2], and 72.)

Appropriately, a Mass for the repose of the soul of Justine Ward (deceased November 27, 1975) was sung at the Abbey of Solesmes in January, 1976, since the Missal rubrics would not permit it during Advent. An obituary notice is read on each anniversary in the refectory in appreciation of her support of the cause of Gregorian Chant and, on that day, her name is read aloud in the Prayers of the Faithful.

NOTES AND SOURCES

Chapter 1

1. J.B. Ward, *Father J.B. Young, S.J.* (*Catholic Choirmaster*, 1924, pp. 120–124) Cf. Appendix No. 59.

2. J.B. Ward, *William Pardow of the Company of Jesus,* Longmans Green, New York, 1914; new impression 1921.

3. J. Kelly, *La Réforme grégorienne aux Etats Unis* (*Rev. Gr.*, 1920, p. 69); L.P. Manzetti, *Echoes of the Gregorian Congress* (*Cath. Choir*, 1920, p. 114). (Cf. *Rev. Gr.*, 1921, p. 159 and Appendix No. 13).

4. J.B. Ward, *Thomas Edward Shields, biologist, psychologist, educator.* Charles Scribner's Sons, New York, 1947. (Cf. Alain Lapy dom Agaësse. Un Grand Educateur: *Revue Gr.*, 1947, p. 196.)

5. *A response to the call of Pius X*, Blanche M. Kelly. New York City (1922). Justine Ward indicates the year 1916 in her brochure *The Dom Mocquereau Schola Cantorum Foundation Inc. and the Catholic University of America at Washington, DC.* (Catholic University of America), p. 1, Cf. Appendix No. 32.

6. Une conférence de Madame Ward à l'Institut Grégorien (de Paris), in *Rev. Gr.*, 1924, p. 160 (Cf. *Rev. Gr.*, 1925, p. 76). Cf. Appendix No. 37.

7. It would have been necessary only to change the address of the telegrammed invitation! (Oral memory frequently confirmed.)

8. Cf. No. 5 supra.

9. The Ward Journal indicates that D. Mocquereau arrived on May 16, that he stayed in Albany (Religious of the Sacred Heart) on June 13 and 14, and returned to France on June 22.

10. D. Mocquereau's lecture was published in French: La pensée pontificale et la restauration Grégorienne, in *Rev. Greg.*, 1920, p. 181 and 1922, pp. 9, 46. English text in Appendix No. 7.

11. D. Mocquereau commented on a formula from the Congress Vota which alluded to the precariousness of the Vatican Edition of Gregorian chant. He insisted that it should be clearly mentioned that it is *compulsory*. (Mocquereau to Ward, Sept 7, 1920, Ward to Mocquereau, St. Francis Camp, August 19, September 9 and 15, 1920, Westbrook, Oct. 21, 1920.) Cf. Appendix Nos. 3 and 4.

12. Ward, *Solesmes and a Centenary*, in the *Benedictine Review* (1950, p. 21), and the *Catholic Choirmaster* (1950, p. 108, Cf. Appendix No. 64) and in French in *Le Lutrin* (Geneva, 1950, p. 13) under the title: *Solesmes and Dom Mocquereau.*

13. Justine Ward later resided in Wentnor (Ward Journal, June 19, 1921), then in Fishborn House (Journal, Nov. 14, 1921).

14. Benedictines of Stanbrook, *In a great Tradition, tribute to Dame Laurentia McLachlan*, 1956. In French: J. de la Forêt-Divonne: *Au pied de la grille. Bernard Shaw et l'Abbesse Laurentia*, Spes, 1961. Cf. Benoît du Moustier: *L'Abbesse Laurentia McLachlan, une 'Mocquereau Anglaise'* in *Le Lutrin*, 1957, p. 34.

15. Stanbrook, 1905, 1926. The first edition was translated into French (Desclée 1906), German and Italian.

16. T.R.P. Dom Augustin Gatard, in *Rev. Gr.*, 1920, p. 204.

17. *Rev. Gr.*, 1922, p. 69.

18. Conférence prononcée a l'Institut Grégorien de Paris le 14 Mars, 1896 (Solesmes, Imprimerie, 1986). English text in the Appendix: *The Art of Gregorian Music, its aims, methods and characteristics*, in *The Catholic Education Press*, 1922. Appendix No. 8.

19. *Music Fourth Year. Children's Manual. Gregorian Chant according to the principles of Dom André Mocquereau*, The Catholic Education Press, Washington, 1923.

20. *L'enseignement du chant grégorien aux enfants par la Méthode Ward* in *Lutrin*, p. 66. Report given by J. Ward to the Congress of Mexico. Cf. infra, Chapter V.

21. App. *Catholic Choirmaster*, 1920, p. 109.

22. Gabriel M. Steinschulte, *Die Ward-Bewegung*, p. 562.

23. Cf. supra and Appendix No. 8.

24. Monographies Grégoriennes IV, Desclée, 1923. English translation: *The Rhythmic Tradition in the Manuscripts*, Desclée, 1952.

25. On July 5, 21 (New York) and July 30 (Westbrook), August 6 (Westbrook), 7, 11, and 29 (New York), Sept. 1 (Westbrook), 7 and 12, 1922 (Washington).

26. No letter from J. Ward written in 1922 was kept by Dom Mocquereau.

27. *Documentation Catholique*, 1922, col. 1456 and foll. Cf. 1921, col. 360–362, 1923, col. 712, 1181.

28. On this subject: Lacombe House, Mocquereau, Feb. 18, March 4 and 22, 1922; Coudreuse Oct. 1, Nov. 20 and Dec. 29, 1922; Asnières, Oct. 1, and Dec. 29, 1922; Sablé Dec. 29, 1922 (railroad station), Feb. 12 and 17, 1923. Ward Journal, Dec. 29, 1922, Feb. 16 and March 17, 1923. In 1924, J. Ward's letterhead indicated "3 quai National" (today rue Léon Legludic).

Chapter II

1. Appendix No. 35, copy of a letter of Monsignor P. Hayes, Archbishop of New York, recommending Justine Ward to the Rector.

2. *The Blessing of the Pius X-Hall,* in *Cath. Choir.*, Dec. 1924, p. 141; *Rev. Gr.*, 1925, p. 76. Cf. Blessing of the Piux X Hall (program). Appendix Nos. 18 and 19.

3. Miss Aileen Tone was the translator of the 1st volume (perhaps even the 2nd volume, not printed).

4. Journal
   22 Feb. 1927: Differences with Dom M. "new . . . contradicts old"
   24 Feb. 1927: Stormy interview with Dom M. + Dom Gajard
   27 Feb. 1927: Idem
   28 Feb. 1927: 3rd interview, Dom M. + G.
   1 March 1927: Dom Mocq. decides to omit page

5. "Un perfectionnement de détail dans la chironomie grégorienne."

6. G. Steinschulte, *Die Ward—Bewegung,* G. Boose, Regensburg, 1979, p. 298.

7. England (*Rev. Gr.*, 1927, p. 39); Dublin and New Zealand (Ward, Mora Vocis, Jan. 31 and April 16, 1929); China (Ward, Mora Vocis, Dec. 26, 1928); Serravalle (Ward, Mora Vocis, Jan. 16 and April 16, 1929).

8. *Le Nombre Musical Grégorien II*, by Dom André Mocquereau, in *Cath. Choir.*, July–Sept. 1928, p. 95. Article first published in *The Commonweal*. Cf. Appendix No. 60.

Chapter III

1. See in *The Catholic Choirmaster*, April–June 1929 (No. 2): *The Mocqureau Schola Cantorum Foundation, Inc.* (pp. 52, 54); *The Rev. Wm. J. DesLongchamps appointed Dean of Liturgical Music School in Washington* (pp. 54–55); *The New Schola Cantorum* (pp. 55–56); A School of Liturgy (p. 56). Cf. Appendices Nos. 24, 25, 26, and 27.

2. G. Steinschulte, p. 181.

3. M. Bragers, from this Institute, had already spent several weeks at Solesmes, as other persons also did (*Rev. Gr.,* 1929, p. 255).

4. Ward, Mora Vocis, April 29; S. Francis, June 2, 1929. Cf. *Rev. Gr.,* 1929, p. 255; article by Dom Mocquereau, with photograph.

5. *The Dom Mocquereau Schola Cantorum Foundation, Inc.* in *Cath. Choir.,* April–June 1929, p. 52 (cf. Appendix No. 24). (Cf. Ward letters, Mora Vocis, May 7; St. Francis, June 10, 1929 about an article by Nicolas Montani.) (Also, letter from Rev. W.J. Longchamps to Dom Cozien, Abbot of Solesmes, June 28, 1929, in Appendix No. 23.)

6. *Fondation d'une Schola Cantorum et d'une Ecole de Musique sacrée à l'Université Catholique de Washington, F.U.,* by D.J. Gajard, in *Rev. Gr.,* 1929, p. 161.

7. *The Dom Mocquereau Schola Cantorum Foundation, Inc., and the Catholic University of America at Washington, D.C.* (Privately printed for the Trustees of the Catholic University of America) (Appendix No. 32).

8. Journal 13/1. Beginning of Dom M. last illness—15/1 Cable announcing Dom M. grave illness—17/1 Cable from Dom M. saying himself "Dr. notes improvement."—18/1 Cable Dom M. died this morning—20/1 Dom M. buried at Solesmes.—3/2 Article Mocquereau "Orate Fratres."

9. *"The Last Days of Dom Mocquereau. From various letters received from Solesmes"* in *Catholic Choirmaster,* Vol. XVL, March 10, 1930. No. 1, p. 3. This article is followed by the translation of another article by Marcel Cochét, published in the newspaper *La Croix* on Jan. 30, 1930. (Cf. Appendix No. 61).

10. Obituaries for Dom Mocquereau by Jean de Valois, in *La Petite Maîtrise,* Paris, March 1930, p. 13, and by Dom Gabriel Tissot in *Revue Liturgique et Monastique,* Maredsous, 1930, p. 239.

Chapter IV

1. Dom Antony Bonnet, Notice sur le Grand Orgue de l'Abbaye de Solesmes, *Lutrin,* 1946, p. 49. (Cf. Appendix No. 51).

2. Cf. the brochure edited on this occasion: *Il Grande Organo del Pontificio Istituto di Musica Sacra, Roma, 1933—Un orgue monumenta offert au Souverain Pontife* in *La Croix,* April 20, 1933.

3. H. Potiron, *Le Nouvel Antiphonaire Monastique* (*Rev. Gr.,* July–August 1934, pp. 121–129).

4. D. Pierre Combe, *Histoire de la restauration du chant grégorien d'apres des documents inédits: Solesmes et l'Édition Vaticane,* Abbaye de Solesmes, 1969.

5. *Du rôle et de la place de l'accent tonique latin dans le rythme grégorien* (Paléographie Musicale, Vol. VII, 1901, p. 128).

6. *Examen des critiques dirigées par D. Jeannin contre l'Ecole de Solesmes* (Monographies Grégoriennes VII, Desclée, 1926, p. 102; *Rev. Gr.,* 1925–1926).

7.[1] Cf. J. Ward *Faut-il accompagner le chant grégorien?* In Le Lutrin, 1953, p. 36 Extract from French translation by D. Agaesse. *Chant Grégorien,* vol. II.

7.[2] See Dr. Roland Boisvert *Replies to the Open Letter From Solesmes,* in *Cath. Choir.,* 1938, p. 139. (Cf. Appendix No. 48.)

8. J.B. Ward, *The Death of the Right Rev. Abbot Dom Ferretti, O.S.B.* in *Cath. Choir.,* 1938, p. 111. Cf. Appendix No. 62.

Chapter V

1. The Abbey's collection ends with No. 3 of the IVth Volume (1946) and we do not know what this article by D. Gajard is about.

2. *Mater Ecclesia,* V, No. 1. Article reproduced in *Gregorian Chant* II, p. 24.

3. It was planned at first, that D. Gajard would come to Washington before the Congress, for All Saints Day (Stockbridge, Sept. 24, 1949).

4. *Anuario de la Comision Central de Musica Sacra de Mexico* (French version, p. 31, and Spanish translation, p. 191). Shortened French version published in *Le Lutrin,* 1949, p. 66.

5. Published as *La Méthode de Solesmes* by Desclée et Cie, 1951; as *The Solesmes Method* by the Liturgical Press, 1960, Collegeville, Minn.

Chapter VI and Conclusion

1. The recordings were made by the Schola, reinforced with other good voices.

2. A few years before, in 1955, four students of Justine Ward, Sister Rose Vincent and three of her friends, all of them nuns of Loretto, had already come for a sojourn at the Abbey under Dom Gajard's direction.

3. *Année Liturgique,* Vol. I, *General Foreword.* This "summa includes 15 volumes. Publication began in 1841 and there were many editors (for example, 20 for the volume on Passion) and several translations, including an English one made by Dom Laurent Shepherd, of the English Benedictine Congregation.

4. Joseph Samson, *Propositions sur la Qualité* (Acts of the Third International Congress of Sacred Music, Paris 1957).

5. F. Kosch, *Le voyage de dom Gajard en Autriche* in *Rev. Gr.,* 1952, p. 43 (article published in *Musica Orans* of June 1952, p. 3).

APPENDIX I - REFERENCE SUMMARY

Appendix Number	Page Reference	Appendix Number	Page Reference
1	3	43	63
2	4	44	65
3	25	45	134
4	137	46	90
5	8	47	135
6	4	48	79
7	137	49	84/139
8	15/138	50	90
9,10,11,12	5	51	139
13	137	52	94
14	16/17/18	53	98
15	6 (Par. 4)	54[1]	112
16	16	54[2]	135
17[1]	17	55	99
17[2]	18	56	135
18,19	138	57	135
20	32	58	121
21,22	50	59	137
23	139	60	138
24,25,26,27	138	61,62	139
28	63	63	92
29	62	64	7/10/12/89/99/137
30,31	63	65	44
32	137/139	66	37/66/89/90
33,34	84	67,68,69	66
35	138	70	32
36	28	71	61/405
37	31/137	72	135
38	34	73	406
39,40	36	74	135
41	44		
42	40		

APPENDIX II - CONTENTS*

INTERNATIONAL GREGORIAN CHANT CONGRESS, NEW YORK, 1920

PROJECT FOR FOUNDING A MONASTERY FROM SOLESMES IN THE UNITED STATES

*Numbers 4, 14, 15, 31, 36, 37, 39, 45, 51, 53, 55, 73, 74, translated by Theodore Marier.

THE PIUS TENTH SCHOOL OF NEW YORK

18. "The Pius X Hall of Liturgical Music", *The Catholic Choirmaster,* December, 1924, p. 141.

19. "Blessing of the Pius X Hall by His Eminence, Patrick Cardinal Hayes." Order of Ceremony, November 6, 1924.

20. "Officium Pastorum", a Nativity Play of the XIII Century, sent to Justine Ward by Dom Mocquereau. Christmas, 1928.

21. Program of concert given by singers from the Pius X School of music at The National Shrine of the Immaculate Conception, Washington, D.C., November 20, 1928. (Handwritten notes by Justine B. Ward)

22. Program given at Divinity College, The Catholic University of America, by singers from the Pius X School of Liturgical Music under the direction of Justine Ward. Program annotations by Mrs. Ward.

SCHOOL OF LITURGICAL MUSIC IN WASHINGTON

23. Letter from Rev. W. J. DesLongchamps to Dom Cozien, Abbot of Solesmes, June 28, 1929.

24. "The Dom Mocquereau Schola Cantorum Foundation, Inc.", *The Catholic Choirmaster,* April–June, 1929, p. 52.

25. "The Rev. Wm. J. DesLongchamps Appointed Dean of Liturgical Music School in Washington", *The Catholic Choirmaster,* April–June, 1929, p. 52.

26. "The New Schola Cantorum", *The Catholic Choirmaster,* April–June, 1929, p. 55.

27. "A School of Liturgy", *The Catholic Choirmaster,* April–June, p. 56.

28. "The School of Liturgical Music", design sent to Dom Mocquereau by Justine Ward.

29. Letter sent to all Ordinaries from Monsignor James H. Ryan, Rector of The Catholic University of America, September 3, 1929.

30. Justine Ward to Msgr. James H. Ryan, Rector, January 5, 1930, memorandum of the Dom Mocquereau Schola Cantorum Foundation. (Copy)

31. Justine Ward to Dom Cozien, Abbot of Solesmes, February 15, 1930. (Translation)

32. "The Dom Mocquereau Schola Cantorum Foundation, Inc., and The Catholic University of America at Washington, D.C." Privately printed for the Trustees of The Catholic University of America. Memorandum of Justine Ward.

33. "Dom Mocquereau and the Founder of the Pius X School", Brother A.S.S., *The Catholic Choirmaster,* March, 1936, p. 55.

34. "Questions and Answers" to the editor from Justine B. Ward, *The Catholic Choirmaster,* June, 1936, p. 55. Response to the preceding.

VARIOUS ITEMS

35. Archbishop Patrick Hayes to Monsignor Charles A. O'Hern, Rector of the North American College in Rome, December 6, 1923. Copy sent to Dom Mocquereau.

36. Errata in the English terminology of the *Nombre Musical Grégorien.* Memorandum from Justine Ward to Reverend Mother Laurentia McLachlan, February, 1924. (Translation)

37. "A Lecture by Mrs. Ward at the Gregorian Institute of Paris," *Revue Grégorienne,* 1924, p. 160. (Translation)

1927

38. Justine Ward to Dom Mocquereau, Sablé, March 5, 1927.

39. "The Undulating Thesis and the Undulating Arsis", memorandum from Justine Ward to Dom Mocquereau, April 9, 1927. (Translation)

40. Declaration, Dom Mocquereau to Justine Ward, Solesmes, March 12, 1927.

1928

41. Justine Ward to Dom Gajard, Mora Vocis, March 7, 1928, commenting on his review of *Le Nombre Musicale.*

42. Dom Mocquereau to Justine Ward, Solesmes, August 22, 1928, well-known letter concerning the visit of Pius X students to Solesmes.

1930

43. Justine Ward to Dom Gajard, Mora Vocis, January 22, 1930, on the death of Dom Mocquereau.

44. Justine Ward and Mother Georgia Stevens, Pius X School, February 20, 1930, with members of the staff and the Schola Cantorum on the death of Dom Mocquereau, to Abbot Cozien.

1935

45. Justine Ward to Dom Gajard, Sablé, August 8, 1935, concerning his brochure "Editions Rythmiques". (Translation)

46. Ward Method demonstration, Paris, April 8, 1935, announcement.

47. "New Papal Honors Conferred on Justine B. Ward", *The Catholic Choirmaster,* June, 1936, p. 112.

1938

48. "The Accompaniment of Gregorian Chant", Roland Boisvert, Mus. Doc., *The Catholic Choirmaster,* March, 1938, p. 3, with annotations by Justine Ward.

49. "An Important Communication from Solesmes". Dom Gajard defines the position of Solesmes, *The Catholic Choirmaster,* June, 1938, p. 51. Reply to the preceding.

1941

50. Justine Ward to Dom Gajard, Sablé, May 6, 1941, announcing her departure for America.

1946

51. "Notice Regarding the Great Organ of the Solesmes Abbey", by Dom Antony Bonnet, *Le Lutrin,* 1946, p. 49. (Translation)

52. Program of a Solemn Service of the Vespers at The Catholic University of America, May 15, 1946, for Dom Gajard.

1948

53. Justine Ward to Dom Gajard, Stockbridge, Massachusetts, July 23, 1948. Detailed program to Dom Gajard in view of his stay in America. (Translation)

54[1]. "Solesmes and the Gregorian Chant", prospectus in English prepared by Justine Ward for the recordings.

54[2]. Liturgical Music Award — 1948, *The Catholic Choirmaster,* June, 1948, p. 59.

1949

55. "Centennial Celebration at Solesmes of Dom Mocquereau's Birth and Baptism", *Revue Grégorienne,* Dom Pierre Combe, 1949, p. 167. (Translation)

1954

56. Archbishop A.G. Cicognani, Apostolic Delegate, to Mrs. Ward, Washington, January 27, 1954. Apostolic Blessing and Felicitations. (Copy)

1965

57. Justine Ward to Dom Gajard, Washington, December 21, 1965.

1971

58. Justine Ward to Dom Gajard, Washington, May 23, 1974, regarding resignation of Dom Gajard as choirmaster.

VARIOUS ARTICLES BY JUSTINE WARD

The Catholic Choirmaster

59. "Father J.B. Young, S.J.", December, 1924, p. 120.

60. "Le Nombre Musical Grégorien II", by Dom André Mocquereau. A review by Justine Ward. July–August, 1928, p. 95.

61. "The Last Days of Dom Mocquereau", from various letters received from Solesmes, March 1930, p. 3.

62. "Death of The Right Reverend Abbot Dom Ferretti, O.S.B.", President of the Pontifical Institute of Sacred Music, September, 1938, p. 111.

63. "Solesmes and the War", Justine B. Ward, December, 1941, p. 155.

64. "Solesmes and a Centenary", Justine Ward, September, 1950, p. 108.

The Ecclesiastical Review

65. "Studies and Conferences — Twenty Five Years — Authority and Obedience", Justine B. Ward, May, 1928, p. 503.

Orate Fratres

66. "Dom André Mocquereau of Solesmes", March, 1930, p. 199.

VARIOUS DOCUMENTS

67. "Liturgical Scholar Led in Restoration of the Gregorian Chant", anonymous. *The Catholic Choirmaster,* May, 1930, p. 8 and p. 35.

68. "Solesmes: Abbey of", L. Robert, *The New Catholic Encyclopedia.* (1963 ?), p. 418.
    Music of", P. Combe, *The New Catholic Encyclopedia,* (1963 ?), p. 418.
    Biographical sketches of Dom Gueranger and Dom Gajard.

69. "Mocquereau, André", Pierre Combe, *The New Catholic Encyclopedia*, p. 988.

70. "Pius X School of Liturgical Music, College of the Sacred Heart — Its Growth and Development", Mary Manly, B.A., from the *Signet.*

71. "The People's Plainsong" from *The London Times,* February 9, 1929.

72. Two Citations
    A   Plain Chant Award Made at Capital, *The Catholic Choirmaster*, 1929, p. 95.
    B   Justine Bayard Ward, Doctor of Humane Letters at Annhurst College, Connecticut.

73. Justine Ward to the Ward Method Teachers, Washington. (No date) (Translation)

74. Historical Account of the Ward Method, 1916 to 1986.

ARCHBISHOP'S HOUSE,
452 MADISON AVE.,
NEW YORK.

arrivé le 25 Mars

February 18, 1920.

Rev. Dom Mocquereau, O.S.B.,
        Quarr Abbey,
            Ryde,
                Isle of Wight, England.

Reverend dear Dom Mocquereau:—

            It affords me as Archbishop of New
York great pleasure to extend to you a most cordial
invitation to come to America for the purpose of
directing the INTERNATIONAL CONGRESS OF GREGORIAN
CHANT to be held in St. Patrick's Cathedral, New
York City, June 1st, 2nd and 3rd, 1920, under the
auspices of the Pontifical Institute of Sacred Music,
whose Auxiliary Committee here, with the Society of
St. Gregory, have been making great preparations for
a magnificent program.

            I trust that you will find it con-
venient to come as the guest of the Committee, and
that you may be accompanied by the Rev. Dom Gatard,
O.S.B., with the understanding that you are to be
the guests of the Committee from the time of your
departure from the other side.

            The Committee will enter more fully
into details, as to your journey, than it is possible
for me in this note of invitation to outline.

            With sincere best wishes, I am,

            Faithfully yours in Christ,

                    ♦ Patrick J. Hays

                    Archbishop of New York.

HT

18 EAST TENTH STREET

le 25 mars 1920

No. 2

Très Révérend Père –

Depuis déjà longtemps je cherche a vous exprimer la grande reconnaissance et la joie de tous nos cœurs Américains de l'honneur que vous nous faites en traversant la mer pour venir diriger nos premiers pas dans la voie liturgique et encourager votre amour (tout jeune encore!) pour le Chant sacré de l'Église. Mais les mots sont si froids et si plats – il me faudrait des belles neumes pour vous l'exprimer! Aussi je me suis réfugiée dans le silence – ou mieux en quelque mots télégraphiques; mais de peur que vous ne me pensiez ingrate n'a donné le courage de vous écrire!

Vous devineriez facilement la joie que nous éprouvons tous de votre grande bonté envers nous quand je vous dit que votre présence seule pourrait faire réaliser le rêve des amants du Plain chant en Amérique en rassemblant toutes les petites flames solitaires pour les réunir dans un grand feu ardent –

Vous n'allez pas attendre la perfection, n'est-ce pas! parce que je ne voudrais pas que vous souffriez une désillusion – mais vous trouverez beaucoup de bonne volonté et même de l'enthousiasme, surtout entre les Religieuses – et l'avenir est entre leurs mains. Elles passeront la belle flame aux enfants – elles le font déjà – et c'est notre première pour l'avenir. Vous verrez peut-être 5,000 petits enfants, qui viendront prendre part au congrès. Ces petits êtres vous feront plaisir je le crois vraiment.

Comme le Saint Père nous a dit les enfants donnent le bon exemple – Entre eux il n'y a pas de petit vanité personnelle qui est malheureusement si présente aux efforts des congréssistes plus âgés. Nous en souffrons déjà pour les chers congrès – sans doute il faut toutes ces souffrances et ces fatigues de corps et d'esprit pour faire une œuvre de Dieu – mais c'est accablant – et cela est une véritable excuse envers vous, très Révérend Père, car la fatigue et la faiblesse m'ont empêchée de vous écrire et j'ai laissé au bon Docteur Gilles le plaisir de vous donner tous les détails du congrès.

Vous allez nous ouvrir tout un monde de beauté, cher Dom Mocquereau – Nous n'avons jamais connu la Liturgie en Amérique – ce n'est pas une chose négligé tant qu'ignorée. Il faut la créer ici – Quelle joie et quel

humour que vous daignez guider nos premiers pas – et ce sont les premiers pas qui content. Nous allons tâcher de ne pas trop vous fatiguer, mais de si bien préparer tout d'avance que nous puissions vous donner un peu de consolation – Et puis Dom Gatard corrigera nos erreurs – et nous tâcherons de bien faire que vous soyez content de vos petits Américains. Une vieille Religieuse du "middle West" m'écrit que le rêve de sa vie a été de vous voir, et qu'elle a la permission de son Supérieur de faire le voyage et prendre part au congrès. Et puis... nunc dimittis! Vous voyez que vous êtes le bien venu!

J'espère que vous pouvez comprendre mon mauvais Français – mais du moins, croyez, cher et Révérend Père, que quoique je ne l'exprime si mal j'ai le contentement plein de reconnaissance pour cette grande bonté que vous montrez envers nous. Votre dévouée en Jésus Seigneur

Justine Ward

ST. FRANCIS CAMP
 LITTLE MOOSE LAKE
  OLD FORGE, NEW YORK

Reçu le 1 7bre
Répondre le
2 7re

August 19, 1920

Dear Reverend Father Dom Mocquereau:

Since writing you at length a few days ago several things of importance
have happened which I think I should tell you.

I have received a very nice letter from Mr. Fischer showing the best of good
will as regards the handling of the publications of Mssrs. Desclée and
Company. On the other hand, I have just seen the Very Reverend Dr. Shields
of the Catholic University who tells me that he had a talk with the Very
Reverend P. Dom Gatard during his visit in Washington at which time he
suggested that the University should handle this matter themselves. He would
be willing to see that a good English translation was made for use in this
country and would be able to distribute the books broadcast as part of the
educational propaganda of the University itself. This has many advantages
and I thought I would like to tell you of this offer of his so that you might
judge which proposition you would yourself prefer. Dr. Shields has been, as
you know, publishing a series of educational books for our Catholic schools
among which my music course is numbered and these books are sold to the
Sisters and the various religious orders directly, eliminating entirely the book-
sellers profit. There is also a certain dignity in the University sponsoring the
Solesmes books and distributing them through the whole educational field.
Doctor Shields will be entirely delighted to do this and also to publish the
NOMBRE MUSICALE in English translation.

Naturally my only interest in the whole matter is to see that the books are
available in America as rapidly and as conveniently as possible. I do not want
to seem to go back on Mr. George Fischer as urging the thing, and after his
very cooperative, nice spirit, but we have, of course, with Mr. Fischer got a
commercial proposition pure and simple and I thought before anything definite was settled that you ought to be informed of Dr. Shields' willingness to
handle the matter at the University and be in a position to judge as to which
would seem most advisable. I have sent a very brief letter to Mssrs. Desclée
and Company telling them that another propositon has been made and that I
have written to you about it. I did not tell Mssrs. Desclée from whom the
proposition came as I thought it better that you should judge and communicate with them if you think wise. I asked them to keep this second matter
confidential until they should hear from you so that if you prefer to proceed
with Mr. Fischer nothing has been done which would interfere in any way.

It also occurred to me that possibly we might deal with Mr. Fischer for the
present edition in Latin and let the University handle the books with the
English translation. My position, of course, is rather difficult in the matter as
I do not wish to treat Mr. Fischer badly. On the other hand, the proposition
with Dr. Shields seems to me so very advantageous and likely to bring about
the wide circulation of the Solesmes books to precisely the best sources, that
is, to the religious orders of this country.

As I wrote you in my previous letter nothing has been heard from Monsier Bonnaire regarding the Paléographie Musicale. I fear greatly that if he has written the letter it has gone astray and I am very anxious not to miss the opportunity of securing the two copies of the complete Paléographie. I am therefore sending you a cable tomorrow asking whom I could address in the matter. It is so important that we should have these complete copies and not lose by any delay the opportunity we have of securing them through your very great kindness, dear Father.

The Very Reverend Dr. Shields who is here with me now tells me that Dom Gatard made a great success during his lectures in Washington and that everybody was delighted with his classes. There were nearly four hundred Sisters from all parts of the United States, Canada, Puerto Rico, Mexico, etc., etc. It has given a splendid impetus to the whole movement. I also had a letter from Dom Gatard himself in which he was very much pleased with the reception he had received in the Diocese of Toledo. All the Organists and the Sisters of the teaching communities had been assembled by the Bishop and were deeply interested. You see that the benefit of your visit and that of Dom Gatard still continues to help along the good cause of Gregorian restoration.

Please forgive that I am writing in haste and in English. I did not want to delay a moment in sending you these various pieces of news.

One last, and less cheerful piece of news. The Committee of the Clergy who represented His Grace the Archbishop of New York for the Gregorian Congress have taken it into their heads to change the resolutions of the Congress so that instead of recommending the adoption of the Vatican Version and the rhythmic signs of Solesmes we are now apparently quoted as having urged "when a definitive edition shall be issued" it shall be introduced as rapidly as possible. I fear that this change has been instigated by the few but rather energetic followers of the Ratisbon version. I have protested against this change being made as it will make the Congress rather ridiculous all over the world. I do not know yet what the Committee of the Clergy will do and therefore I have written to Father De Santi that should the resolutions be forwarded with this change that it was not the will of the Congress and I am sure he will see that the Holy Father does not misunderstand us. The matter has troubled me greatly as you can well imagine but I am quite powerless to do anything further.

With my very best remembrances and deepest gratitude for all your great kindness, dear Reverend Father, I remain.

Faithfully yours,

Justin B.

Very Reverend P. Dom Mocquereau
Quarr Abbey
Ryde, Isle of Wight
England

Excerpt of a letter of Dom Mocquereau to Justine Ward. Quarr Abbey,
September 2, 1920, with regard to the resolutions of the New York
Congress.

(1°) Amendments to the Congress resolutions. They are already published
in two worlds and now they are to be changed!! Last night, I sent you a
dispatch giving you the thought of Most Rev. Dom Paolo Ferretti, Consultor
of the Sacred Congregation of Rites, President of the Chant Commission,
close to the same congregation in Rome. Here are the declarations which I
wrote from his dictation, for he has been staying here now for almost two
months: "I know from certain knowledge that in Germany, Austria and
German Switzerland, there are oppositions to the Vatican Edition, even on
the part of certain bishops, under the pretext that this edition is not
finished, that all the books have not yet appeared. I know that the
complaints of ecclesiastics and religious have arrived in Rome against a
bishop whom I could name, because this bishop does not permit the use of
the Vatican Edition (under the pretext described below). It is said that
Pustet of Ratisbon, profiting from this underhanded opposition, is not
afraid to reprint surreptitiously their old editions. The proposals of changes
in the Congress resolutions are only ramifications of these underhanded
dealings; one cannot be associated with them. The truth is that each new
book of the Vatican Edition that appears is obligatory as the decrees and
the very clear prefaces on this point prove. There is no need to wait in
order to adopt the books that are already in print. If the oppositions
continue, added the Most Reverend Ferretti (who has had in hand all the
relevant documents), the Congregation will make even clearer declarations
in this matter.

These are the words of the official prelate, who in Rome is certainly
the most knowledgeable in that which comes to the attention of the
Congregation of Rites regarding the chant.

As for Solesmes, it goes without saying that we can no longer follow the
Congress, if it goes off the track in this way . . . If the new resolutions were
adopted and published, I would be obliged to protest publicly that Solesmes
is absolutely opposed to a resolution that is opposed to the decrees of the
Holy See, and which would compromise in Rome the clean reputation of
his Grace, the Archbishop of New York.

ST. FRANCIS CAMP
  LITTLE MOOSE LAKE
    OLD FORGE, NEW YORK

                                                                September 4, 1920

Reverend dear Father:—

        I have had the privilege of spending the last few days with Mrs. Ward. We were
occupied for the most part in discussing plans for the spread of Gregorian music in this country.
The great impetus given to the movement by the gracious visit of yourself and Dom Gatard on
the occasion of the International Congress of Gregorian Chant must not be lost.
        I need not remind you that Mrs. Ward and I have been doing everything in our power
for many years to bring about the restoration of Gregorian music. The most important part of
the work, in my judgment, has been the development of foundations of musical education among
the children of our Catholic schools.
        The purpose of the Catholic Education Press is to publish and supply to our Catholic
Schools and Churches all books and charts which would prove helpful in the restoration of
Gregorian music and the renewal of the content and method of the curricula of our schools.
        It seems to us that the Catholic Education Press could handle the Solesmes books in this
country to greater advantage, perhaps, than any other firm. I am aware that some negotiations
have been taken up in the matter with Fischer Brothers of New York City. I do not wish to
interfere with anything that has been done, but it gives me great pleasure to offer to you and to
your publishers the assistance and cooperation of the Catholic Education Press. I will be glad to
handle the American Agency for all your publications, or (if your publishers do not see fit to
establish an American agency with exclusive privileges) I will be glad to carry your books in
stock, provided I am allowed the usual jobbers' discount. This would not prevent the books being
sold to other publishing houses in this country at the same rate they are sold to us, but it would
necessitate the addition of the trade discount on all books sold by Desclée & Cie. directly to individual customers.
        We have on the list of our customers at present most of the Catholic churches and
schools of the United States and feel that we could reach them more readily than anyone else.
        I understand that you are desirous of publishing an English version of some of your
books. When talking to Dom Gatard, on the occasion of his visit to the University, I offered
you, through him, to publish English translations of whatever works you desire published in this
form. I now renew this offer directly. We can have the translation made in this country if you
desire, and submit the finished work to you. We would of course arrange to pay you the same
royalty that you are now enjoying on the French Editions.
        I should be much pleased if you would take this matter up with your publishers and let
me have an answer at your convenience.
        Please address the reply to my home address:
                T.E. Shields
            Catholic University of America
                Washington, D.C.

Very sincerely yours in Xto.   *Thomas Edward Shields*

Reverend P. Dom André Mocquereau
Abbeye St. Pierre de Solesmes
    Quarr Abbey
        Ryde.
            Isle of Wight

THE INTERNATIONAL CONGRESS OF GREGORIAN CHANT ❡ ❡ ❡ TO BE HELD AT THE ❡ ❡ ❡ CATHEDRAL OF SAINT PATRICK ON JUNE FIRST, SECOND & THIRD ❧ ❧ ❧ ❧ MCMXX ❧ ❧ ❧ ❧

UNDER THE AUSPICES OF

THE MOST REVEREND PATRICK J. HAYES, ARCHBISHOP OF NEW YORK

DIRECTORS

THE REV. DOM MOCQUEREAU, O.S.B.
THE VERY REV. DOM GATARD, O.S.B.

GRAND ORGAN

M. JOSEPH BONNET

PATRONS

HIS EXCELLENCY JOHN BONZANO, D.D.
Apostolic Delegate
HIS EMINENCE CARDINAL GIBBONS,
Archbishop of Baltimore
HIS EMINENCE CARDINAL O'CONNELL,
Archbishop of Boston
MOST REV. J. J. HARTY, D.D.
Bishop of Omaha
MOST REV. HENRY MOELLER, D.D.
Archbishop of Cincinnati
MOST REV. J. J. KEANE, D.D.,
Archbishop of Dubuque
MOST REV. E. J. HANNA, D.D.
Archbishop of San Francisco
MOST REV. D. J. DOUGHERTY, D.D.
Archbishop of Philadelphia
MOST REV. AUSTIN DOWLING, D.D.
Archbishop of St Paul
RT. REV. C. E. McDONNELL, D.D.
Bishop of Brooklyn
RT. REV. M. F. BURKE, D.D.
Bishop of St. Joseph
RT. REV. P. J. DONOHUE, D.D.,
Bishop of Wheeling
RT. REV. M. J. HOBAN, D.D.
Bishop of Scranton
RT. REV. J. J. MONAGHAN, D.D.
Bishop of Wilmington
RT. REV. P. J. MULDOON, D.D.
Bishop of Rockford
RT. REV. T. F. HICKEY, D.D.
Bishop of Rochester

RT. REV. VINCENT WEHRLE, D.D.
Bishop of Bismark
RT. REV. J. J. O'CONNOR, D.D.
Bishop of Newark
RT. REV. JOSEPH SCHREMBS, D.D.
Bishop of Toledo
RT. REV. D. J. O'CONNELL, D.D.
Bishop of Richmond
RT. REV. P. A. McGOVERN, D.D.
Bishop of Cheyenne
RT. REV. T. J. SHAHAN, LL.D.
Rector, Catholic University
RT. REV. FERDINAND BROSSART, D.D.
Bishop of Covington
RT. REV. P. R. McDEVITT, D.D.
Bishop of Harrisburg
RT. REV. W. T. RUSSELL, D.D.
Bishop of Charleston
RT. REV. T. J. WALSH, D.D.
Bishop of Trenton
RT. REV. J. T. McNICHOLAS, D.D,
Bishop of Duluth
RT. REV. JOSEPH CHARTRAND, D.D.
Bishop of Indianapolis
RT. REV. C. E. BYRNE, D.D.
Bishop of Galveston
RT. REV. J. B. JEANMARD, D.D.
Bishop of Lafayette
RT. REV. E. F. GIBBONS, D.D.
Bishop of Albany
RT. REV. WILLIAM TURNER, D.D.
Bishop of Buffalo

"It is a great bond of unity when an immense number of people raise their voices in a single chorus."
(St. Ambrose)

The International Congress of Gregorian Chant is not primarily a musical event. It is a Triduum of public worship by means of the liturgy sung by the voices of a united people.

It restores, according to the wishes of the Holy See, a custom once universal in the Church, but new to Catholics in America: the congregational singing of the Mass and other offices.

The people were not always silent onlookers at the liturgical drama. Their part originally was akin to that of the chorus in the Greek drama; they responded to the prayers of the priest with a shout of approval—"Amen", with a burst of joy—"Alleluia!" The Kyrie was their own plea for mercy, the Credo their own act of faith. But for generations the voice of the people has been hushed. The Church is restoring to them their musical birthright.

"The most ancient and correct ecclesiastical tradition in regard to sacred music encouraged the whole body of the people to take an active part in the liturgical services, the people singing the common of the Mass, while a Schola Cantorum sings the varied and richer parts of the text and of the melodies, thus alternating with the people." (Pius X 1912)

Since the Renaissance, public worship has suffered a gradual deterioration. Stealthily the principle of art for art's sake has crept into our churches through the choirs. Music has been treated as an end rather than as a means, and both music and prayer have suffered. The liturgy, the complex of public worship through words, through gesture, through color, through sound—is the most powerful means towards conversion and sanctification. The arts as humble handmaids of the Lord, are admitted, not for their own sakes, but "to add life and efficacy to the thoughts," and by so doing, to "train and form the minds of the faithful to all sanctity." (Pius X) Music must be primarily prayer, and furthermore, liturgical prayer, vesting itself with the exact form and spirit of liturgy. "These qualities are to be found in the highest degree in Gregorian Chant, which is consequently the chant proper to the Roman Church." (Pius X)

"Special efforts are to be made to restore the use of Gregorian Chant BY THE PEOPLE so that the faithful may once more take an active part in the ecclesiastical offices as was the case in ancient times."
(Pius X 1903)

Gregorian Chant, being unison music, can be sung by the entire people, even by little children. Five thousand of these children will take part in the Congress in St. Patrick's Cathedral, and as many adults—delegates from all over the United States and Europe. The seminaries of Baltimore, Rochester, Cleveland, and others will co-operate with those of New York and

Brooklyn in singing the offices. Hundreds of delegates from Religious Communities from all over the country will take part in the singing. The laity are rehearsing to fit themselves to join in the singing of the Psalms.

For three days the body of St. Patrick's Cathedral will be filled with these singers under the direction of the greatest living authority on Gregorian Chant, the venerable Benedictine Monk, Dom Mocquereau, with his pupil Dom Gaturd, Prior of Farnborough Abbey. Dom Mocquereau, more than any single figure has contributed by his researches to the restoration of the Gregorian melodies to their original purity in the form now embodied in the Vatican edition of the Gradual, which, since its publication, has become a matter of musical dogma to the Church.

New York is honored by its selection for the site of this historic event. His Grace Archbishop Hayes has taken the matter under his special protection and has offered St. Patrick's Cathedral to be the scene of this triduum. The most distinguished names in the American Hierarchy are its patrons. An equally distinguished list of the laity are now invited to co-operate as patrons, who will have the privilege of inviting to this city, as their guests, the delegates from the Seminaries and Religious Communities, whose poverty would otherwise make it impossible for them to have the privilege of studying under the great master, Dom Mocquereau. No more rapid and effective method could be devised to further this great educational movement in the Church than through the bringing of these many groups together for the Congress, which proposes not only to give a model of what the Holy See desires, but a practical illustration of how this result may be most easily obtained.

For many years the Society of St. Gregory and the Auxiliary Committee of the Pontifical Institute of Sacred Music have been laying the foundation for a Congress such as this. The Holy See has approved their work, expressing itself in regard to the latter Society in the following words:

"Gregorian Chant has always been regarded as the supreme model for sacred music, so that it is legitimate to lay down the following rule: the more closely a composition for church approaches in its movement, inspiration and savour the Gregorian form, the more sacred and liturgical it becomes; and the more out of harmony it is with that supreme model, the less worthy it is of the Temple." (Pius X)

*"The ancient traditional Gregorian Chant must therefore in a large measure be restored to the functions of public worship, and the fact must be accepted by all that an ecclesiastical function loses none of its solemnity when accompanied by this music alone."
(Pius X 1903)*

"What is more pleasing to God than to hear the whole Christian people sing to Him in unison." (St. Clement of Alexandria)

"Now that the necessity of a complete change in the order of things has come to be universally appreciated any abuse in the matter becomes intolerable and must be removed."
(Pius X to Cardinal Vicar of Rome 1903)

"The Holy Father, not only takes pleasure in pointing out this praiseworthy propaganda, an act of filial adhesion to His Supreme Authority, but He admires also this proof of a noble apostolate for the decorum of divine worship in order that the faithful may live the life of the sacred liturgy by experiencing, through the mysteries of religion, that sublime elevation towards God which revives the Faith and betters the practice of the whole Christian life.

"Therefore, His Holiness commends all the members of the Auxiliary Committee of New York, and with best wishes for a happy extension of the work, grants to them, with paternal benevolence, the Grace of the Apostolic Blessing."

Funds, of course, will be needed to carry out the program of the Congress. They will not be less than twenty-five thuosand dollars and will be devoted entirely to the expenses of the Congress. These will be principally the traveling and living expenses of the large number of seminarians and delegates from religious communities who will come to New York to take part in the Congress and whose time and services will be devoutly and freely offered in this endeavor to prove and to restore the simplicity, beauty and efficacy of the Church's liturgy.

This appeal will become more and more deserving as it reveals itself in the Congress on June first, second and third and we invite you to contribute to this fund as generously as you may. Meanwhile we must rely on those who see the things invisible. We are,

Sincerely yours,

Mrs. NICHOLAS BRADY	Mr. JOHN G. AGAR
Mrs. WINTHROP CHANLER	Mr. JAMES BYRNE
Mrs. JOHN C. MOORE	Mr. BOURKE COCKRAN
Mrs. HERBERT D. ROBBINS	Mr. JOSEPH P. GRACE
Mrs. WILLIAM F. SHEEHAN	Mr. WILLIAM GUTHRIE
Mrs. CORNELIUS TIERS	Mr. ADRIAN ISELIN
Mrs. CABOT WARD	Mr. CLARENCE MACKAY

LIST OF THOSE TAKING PART IN THE CONGRESS

VISITING RELIGIOUS ORDERS

Baltimore, Md. ....Notre Dame Sisters
Buffalo, N.Y. ....Grey Nuns of the Holy Cross
Chestnut Hill, Pa. ....Sisters of St. Joseph
Elizabeth, N.J. ....Benedictine Sisters
Garrison, N.Y. ....Friars of the Atonement
Garrison, N.Y. ....Sisters of Atonement
Joliet, Ill. ....Franciscan Sisters
Merion, Pa. ....Sisters of Mercy
New Rochelle ....Salesians of Venerable Dom Bosco
Philadelphia, Pa. ....Franciscan Sisters
Pittsburgh, Pa. ....Sisters of Mercy
Scranton, Pa. ....Sisters of Immaculate Heart
West Chester, Pa ....Sisters of Immaculate Heart

SEMINARIES

Yonkers, N.Y. ....St. Joseph's
Baltimore, Md. ....St. Mary's
Cleveland, Ohio ....St. Mary's
Metuchen, N.J. ....Brothers of Sacred Heart
Notre Dame, Ind. ....Holy Cross
Rochester, N.Y. ....St. Bernard's

CHOIRS

New York, N.Y..........Blessed Sacrament Choir
Philadelphia, Pa. ....Palestrina Choir

SCHOOLS

New York City:
Academies of the Sacred Heart
    "Manhattanville"
    "Maplehurst"
St. Adalbert's School
St. Ambrose School
St. Anthony's School
Annunciation School
Blessed Sacrament School
St. Catherine's Academy
St. Catherine's School
St. Catherine of Sienna's School
St. Francis School
St. Francis Xavier School
St. Gregory's School
Holy Rosary Academy
Holy Rosary School
St. Ignatius Loyola's School
St. Jean Baptiste School
Our Lady of Angels School
Our Lady of Lourdes School
St. Nicholas School
St. Thomas Aquinas School
St. Stephens' School
St. Vincent Ferrer School
St. Walburga's Academy
  New Rochelle:
Blessed Sacrament School
St. Gabriel's School
College of New Rochelle
Mt. Loretto Convent
    Princess Bay, Staten Island

Brooklyn:
St. Brigid's School
St. Catherine's of Alexandria's School
St. Cecilia's School
Holy Name School
Holy Cross School
Immaculate Heart School
St. John's School
St. Michael's School
Queen of All Saints' School
St. Thomas Aquinas School
St. Rose of Lima's School

St. Mary's School
    Long Island City

Blessed Sacrament School
    Yonkers, N.Y.

Convent of Good Counsel
    White Plains, N.Y.

Benedictine Academy
    Elizabeth, N.J.

Our Lady of Good Counsel School
    Newark, N.J.

Rosemount Hall
    So. Orange, N.J.

St. John's School
    Paterson, N.J.

Academy of Mount St. Joseph
    Chestnut Hill, Pa.

Academy of the Sacred Heart
    "Kenwood", Albany

PROGRAMME of

Tuesday, June the first.

AT 11.00 A.M. SOLEMN PONTIFICAL MASS.
                    VOTIVE MASS OF THE HOLY GHOST.

1. *"Sacerdos et Pontifex". At the reception of the Most Reverend Archbishop. By Schola and people.*

2. *"Veni Creator". During the vesting. The Congregation singing the even verses, the Schola the odd verses.*

3. *Proper of the Mass by St. Bernard's Seminary, Rochester.*

4. *Ordinary of the Mass (Missa de Angelis, No. VIII) by 3500 children from 47 Schools.*

AT 2.30 P.M. IN THE CATHEDRAL COLLEGE HALL.

Lecture by Dom Mocquereau and Dom Gatard on "The Popes and the Restoration of the Roman Chant".

AT 3.30 P.M. LECTURE BY THE REV. DR. EDWIN RYAN

on "The Vestments of the Roman Rite and Their Historical Development".

AT 5.00 P.M. SOLEMN PONTIFICAL VESPERS AND COMPLINE.

St. Bernard's Seminary, alternating with the Congregation (consisting of Seminarians, Religious Orders, Colleges, Academies, Schools and Volunteer Singers all having received special training) in the Psalms and Hymns.

AT 8.00 P.M. IN THE CATHEDRAL COLLEGE HALL.

Public Discussion (conducted by the Rev. Dr. Ryan) on Gregorian Music and Congregational Singing.

COMMITTES:

Auxiliary Committee to the PONTIFICAL INSTITUTE OF SACRED MUSIC

Archbishop's

Rt. Rev. Monsignor JAMES H. McGEAN   Rt. Rev. Monsignor EDWIN

the CONGRESS

Wednesday, June the second.

AT 11.00 A.M. SOLEMN PONTIFICAL REQUIEM MASS
(for Those Who died in the War)

1. *Proper of the Mass by St. Joseph's Seminary, Dunwoodie.*

2. *Ordinary of the Mass and Sequence by the Congregation (consisting of Seminarians, Religious Orders, Colleges, Academies and Schools).*

AT 2.30 P.M. IN THE CATHEDRAL HALL.
Lecture on "The Liturgy in the Education of Children" by the Very Reverend Dr. T. E. Shields.

AT 3.30 P.M. DEMONSTRATION OF SCHOOL MUSIC
by the children of the Schools of Our Lady of Lourdes and the Annunciation.

AT 5.00 P.M. SOLEMN PONTIFICAL VESPERS AND COMPLINE.
St. Joseph's Seminary, Dunwoodie, and Congregation as on June the first.

AT 8.00 P.M. IN THE CATHEDRAL COLLEGE HALL.
Continuation of the Public Discussion as on June the first.

Thursday, June the third.

AT 11.00 A.M. FEAST OF CORPUS CHRISTI.

1. *"Sacerdos et Pontifex" and "Veni Creator" as on June the first.*

2. *Proper of the Mass by St. Mary's Seminary, Baltimore.*

3. *Ordinary of the Mass ("Cum jubilo" Mass of the B.V.M. No. IX) Sequence, "Pange lingua" and "Te Deum" by Congregation as before.*

THE CONGRESS CLOSES WITH THIS SOLEMNITY.

THE SOCIETY OF SAINT GREGORY OF AMERICA

Committee

M. SWEENY, *Chairman*   REV. JOSEPH H. MCMAHON, Ph. D.

International Congress of Gregorian Chant
St. Patrick's Cathedral, New York, N. Y.

June 1, 2, 3, 1920.
by the

Auxiliary Committee to the
Pontifical Institute of Sacred Music

Saint Gregory Society
of America

Director of Chant: Very Rev. Dom Mocquereau
Prior of Solemnes now at Quarr Abbey, Isle of Wright

Grand Organ: Monsieur Joseph Bonnet
Concert Organist of St. Eustache, Paris

DAILY PROGRAMME.

LITURGICAL.

MORNING: Solemn Mass { *Common and Responses: The people in unison.*
10 A. M.   { *Proper: Visiting Choirs.*

AFTERNOON: Vespers { *Psalms: The People.*
4.30 P. M.   { *Antiphons: Visiting Choirs.*
                    { *Hymns: The People.*

EVENING: *Compline, 7.30 P. M. Psalms and Hymn: The People.*

EDUCATIONAL.

between 2 and 4 P. M.

1. LECTURES AND PRACTICAL DEMONSTRATIONS.

The Liturgy as Social Force.
The Liturgy as Educational Force.
The Chant as the People's Musical Medium.
The Place of the Organ in Liturgical Offices.
Sacramental Art and the Education of the Symbolic Sense.
Music in our Schools with Demonstrations.
Music in our Seminaries with Demonstrations.
Popular Singing Societies—Demonstrations.

2. EXHIBITS.

Vestments according to Rubrics.
Altar adornment according to Rubrics.
Church decorations according to Rubrics.
Architecture according to Rubrics.
     (illustrated by pictures and slides)

MUSICAL PROGRAMME FOR MASS.

June 1.

VOTIVE MASS OF THE HOLY SPIRIT.

a.) *Veni Creator: By people and Scholae.*
b.) *Missa de Angelis: School children and congregation.*
c.) *Proper: Votive Mass to the Holy Spirit: Visiting Choirs.*

June 2.

MISSA PRO DEFUNCTIS [*for the soldiers who died in the war*]

Common: By the People.
Proper: By visiting Choirs.
Sequence: Dies Irae: By people and choirs.

June 3.

FEAST OF CORPUS CHRISTI

Common: Mass of B. V. M. (Cum Jubilo) The People.
Proper of the Feast: By Visiting Choirs.
Sequence, Lauda Sion, by People and Visiting Choirs.
Procession, Pange Lingua, by People Choirs and Children.
Te Deum   "   "   "
Tantum Ergo   "   "   "

The Congress will conclude with Benediction on the morning of June 3.

(Reprinted without change of paging from The Catholic Educational Review for September, 1920)

THE PAPAL ATTITUDE TOWARD THE RESTORATION OF GREGORIAN CHANT[1]

Amid the solemn religious and musical ceremonies which are unfolding before our eyes, a feeling of profound gratitude to the goodness of God is awakened in the hearts of the two monks of Solesmes who are called by your kindness to occupy a place of honor among you. This celebration truly realizes even beyond their hopes the ideals pursued by Dom Gueranger and his sons for well nigh a century, namely, that in all Catholic Churches there should prevail the Roman liturgy and with it its faithful companion, the pious, sweet Gregorian Chant. This musical language, most fit for divine worship, we hear each day uttered carefully and lovingly by the lips of artists and of children, by the lips of the whole people—how can we fail to be moved with joyous gratitude unto the Lord who deigns thus to bless and reward our labors?

Moreover, gentlemen, is it not an exquisite Providence which brings us here in this land, to rejoice in this sacred music? Well, I know: *Domini est terra,* the earth is the Lord's· for Him there is neither Old World nor New; but to us old monks, who, more than fifteen centuries ago, took root in ancient Europe, who live habitually in quiet within the four walls of their monastery, there is an exotic flavor, an added charm—in finding again beyond the Atlantic, in the New World in New York, at St. Patrick's, brothers in faith, praising the same Lord in the same Gregorian modes and rhythms which nursed the piety of their ancestors and were the joy of early Christianity.

---

[1] Paper read by Dom Mocquereau at the International Gregorian Congress, held in New York City in June, 1920.

These joys, religious and artistic, we owe, gentlemen, to
you: first to His Grace, the Archbishop of New York, who
so kindly invited us to your celebration, whose extreme benevolence has made this Congress possible, and who has shown in
many ways his keen and enlightened interest in its success,
whose assiduous and unselfish labors have prepared these
festivities; to the Seminarians, who, under the able direction
of renowned professors of music, have been taught to render
the Gregorian Chant with all the perfection of rhythms; to
those numerous children, trained with great self-denial by their
teachers, and also to these men and women who attended the
practices, sacrificing a well-earned rest, and whose rendition of
the melodies will demonstrate the possibility of congregational
singing, and next to the committees. The prominent place
you have reserved for us at the head of your choirs is a reward
which Solesmes—for it concerns the Community of Solesmes
as a whole—would never have dared to claim, and for which
we shall ever remain proud and grateful.

The American Gregorian festival which we are attending
brings vividly to my mind a festival in Rome in 1904 at St.
Peter's, over which presided Pope Pius X. This was the beginning of the restoration of Gregorian Chant, and in the whole
history of reform two dates glow with incomparable splendor—
1904 and 1920; two names stand out—Rome and New York;
Rome as sovereign, giving the impulse and signal for the universal renaissance—New York answering that call with all
a young nation's energy and enthusiasm of faith and love;
New York, by its example, arousing the New World to follow
in its path and in the path of Rome.

Rome, gentlemen, we cannot forget in these festal days,
for her Pontiffs have been the foremost instruments of the
Gregorian restoration: Pius IX and Leo XIII prepared and
began it: Pius X and Benedict XV, now reigning gloriously,
have accomplished it. What thanks we owe them! The Benedictines of Solesmes and their friends will remember always
that in troublous times these Roman Pontiffs protected them—
at need, defended them—and finally approved their efforts with
a favor so mighty and so unreserved as must needs carry all
others along with it.

Restoration of Gregorian Chant

It is precisely this position on the part of the Holy See which has determined my choice of a subject. I should like to trace for you in its large outlines the eventful history of the Gregorian renaissance, that I may show you, dominating the fluctuations of events and the clash of ideas, the *Papal attitude,* transmitted faithfully from Pope to Pope, always the same, revealing or veiling itself according to the pressure and exigency of circumstances, always encouraging our scientific investigations and our practical experiments, and ending, by dint of prudence and patience, in surmounting every opposition and every obstacle.

This account will be, on the part of the Benedictines, a public act of gratitude to those great Popes; may it bring into being in the hearts of my listeners the grateful feelings which inspired it; for our rejoicings of today are the fruit of their struggles and of their labors.

This said, I shall turn at once to my subject.

Toward the middle of the nineteenth century, thanks principally to the work of Dom Gueranger, the reestablishment of the Roman liturgy in France was a *"fait accompli."* What was next required was the restoration of the Gregorian melodies.

In the course of centuries, the original form of these chants had been seriously altered; more than twenty editions, each different from the other, divided the Catholic world among them; tradition evidently was not to be found in this chaos. The most ancient manuscripts, then, must be consulted if we were to find again the ancient form in its integrity and beauty. Dom Gueranger did not draw back before this new task; with the help of his sons, he felt confident of accomplishing it. They set to work. Some of the monks visited libraries, copying, tracing the ancient manuscripts; the work was slow and laborious: at that time photography had not come to the aid of science. But no matter; they took their time, for they wished to work well, very well; it was for the Church and for the beauty of divine worship that they toiled.

The Benedictines, however, were not alone in their work. The idea of restoring the Gregorian melodies haunted men's minds; it was the order of the day. In several dioceses, the

THE CATHOLIC EDUCATIONAL REVIEW

expectation was that it could be done at once. There was hardly a notion of its difficulties!

In 1848, the Archbishops of Rheims and of Cambria submitted to Pius IX, then in exile at Gaeta, the plan of an edition which was to reproduce in their entirety the melodies according to the manuscripts. Pius IX approved, and when a few years later this edition was published, the Pope, in several Briefs, congratulated the authors and editors of this publication, "which restores at last," he said, "the Gregorian Chant in its pristine majesty and perfection," *in majestatem pristinam et perfectionem.* (Brief to the publisher, August 23, 1854.)

And this was really the case: the members of the commission in charge of the edition had worked over the manuscripts, and, in general, had followed them. But they departed from them in certain passages and thus made a new edition necessary. This the monks of Solesmes soon perceived, and they patiently continued their researches.

The praise of Pius IX determined some twenty dioceses to adopt the books of Rheims and of Cambria.

The attitude of Pius IX reappears in numerous documents of this period: I shall mention only his Brief to the Reverend Father Lambillotte, who sent to the Pope, as an offering (*en hommage*), his lithographed reproduction of the precious manuscript in the Gregorian Neums, preserved in the library of St. Gall. After the customary praises and thanks, the Brief adds these significant words: *"Adsit laboribus studiisque tuis benignissimus Dominus, ut revera proficiant ad majestatem et gravitatem cantus ecclesiastici ubique restituendum."*

"May the most kind Lord aid your labors and your studies, that they may truly help to restore everywhere the majesty and the solemnity of ecclesiastical song."

The Pontifical intention surely, then, has for its final goal, restoration, and restoration exact and entire. This is evident, because the good wishes here formulated apply especially to the reproduction of manuscripts, the scientific basis of an exact restoration. The Holy See has pointed the way, and there is naught left but to follow it.

All then seemed well begun: investigation could continue;

RESTORATION OF GREGORIAN CHANT

with time, labor and the support of Rome, the goal could not
but be reached. But no work of man can succeed and endure
which has not been tried as by fire, and from its touch received,
as it were, a consecration. Gregorian art, at its renaissance,
was destined to receive that consecration.

In the seventeenth century—in 1614, to be exact—the period
of greatest decadence for the Gregorian Chant, there had been
published a very poor edition, called the Medicean edition.
On the title page, the publishers had smuggled in, as it were,
the name of Paul V; moreover, there was a false legend at-
tributing its editorship to Palestrina. In spite of the recommendation of these two great names, it had, in its time, no
circulation.

In the nineteenth century two publishers conceived the idea
of reprinting it. A first attempt was made in Belgium between 1848 and 1855; the publisher issued his books at his
own risk. Their success was mediocre. In France, one diocese
only accepted them (Cahors).

Twenty years later a new publisher appeared. More skillful
than the first, he surrounded himself with every precaution in
order to succeed: he took as his adviser a man who, in the
ecclesiastical musical world, enjoyed undisputed authority, but
who was absolutely ignorant of the Gregorian Chant; then he
addressed himself directly to Rome. He proposed to the Sacred Congregation of Rites the printing of a great folio edition
of the Medicean Gradual and begged the Holy Father to grant
him certain privileges for this edition, which would cost him
enormous sums!!! . . . and might easily cause his ruin if he
were not helped.

Pius IX granted, through the Sacred Congregation of Rites,
a privilege of thirty years (Brief of October 1, 1868) upon condition that at least one reviser of the said Congregation approve and sign each printed page.

In short, it was in the beginning a simple permission to
print; but the publisher did not stop there: he took advantage
of every circumstance to beg new favors; Brief succeeded
Brief, Decree succeeded Decree, each going beyond the last;
soon the new edition became quasi-official, then actually official—Pius IX approved, Leo XIII did likewise. It was even

THE CATHOLIC EDUCATIONAL REVIEW

recommended to the Ordinaries, though not *prescribed,* nor ever will be; upon this point Rome will not yield.

Henceforth, what were to become of the plans of Pius IX, which had been so favorable to the restoration of the melodies in their integrity? Was there not a manifest contradiction between the first declaration and the new one?

No, gentlemen, the Pontifical attitude did not change. Pius IX, when he gave his approval to the Neo-Medicean edition, considered himself to be furthering his object; for he was told that this edition contained the ancient version of the Gregorian melodies. He was deceived, and with him the Sacred Congregation of Rites.

This is evident from two of the briefs to the publisher. It is an important point, for here we have the source of that error which has caused so much disturbance and the responsibility for which must rest wholly upon the publisher and his adviser. First let us glance at the Brief of January 20, 1871. The publisher has finished the octavo edition of the *Gradual:* The Sacred Congregation strongly recommends it, says the decree, *maxime commendat,* to the Ordinaries, because it may help much to amplify divine worship and to apply the *genuine* Gregorian Chant to the liturgy of the Church: *ad genuinum cantum gregorian in liturgia adhibendum.*

Note the word *genuinum,* genuine, authentic, ancient. If you think the true sense of this word debatable, here is the Sacred Congregation's own commentary upon it, in a new Brief of August 14, 1871, the same year as the foregoing. The printing of the first folio volumes of the Gradual *ad instar editionis Mediceae* is now ended; of course the publisher asked for a Brief, and got it. Listen: "Inasmuch as this edition contains the Gregorian Chant, which the Roman Catholic Church has *always* kept, and therefore, by reason of *tradition,* may be held to be more in agreement with that which the Sovereign Pontiff, Saint Gregory the Great, had introduced into the sacred liturgy . . . therefore, the Sacred Congregation of Rites recommends it very strongly to the Ordinaries. . . ."

In 1871, then, the Sacred Congregation of Rites believed,

Restoration of Gregorian Chant

and so did Pius IX, that the *Medicean Gradual* contained the true Gregorian Chant.

Numerous articles were thereupon published praising the Neo-Medicean edition; and at these the musical world was much troubled; for within a quarter century Gregorian science had made such progress that blunders like these could no longer be committed without rousing warm protests. These protests were not without effect, for the two briefs which I have just quoted were not long in disappearing from circula-tion, and later decrees, when they mentioned the Medicean Chant, had recourse to vaguer terms, like "Gregorian Chant," "Roman Chant."

Such mistakes are regrettable, doubtless, but easily ex-plained. The case was one in which archaeology and palaeog-raphy were to be applied to the restoration of an art; and in this purely scientific field ecclesiastical authority was bound to rely upon specialists. I have mentioned the specialists who gave the information—the publisher and his adviser—and I shall not dwell upon the point. Let us observe only this: that the authorities, in so far as they merely *recommended,* and de-spite all urging, resolutely refused to *impose,* the new edition upon the churches, said plainly enough that they were holding to their principles, and were reserving the right to reverse their first decision upon riper consideration, as soon as the great works of restoration, then under way, should have reached their full maturity.

Meanwhile, however, the Medicean edition, with its thirty-year privilege, seriously threatened the full restoration of the Gregorian melodies, or at least delayed it a long while. Dom Gueranger had not concealed his feelings about this make-shift; nor did it, when it appeared, cause him to change them; his monks, under his encouragement, continued their research only the more energetically; but the great Abbot passed away in 1875 before he could see its effect.

The first result to be published was the volume which ap-peared in 1880, under Dom Couturier, his successor (1875-1890): *Les Mélodies Grégoriennes d'apres la tradition,* by the Reverend Father Dom Joseph Pothier, a Benedictine monk of Solesmes.

From this beautiful work two facts appeared clearly:

First: the traditional melodies of the Roman Church were preserved in manuscripts and could be read;

Second: the practical rules which must govern their rendition had been rediscovered.

Finally a new edition of the Chants was announced as in press. It has been said that there was nothing very new in this work. That may well be. Rheims and Cambria had already translated the ancient manuscripts fairly adequately; Canon Gontier, at the Congress of Paris in 1860, and in his excellent *Methode*, had already enunciated the fundamental rules which Dom Joseph Pothier repeated, but in the latter's books these two points were more solidly established, more fully developed. Be that as it may, this book had an absolutely unexpected success. It was translated into German and into Italian, and worked a veritable revolution in the rendition of plain song. All the new books of practical *Method* attached themselves to the teachings of the monk of Solesmes.

This success was undoubtedly due to the intrinsic value of the work, but it must be said too that the book had the luck to appear at exactly the right moment, at the very time when increasing opposition was arising against the new Medicean edition. This opposition was confused, without a leader, without any definite theory: there were protests, there was turmoil, there were agitations, but there was no plan. And behold, suddenly there arises a leader possessing a theory, a leader who promises an edition conforming to the manuscripts, a leader finally who belongs to the Abbey of Solesmes, and Solesmes means absolute devotion to the Holy See. Instantly all rally about him, under the protection of the name of Solesmes; all are reassured and believe that they may legitimately love the melodies in their primitive purity, fight for them, and choose them in preference to the mutilated and altered chants which are merely recommended, and that for only thirty years. So, bit by bit, a Gregorian army is formed, prepared to show its valor in favor of antiquity.

This state of mind was demonstrated in a striking manner at the European Congress, held at Arezzo, in September, 1882. Dom Joseph Pothier and his teachings were applauded and

Restoration of Gregorian Chant

acclaimed in the presence of representatives and partisans of the Neo-Medicean edition. A Mass, sung from the printer's proofs of the Solesmian *Liber Gradualis,* roused the audience "like an echo of ancient times." In short, the first resolution formulated by the Congress was the following: "That choral books should henceforward conform as closely as possible to the ancient tradition!" This was unanimously adopted with the exception of three votes.

Two days after this vote, which its opponents declared schismatic, the Congress almost as a body betook itself to the feet of the Sovereign Pontiff. What would be the attitude of Leo XIII? The survivors still remember it. He had naught but words of praise for the zeal and the labors of the Congress, for the encouragement of the search for tradition; and he showed a special kindliness toward Dom Joseph Pothier and the Benedictines who were present.

Here again we see the Papal attitude.

If you raise as an objection the approbation given earlier by the same Pontiff to the Neo-Medicean edition, I answer in the words of Leo XIII himself to Cardinal Caverot, Archbishop of Lyons, who had questioned him on this subject:

With regard to what you add in the matter of the books of Gregorian Chant published at Ratisbon, you need have no uneasiness. When recently there was presented to us a copy of this edition, executed with care and vised by the Sacred Congregation of Rites, *we could not but recommend this work both in speech and in writing—Non potuimus opus voce ac scriptis non commendare*—in view especially of the enormous expenditures which had to be made to undertake it and to bring it to a conclusion. However, there is no need to infer that all Cathedral churches have been forced to procure copies of that edition.

The Congress of Arezzo and the words of the Holy Father echoed loudly throughout the world; these words brought joy and hope to all who labored at the Gregorian restoration. Alas! this joy was not of long duration.

The adversary was watchful: this declaration took him by surprise; he must not let it go farther. He knew that the edition of the Solesmian *Liber Gradualis* was forthcoming.

It had to be nipped in the bud. He soon succeeded in ob-

THE CATHOLIC EDUCATIONAL REVIEW

taining from the Sacred Congregation of Rites action more important and more decisive than all preceding briefs: this was the decree *Romanorum Pontificum sollicitudo* of the 10th of April, 1883.

(*a*) This decree disapproved sharply all the resolutions of the Congress of Arezzo—especially the one concerning the exact restoration of the melodies.

(*b*) It approved as the only legitimate and authentic chant of the Roman Church the edition of Ratisbonne, since it must be called by its name.

(*c*) It recommended it strongly to the Ordinaries, *but always without imposing it;* even now the Neo-Mediceans had not been able to gain this point. Rome stood firm.

(*d*) It accorded, however, full liberty for theoretical and archaeological study of the liturgical chant.

It contained this sentence: "Consequently, there should no longer be either doubt or discussion upon the authenticity and the legitimacy of this form of chant among those who are sincerely submissive to the authority of the Holy See.

His Holiness approved the decree on the 26th of the same month. I hasten to tell you that the Sacred Congregation of Rites recalled this decree some years later, as soon as it realized that the facts upon which it was based were false.

But at the time of its appearance it retained its entire weight and authority. The Medicean camp was exultant; listen to one of its leaders: "As a glorious trumpet blast, triumphant yet peaceful, succeeds the alarming uproar and confused cries of battle, so resounded the Pontifical decree, '*Romanorum Pontificum,*' on the 26th of April, 1883."

It was indeed terrible; there was consternation, there was stupor everywhere among the friends of Solesmes, for Solesmes was directly aimed at. This was, so it seemed, the annihilation of all hope. A bitter time, the bitterest time in the history of Gregorian restoration—a time of. surrenders, of discouragements, and of painful defections. The periodicals most devoted to the Gregorian cause made it a duty—and who could blame them—to adhere to the decree "fully, absolutely, and without mental reservations or subterfuges of any kind." (*Musica Sacra,* of Ghent, 1883, page 92.) Canonists and

Restoration of Gregorian Chant

theologians, among them some who were in high office, most
of them perfectly incompetent musically—and for that very
reason all the more severe and cutting towards Solesmes—
interpreted it, some with restraint and moderation; others
with an implacable rigor which drew them to conclude that
the Ordinaries were under a *moral obligation* to adopt books
that were so earnestly recommended.

Under these distressing circumstances, the *Liber Gradualis*
was being completed at Tournai. It behooved the Abbot of
Solesmes, Dom Couturier, to publish it. What should he do?

This tender, straightforward, strong man was never wont
to draw back before his duty. He was the Abbot General of
all the monasteries of the Congregation of France; it was in
that capacity that he was to act; upon him would rest all the
responsibility.

(*a*) First of all, he inquired even at Rome itself as to the
Papal intent, and this in all intimacy and frankness; he
learned it and it reassured him.

(*b*) Besides, the Decree merely *recommended* the Neo-Medicean, but did not impose it: so there was freedom.

(*c*) Moreover, the great Religious Orders—the Carthusians,
the Cistercians, the Dominicans—have each their traditional
Chant: why should not the Benedictines, more ancient than
any of them, have theirs?

(*d*) The Bishop of Tournai had without hesitation given
his *Imprimatur* the 23d of May, 1883, less than a month
after the publication of the Decree.

And the Abbot published the *Liber Gradualis* with a calmness, boldness, and prudence, which is revealed to us by the
title itself: "Liber Gradualis a S. Gregorio magno olim
ordinatis, postea summorum Pontificum auctoritate recognitus
ac plurimum auctus, cum notis musicis ad majorum tramites
et codicum fidem figuratis ac restitutis in usum. Congregationis Benedictinae Galliarum praesidis ejusdem jussu editus
Tornai 1883." "Gradual, formerly arranged by St. Gregory
the Great; afterward recognized and much augmented by
authority of the Supreme Pontiffs; with music composed in
the ways of the ancients and restored according to the manuscripts, for the use of the Benedictine Congregation of France,

Published by order of its Abbot General. Tournai . . . 1883."

In this title every word counts: It is frank, for it does not conceal the fact that the new *Liber Gradualis* contains melodies of St. Gregory the Great restored according to the manuscripts;

It is bold, because it says so one month after the decree which disapproved these melodies;

It is prudent, because the *Liber Gradualis* did not in the least claim to impose itself upon the universal church, but was published by order of the Abbot of Solesmes, for the special use of his congregation.

I do not believe that I exaggerate, gentlemen, in saying that this was the serious moment in the history of the restoration. In so acting, Dom Couturier laid the official foundation upon which, after long and painful struggles, was to be based the liberating Motu Proprio of Pius X in 1903.

What would have happened if the Abbot of Solesmes, intimidated, paralyzed by discouragement and the loss of our friends, had stopped the publication of the *Liber Gradualis?* I know not. The Lord has a thousand means of reaching His ends. By this courageous act of faith in the final triumph of truth in the bosom of the Roman Church, our Abbot pierced the future and made certain the restoration of the liturgical melodies. Let us salute in passing the noble figure of this worthy successor of Dom Gueranger, to whom we owe so great a benefit.

The publication of this *Gradual* excited great irritation at Ratisbon. Naturally, for it was so much to the interest of the partisans of the Modern Mediccan edition to spread the belief that *their* edition contained the *Cantum Gregorianum "quem semper Ecclesia Romana retinuit, proindeque ex traditione conformior naberi potest illi quem in Sacram Liturgiam summus Pontifex sanctus Gregorius invexerat."* (Brief of August 14, 1871.) And now our attempt, now our labors, by re-establishing the Gregorian version in its primal purity, publicly gave them the lie direct. Henceforth, they felt, Solesmes was their enemy; nothing was left undone which might destroy its work, and represent the monks of that monastery as sons "in revolt" against the authority of the Holy See.

RESTORATION OF GREGORIAN CHANT

As for our friends, their courage had been slightly renewed by the action of the Abbot of Solesmes. Magazines, assemblies, and congresses discussed how the *Liber Gradualis* and the practical Method of Solesmes might be turned to account without disobeying the decree, so as to make the best possible use of the faulty editions spread throughout the various dioceses. But the comparison itself only led to a higher estimate of the primitive version of St. Gregory and to a severe criticism of all those modern editions, today defunct, which contained but a bare skeleton of the ancient liturgical melodies.

So much for the public. But what thought Leo XIII, the Holy Father?

His first act was praise, unreserved praise. On March 3, 1884, a few months after the publication of the *Liber Gradualis*, His Holiness addressed a brief to Dom J. Pothier, in which he praised the zeal and the intelligence of the author "in interpreting and explaining the ancient monuments of sacred music in their exact and ancient form, etc." The Holy Father added, moreover: "The Roman Church judges worthy to be always held in high honor this type of sacred melody, which is recommended by the name of St. Gregory the Great."

These words brought the monks of Solesmes relief and comfort. The Pope was saying all that he might say under existing conditions, in view of the thirty-year privilege accorded the Medicean edition; we could expect no more. He said: "Let them pass: hands off!" It was a permission to go on. We were reassured: we had only to sing in our Benedictine churches the Benedictine edition, and to continue our labors in peace.

Unfortunately this excellent situation was well-nigh compromised by ill-advised friends, who tried to interpret this brief as an appreciation almost equivalent to that given the Neo-Medicean edition. Their comments were imprudent and excessive; and we took no part in them. Our adversaries exaggerated these still more—used them to their own advantage—and on May 3 of the same year they obtained a second brief addressed to Dom Joseph Pothier, and explanatory of the first.

THE CATHOLIC EDUCATIONAL REVIEW

In this the Holy Father confirmed the praises contained in his first brief: "However," said His Holiness, "in order to prevent this Letter from giving occasion to false interpretations, We have thought best . . . to notify you . . . that We have had no intention of departing, in any particular whatever, from the published Decree . . . *Romanorum Pontificum sollicitudo,* and that We had not intended to approve, for use in the Sacred Liturgy, the Gradual which has been offered to Us. . . . " etc.

Which means clearly enough: Rome has given its approval and a privilege for thirty years to the Neo-Medicean edition. I cannot now approve another. Wait; be patient!

This letter simply put things back *in statu quo.* The *Liber Gradualis,* praised by the Holy Father, was to stand on its own feet, and to move slowly over the whole world, despite the innumerable obstacles raised by its adversaries. The Gregorian melodies by their own beauty were to win the esteem of all Catholic musicians. With time, success would be assured.

Still, this success must be made ready and hastened. After all, canonical discussions of briefs, of decrees, of personal interpretations, were secondary; the chief question lay in the intrinsic value of two opposing editions. If we should succeed in proving clearly that the melodies of the Neo-Medicean were but a wretched caricature of the primitive chants, the game would be won: at one stroke all decrees would crumble; for Rome, once in possession of all the elements of the question, would never permit, as events have well shown, that chants unworthy of divine worship should be used in Catholic churches. Mistress and guardian of the Arts, she holds these sacred melodies in trust; and will restore them to honor as soon as they have been restored to their ancient beauty, and have been proved authentic, not only *canonically,* but *historically.*

To this purely scientific field, then, the combat was to be transferred; there we were certain of victory. Besides, the modern Mediceans were triumphant enough to draw us thither. After their supreme claim of *authority,* which for reasons of

Restoration of Gregorian Chant

respect we would not answer, their favorite arguments were
these:

(a) That the edition of Solesmes could not obtain the chant
of St. Gregory, because that chant was lost.

(b) That even were it found, the manuscripts which contained it could not be deciphered.

To these unfounded assertions an answer was needed, but
one to which no reply was possible. Newspaper articles—
reviews? Everybody was tired of them. This kind of light
weapon would no longer do. The struggle had lasted fifteen
years (1868-1884). It must end. Fifteen years more and the
famous thirty-year privilege would expire: by that time Rome
must be made to see the light, and so clearly that Truth, as
mistress, would triumph there.

But what engine of war could overturn all obstacles and
hasten victory? A sort of scientific "tank" must be found,
powerful, invulnerable, capable of crushing all hostile
arguments.

A few young monks of Solesmes conceived this new machine
and devoted themselves to its launching. It was called
Paléographie Musicale. It was to publish in phototype the
principal manuscripts of the Gregorian Chant, with commentaries.

Dom Couturier, still our Abbot, upheld us with all his
might. At Rome itself, His Eminence Cardinal Pitra enthusiastically applauded us; and for our part, in order to demonstrate that we were submissive sons of the Holy See and
that we were undertaking this great work only for the honor
and glory of the Holy Church, we turned our eyes towards
its august head, praying him to bless our work and to accept
it in homage. The name and the blessing of Leo XIII, placed
at the head of our paleographic collection, gave it its best
protection.

The first volume to be published was a Gradual of the
tenth century, from the library of the Abbey of St. Gall,
which, about 790, had received the Roman Chant directly
from Rome. Comparison of this manuscript with our *Liber
Gradualis* proved that we had reprinted, note for note, group
for group, the true melodies of the Roman Church.

THE CATHOLIC EDUCATIONAL REVIEW

A proof so decisive should convince, it would seem, the most obstinate. It did not. The Neo-Mediceans contended that a single manuscript proved nothing; that, moreover, manuscripts scattered over the whole world *did not agree* among themselves; and that, in view of these divergences, the restoration of the true Gregorian Chant was impossible.

How was an assertion so unfounded to be refuted? How publish the hundreds of manuscripts dispersed in the libraries of every land?

Nevertheless, the challenge was accepted. A piece of music was chosen (the melody of the Response—Gradual *Justus ut Palma*), and reproduced from 219 antiphonaries of diverse origins, dating from the ninth to the seventeenth century. In this inquiry, all the churches, Italian, Swiss, German, French, Belgian, English, Spanish, were called to witness; and all testified in favor of the Gregorian musical tradition of the Roman Church by contributing to our collection with the exception of some insignificant variants of detail, *always the same melody*—that of the Solesmian *Liber Gradualis*.

The proof was established for all right-thinking minds.

When the Benedictines had ascertained the outward form of the melody and its historical authenticity, they went further. By means of exact analyses, which entered into minutest details, they rediscovered the laws of composition of this ancient musical language—the rules whereby the words were applied to the melody; the rules of tonic accent; the rules regarding weak penultimate syllables; the rules governing the *cursus* in the melody, as conforming to the cursus of the text.

In the structure of these chants, they established a whole series of ingenious and artistic processes transferred from language to music: for example, in a certain given melodic formula, suppressions or additions of notes required by modifications of the text; or again, contractions or permutations of notes or groups; all of which the composers employed according to rules which were completely and adequately verified by numberless examples drawn from the most ancient Gregorian pieces.

These unexpected discoveries came just in time. In them the defenders of Gregorian art had the luck to possess a

Restoration of Gregorian Chant

whole armory of weapons of the finest temper, a full array of evidence, new and irrefutable, to bear witness against the Neo-Medicean edition, and to save from shipwreck this art, this priceless treasure of the Church. Until then the *Paleographic Musicale* had worked defensively and reconstructively; henceforth, it was in a position to take a vigorous offensive, and to become that engine of war of which I just spoke to you, destined to annihilate the spurious Gregorian Chants of the edition of Ratisbon.

To accomplish this, all that was needed was to set up comparative tables between the two editions. On the one hand, the ancient version with a short account of its laws of composition; on the other hand, the Neo-Medicean version, with its mutilations and its absolute ignorance of the rules. There was no need of talk; the mere sight of the tables carried conviction.

The Caecilia of Colmar summed up clearly the impression generally made by this synoptical arrangement: "The fifth table presents a musical phrase of the Vth mode, under the melody of which are placed twenty-three different texts. Here we find *intonation, recitation,* and *cadence,* perfectly distinguished: a definite musical structure. But while a single musical phrase of the manuscripts suffices for these twenty-three texts, the Ratisbon edition brings in a different chant for each of them, with important and arbitrary changes in the beginning, the middle, and the end of the versicle. A glance is enough to show that the Ratisbon edition, which, by reason of its abbreviations, is supposed to make Gregorian Chant easier, on the contrary, increases its difficulties frightfully. While the manuscripts give memory its proper function, by allowing a large number of texts to be grouped under a single melody, the Ratisbon edition absolutely rejects all the assistance that memory might afford, forces it to begin the study of the chant all over again for each new text, and, what is more, confuses and puts out the most practised musician."

These tables were the *coup de grace* of that poor edition: from the scientific point of view there was nothing left of it.

At the same time, they refuted all the empty arguments upon which it claimed support.

THE CATHOLIC EDUCATIONAL REVIEW

It was supposed to have superior artistic beauty, but now it was proved to be only confusion and disorder.

It was supposed to be easier; and now by this disorder, it was shown to have multiplied difficulties "frightfully."

All that remained was its canonical authority; and in proportion as all other arguments crumbled under their feet, the partisans of the Neo-Medicean clung to this one. To all objections they kept answering: "Authority! authority!" To this, out of respect, we had no desire to answer; we kept waiting until Providence should furnish us the opportunity to enter into direct relation with this authority, which always and in all things seeks the truth. And now the hour of this beneficent Providence had come.

The first four volumes of the *Paléographic Musicale*, containing the researches of which I have spoken, had been published in five years, 1889-1894; with them hope had once more, little by little, taken possession of our hearts, and with our friends we could see dimly a favorable outcome for our painful ordeal. In the meanwhile, the search for the two hundred *Justus* had required us to make journeys to the libraries of Europe. We could not neglect Italy, Rome above all; and in 1890 Dom Couturier had sent thither two young monks, whom I am permitted to name, Dom Cabrol and myself—Dom Cabrol, now Abbot of Farnborough. They arrived in Rome toward the end of January, 1890. Their single aim was to reap the harvest of manuscripts and of *Justus* for the second and third volumes of the *Paléographic,* and they were resolved to hold to this aim.

A personal recollection: On the road to Turin, a kind Salesian had given me the address of the Reverend Father A. de Santi, Jesuit of the *Civiltà Cattolica*, to whom in 1887 the Holy Father had entrusted the task of treating in this review questions of religious music, and to *defend*, I was told, the *Neo-Medicean edition*. Father de Santi was already an important person, and the day after our arrival in Rome we paid him a visit. A long conversation showed us that the person with whom we had to deal was not blinded by passion, and was not beyond conviction: what he sought was the truth. He acknowledged the order which we had received from Leo

Restoration of Gregorian Chant

XIII, and he desired to obey it. While he recognized, in his candor, the superior value of our *Method,* he did not appreciate as yet the superiority of the Solesmes edition, and for the time being he desired to study, that he might best serve the cause of art and of the Church. Altogether, he was the Holy Father's right-hand man, and through him it might perhaps be possible to reach His Holiness and in time to enlighten him upon the true state of affairs.

But the situation was about to change, and events were to move quickly. The two Benedictines had taken up quarters at the French Seminary of Santa Chiara. They were careful not to make the slightest propaganda. At Rome, they thought, it was only proper to be prudent. How simple minded they were! They had been at the seminary only a fortnight when the Reverend Father Superior invited them to give a lecture to the pupils upon the subject of the Chant. Surprise, hesitation on the part of the Benedictines. The Superior insisted—reassured them as to the danger. In short, the lecture was given—purely scientific, you may well believe. Attracted by this beginning, some of the students had themselves initiated into the secrets of Gregorian melody. Astonished and delighted, they saw their numbers grow, a Schola was formed, and with the *Liber Gradualis* of Solesmes in their hands, its members sang the Mass *Reminiscere,* and sang it successfully.

This beginning encouraged our young people, and they prepared the magnificent *Mass Laetare;* I drilled them; they were enthused; they wanted an audience. Behold! They have become apostles. They invited their fellow students in the Roman College, and *Laetare* Sunday found the pupils of the various colleges of Rome assembled in the Chapel of the French Seminary. All colors are represented there; several even are clad in red. They and their choirmaster were Germans, destined to propagate the Neo-Medicean edition. The Reverend Father de Santi was present, well placed, surrounded by musical authorities. Our Schola outdid itself; the performance was a triumph for our ancient Gregorian Chant. "It is evident," said Father de Santi after the Mass, "that this Chant will one day be that of the Roman Church."

The Catholic Educational Review

At once the Superior decides definitely that the Schola is to be maintained: It is to sing from the *Liber Gradualis* of Solesmes, and the Solesmes *Kyriale* was adopted for the whole choir. And this at Rome!

Henceforth every Sunday drew new hearers to Santa Chiara. All were struck, all were ravished with the beauty of the Gregorian melodies. Soon the French Schola became well known at Rome; it was often invited to take part in ceremonies, and before very long even had imitators and rivals. Its head at that time was a young student, the Abbé Ginisty, today Bishop of our glorious city of Verdun. He himself later told the story of this introduction of the Solesmian Gregorian Chant into the French Seminary: "It is the sweetest memory of our clerical youth," he wrote in 1904, under Pius X, "and also the greatest honor, to have been at Rome itself . . . among the workers—among the least of them, it is true—for this restoration which is today being completed; and we are happy to have helped to realize in, though but a narrow sphere, yet precisely and in advance the very program marked out by the Sovereign Pontiff (Pius X)."

The next year, 1891, offered to the Benedictines and to the Schola of the French Seminary a providential occasion for the winning of fresh victories. The Holy Father, too, took advantage of it to manifest his attitude in a manner as striking as possible under the circumstances. A great Congress was to be held in Rome for the thirteenth centenary of the exaltation of St. Gregory, and in this, naturally, the Gregorian Chant held a prominent place. On the 29th of January, at the inaugural session at the French Seminary, in the presence of the Prefect of the Congregation of Rites and of Cardinal Parocchi, the Pope's vicar, the Reverend Father Grisar, of the *Civiltá,* publicly praised the book of Melodies Gregoriennes, by Dom Joseph Pothier; made formal mention of the liturgical and musical studies of the Benedictines of Solesmes and of their Paléographie Musicale; and, finally, he was not afraid to congratulate the young students of the Seminary. "It is known in Rome," said he, "with what artistic perfection and with what deep piety they render in their Church of Santa Chiara the ancient Gregorian melodies."

RESTORATION OF GREGORIAN CHANT

Such an opening of the celebration gave reason to anticipate that it would be truly worthy of our great St. Gregory; and indeed, on the 5th day of the following March, at another session, it was the students of the *Vatican Seminary* who offered to the Sovereign Pontiff a "specimen of sacred music," under the direction of the Reverend Father de Santi. The first part of the program took up the Gregorian Chant. Father de Santi, in bold outlines, sketched its history and made a comparison, striking in its truth, between Gregory the Great and Leo XIII; the first of whom presided at the organization of its melodies, and the second at their renaissance: The *"Revertimini ad fontes S. Gregorii,"* he said, in substance, "is the pass-word given out by the Pontiff; under his rule, archaeologists have searched antiquity, have discovered and have deciphered the manuscripts; better still, they have rediscovered the rhythm and restored the life of the ancient melodies." "The Gregorian notes," the orator exclaimed, carried away by his subject, "were like unto that field of scattered and dry bones which Ezekiel saw: *Fili hominis, putasne vivent ossa ista?* 'Son of man, dost thou think these bones shall live?' and a new Ezekiel came and answered: *'Ecce ego intromittam in vos spiritum et vivetis.'* 'Behold, I will cause breath to enter into you and ye shall live' (Ezekiel, 37). This new Ezekiel is Dom Joseph Pothier, of the Abbey of Solesmes"; and the orator developed this thought with irresistible eloquence.

Then Father de Santi rendered with his own choir two Gregorian melodies whose texts formed a part of the archives of St. Peters, and which conformed in every respect to the *Gradual* of Solesmes. Thenceforward his Schola followed the example of the French Schola.

Other similar renditions followed at Rome during the month of March. Cardinal Parocchi officially invited the French Seminary to adorn with its chants the celebrations of the centenary of St. Gregory upon the Caelian on the 11th and 12th of April. At the same time he directed an invitation to the Right Reverend Abbott of Solesmes, Dom Paul Delatte, begging him to be present personally or by his representative at these Gregorian celebrations.

THE CATHOLIC EDUCATIONAL REVIEW

In answer to this invitation, Dom Pothier and Dom Moc-quereau left for Rome, and on the 5th day of April were at the French Seminary. Hardly had they arrived when they began rehearsals. The students, happy and proud of the privilege which the Cardinal Vicar had granted them, desired to show themselves worthy of such confidence. They devoted themselves with zeal and singleness of heart to all the drilling which was required of them. Well they knew that from their chants, from their successes, a great good might ensue for the Gregorian cause, whereof they were the chief promoters and chief representatives at Rome.

The effect of the Mass was decisive. "The students of the French Seminary," said *La Civiltá Cattolica*, "rendered their program admirably. They caused all their hearers to sense the beauty of the Gregorian melodies in their true rhythm, which to a large portion of the audience seemed a musical novelty, or rather a return to antiquity, deserving of the highest praise. Of this, we can bear witness, not only for ourselves, but in the name of many competent Maestri and good judges, with whom we have conversed about this rendition." The whole press was unanimous in its approval.

But the young artists were to receive a much higher reward. I quote Monsignor Ginisty, Bishop of Verdun, who was then their head: "To crown these celebrations worthily, the Sovereign Pontiff deigned to receive in private audience the members of the Congress, who were presented to him by Cardinal Parocchi. In a *written* address, His Holiness heartily praised the organizers of the Centenary, and was pleased to recognize officially its success. As regards sacred music, the Sistine Chapel received well-deserved compliments; and then Leo XIII expressed his great satisfaction in that the French Seminary had during the Gregorian celebrations sung on the Caelian Hill the Chant of St. Gregory, *restored to its pristine purity.* "richiamato alla sua antica purezza."

These words were not only a reward, but a reassurance and a ground for hope. At last we Benedictines and our friends were no longer "in revolt," no longer "Jansenistes," no longer "heretics" (for all this was at one time said of us); on the contrary, our feet were set upon the good path—we had

Restoration of Gregorian Chant

heard it from the mouth of the Holy Father himself—in the path marked out by the successor of St. Gregory. We were merely profiting by that liberty which he had so often affirmed, and which now kept assuring us that with the aid of God, a complete victory would not be long deferred.

We had to leave Rome, to be sure, but we left there a group of friends, devoted to the Gregorian cause, with the Reverend Father De Santi at their head. We knew that we had the confidence of the Holy Father. It was to him that the Vatican would send bishops who wished information upon the question of liturgical chant. During our sojourn, an English-speaking archbishop had gone to see him upon such an errand at the *Civilitá* and said to him: "I no longer understand how things go in Rome. Only a few years ago (1883) you were inviting us vehemently to take the Medicean edition, and here today all the honors are going to Solesmes. Yesterday the Cardinal Vicar (Parocchi) was telling me himself that the Medicean edition was the worst of all." And the good archbishop continued his lamentations. The Reverend Father De Santi enlightened him, consoled him, told him the whole truth; and the prelate went away distressed at having adopted the Neo-Medicean in his diocese, foreseeing that very soon he would have to discard it.

The Gregorian Centenary celebration was soon echoed throughout the world. The phrases: "Revertimini ad fontes S. Gregori," and "Richiamato alla sua antica purezza," were repeated in newspapers, periodicals, and speeches, and hopes were raised high everywhere. Our friends kept growing bolder and bolder; in the years which followed (I can only sum up rapidly now), Gregorian Congresses and performances were multiplied; and the admirers of the restored melodies became innumerable.

It was just during these years, 1892, '93, '94 and the *Paleographie Musicale* was publishing those comparative tables which proved fatal to the Medicean edition; the accusing light upon its faults exasperated its partisans; feeling that it was mortally wounded, they resolved to do the impossible in order to save it; and they had recourse to their single engine of war —authority.

THE CATHOLIC EDUCATIONAL REVIEW

At Rome, they were still very powerful. There, one man above all others gave them trouble—a Jesuit, the Reverend Father de Santi; they determined to get rid of him, and finally obtained his removal. On January 20, 1894, he left Rome, armed, to be sure, with the paternal benediction of the Pope, and remaining attached, at the Holy Father's express desire, to the board of editors of the Civilta Cattolica. And his exile, if so it may be called, was to last but a few months.

Yet it was a bad beginning for the year, and it was to lead to worse, for the Mediceans meant to make good use of his absence.

This regrettable event did not damp the ardor of the Gregorianists; the light was so plain for right-thinking and well-informed minds, that the most earnest men, even certain canonists, as well as the most authoritative reviews, dared to demand openly the repeal of the decree *"Romanorum Pontificum sollicitudo"* (1883) and of the privilege of the publisher. And in this it was the spirit of faith, it was the Catholic spirit alone, that caused them to act and speak frankly and boldly. Let me give you an example:

The *Musica Sacra* of Ghent, published in Belgium under the patronage of the bishops, wrote these noble and loyal words (March, 1894, p. 65): "Moved by love of Holy Church—a sincere love which alone has guided us in these painful controversies—we believe it our duty at last to say a word, in all frankness and calmness, against such violent tirades and disingenious dealings. Yes, the honor of the Sacred Congregation is concerned, but in a sense quite the opposite of that which is supposed. (It was believed that to alter their decision would be to forfeit honor): the honor of the Sacred Congregation demands that it repeal the decrees relative to the privileges of the Ratisbon publisher." And the editors went on to set forth, from the canonical point of view, the reasons which required such repeal. I shall spare you these reasons, gentlemen, and say merely that the editors had no difficulty in proving their point. In France, in England, even in Germany, other voices were heard, insisting upon the same point.

The answer, gentlemen, was a new decree: *"Quod Sanctus*

Restoration of Gregorian Chant

Augustinus," published July 7, 1894. It maintained the preceding decrees, and particularly that of 1883. . . . recommended anew to ordinaries the Neo-Medicean edition; but this time again it imposed nothing, and left action free. On this point, the Holy Father, despite the reiterated efforts of our adversaries to have their edition *imposed* upon the Catholic world, had remained inflexible: once more he showed what would be his final attitude when the thirty year privilege should have expired.

The Catholic world received this document quite differently from that of 1883. The former, it will be remembered, had produced a profound stupor; the new one brought sadness without surprise; the movement of the Renaissance was scarcely retarded; rather it continued with even greater energy than in the past. The debates which had lasted for more than eleven years had thrown such light upon the *scientific*, *canonical* and *practical* situation, that doubt was no longer possible about the happy issue of this crisis. The enthusiasm in favor of the ancient melodies was too sincere, too universal, to be stopped: the new Decree came too late. Victory had already been virtually attained. Moreover, men's eyes were no longer turned toward the Sacred Congregation of Rites; they were directed to the Vatican.

Now the entire world knew that in the Vatican Seminary the Gregorian melodies, so eagerly sought elsewhere, had found asylum, and that with the supreme authorization of the Roman Pontiff, the pupils of this seminary, pontifical among all others, admired them and skilfully and lovingly performed them. Besides, all knew that when the new Decree had appeared, the Holy Father had sent word to the Vatican Seminary to change none of its habits, and to continue as in the past to chant from the books of Solesmes.

A remarkable coincidence, and a consoling one for us: The very day, the 7th of July, when the Decree was promulgated at Rome, there arrived at our abbey a young priest named Dom Lorenzo Perosi, sent by His Eminence the Cardinal Joseph Sarto, Patriarch of Venice, our future Pius X, to learn the Gregorian Chant of Solesmes. Some years later he was to be at the head of the Sistine Chapel.

THE CATHOLIC EDUCATIONAL REVIEW

The French Episcopacy, for its part, was moved no more
by the second Decree than it was by the first. In France the
dioceses, finding themselves all supplied with editions at the
time when the thirty year privilege began (in 1870) took
advantage of the liberty allowed by Rome to maintain the
status quo. Of eighty-four dioceses, two only accepted the Neo-
Medicean edition out of devotion and love for the Holy See,
and with eyes closed.

However, the Gregorian movement was ever gaining in
volume. A little more and the rising tide would carry everything with it. Even in Rome, the Vatican Seminary had imitators: at St. Anselm, at the French Seminary, at the South
American Seminary, at the *Collegio Capranica,* etc., etc. Sometimes, here and there, out of prudence, out of deference for
certain high and zealous Mediceans, the books of Solesmes
were for a time closed; then, the danger past, the rougish
younger set took to them again with greater joy and ardor.

The great Orders, Dominican, Cistercian, Franciscan, and
almost all the Benedictine Congregations, both of men and of
women, were coming back to the ancient melodies. The Carthusians had never given them up, and the Lazarists cultivated them with passion in their house at Paris and in their
Seminaries and missions. As to the churches, it would take
too long to enumerate the endless list of dioceses, cathedrals,
parishes, universities, seminaries large and small, religious congregations of both sexes, which henceforth used them in the
Mass. Decidedly, the old Roman melody had made its way
everywhere—in Italy, in Switzerland, in Germany, even in
Bavaria—two steps away from the citadel of Ratisbon; in Austria, in Spain, in England, where His Eminence Cardinal
Vaughan would have no other chant but that of Solesmes when
he decided to celebrate the divine office every day in his Cathedral. That is not all: henceforth, the Gregorian Chant
spread beyond the borders of Europe and was heard in Africa,
in Asia, in America.

In Europe a number of writers and artists of the lay world
took pains to give it prominence: Charles Bordes in his
Tribune de St. Gervais, founded in 1895; Camille Bellaigue
in the *Revue des Deux Mondes,* Laloy, Combarieu, etc. It was

RESTORATION OF GREGORIAN CHANT

taught at the Catholic University of Freiburg, in the Catholic Faculty of Paris. The greatest artists and composers of this period: Gounod, Guilmant, Capocci, Perosi, Tinel, Vincent d'Indy, and the rest, labored at its restoration and sought in it their most notable inspirations.

Even the Anglican Church did not remain alien to the movement. In August, 1897, twenty-three Anglicans arrived at Solesmes for the purpose of hearing the choir of monks and of learning the theory and practice of Gregorian Chant. Two of them had already made their first appearance at the abbey in 1894, Mr. Briggs and Dr. Gibbs, whom I am happy to greet here, one of the organizers of this Congress. These voyages of our neighbors from across the Channel gave us great consolation because they furnished an occasion for several of them to return to the Roman Church.

Our little printing-office at Solesmes could not satisfy the demands which came to it from everywhere. The *Liber Gradualis,* timidly published in 1883 for the use of the Benedictine Congregation in France, had been reprinted in 1895 for the entire Church. Antiphonaries Roman and monastic, and Vesper books, had been brought forth, likewise a *Liber Usualis,* a parochial Mass book for small churches and for colleges, and then extracts from these books: a Kyriale, various services, a Holy Week book, etc.—in short, a whole series of Gregorian publications whose diffusion has showed plainly enough that the Gregorian melodies were more and more in favor with the Christian public. It became more and more evident that, thank God, these crises were about to end, and that triumph was near.

Ever since the year 1891, the year of the Congress for the Centenary of St. Gregory—some excellent minds in Rome had realized that from the beginning of this affair they had been badly advised. They regretted above all, in silence, the publication of the Decree *Romanorum Pontificum sollicitudo* of 1883. The new edition of Gardellini, *"Decreta Authentica Congregationis Sacrorum Rituum,"* was being prepared; and there was some thought of not inserting this decree, and of thereby suppressing it. The events of 1894 put an end to this project. In 1899, at the very time when the Decree was to be

THE CATHOLIC EDUCATIONAL REVIEW

reprinted in the third volume of the collection, some of our friends raised anew at Rome the question of opportuneness. Several memoirs were presented to Cardinal Mazella, Prefect of the Sacred Congregation of Rites, who was well disposed toward Solesmes; one of them was signed by the pious Cardinal Richard, Archbishop of Paris. All were well received, and the suppression decided upon; in fact, in March, 1899, the sheets of the new edition went through the press, and the Decree of 1883 did not appear there.

The Decree of 1894 of *Quod S. Augustinus* was maintained out of regard for the cardinal who had signed it, and who was still living; but it was modified and softened so as to be rather favorable to the Gregorian thesis.

This victory, although incomplete, emboldened our friends to dare everything; besides it took from our adversaries their magnificent self-confidence. Shortly thereafter, the young Maestro Perosi achieved a truly bold stroke. Upon the occasion of the success of his Oratorio, the "Resurrection of Christ," Leo XIII had named him perpetual Master of the Sistine Chapel. In announcing this news to us, a friend wrote on his behalf that he had "firmly resolved to labor with all his powers . . . for the complete and early triumph of Solesmes." To this letter Dom Lorenzo Perosi had taken care to add his signature (December, 1898). On the 28th of May following (1899) the young Maestro kept his word, on the very day he took office. Upon the solemn occasion of the opening of the Council of (South?) American bishops in Rome in the Sistine Chapel, under his direction, in the presence of the Holy Father, the singers of the famous Schola performed for the first time in centuries several Gregorian melodies "brought back to their primitive purity." Thanks to Dom Perosi and to his devotion, the chants so long sung before Roman Pontiffs had once more taken their place, and had penetrated at last to the innermost sanctuary of the papacy.

We reach the eve of the year 1900, which brought the end of the thirty-year privilege. For the last year, a final and mighty effort to save the recommended edition was to be expected.

The Mediceans knew beyond a doubt, by the repeated checking of all their activities that neither the Sovereign Pontiff

Restoration of Gregorian Chant

nor the Congregation of Rites would ever consent to impose the abridged songbooks upon the Catholic world; and they gave up the idea. But, at least, they thought, could they obtain this imposition for the diocese of Rome? Their books had been edited by Palestrina; they contained the Chant of Paul V, which had become for thirty years, the "official" chant, the distinctively "Roman" chant; moreover, the publisher had struggled, toiled, suffered for the Holy See, for Rome. Did he not deserve a reward? For the future it would be a stepping stone: the example of Rome could in the long run carry with it other Catholic dioceses. It was a last card to play.

To prepare and assure the carrying out of this plan, zealous workers went to seminaries, colleges, and monasteries where the Gregorian melodies were being cultivated; they recalled the recommendations in favor of the "official" edition, the "Roman" edition which soon they added, would be imposed upon the diocese of Rome! These visits, this advice, which could not be overlooked, once more troubled men's spirits: the whole year 1900 was a painful one in Rome for those who favored the restoration.

At about this time also Monsignor Carlo Respighi, the Pontifical Master of Ceremonies, by the help of documents recently discovered, attacked sharply, and overturned the thesis of Ratisbon which affirmed that "Palestrina authority for the Medicean edition." His article, first published at Madrid in a Spanish review (*Ciudad de Dios*, September 1899) was later reprinted in Rome by the publishing house of Desclée. Soon after, at the beginning of 1900, the Reverend Father Dom Raphael Molitor, of the Abbey of Beuron, brought new proofs to the debate, and upon this point attained absolute demonstration. Thus, the last historical rampart behind which the Neo-Medicean edition kept sheltering itself was breached.

There remained the danger, serious and threatening—of imposition upon the diocese of Rome. Once again this danger was momentarily removed. After repeated and urgent proceedings against the plan, high authority declared that "if the imposition upon Rome had been decided, at least it would be deferred for the time being." The threat was still imminent. Yet we were almost at the end of this thirty year

THE CATHOLIC EDUCATIONAL REVIEW

crisis, and it was destined to be followed by a peace which
was to be complete and definitive.

At the beginning of January, 1901, the seminaries were still
laboring under this painful impression. To dissipate it His
Eminence Cardinal Parocchi requested of the Holy Father,
January 12, 1901, a declaration of policy with regard to the
Gregorian question; he wished to give a pertinent answer to
the rectors, who kept incessantly consulting him. The Holy
Father answered: "Say from Us that they are to stop troubling
the colleges; say to the rectors and to others who are interested in the colleges that they are not to disquiet themselves,
but are to sing and cause to be sung whatever they deem best
and most suitable. . . New Decrees? No, We shall issue
none; We must find a way other than that which has been
followed hitherto; and upon this We ourself shall take
thought."

The orders of Leo XIII were carried out punctually, to the
delight of all. Only a few days after these words of deliver-
ance had been pronounced, we at Solesmes were officially invited to send to the Holy Father without delay a memorandum
relating in some detail all our labors—scientific, theoretical
and practical, in favor of the Gregorian Renaissance. At the
beginning of February the same year, this memoire, signed by
the most Reverend Abbot Dom Paul Delatte, in the name of
the Paleographic School of Solesmes, was in the hands of Cardinal Satolli, Prefect of the Sacred Congregation of Studies,
who undertook to present it to the Holy Father. It was presented on the 23 of March and was kindly received. Finally,
on the 17 of May following, His Holiness answered by the
Brief "Nos Quidem," addressed to the most Reverend Father
Delatte, Abbot of Solesmes.

Permit me, gentlemen, to read you the estimate of this decisive brief given by the Civiltá Cattolica:

Those who have kept up with the facts of the thirty-year
controversy upon Gregorian Chant will be forced to admire
in this very important document the lofty wisdom, together
with the exquisite delicacy of wording and phrasing, with
which His Holiness has deigned to resolve a question which
long seemed insoluble, or at the very least, and in many ways,
exceedingly thorny.

Restoration of Gregorian Chant

Leo XIII praises amply the long and arduous labors which the Benedictines have devoted to the restoration of the traditional melodies of St. Gregory, as they are found in the ancient books of the Church, and this not only from the point of view of purely theoretical studies, but also from that of practical daily use in the sacred liturgy. Today this use has already spread far and wide, thanks to the beautiful and careful editions of liturgical chant published at Solesmes, and to the remarkable ease with which Gregorian melodies may be rendered in accordance with the method taught by these monks.

Consequently the beauty and the sweetness of these original melodies, as well as the virtue which they possess in themselves to clarify and vivify the words of the liturgy, and thereby to arouse religious feelings in the soul of the faithful—all these are expected by the Sovereign Pontiff to enhance notably the splendor of our worship. With this in view, he sets up the work of the Benedictines of Solesmes as a pattern of Gregorian studies, and in words of great kindness exhorts all who feel themselves capable of doing anything in this matter, especially the members of the clergy, both secular and regular, to concur together, by efforts undertaken *solerter et libere,* skillfully and freely—with the assurance that they will be useful, and without any fear that they shall henceforth find themselves in any manner thwarted, provided that they keep always mutual charity and the submission and respect due to the Church.

The brief, "Nos Quidem," is therefore not only a well deserved eulogy of the monks of Solesmes, it is also a lesson for us all. It points the way which for the future should be followed by all friends of the Gregorian melodies, the only way which can lead to acceptable results, that is, the way of knowedge and of skill, of history and of tradition.

The struggle has ended; the Papal intent is triumphant; the Catholic world accepts it with joy and at once sets to work to realize it.

Among those who set to work without delay, I am happy to mention in the very first place His Eminence Cardinal Gibbons. I read from the Roman correspondence of the *Univers* of Paris: "Last Sunday (June 9, 1901) (consequently only a few days after the publication of the brief *Nos Quidem*) His Eminence Cardinal Gibbons, accompanied by two Sulpician priests, paid a visit to the Latin American *Collegio Pio,* which is the South American Seminary. The cardinal had expressed a wish to hear Gregorian melodies chanted by the students according to the method of the Benedictines of Solesmes. . . . At the end of this musical performance, His Eminence made an address to the students of the Latin American college, and

The Catholic Educational Review

commented upon the very recent Brief of Leo XIII to Dom
Delatte, adding that what he had just heard confirmed him
in his intention to introduce into the Baltimore Seminary the
traditional melodies of the Church according to the method
of Solesmes."

It seems to me, gentlemen, that the germ of the magnificent
ceremonies which are unfolding before our eyes was in the
decision taken by His Eminence Cardinal Gibbons. His Eminence followed out obediently the intent of the Holy Father
as soon as that was fully manifested, and his obedience drew
America in its train. *Vir obediens loquetur victorias.*

And now, gentlemen, you know the rest. Events are still
too recent not to be in everybody's memory. It is enough to
recall them rapidly—they speak for themselves with an eloquence of their own.

Leo XIII (20th July, 1903) did not have time to finish his
plans for restoration. Providence reserved this joy for his
glorious successor, Pius X, and you know what eagerness and
what liberality he brought to this work. Scarcely upon the
Pontifical throne, this new Gregory launched his memorable
Motu Proprio upon sacred music at the feast of the Roman
virgin, St. Cecilia, November 22, 1903. There the place of
honor was held by the Gregorian melodies. February 24,
1904, upon the order of the Holy Father, the Sacred Congregation of Rites declared that the editions of Solesmes were in
conformity with the *Motu Proprio.* Then came April, 1904,
the unforgettable festivals upon the Centenary of the death
of St. Gregory the Great, with the Papal Mass at St. Peter's
on Monday, the 11th of April, "festivals which were celebrated," Pius X said afterwards, "in order to consecrate
the beginnings of the restoration of Gregorian Chant." This
Mass was the culminating point of this apotheosis of the ancient Gregorian melodies. I was there, gentlemen. It was
incomparable; nothing in the most beautiful dreams of our
days of toil came near the triumphal, the royal, the pontifical
glories which in honor of Gregory the *Incomparable,* "*Viri
incomparabilis,*" says the Martyrology, were unrolled before
us. Then, to crown the whole, to perpetuate in the ceremonies
of all the churches the songs which had just been honored,
came the *Motu Proprio* of the 25th of April, which decrees

Restoration of Gregorian Chant

and organizes the Vatican edition, and marks out the general rules according to which it is to be composed. Finally on the 22nd day of May there issued a new brief to the Most Reverend Dom Delatte, which entrusts to the Benedictine Congregation of France, and especially to the Monastery of Solesmes, the editorship of this new edition.

Before receiving his eternal reward, Pius X had the consolation of approving and imposing the Gradual and Antiphonary. He also gave his blessing January 4, 1911, to the beginnings of the Pontifical School of Sacred Music at Rome, upon which he built the greatest hopes for the realization throughout the whole world of the prescriptions of the *Motu Proprio.*

Benedict XV continues today the tradition of Pius X: "It is at least an equal kindness which the school has met with at the hands of His Holiness, (who) considers it as a very precious heritage from his holy predecessor."

Furthermore, the Vatican Edition is making progress: the editing of the books which are still to appear continues to be entrusted to the Benedictines of the Abbey of Solesmes at Quarr Abbey. Under the reigning Pope there have already appeared, 1916, the chants of the Passions, *Cantus Passionis Domini Nostri Jesu Christi,* restored to their pristine simplicity. The work upon the *Liber Nocturnalis* is well advanced. In a few months the Vatican Press will give us the book containing the entire Holy Week services, and the remainder will follow shortly. And thus will be completed the ideal of the last four Roman pontiffs.

My part as historian has ended; will you now, gentlemen, permit me to be a prophet? In the presence of so magnificent a manifestation, there is no need of a light from on high to pierce the future. In the question of Gregorian music, Rome is your signal light, the *Motu Proprio* your guide; the whole American Catholic people with their bishops at their head show today that they are determined to follow it. Very soon, to serve this general desire, you will have in your seminaries, your parishes, your communities, many professors able to teach you. Neither knowledge, nor devotion, nor even money will be wanting to bring to its accomplishment this great artistic and liturgical work. Doubtless there will be difficulties, there will be contraditions, there will be faintings by the way; you will need patience, you will need time; but you will triumph in the end because you are Americans and Roman Catholics, and because you know how to will and to achieve. Yes, it will not be long, for in your country things move quickly —it will not be long before the United States and all the nations of America shall sing unanimously the ancient Gregorian Chant, the joy of the ancient Christian world. This is my prophecy! It shall be fulfilled—it shall be fulfilled to the Glory of God.

The Art of Gregorian Music[1]

I

ITS AIMS, METHODS, AND CHARACTERISTICS

Plato has given us an excellent definition of music. "It is," he says, "art so ordering sound as to reach the soul, inspiring a love of virtue." He would have the best music to be that which most perfectly expresses the soul's good qualities. "It is to serve no idle pleasures," he says in another place, "that the Muses have given us harmony, whose movements accord with those of the soul, but rather to enable us thereby to order the ill-regulated motions of the soul, even as rhythm is given us to reform our manners, which in most men are so wanting in balance and in grace." This was the high ideal which the Greeks had of music. It was, in their conception, the expression of order in all things: far from regarding it as a mere pastime, they made it the indispensable foundation of civilization and morality, a source of peace and of order for the soul, and of health and beauty for the body. Their masters were insistent that "rhythm and harmony should be so identified with the minds of the young that as they became more balanced and composed, they might be better able to

[1]The present article is the first of a series of translations of writings by the Reverend Dom Andre Mocquereau, O.S.B., of Solesmes, which are to be published by the Catholic Education Press with a view to making available in the English language the scholarly and scientific works on Gregorian Chant which have hitherto been available to French readers only.

The Art of Gregorian Music has been selected as a suitable beginning because it deals on broad lines with the principles underlying the restoration of the liturgical chant of the Catholic Church. The paper was originally read before the Catholic University of Paris in 1896 and thus antedated by nearly a decade the official action of the Holy See. In spite of this fact the translators have thought best to reproduce the paper without any attempt to bring it up to date in detail, partly because of its historical interest, but chiefly because, dealing as it does with the subject on broad and general lines, it forms an ideal introduction to the more detailed study of the liturgical chant which will follow in the monumental work of Dom Mocquereau: *Le Nombre Musical Gregorien.*

speak and act aright. For, as a matter of fact, man's whole being has need of rhythm and of harmony."[2]

The very nature of that music, its dignity and simplicity, its gentle, tranquil movement seconded the master's endeavors, and led, as it were, naturally to the desired end. "The ancients," says Westphal, "never attempted to express the actual and passionate life of the soul. The noise and bustle whither modern music carries our fancy, the representation of strife and strain, the portrayal of those opposing forces which contend for the mastery of the soul, were all alike unknown to the Greek mind. Rather was the soul to be lifted into a sphere of idealistic contemplation, there to find peace with herself and with the outer world, and so to rise to greater power of action."[3] Greek music may not always have remained faithful to this ideal, but it is enough to know that in its primitive purity it rose to such heights.

The Catholic Church, that society of souls established by our Lord Jesus Christ, is the depository of all that is good and beautiful in the world. She inherited the traditions of antiquity, and gave a foremost place to the art of music, using it in her liturgy as well as for the instruction and sanctification of her children, no light task indeed when one recalls the state of society when that peaceful conquest was begun. But Holy Church set her strength and her hope in her divine Head, that true Orpheus, whose voice has power to charm the beasts, and melt the very rocks. She had, moreover, treasured those words of St. Paul: "Teach and admonish one another in psalms and hymns and spiritual canticles." In the mouth of the great Apostle this precept had all the force of law: rightly, therefore, may music be considered a constituent element of the Church's worship. St. Dennis was of this opinion, and none have treated of the divine psalmody with greater insight than he. It was, in his conception, the preparation for the deepest mysteries of the faith. "The hallowed chant of the Scriptures," he writes, "which is essentially a part of all our

[2]His Eminence Cardinal Penaud commented upon these last few lines in his impressive and charming pages upon the rôle of music in education. I feel bound to call attention here to this book, the title of which is: Eurythmie et Harmonie, Commentaire d' une Page de Platon. Paris, Téqui, 1896.
[3]Westphal, Metrik, I, p. 261.—Cf. Gervaert, Histoire et théorie de la musique de l'antiquité, I, p. 36.

mysteries, cannot be separated from the most sacred of them all (he is speaking of the mystery of the Eucharist or Synaxis). For in the whole sacred and inspired Book is shown forth God, the Creator and Disposer of all things." St. Dennis then describes that great drama at once human and divine which is enacted in our sacred books, and in the liturgy, and continues: "Wherefore the sacred chants form, as it were, a universal hymn telling forth the things of God, and work in those who recite them devoutly an aptitude for either receiving or conferring the various sacraments of the Church. The sweet melody of these Canticles prepares the powers of the soul for the immediate celebration of the holy mysteries, and by the unison of those divine songs, brings the soul into subjection to God, making it to be at one with itself and with its fellows, as in some single and concordant choir of things divine."[4] Peace, strength, purity, love: in very truth, the music of the Christian Church soars to greater heights than that of the ancients.

Is it possible, however, for any music of man's making to realize this ideal? Can modern music do so? If the question were put, no doubt the answer would be, *"Quo non ascendam?"* What shall hinder it? Were you to enquire of M. Combarieu, who has plunged more deeply than any other critic into the potentialities and ideals of music,[5] he would doubtless reply that this high ideal does not transcend its powers. But although I both admire and respect the views of this distinguished musician, I cannot share them. I know modern music well: it cannot, in its present form, rise to the heights of the Christian ideal. And if you name those great creators of the classic symphony, Haydn, Mozart, Beethoven, Berlioz, I must again answer in the negative. Those eagles of their art never attained to the tranquil spheres of Chris tian music. They had indeed force of conception, inspiration, the flight of genius: some had, moreover, the light of faith, the flame of love; one thing only was lacking, and that was a language so pure, so free from all earthly alloy, as to be able to echo faithfully that divine calm, that ordered peace, that ever attuned melody which rings in the heart of Holy

---

[4] S. Dionysius Areop. De Eccl. Hierarchia. Ch. III.
[5] *Jules Combarieu, des Rapports de la Musique et de la Poésie considerées au point de vue de l'expression.* (Paris, Alcan.) Ch. IV.

Church, and reminds the exiles of earth of the tranquil, endless harmonies of the heavenly Jerusalem.

Far be it from me that, in thus criticising these great composers, I should seem to disparage them. To disown them
would be to disown my dearest memories. Often, as a child,
I was lulled to sleep to the sound of the sonatas, the trios and
the quartets of Beethoven, Mozart, or Haydn. And when I
grew to man's estate, I took my place as 'cellist in an orchestra
conducted by that revered master, M. Charles Dancla, a professor at the Conservatoire. I know the power of orchestral
music. At Pasdeloup, and at the Société du Conservatoire
more especially, I was alternately swayed, overwhelmed,
soothed and entranced; it is the conviction born of this experience that enables me to assert today that the ideals of Christian art are not, and cannot be, found therein.

Is, then, this ideal realized by Palestrina? A few days
hence, in this very place, M. Bordes, one of the greatest
authorities on this subject, will, no doubt, answer this question.
Moreover, M. Camille Bellaigue has already treated of the
characteristics and the beauties of Palestrina's compositions
in the *Revue des Deux Mondes*. One remark, however, I will
allow myself: The Church could not have allowed sixteen
centuries to elapse before she found a chant befitting her
worship.

Shall we, then, find what we seek in the Gregorian chant?
I venture to think so: nevertheless, it must be borne in mind
that this hallowed chant has in our days so fallen into dis-
repute, and is so condemned and discredited that to present
this patrician outcast as the most artistic and finished realization of the Church's prayer would seem folly. That music
which, in the days of its glory, was so full of beauty, is today
unrecognizable. Like the Master whom it hymns, the chant
is come to the hour of its passion. "*Non est species ei, neque
decor, et vidimus eum et non erat aspectus et desideravimus
eum.*" There is neither beauty nor comeliness: the music which
we hear in our churches does not attract us: it is an object
of contempt: "*Unde nec reputavimus eum.*"[6]

And yet, notwithstanding its sorry plight, something of the

---

*This was written in 1896, before the time when Pope Pius X restored
the Gregorian melodies officially, in a version which has been made
binding upon the universal Church.

ancient power and majesty remains. You have but to read the impressions recorded by Durtal in Huysman's book, "En Route," to see that the chant is still able to turn souls to God. Along the way, bestrewn with relics and with blood, are yet some faithful ones who pray and hope beside the grave where the chant awaits the day of resurrection. That day, gentlemen, has already dawned: A day real enough, even if not all glorious and resplendent as that of the Master. In many places the chant, even now is heard. Rome has summoned it to the venerable feasts of St. Gregory: it is installed in the Vatican; Venice has restored it to its former place beneath the dome of St. Mark's. Everywhere the chant is found: in Belgium, in Germany, in England, in Spain, in America. It is used by all the great religious orders; in France it has invaded all our churches. It has existed in a quiet way in Paris for some years, and today you meet it at the Institut Catholique, so that it may be said to have fairly established itself in the very stronghold of intellectual culture. You are soon to hear the chant for yourselves, and I trust that its artless, unaffected beauty will go straight to your hearts. But before you do so, you will allow me, I hope, a few words by way of introduction.

The chant is invariably set to words. Among the ancients music was regarded as the auxiliary of poetry: "It was speech raised to the highest term of power, acting simultaneously upon the sensitive and intellectual faculties."[1] Unconscious of its own power, music did not at once throw off the yoke of centuries in the first ages of Christianity. Indeed, had it existed as a separate art, the Church would not have made use of it. Music without words would not have served her end, which is to give her children not sacred melodies only, and vague musical impressions, but also theological and philosophical truths, and definite acts of faith, of love and of praise, which music alone could never formulate.

The primitive conception of music was therefore perfectly adapted to the Church's purpose. Set, as it were, at the confluence of those two streams of civilization, the Jewish and the Graeco-Roman, the Church, with her rare insight, borrowed from the music of both whatever was most suited to her pur-

---

[1] *Lamennais. Esquisse d'une philosophie*, III, p. 293.

pose. The words, and also the whole scheme of her psalmody, were taken from the books of Holy Scripture, that treasure the Church had received from the Lord's hands. The psalmody of the Roman office, indeed, with its verses and strophes characterized by antiphons, which serve as refrains, has a most unmistakable Jewish flavor. The Psalter stood forth above all others as the book of divine praise: the Church added thereto songs of her own making. This is not the place to remind you of the surpassing beauty of the Liturgy: it ought, nevertheless, to be done, for, in order fully to fathom the meaning of the chant, it is imperative that we should understand, love, and live those hallowed canticles. For it must ever be borne in mind that they are the essential part of plainsong.

But however great their beauty, the mere recitation of the words does not suffice. The Church does not merely know her dogmas: she loves them, and therefore she must sing them. "Reason," wrote Joseph de Maistre, "can only speak; but love sings." But the Church sings for yet another reason. Although the word of God has such power that it would seem that the mere hearing would enthrall both mind and heart, it is, alas, addressed to mortal men, to souls dull and heedless, buried, as it were, beneath the covering of flesh and sense, which must be pierced before it can touch them. And therefore the Church summons to her aid that most subtle and penetrating of all arts, music. Albeit inferior to speech in the world of the intelligence, it reigns supreme in the world of sense, possessing, as it does, accents of matchless strength and sweetness to touch the heart, to stir the will, and to give utterance to prayer.

It was from the Graeco-Roman stream that the Church borrowed the elements of her music. She chose diatonic melody because of its dignity and virility, for chromatic and inharmonic melodies accorded but ill with the pure worship of God. It is, moreover, probable that the Church adapted her songs to the Greek modes and scales; to what extent, however, it is impossible to say. It has been recently asserted, though without any sort of proof, that the pagan airs or nomes, were adopted by the Church, and used by the early Christians, but this assertion is in manifest contradiction with all that we know of the Fathers, and of the Councils, as well as with the mind of the Church. Until further information comes

to hand, I incline to think that the airs to which our antiphons are set, whether simple, florid, or neumatic, are in very
deed of the Church's own composition.

Whether this be so or not, of this marriage of Jewish poetry
done into Latin, with the chant, was born a new art, perfect
in its kind, which, though imbued with the principles of
antiquity, was nevertheless well fitted to serve the Church's
purpose. One of our modern poets[8] most aptly describes it:

Beau vase athénien, plein de fleurs du Calvaire.

And so it is: Like the music of the ancients, its offspring is
simple and discreet, sober in its effects; it is the humble
servant, the vehicle of the sacred text, or, if you will, a
reverent, faithful, and docile commentary thereon. Even as
a healthy body is an instrument perfectly fitted to serve the
soul, and to interpret its workings, so the chant interprets the
truth, and gives it a certain completeness which words alone
could not achieve. The two are bound up together: the word
sheds the rays of intellectual light upon the mysterious shadow
world of sound, while the melody pervades the words with
deep inward meaning, which it alone can impart. Thus
mingled, one with the other, music and poetry ravish man's
whole being, and uplift the soul to the blissful contemplation
of truth.

Before we pursue our subject further, you ought to hear
some examples of plainsong. The real value of a statue
cannot be estimated from a description, however graphic.
And so I propose setting before you a fair statue of ancient
church music, not mutilated, but restored, living, and complete. It will be easier for me afterwards to make you admire
the dignified simplicity, the harmony and proportion, of its
lines, and the pervading sweetness of its expression.

To aid me in this attempt, the execution of the chant should
be perfect. The voices should be pure, flexible, and trained
as in the great academies of the capital. Nevertheless, I
have thought it better not to choose trained singers for my
purpose. Not that I consider art to be a negligible quantity
in the execution of plainsong. On the contrary, it is a point
on which many, unhappily, have fallen into regrettable ex-
aggerations which are only calculated to discredit the chant.
But on this occasion, in order to prove that a lengthy train-

[8]Victor de Laprade.

ing is not an indispensable condition, and, at the same time,
to show what results may be attained by such ordinary means
as may everywhere be found, and in the conviction, moreover,
that culture and intelligence will always give a better rendering than mere art, however perfect, I have chosen some young
men who would be much astonished were I to introduce them
to you as great artists. I therefore refrain from doing so;
this, however, I may say of them, they have the type of soul
which can appreciate and render these holy melodies.

[At this point the Schola sang the following simple chants:
An Ambrosian *Gloria in excelsis*, the Ambrosian antiphon
In Israhel, followed by the psalm *Laudate Pueri*, and the
Gregorian antiphon *Cantate Domino* with the *Magnificat*.]

II

Gentlemen, you have been listening to plainsong in this
simplest form. We shall now be able to study its features, its
aspect, and expression. If it be beautiful, wherein does its
beauty lie—is it of earth or of heaven? And if this beauty
be something heavenly, if it act upon our souls like a gentle
and refreshing dew, how does it go to work? What are its
means of action, the elements of which it makes use? This
we must first ascertain by a rapid analysis of details. I do
not propose to do more today than to sketch these in brief.

When I was speaking a little while ago of the marriage of
words and music in the chant, I omitted to say that some
modern critics have drawn a somewhat surprising conclusion
from this fact. They allege that this intimate connection between text and melody is precisely the principle underlying
modern musical drama, which has reached its zenith in the
works of Richard Wagner. The famous composer, alluding to
his opera, "Tristan and Isolde," says: "In 'Tristan' the fabric
of the words has the full compass planned for the music: in
fine, the melody is already constructed in poetic form."[9] But
may not Wagner's rule be applied most exactly to plainsong?
Whereupon the critics forthwith leap to the conclusion that
Gregorian music is Wagnerian music and vice versa.

To maintain such a conclusion, however, it is evident that
one or other of the terms of the comparison must be omitted.

---

[9]*Richard Wagner. Lettre sur la musique à M. Frédéric Villot.*

The snare into which the critics have fallen is obvious. They should have foreseen that although the principles which govern Gregorian and Wagnerian music are identical, the same principles in application may attain widely differing results. And, as a matter of fact, have you not noticed that as we listen to these melodies, our habits, taste, and judgment are utterly nonplused? The truth is that, there, a wide gulf separates the chant from Beethoven's overpowering symphonies and Wagner's fantastical dramas. Though the expression of beauty be the end of both, the two arts lie at opposite poles, literary and musical terms, tonality, scales, time, rhythm, movement, the very ideals differ, as analysis will show.

Take the first element: unison. Plainsong is unisonous; it it simple, clear, luminous, stripped of all disguise: all can understand it, the most fastidious artist as well as the man in the street. It does not lurk beneath the obscure and whimsical maze of the myriad sounds of an orchestra, hardly to be followed, even by cultivated ears. Harmony, in the modern meaning of the word, is unknown: it relies upon its own intrinsic charm to move and enthrall us. Plainsong is like a great, still-flowing river: the sacred text is broadly reflected on the surface: the clear, limpid stream, so to speak, is unison; the sonorous waves of an accompaniment, harmonious though they be, sadly trouble the surface and sully those limpid depths. This alone were enough to differentiate it from all modern music. But what follows is still more characteristic.

It will be well at this point to bring to mind some principles which have been most ably exposed by M. Mathis Lussy, in his treatise on "Expression in Music." I quote them in an epitomised form:

"Modern music is composed of three principal elements—

"1. The Scale, or tonality, in the two modes, major and minor.

"2. Time, that is, the periodic recurrence at short intervals of a strong beat, breaking up a piece of music into small fragments, called measures, of equal value or duration.

"3. Rhythm, that is, the periodic recurrence of two, three, or four measures of the same value so as to form groups or symmetrical schemes, each of which contains a section of a musical phrase and corresponds to a verse of poetry.

"These three elements impress upon our consciousness a threefold need of attraction, of regularity, and of symmetry.

"No sooner has the ear heard a series of sounds subject to the laws of tonality, of time, and of rhythm, than it anticipates and expects a succession of sounds and analogous groups in the same scale, time, and rhythm. But, as a rule, the ear is disappointed of its expectation. Very often the group anticipated contains notes extraneous to the scale-mode of the preceding group, which displace the tonic and change the mode. Or, again, it may contain notes which interrupt the regularity of the time, and destroy the symmetry of the original rhythmic plan. Now, it is precisely these unforeseen and irregular notes, upsetting tone, mode, time, and the original rhythm, which have a particular knack of impressing themselves upon our consciousness. They are elements of excitement, of movement, of force, of energy, of contrast: by such notes is expression engendered."

It must be admitted that this theory contains a certain measure of truth, but can it be said to be complete? Are not order, calm, and regularity most potent factors of expression, even in modern music? Moreover, if expression must be denied to all music which does not employ such elements of excitement, then it must be denied to Gregorian music, which rejects, on principle, all such expedients, being thereby distinguished from all compositions of modern times. The comparison and the scrutiny of the three elements of which we have been speaking will be a convincing proof of this assertion.

We will deal first with tonality. It is well known that Gregorian tonality is very different from that of modern music. In the latter are found diatonic and chromatic intervals, major and minor modes, discords, the leading note, modulations, and constant irregularities of tone. What is the result? Agitation, excitement, frenzy, passionate emotional and dramatic expression; in short, the violent and excessive disturbance of the hapless human frame.

Gregorian tonality, on the contrary, seems ordained to banish all agitation from the mind, and to enfold it in rest and peace. And since the chant is all in unison, discord, that most effective element of expression, is unknown. It follows that the leading note is also debarred; and as a matter of fact, long before there could be any question of its use, anything resembling such a note was excluded by the rules laid down for the composition of the chant. In plainsong, the cadence is never made by approaching the final from the semitone below: a whole tone must invariably be used in such a case. This rule gave the cadence a certain dignity and fullness of expression to which modern music cannot attain by means of the ordinary rules of composition.

Gregorian tonality likewise proscribes the effeminate progressions of the chromatic scale, admitting only the more frank diatonic intervals. These intervals are arranged in scales, eight in number, called modes, the distinct characteristics of which evoke varying impressions and emotions. Bold or abrupt changes from one mode to another are also proscribed, though the chant is by no means lacking in modulations, for these are essential in any music. In plainsong, the modulation is effected by passing from one mode to another. Some compositions borrow the sentiments they seek to interpret from several modes in succession: the mere change of the dominant or reciting-note is enough to give the impression of a true modulation. These changes of mode are effected very gently: they move and mildly stimulate the soul, without either shock or disturbance.

You must not be surprised that the means employed should be so simple and elementary: it is to the higher faculties of the soul that the chant makes appeal. It owes its beauty and dignity to the fact that it borrows little or nothing from the world of sense. It passes through the senses, but it does appeal to them: it panders neither to the emotions nor to the imagination. Plainsong is capable of expressing the most tremendous truths, the strongest feelings, without departing from its sobriety, purity, and simplicity. Modern music may perhaps arouse and voice coarse and violent passions, although I grant that this is not always the case. The chant, however, cannot be so abused: it is always wholesome and serene: it does not react upon the nervous system.

Its frank diatonic tonality, and the absence of chromatic intervals, whose semitones give an impression of incompletion, seem to render plainsong incapable of expressing anything but the perfection of beauty, the naked truth, "yea, yea, and nay, nay." For the unyielding diatonic scale has a certain angelic quality which never varies: an ear accustomed to its matchless candor cannot tolerate melodies, sensuous even when the love of God is their theme.

If from the study of sounds and their progression, we proceed to analyze their duration and intensity, we shall find that the contrast between plainsong and modern music is as great as before.

In modern music the simple beat, that is, the unit of time which, when once adopted, becomes the form of all the others, may be divided indefinitely. An example will serve to make my meaning clear. A bar, or measure, in simple duple time is composed of two crochets: each crochet constitutes a beat, and may be divided into two quavers; these again into semiquavers, demisemiquavers, and so on, until the subdivisions become infinitesimal. It is easy to see how such facility of division may introduce much mobility or instability into modern music.

In plainsong, on the contrary, the beat, or pulse, is indivisible: it corresponds to the normal syllable of one pulse, and cannot be divided any more than a syllable can be. Thus, in writing a piece of plainsong in modern notation, the crochet becomes the normal note and unit of time; it must never be broken up into quavers. I have no hesitation in declaring that plainsong is syllabic music, in the sense that the syllable is the unit of measure, and that not only in antiphons, where each note corresponds to a syllable, but also in vocalizations (melodic passages or neums), where the notes, momentarily freed from words, remain subject, nevertheless, to the time of the simple beat, previously determined in the syllabic passages.

This approximate equality of duration is the inevitable consequence of the intimate connection which existed among the Greeks between the words and the melody. It is explained by a fact familiar to all philologists and grammarians, namely, the transformation which the Latin language underwent during the first years of the Christian era. Quantity, once paramount in poetry, and to a certain extent, in Ciceronian prose, eventually gave place to accent. Little by little the short and long syllables came to have the same value: in prose as in poetry, syllables were no longer measured, but counted. Quantity was no more. In actual practice, the syllables were neither short nor long, but of equal duration, strong or weak, according as they were accented or unaccented.

An evolution of such import was bound to react upon the music of the Church, which was in its infancy at the time that these changes were being effected. Plainsong was modeled on the prose of the period: it therefore adopted its rhythm, from its simplest elements, the primary fundamental pulse, for example, to its most varied movements. And just as there were two forms of prosody, the one metric, the other tonic; two forms of prose, and two "cursus," so there were two forms of music, the metric and the tonic; the latter, like the tonic prose and cursus, was based upon the equality of notes and syllables.

It must be understood that this equality is not a metronomical equality, but a relative equality—the mean duration resulting from all the syllables taken as a whole, and pronounced in accordance with their material weight: this, to the ear, produces a distinct sense of equality. Nevertheless this equality becomes more rigorous as the melody frees itself from the text, for then the shades of inequality caused by the varying weight of the syllables, entirely disappear and make way for more equal musical durations.

It is not to be inferred from this fact that the notes are all equal in length. As a matter of fact, though a beat may never be divided, it may be doubled and even trebled. Just as in embroidering upon canvas, the same color in wool or silk may cover several stitches, so upon the canvas of the simple beat, the same note may include two, three or four stitches and thus form a charming melodic scheme.

Adequate attention has not been paid to this fundamental distinction between plainsong and modern music, notwithstanding the fact that it influences in no small degree the whole movement of the phrase and the expression as well. It is to the indivisibility of the beat that the Roman chant owes, in great measure, its sweetness, calm, and suavity.

Since Latin is the language of the Roman liturgy and the Latin syllables are the prima materies of Gregorian rhythm, it will be well to examine the nature of the Latin accent at the period when the Gregorian melodies were written, drawing attention to important differences between the character of the tonic accents at that date and in more recent times.

Now the Latin accent has not the same force as is usually attributed by modern musicians to the first beat of the measures, not as the accent in the Romance languages. In Latin, the accent is indicated by a short, sharp, delicate sound which—inasmuch as it is the soul of the word—might almost be called spiritual. It is best represented by an upward movement of the hand which is raised only to be lowered immediately. In modern music this swift flash is placed on a ponderous material beat, crushing and exhausting the movement. This surely is a misconception. For the Latin accent is an impulse or beginning which requires a complement: this, as a matter of fact, is found in the succeeding beat. It is therefore most aptly compared to the upward movement of the hand in beating time, no sooner raised than lowered. In modern music, however, this impulse or beginning is placed on the second and downward beat, on which the movement comes to rest. And this again is surely a misconception.

Nor is this all: for the Latin accent is essentially an elevation of the voice: which plainsong—that faithful interpreter—translates constantly by a rise of pitch; and, once more, the upward movement of the hand corresponds and gives plastic expression to the lifted accent. But modern figured music, misled by the ponderous weight of the stroke by which the Latin accent is so often emphasized as well as by the downward movement of the hand, represents this accent by lowering the pitch of the note. Have we not here a complete reversal of the text—both melodically and rhythmically, which is unjustifiable even from a purely musical standpoint?

In fine, Gentlemen, in modern music the character of the accent is utterly transformed: melody, rhythm, delicacy and joyous impulse, all are lost, and converted into the Romance accent. Hence there arises between words and music a continual conflict, an initiating apposition, which, albeit imperceptible to the inattentive and uncultured public, is none the less painful to those who appreciate the characteristics of the Latin accent, and the rhythm of the Latin phrase. It is, in fact, an outrage to the ideal which one has a right to expect in every artistic or religious composition. A very few months of familiarity with plainsong would suffice to make you grasp fully these statements. As one listens day after day to the chant, the mind opens to the appreciation of that music, the

rhythm and style of which are so essentially Latin: very soon
the judgment appraises it at its true value, and ultimately
the exquisite feeling, the consummate skill behind that fusion
of words and melody become apparent, and scholars and
musicians alike applaud its artistic perfection. On the other
hand, a closer knowledge of plainsong makes us discover in
modern religious music—beneath the real beauty of some of
the compositions—the awkwardness, the unconscious clumsi-
ness, of this mixed romance Latin rhythm which disfigures
even the noblest musical inspirations.

We are now come to the succession of groups, of sections of
the phrase, and to the phrase itself; that is to say, to rhythm
properly so-called. You may already have noticed that in
the Gregorian phrase the groups of two pulsations or of three
do not succeed each other so uniformly, nor so regularly as
in figured music. In plainsong, a mixture of times is the
rule, whereas in figured music it is the exception. The ancients, who were familiar with this mixed rhythm, gave it the
name of numerus, number, or rhythm. Impatient of restric-
tion and constraint, plainsong shook off the trammels of symmetry: thus in the course of the melody, the groups of two
notes or of three or of four, etc., succeed each other as
freely as in oratorical rhythm. Any combination is admitted provided it be in harmony and in proportion. "This
proportion," says Dom Pothier, "is based upon the relation in
which the component parts of the song or speech stand to
each other or to the whole composition."[10] Nevertheless, the
chant does not altogether disdain measure and successions of
regular rhythm: but these are never cultivated to the extent
of accustoming the ear to them and making it expect the
recurrence of regular groups. Never is the ear shocked or
surprised. The measures and rhythm succeed one another with
amazing variety, but never at the cost of smoothness. There
are no syncopations, no broken rhythms, nor yet any of those
unexpected, irregular, unnatural effects, which break the ordinary movement of the phrase[11] by introducing elements of
agitation, of strife, and of passion. All this is unknown in
plainsong. All the accented pules, whether of the measure or
of the rhythm, all the notes which give expression such as the

[10]*Dom Pothier, Melodies Gregoriennes,* p. 175.
[11]*Mathis Lussy, Traité de l'expression musicale.*

pressus and the strophicus, although scattered irregularly over the texture of the melody, are invariably found in their regular place at the beginning of the measure. This solid foundation of regular rhythm gives the Roman chant that calm, dignity and evenness of movement which become the sacred liturgy.

Was I not right in saying that the art of Gregorian music had little in common with the art of modern music? Henceforward no one will confuse Wagner's methods with those which animate the Gregorian chant. And if we would define the results which issue from this analysis, we shall form the following conclusions:—

Gregorian music disclaims, or rather rejects on principle all elements of confusion, agitation, or excitement: it courts, on the other hand, all that tends to peace and calm.

It will be well, after having thus analyzed the details of the chant, to view it as a whole, and to study its main distinctive features. To refresh us, however, after these somewhat dry researches, the Schola is kindly going to render the melismatic pieces mentioned in the programme, namely, the communion *Videns Dominus,* and the Introits *Reminiscere* and *Laetare.*

III

The most striking characteristic of plainsong is its simplicity, and herein it is truly artistic. Among the Greeks, simplicity was the essential condition of all art; truth, beauty, goodness cannot be otherwise than simple.

The true artist is he who best—that is, in the simplest way—translates to the world without the ideal conceived in the simplicity of his intellect. The higher, the purer the intellect, the greater the unity and simplicity of its conception of the truth: now, the closest interpretation of an idea which is single and simple is plainly that which in the visible world most nearly approaches singleness and simplicity. Art is not meant to encumber the human mind with a multiplicity which does not belong to it: it should on the contrary tend to so elevate the sensible world that it may reflect in some degree the singleness and simplicity of the invisible. Art should tend not to the degradation, but to the perfection of the individual. If it appeals to the senses by evoking impressions and emotions which are proper to them, it only does so in order to arouse the mind in some way, and to enable it to free itself from and rise above the visible world as by a ladder, cunningly devised in accordance with the laws laid down by God Himself. Whence it follows that plainsong is not simple in the sense that its methods are those of an art in its infancy: it is simple consistently and on principle.

It should not be supposed that this theory binds us to systems long since out of date: the Church in this matter professes the principles held by the Greeks, the most artistic race the world has ever known. In their conception, art could not be otherwise than simple. Whenever I read Taine's admirable pages on the simplicity of Greek art, I am constantly reminded of the music of the Church. Take for instance, the following passage: "The temple is proportionate to man's understanding —among the Greeks it was of moderate, even small, dimensions: there was nothing resembling the huge piles of India, of Babylon, or of Egypt, nor those massive super-imposed palaces, those labyrinthine avenues, courts, and halls, those gigantic statues, of which the very profusion confused and dazzled the mind. All this was unknown. The order and harmony of the Greek temple can be grasped a hundred yards from the sacred precincts. The lines of its structure are so simple that they may be comprehended at one glance. There is nothing complicated, fantastic, or strained in its construction; it is based upon three or four elementary geometrical designs.[12]

Do you not recognize in this description, Gentlemen, the unpretentious melodies of the Gregorian chant? They fill but a few lines on paper: a few short minutes suffice for their execution; an antiphon several times repeated and some verses from a psalm, nothing more. They are moreover so simple that the ear can easily grasp them. There is nothing complicated, weird or strained, nothing which resembles those great five-act operas, those interminable oratorios, those Wagnerian tetralogies which take several days to perform, bewildering and confusing the mind.

The same simplicity is found in Greek literature and sculpture. To quote Taine again:—"Study the Greek play: the characters are not deep and complex as in Shakespeare; there

---

[12]*Taine, Philosophie de l'art en Grèce*, p. 66 et seq.

are no intrigues, no surprises—the piece turns on some heroic
legend, with which the spectators have been familiar from early
childhood; the events and their issue are known beforehand.
As for the action, it may be described in a few words—nothing
is done for effect, everything is simple—and of exquisite
feeling."

These principles, Gentlemen, may all be applied to plainsong.
"No loud tones, no touch of bitterness or passion; scarce a
smile, and yet one is charmed as by the sight of some wild
flower or limpid stream. With our blunted and unnatural
taste, accustomed to stronger wine (I am still quoting Taine)
we are at first tempted to pronounce the beverage insipid: but
after having moistened our lips therewith for some months,
we would no longer have any other drink but that pure fresh
water; all other music and literature seem like spice, or
poison."[13]

You will no doubt ask how so simple an art, from which the
modern means of giving expression are systematically excluded,
can faithfully interpret the manifold and deep meaning of the
liturgical text. Seemingly this is impossible. But here you
are mistaken, Gentlemen. In music, as in all art, the simpler
the means, the greater the effect and impression produced.
Victor Cousin has a telling saying:—"The less noise the music
makes, the more affecting it is." And so simplicity excludes
neither expression nor its subtleties from the chant.

What then is this expression, whence does it spring, and
what is its nature? Let me make yet another quotation,
for I like to adduce the theories of modern authorities in support of the aesthetics of the chant: behind their shelter, I
shall not be exposed to any charge of having invented them
to suit my case. M. Charles Blanc, in his "Grammar of the
Graphic Arts," says that "Between the beautiful and its expression there is a wide interval, and moreover, an apparent
contradiction. The interval is that which separates Christianity from the old world: the contradiction consists in the fact
that pure beauty (the writer is speaking of plastic beauty) can
hardly be reconciled with facial changes, reflecting the countless impressions of life. Physical beauty must give place to
moral beauty in proportion as the expression is more pronounced. This is the reason why pagan sculpture is so limited

[13]*Taine, op. cit.,* p. 113.

in expression."[14] I am well aware, Gentlemen, that in sculpture, more than in any other art, the greatest care must be
taken not to pass certain appointed bounds, if the stateliness
which is its chief characteristic is to be preserved. I am also
aware that in other arts, such as painting or music, it is
legitimate to indulge more freely in the representation of the
soul's manifold emotions. All this I grant, Gentlemen: nevertheless, it must be acknowledged that these distinctions are
very fine indeed, and that in every art, the higher laws of
aesthetics are the same. The laws of musical expression are
analogous to those of plastic expression: there too it may be
asserted that pure musical beauty accords ill with the tonal,
metrical or rhythmic changes of a melody reflecting the manifold impressions of the soul in the grip of its passions. There
too we may say that the more intense is the expression, the
more the beauty of the music as music gives way to moral
beauty. How then are we to reconcile beauty, by its very nature serene and immutable, with the restlessness and versa-
tility which are the essential characteristics of expression?
The problem is by no means easy of solution.

Ancient art, with deeper insight, loved beauty so much that
it shunned expression: our more sensual modern art endeavors
to obtain expression at the expense of beauty. But the Church
in her song has found, it would seem, the secret of wedding
the highest beauty without any change to a style of expression
which is both serene and touching. This result is attained
without conscious effort. For as a sound body is the instrument of a sound mind, so the chant, informed by the inspired
word of God, interprets its expression. This expression is enhanced both by the smoothness of the modulations, and by the
suppleness of the rhythm. And as the melody is simple and
spiritual, so likewise is the expression: it belongs, like the
melody, to another age. It is not, as in modern music, the result
of surprise, of discord, of irregularity or disorder; it does not
linger over details, nor endeavor to chisel every word, to cut
into the marble of the melody every shade of emotion. It
springs rather from the general order, the perfect balance
and enduring harmony of every part, and from the irresistable
charm born of such perfection. Measured and discreet, ample
liberty of interpretation is left to the mind by such expression.

[14]*Charles Blanc, Grammaire des Arts du Dessin, p. 519.*

Always true, it bears the signal stamp of the beauty of fitness:
it becomes the sanctuary, it becomes those who resort thither
that they may rise to the spiritual plane. "No defilement
shall touch it," no dimness, nor stain but a limpid virginal
purity: like the ancient Doric mode, it breathes modesty and
chastity.

It is, moreover, infinite in its variety. "Attingit ubique
propter munditiam suam." What, for example, could be more
artless and expressive than the Ambrosian Gloria which was
sung to you? It turns upon two or three notes, and a short
jubilus. A modern composer would consider it monotonous
and insipid, but to me its simplicity is charming, and its frank
and wholesome tonality refreshing. That joyous neum has a
rustic ring about it that reminds one of the hillsides of Bethlehem and fills me with the joy and peace of Christmastide.
It is indeed a song worthy of the angels, those pure spirits,
and of the poor shepherd folk.

The same characteristics are found in the little carol *"In
Israhel orietur princeps, firmamentum pacis."* It contains but
six short words, yet these suffice to make a melodic composition
of exquisite delicacy and expression. In the Introit *Reminiscere,* you heard the plaintive accents of sorrowful entreaty,
and in the *Laetare,* those of a joy so sweet and calm as to be
almost jubilant. As for the communion *Videns Dominus,* it
has no equal. No melody could express more vividly the
Saviour's tears and His compassion for Lazarus' grief-stricken
sisters, and the divine power of His bidding to death.

In presence of the masterpieces of Greek art, the most dis-
cerning modern artists frankly confess their inability to appreciate them at their true value. To use Taine's words:—
"Our modern perceptions cannot soar so high." And we may
in like manner say of the musical compositions of the early
Church that they are beyond the reach of our perceptions:
we can only partially and gradually comprehend the perfection
of their plan; we no longer have their subtlety of feeling and
intuition. "In comparison with them we are like amateurs
listening to a musician born and bred: his playing has a delicacy of execution, a purity of tone, a fullness of accord, and
a certain finish of expression, of which the amateur, with his
mediocre talents and lack of training can only now and again
grasp the general effect."[15]

---

[15] *Taine, op. cit.,* p. 70.

The finishing touch has yet to be added to this brief outline of plainsong; this suavity, or more correctly, unction, the supreme quantity in which all the elements we have been discussing converge. The product of consummate art, it crowns the chant with a glory unknown in all other music, and it is on account of this very unction that the Church has singled it out for her use: It is this quality which makes plainsong the true expression of prayer, and a faithful interpretation of those unspeakable groanings of the Spirit who, in the words of St. Paul, "prays in us and for us." We sometimes wonder at the secret power the chant has over our soul: it is entirely due to unction, which finds its way into men's souls, converts and soothes them, and inclines them to prayer. It is akin to grace, and is one of its most effectual means of action, for no one can escape its influence. The pure in heart are best able to understand and taste the suavity of this unction. Yet, for all its delectable charm, it never tends to enervate the soul, but like oil, it makes the wrestler supple and strengthens him against the combat: it rests and relaxes, and bathes him in that peace which follows the conquest of his passions.

A last word as to the style of execution best suited to plainsong. There can of course be no doubt that an able and artistic interpretation is eminently suited to music so subtle and so delicate, but I hasten to add that mere technique is not enough: it must be coupled with faith, with devotion and with love. There must be no misunderstanding in this matter. Notwithstanding its beauty, plainsong is both simple and easy: it is within the capacity of poor and simple folk. Like the liturgy and the scriptures, and, if such a comparison be admissable, like the Blessed Sacrament itself, this musical bread which the Church distributes to her children, may be food for the loftiest intellects as for the most illiterate minds. In the country it is not out of place on the lips of the ploughman, the shepherd, or laborer, who on Sundays leave plough and trowel or anvil, and come together to sing God's praises. Nor is it out of place in the Cathedral, where the venerable canons supported by the fresh young voices of a well-trained choir sing their office, if not always artistically, at least with the full appreciation of the words of the Psalmist "Psallite sapienter," Very possibly the chant is neither rendered, understood, nor appreciated in precisely the same manner in a country church

as in a cathedral. But it would be unfair and unreasonable
to expect of village folk an artistic interpretation of which
their uncultured minds have no inkling, since, after all, their
devotion and taste is satisfied with less. But on the other
hand, a suitable interpretation may in justice be expected and
required of them: the voices should be restrained, the tone
true and sustained, the accents should be observed, so too the
pauses, the rhythm, and the feeling of the melody. All that
is needed beyond this is that touch of devotion, of feeling,
which is by no means rare among the masses. With his slender
store of musical knowledge, the village cantor will not, I confess, become an artist. He will not render the full beauty, the
finer shades of the melody: nevertheless, he will express his
own devotion and withal he will carry his audience with him.
For the simple folk who listen to him are no better versed than
he in the subtle niceties of art: neither he nor they can fully
appreciate the chant, but they are satisfied with that which
they find in it: it contents their musical instincts and appeals
to their ingenuous piety.

Is this then all, Gentlemen? Does such an easy victory
fulfill the Church's intentions: is her aim merely to win the
approval of our good peasants? Indeed, such is not the
Church's meaning: she does not rest content with well-meaning
mediocrity: she has her colleges, her greater and lesser seminaries, her choirs, her monasteries, and her cathedrals. Of
these she demands an intelligent rendering of the chant so
dear to her heart, that it may compel the admiration of the
most exacting critics, and be at the same time the most perfect
expression of her official prayer. Here indeed is art most
necessary: here we may despoil the Egyptians of their most
precious vessels, and fairly borrow, without any scruple, from
profane artists, the methods whereby to restore to the voice
its true sweetness and purity. Art teaches us how to use the
voice, to sing the neums softly or loudly as the case may be,
to pronounce the words, to give delicacy to the accents, to
phrase correctly, to bring out the expression and the true meaning of the ideas contained in the words. Art conceals natural
or acquired defects, and restores to nature its primitive beauty
and integrity. In plainsong, the aim of art is to provide the
soul with a docile, pliant instrument, capable of interpreting
its sentiments without deforming them. To attempt to sing

without training or art; "naturally," as the saying goes, would be as foolish an undertaking as to pretend to attain to sanctity without setting any check upon our impulses. Art is to the right interpretation of the chant what the science of ascetics is to the spiritual life. Its proper function is not to give vent to facitious emotions, as in modern music, but rather to allow genuine feeling complete freedom of expression. It is with intent that I use the word freedom, for freedom is simply the being able to yield without effort to the rules of the beautiful, which become as it were natural.

Art then is necessary, but as I have already said it is not sufficient in itself. To sing the chant, as it should be sung, the soul must be suitably disposed. The chant should vibrate with soul, ordered, calm, disciplined, passionless: a soul that is mistress of itself, intelligent and in possession of the light; upright in the sight of God, and overflowing with charity. To such a soul, Gentlemen, add a beautiful voice, well-trained, and the singing of those hallowed melodies, will be a finished work of beauty, the music of which Plato dreamed, a music which inspires a love of virtue: nay, more, you will have the ideal of Christian prayer as St. Dennis understood it, the realization of the great Benedictine motto:—"Mens nostra concordet voci nostrae." "Let our mind concord with our voice" in the praise of God.

LAUS DEO ET AGNO

THE CATHOLIC CHOIRMASTER

What the International Gregorian Congress has accomplished

ON the first three days of the month of June there convened in New York City the first great International Congress of Gregorian Chant, to be held in this country. Its announcement was a herald of a new and brighter hope for pure Church Music in this country, and great things were expected of it. It has now passed into history and to say that it has exceeded the expectations of the most sanguine, no one can deny. Never before has such Church Music been heard in this country. Under the supervision of the great champion of Gregorian restoration the Rev. Dom A. Mocquereau, and the direction of the Very Rev. Dom A. Gatard, whose name is synonymous with the best traditions of Solesmes School, the vast choir of thousands in St. Patrick's athedral, New York City, thrilled all who were present with the most wonderful rendition of Gregorian Chant, the most sublime exemplification of the art of music in it highest and noble form.

That the success which crowned this memorable event will be attended by the most beneficial results there can be no doubt. The stimulus imparted to pure Church Music by this great and inspiring Congress will be felt throughout the country. It will give church musicians a new impulse a new consciousness of strength, a new taste of the joy of unity of effort, a new love of co-operation and a deeper sense of the divine significance and power of music, than they ever had. Education has come out of it. It has planted well and wisely for the future. It has given to many a new belief in a style of music hitherto almost universally neglected in this country. Many now will have faith in the sublime Gregorian melodies, who never had much before; they for the first time will respect them as a high and holy influence, who very likely looked upon them as at the best, an innocent primeval form of music. We shall no longer have to plead against such odds to claim that Gregorian music and Gregorian masterpieces have their permanent and honored seat among the productions of the masters of modern time. We begin to see how music, freely and divinely from within, inspires the instinct of fond and child-like reverence for something high and holy. So far as the International Congress has wrought this conversion, among unbelieving and indifferent musicians and among those who were positively hostile to it, even among our clergy, it has done an incalculable good; and if for this alone, we cannot be too grateful

to those who were instrumental in its inception and its success.

A large element in the extraordinary spell which the Catholic Church has always exercised upon the minds of men, is to be found in the beauty of her Liturgy, the solemn significance of her forms of worship and the glorious product of artistic genius in which those forms have been enshrined. For the beauty and grandeur of outward form and embellishment are not superadded from without as though they might be again withdrawn without essential loss; they are the natural outgrowth of the very spirit of the Church, the proper outward manifestation of the idea which pervades her worship. Music is the very breath of the Liturgy itself, acting immediately upon the heart, kindling the latent sentiment of reverence into lively emotions of joy and love. Catholic Liturgy in its conception and history is a musical Liturgy. The text is inseparably bound up with its musical setting like soul and body. The Chant melodies are the very breath of the words. This was realized by those who were fortunate enough to attend the services held at St. Patrick's Cathedral during the sessions of the Congress. In no modern musical works do we find such care of design, such devotion to the highest demands of art, such pouring forth of the rich treasures of intellects trained under the protecting wing of Holy Church. Music the child of prayer, the companion of religion, in ts Gregorian form, is a real mediator between earth and heaven. The sublime renditions of the art of music at the Congress impressed this truth upon the hearers, by giving wings to the soul, elevating the heart and mind, and preparing the way for all good and holy thoughts and aspirations.

O music what a power thou art.
On earth there's naught that can impart
A purer joy to human heart
Nor nobler thoughts inspire.

..The text of the Gregorian melodies is so exalted partaking of the sanctity of the particular Office celebrated, that it must be uttered in tones consecrated to it, and so intimate is this union of tone and language, that in the process of time, these two elements have become amalgamated into a union so complete that no dissolution is possible even in thought. The Chant of the Church is a sort

THE CATHOLIC CHOIRMASTER

of religious folk-song, proceeding from the inner shrine of religion; it is abstract, impersonal; its style is strictly ecclesiastical, medieval, even antique; and because its origin is lost in the mists of the past, it bears, like the ritual itself, the sanction of unimpeachable, traditional authority. To one who understands the whole conception and spirit of Catholic worship, there is a singular appropriateness in the style of the Chant, and when properly rendered, as it was at the Congress, it is the only music that blends most efficiently with the architectural splendor of altar and sanctuary, with incense, lights, vestments, ceremonial action, and all the embellishments that lend distinction and solemnity to the ritual of the Church

———

As the Chant has been preserved to the present day in its integrity, it is a unique and precious heritage which furnishes the strongest evidence of the divine origin of a faith that had triumphed over all obstacles. To the devout Catholic and especially the Catholic priest and musician, the Chant has a sanction which transcends even its aesthetic and historic value, and all may reverence it as a direct creation and a token of a mode of thought, which, as at no epoch since, conceived prayer and praise as a Christian's most urgent duty and as an infallible means of gaining the favor and assistance of God. Every lover of Church music will find a new pleasure and uplift, in listening to its noble strains. He must however listen sympathetically, expelling from his mind all comparison with the modern styles of music to which he is accustomed, holding in clear view its historic and liturgic function. To one who so attunes his mind to its peculiar spirit and purport, Gregorian Chant will seem worthy of the exalted place which it holds in the worship and the love of the most august ecclesiastical institution in the history of the world, Holy Church. Gregorian Chant appeals just as strongly to a person with no musical education as to the greatest artist, for it comes from God. It appeals to all that is finest in us. It brings into the heart, the spirit of prayer, the prime object of all religious music worthy of the name.

———

The success of the International Gregorian Congress was beyond precedent according to the testimony of those who have attended other Congresses in other parts of the world. It was far in advance of the most sanguine anticipation. That it would be a success, no one who was aware of the manner in which it was progressing could for a moment doubt; but that that success was realized to such an unexpected extent was startling to its most earnest supporters. We certainly do not propose to claim for the Congress an absolute perfection; yet was it so near perfection as to challenge the wonder and admiration of those who participated in it or who attended its sessions. All honor and gratitude to those, who without thought of a return, labored to make the Congress the artistic success that it proved to be.

———

One good effect of the Congress will be to stimulate the desire to learn and hear religious music according to the standard desired by the authorities of the Church, on the part of Church musicians, choirmasters and organists. But this cannot be done without stimulating the public taste and elevating the musical standard on the part of those who have already made this grace their study and found it a satisfying and ennobling pursuit. Its influence should and will be felt in every Church Choir in this country worthy of the name, and arouse the members to banish all music unworthy of the House of God. In this direction, it is difficult to estimate the power of the International Congress for good, and looked at from this point of view, it must fill us with hope for the future of Catholic Church Music in our country. All honor to Dom. Mocquereau and Dom Gatard, the great champions of Gregorian restoration.

(Rev.) F. JOSEPH KELLY
Mus. D.

COMMENTS ON THE GREGORIAN CONGRESS

A Non-Catholic—one of the most prominent architects in the country expressed himself in this manner:

"I certainly intend to be back in order that I may come to some of the meetings of the Congress. It would be impossible for me to express my enthusiasm over the whole project. It is one of the most encouraging and heartening things I have known for a long time. I have had this dream for many years, and now it really appears to be taking definite shape. I am not sure that I should not look on this as perhaps the most promising evidence of a new and constructive vitality in society that has shown itself since the armistice."

✪ ✪ ✪

MRS. NATALIE CURTIS BURLIN (Author of original Collection of Folk-Songs of Indians, and Negroes) was present at all the services of the Congress and is quoted as having said that she never before had understood what Religion could mean—the sublimity of the three days, both the singing and Monsieur Bonnet's impressive playing of compositions of such nobility, made an indelible impression.

✪ ✪ ✪

CANON DOUGLAS (Anglican)—is quoted as saying that the Congress was one of the dreams of his life come true.

✪ ✪ ✪

DOM GREGORIO MA SUNOL—Montserrat, Spain.—(Translation) "although it is impossible for me to be present at the Congress I wish to send my thanks for the kind invitation and to express my support of the great and meritorious object of the liturgical Congress.

"In addition to what my personal support may be worth I also takepleasure in expressing the support of our Benedictine Community of Monserrat, of the 'Associacio Gregorianista' of Barcelona of which I am president, of the liturgical review 'Vida Cristina' of which I am editor, and of the 'Association Ceciliana' of Spain of which I am a member.

"Please count me as among the delegates of the Congress and if possible I will send in a paper to be read, but if this should prove impossible, the Rev. Dom. Andre Mocquerau, my teacher, and the Very Rev. Dom Augustin Gatard, my friend, can describe our Gregorian propaganda in Spain."

✪ ✪ ✪

MSGR. EDWIN M. SWEENEY—"Its was a great idea splendidly carried out."

✪ ✪ ✪

A JESUIT FATHER—"How can we ever thank God enough for the truly magnificent way in which he heard our prayers. I feel we shall have to call upon all the angels of heaven to sing a fitting Te Deum... Kindly express to the two Benedictine Fathers my deep admiration and my heartfelt gratitude for the heroism of their undertaking. Monsieur Bonnet did all that could be done with his instrument. To him is due the very idea of this glorious tour de force—and we shall never be able to thank him enough for his truly Christian unselfish devotedness to the holy cause."

✪ ✪ ✪

NUNS.

The Grey Nuns of the Cross of D'Youville College... wish to congratulate the Committee upon the wonderful success of the Congress.

✪ ✪ ✪

A Sister of Saint Joseph—"In the name of all our Sisters who attended the Congress, I thank you. They will never forget their days spent in New York. As for me I felt I had one little taste of the grand Liturgy of the "Church Triumphant." If those days were so grand, what will that great Reunion be?"

✪ ✪ ✪

LAITY

Typical expression—"Rarely have I been so thrilled or uplifted as on that wonderful Wednesday morning of the Requiem Mass. As to the rendition of the Dies Irae it was one of the most sublime things I have ever heard in any Church. The impersonality of the Chant at times was like wood-wind instruments in a forest—a chant of praise-prayer-lifting of heart and voice like the birds singing."

✪ ✪ ✪

H. E. Krehbiel the music critic of the New York Tribune had this to say of the singing on the first day of the Gregorian Congress: "There was something beautiful and spiritually uplifting in the singing of the ordinary of the "Missa de Angelis" at the opening of the recent Congress and lovers of pure church music were no doubt cheered by it in the hope that the next generation might see a restoration of the part which in almost primitive times the congregation took in the office of the Mass..."

During the sessions devoted to Lectures etc. the Very Rev. T. E. Shields, Dean of the Sisters College In Washington spoke on the subject of "The Liturgy in the Education of Children."

Dr. Shields spoke from the psychological and educational point of view, his words having additional weight on account of the very great experience he has had as an educator. The reverend Doctor laid stress on fact that the supreme importance of teaching the liturgy in childhood years was most effectively accomplished through music. That music, when put to such exalted use, was filling its highest, noblest mission, and that it should be made as beautiful as possible as to style or rendition. Nothing is too good to devote to such service, the inculcating in young minds what the liturgy is and bringing to its rendition the best, truest and loveliest resources of genuine art. School music training should make for unforced, good tone quality in singing. The Ward method of treatment of the liturgical chant as the very foundation of future participation in congregational singing. The Ward method of school music was recommended as leading to this, as it embodied instruction in the chant as an integral part of its course.

How are we to bring about a revival of that nearly lost art of congregational singing? It must be done through the children. Every parochial school under proper guidance can become a nucleus of the true traditional singing, which is shown to be beautiful, touching and attractive beyond description. Choirmasters, organists and teachers must drop preconceived ideas about musical rendition come to child singing with a free mind, unhampered by previous training in modern music, realizing that here is a field that demands attention for itself.

By degrees, the little band of priests, organists and choirmasters, trained in the true traditions, will show by example and precept, will spread the knowledge of how best to give this training. In "Le nombre musicale," Don Mocquereau gives the theory and practice of Gregorian rhythm as taught and practiced at Quarr Abbey, where the Solesmes monks have lived since their exile from France. Of that singing, Reverend

Vincent Clement Donovan, O. P., says: "It is like breath from heaven. The innermost soul of every one of the fifty or sixty monks seems revealed in the spontaneous overflow of their song of praise and thansgiving. One does not have to be a musician to realize that they are not singing mere notes, but ideas— the ideas of the liturgy."

To bring something of this noble spirit to the education of our children for the furtherance of their future participation in the services of Holy Church is surely an aim worthy of our greatest zeal and constant effort.

THE CONGRESS OF THE OLD CHANT
AND PLANS FOR CATHOLIC CON-
GREGATIONAL SINGING

DOM MOCQUEREAU'S IMPRESSIONS

Restoration of congregational singing, once
universal in the Roman Catholic Church but
never practiced in Catholic churches in this
country, is the purpose of the gathering this
week (June 1 to June 3) under the auspices
of Archbishop Patrick J. Hayes in St. Patrick's Cathedral of an International Congress
of the Gregorian Chant. The beginning is to
be made by teaching the children, so that
the next generation of Catholics may sing in
church—for the same reason that the wor-
shippers of the present day remain silent.

To direct all this has come to New York
from Quarr Abbey on the Isle of Wight the
Rev. Dom. Andre Mocquereau of the Order
of St. Benedict, regarded as the foremost
authority in the world on Gregorian music.
Assisting him during the congress will be
the Very Rev. Dom. Gatard, also of the
Benedictine Order and Prior of Farnborough
Abbey in England. Dom. Mocquereau, who is
a venerable figure with white-hair, has been
asked to lecture at Harvard University following the congress, and may visit a few
Western cities before returning to his
monastery.

He said that when he was told that he was
to conduct 5,000 children in their singing
of the chant on the first day of the congress
he was appalled.

"But," he added, "at the first rehearsal with
them my fears were changed to enthusiasm,
and I realized that my dream had come true,
and that through the medium of the children
of America the great heritage of congregational singing will be restored to the Church."

"The chant of St. Gregory, Dom. Mocquereau continued, "fell into disuse about
the time of the Reformation, when congregational singing in the Church became the
province of the choir. Up to this time all
Catholic countries had largely, by reason of
their participation in the mass, evinced a
keen interest in music generally, and were

the singing countries of the world. This
constant use of mass music—or, rather, mass
singing—created an understanding and love
for music that had its natural reaction upon
the people.

"From the time of the Reformation, however, when congregational singing became
a thing of the past, a change crept into liturgical music. The works of the composers of
the day, Haydn, Beethoven and others of an
earlier period, began to be used. Many of
them were not composed for church services
and met with objection on the ground that
they did not carry the spirit of prayer, and
hence were not appropriate for ecclesiastical
use.

"The liturgy, the complex of public worship
through words, gesture, color and sound, is
the most powerful means toward conversion
and sanctification. The arts are but humble
handmaidens of the Lord. Music must be
primarily prayer, and, furthermore, liturgical
prayer, vesting itself with the exact form and
spirit of liturgy. These qualities are to be
found in the highest degree in the Gregorian
Chant.

"Pope Pius X. wrote these words in 1912:
'The most ancient and correct ecclesiastical
tradition in regard to sacred music encouraged
the whole body of the people to take an active
part in singing the common of the mass, while
a Schola Cantorum sings the varied and richer
parts of the text and of the melodies, thus
alternating with the people. The Gregorian
Chant always has been regarded as the
supreme model for sacred music, so that it is
legitimate to lay down the following rule:
The more closely a composition for the Church
approaches in its form, inspiration and savor
the Gregorian the more sacred and liturgical
it becomes; and the more out of harmony it
is with that supreme model, the less worthy
it is of the temple. The ancient traditional
Gregorian Chant must therefore in a large
measure be restored to the functions of public
worship, and the fact must be accepted by
all that an ecclesiastical function loses none
of its solemnity when accompanied by this
music alone.'"

June 1.   N. Y. TIMES.

RESOLUTIONS ADOPTED BY THE INTERNATIONAL CONGRESS OF GREGORIAN CHANT, JUNE 1, 2, 3.

1.—We urge that Gregorian Chant be restored to the supreme place assigned to it in the liturgy; without prejudice to other types of music permitted by the Holy See in the Motu Proprio.

2.—We urge that the Vatican Edition be introduced everywhere as rapidly as possible.

3.—We urge that edition containing the rhythmic signs of Solesmes be used as in the Pontifical School of Sacred Music at Rome, and in the Vatican Seminary.

4.—We urge that preparatory training be established in the parochial schools in order to lay a foundation for congregational singing as recommended by the Holy See.

5.—We urge that in each diocese under the particular authority of the Ordinary attention be given to the training of choirmasters, this training to be given whenever possible at Quarr Abbey under the Benedictine Fathers of Solesmes.

6.—We urge that in every diocese schools of liturgy and ecclesiastical music be established according to the model of the Pontifical School of Sacred Music at Rome.

7.—Resolved: That a vote of thanks be conveyed to the Rev. Dom Mocquereau and the Very Reverend Dom Gatard and to their superiors, the Very Reverend Abbot Dom Delatte, Abbot of Solesmes, and the Very Reverend Dom Cabrol, Abbot of Farnborough for their great kindness in making possible the Congress of Gregorian Chant in New York.

8.—Resolved: That the homage of the Congress be conveyed to His Holiness Pope Benedict XV with the gratitude of the Congress for the blessing of the Holy Father, and that a copy of these resolutions be forwarded to His Holiness.

THE CATHOLIC CHOIRMASTER
Echoes of the Gregorian Congress

There has been some discussion concerning the artistic success of the International Congress of Gregorian Chant held in New York City last June.

A Catholic weekly published two articles written by clergymen, who attended the sacred functions held in St. Patrick's Cathedral, in which the writers give their frank views of how the Gregorian melodies were rendered by both the congregation, which was composed of school children and parish choirs and by the Scholas of Rochester, Dunwoodie and Baltimore seminaries, acting respectively each day as liturgical choirs.

I have not the honor to know the musical standing of the reverend writers, nor hence the authority that their criticisms may have in their community. Yet, I venture a reply, due to the readers of the "Catholic Choirmaster" who had not the privilege of attending the Congress and forming for themselves 'de visu et auditu' an opinion of the same.

After quoting an article of Dom Mocquereau, published in the Revue Gregorienne, the first critic remarks rather boldly and, to all appearances, convincingly—to himself—that the Chant, offered during the Congress as a demonstration of proper interpretation, was "slow, mechanical and monotonous"; that the Seminarians were "slaves to the notes" and that "although all of those taking part in the singing were using musical notation with rhythmical characters, these were equally disregarded by all." The broadness of such statements will escape no one, I am sure, and, at first hearing, create the impression that the critic's artistic opinion has a rather personal bearing.

I wish, however, that the reverend writer had taken pains to let the public know his frank opinion also of the rhythmical characters themselves, what meaning he attaches to them and exactly how he opines they should be carried into the rendition of the Chant. That would have been most interesting and besides, would have facilitated the discussion of the question at stake, for, any one who might chance to say just the contrary, namely that the rendition of the Chant was not slow, me-

chanical and monotonous; that the seminarians were not slaves to notes, etc., etc., would deserve as much attention as this critic of the Congress. Indeed let me confront him with the expressed opinion of the discoverer himself of the so-called rhythmical characters, who better than anybody knows what they stand for and how they should be rendered. I beg to quote the very words by which Dom Mocquereau himself expressed to me personally his valuable opinion of how he thought the rhythmical characters—which by the way he calls signs—were rendered by the Scholas, and a fortiori, by the congregation. He said that both were EMPHASIZING the rhythmical signs a little too much, and he spoke especially of the episemas. In other words singers were taking those signs too seriously and had too much regard for them. Now I shall not try to reconcile the two opinions, for they are too far apart. Both the critic and Dom Mocquereau must have had different visuals, as though one was looking at the matter through a telescope and the other through a microscope.

I am not in any way belittling the opinion of that giant on Gregorian questions, whom we have learnt to admire, the Rev. Andre Mocquereau, O. S. B. the founder and editor of the "Paleographie Musicale" and author of "Le Nombre Musical Gregorien," works that will make his name a synonym of musical genius; I desire simply to explain such a wide discrepancy between his opinion and that of the reverend critic of the Congress; and, in my estimation, the reason for such discrepancy, may be found in the fact that the rhythmical signs, as discovered by the School of Solesmes, have had their strong opponents from the very start, and have them still, no matter what the signs mean or do not mean. There are still here and there in the musical world a few living adherents of a school of plainchant, if it can be called a school, or even a system, that held sway in musical circles years before the rediscovery of the traditional melodies. Their rhythmic system, or method, was not to be found in any book, it is true; its principles were not written and explained at all; they were supposed to be known and the rendition of plainchant had to be "thusly." That is, it had to be as primitive as possible, as plain as possible, and the plainer the better. There was but one supreme rule, rather guessed than elucidated scientifically: the singers had to take the utmost care of word accents and make them long, strong and heavy, no matter if affecting a short syllable or otherwise. That was easy enough, of course; but when there was no available accented syllable to thunder upon as in neumatic passages of a single unaccented syllable, then singers were at their wit's end and accents were left to the whim and feelings of the performers, for, mind you, there were no signs to show the places or the rallying points of the rhythm. How a whole choir could thus grasp any form of rhythm is a mystery to me, but very likely it was "in the air." Furthermore, group notes were rushed upon as one would run on burning coals, and the last note was invariably made a long note, a place of rest, especially when affected with a stem, then it was likely bombarded altogether. Descending groups were slid as though they had been inclines of a racer dip. They had to be for they were written with diamond notes, you know. The whole of the system—or absence of it—was called interpretation, and so they were avoiding a slow, mechanical and monotonous rendition. They certainly were not slaves to the notes.

So no wonder, when the Benedictines of Solesmes, after almost a half century of scientific researches came out with the traditional theory of rhythm based on the prosodical or metrical cursus of the ancient theorists as a foundation to an oratorical form of rhythm; when they promoted a smooth and even flow of notes embellished with light accents, rather short than long, according to the precepts of the ancient grammarians, but strong enough to mark the swift movement of the melody; when they suggested an impassiveness of feelings in rendering the Church melodies as best fitting the prayerful attitude of the worshipers, the so-called musicians, who had been in the habit of holding artistic opinions "that were in the air" as the nec plus ultra of musical science and interpretation, were nonplussed and demurred. Some do so yet. I fear it was with such a prejudiced attitude that some of them came to the International Gregorian Congress of New York. The Congress did not

meet with their standard. The rhythmical signs were thought disregarded because not thundered as accents of old, and naturally passed unnoticed to heir ear. Seminarians were thought slaves to the notes, because they did not take liberties with groups of notes and the whole thing appeared slow, monotonous and mechanical. I am not trying to say that the rendition of the plainchant by the Scholas and, a fortiori, by the congregation, was perfect in every respect; in my humble opinion it was not. It never will be. There is no Church choir that can boast of rendering music perfectly. But, in the present case, the trouble was not so much with the rendition as with the mind of the critic. I think, for neither Scholas nor congregation cared to meet his standard of musical interpretation of the chant.

As was expected, the critic encountered contradiction. A second clergyman wanted to come to the rescue of the so-maligned Congress for the sake of the good that really was in it. While he pointed out especially, with words of high praise, the work of St. Mary's Schola of Baltimore, he seemed to have been unable to divest himself of the opinion, which, very likely, must be rampant in their section of the country, that the rhythmical characters of Solesmes were the cause of the apparent monotony and mechanical way in which the Gregorian melodies were rendered in New York. To explain, however, the difference that he had detected in the singing of St. Mary's Schola and that of the others, he surmised that the Baltimore singers were not following exactly the Solesmes interpretation but "gave the only true interpretation of the Roman Rhythmic School." This time it was my turn to be nonplussed. In spite of the great honor bestowed upon my humble work with the Baltimore Schola, I could not help wondering at my being hailed as a champion of the Roman Rhythmic School, coming out of the Congress with St. Mary's Schola flying the Roman colors. The whole thing is fresh news to me, indeed.

The Benedictines, with Dom Pothier, under Pope Pius X., and now Dom Mocquereau with the monks of Solesmes, under Pope Benedict XV., are the compilers of the official books of Gregorian Chant called the Vatican

Edition. It is true the rhythmical signs as yet are not officially approved by the Holy See, but neither are they condemned by any means. In my opinion, this is a providential circumstance, for the last word in interpretation of the Gregorian, through these signs, has not yet been said. Many questions of details and application remain to be pondered over and elucidated. Certainly rhythmic signs are badly needed in plainchant as they are in figured music, yet while some musicians do not object to have their figured music books marked with all kinds of interpretation signs, they will object to signs in behalf of the interpretation of plainchant. It is a strange anomaly; unless they think that plainchant is not an art. At the Pontifical High School of Church Music, in all the Catholic Institutions, Colleges, and Convents of Rome, the editions with rhythmical signs are rightly used with the consent of the Ecclesiastical authorities. Furthermore, I have never heard that Roman singers and musicians had a Rhythmic School of their own, in contradistinction to that of the Benedictines of Solesmes, as exemplified by the signs of Dom Mocquereau. Indeed the manuscripts found with rhythmical signs are all of Italian, I may say, Roman origin, although they have been written outside of Rome and Italy, especially in the famous schools of St. Gall and Metz, for instance.

These schools were founded by Roman scholars and singers sent by the Popes to establish the Roman Chant in foreign countries. So far only manuscripts copied in foreign schools had been found with rhythmical signs, but lately manuscripts of full Italian origin were found with signs also, thus proving the common Roman origin of the signs themselves. Now these are the very signs that Dom Mocquereau and the monks of Solesmes try to interpret and give to the musical world. They have no intention of giving them as of a foreign origin or make them bear a French or German interpretation.

In a lecture given at the recent International Congress of Church Music, held at Tourcoing, France, in September, 1919, Dom Mocquereau said that the "free rhythm of the Gregorian melodies is of Latin and Roman origin, although having its root planted in the remotest antiquity." Furthermore, he calls the

Solesmes method of interpretation the "Roman method."

Personally, I have tried to follow very closely the question of Gregorian rhythm since they began to be agitated among church musicians. I have tried hard to get at the root of Dom Mocquereau's contentions, to understand neither more nor less than he meant by them; I have tried to put them to a test by applying them to modern music also, and even to the other arts of moving nature, as dance and oratory. I have found them sound to the core and in perfect hamony with the practice of the best interpreters of music and elocutionists. These artists are few indeed; the very best only and unconsciously at that, (since rhythm is neither taught nor studied in a scientific way in even the greatest conservatories of music), chance to hit upon the rhythmical principles as they were understood by ancient grammarians, rhetoricians, musicians, and dancers and recently by Dom Mocquereau. These principles have solved to my mind, many difficulties that had troubled me in the past. I may say I never understood music in all its designs divisions, forms and proportions of rhythm until I succeeded in grasping the true meaning of the rhythmical signs of the prosodical cursus as discovered by Dom Mocquereau. Even the tonic cursus, which modern plainchantists think is the only one worth their attention, has in the prosodical cursus a foundation on which it can build its own more modern rhythmical structure. I have therefore come to the conclusion that to make plainchant, figured music, and oratorical art true artistic creations we should turn to the scientific rhythm of the ancients, and thank Dom Mocquereau for having lifted the veil that had hidden it from the musical world for so many centuries. I have concluded that we should consequently, beware of cheap and amateurish modern opinions in this regard. I am sure that time will tell; although so far some seem to have but reached the stage of wonderment at the new thing. They seem yet to assume no better attitude, than the one taken by the country school boy, who had never seen a railroad engine. Though the teacher had explained to him the principles of steam action motion, and mechanism, he was nonplussed and demurred, saying he was sure the teacher was correct, but he could not understand how an engine could run without horses.

It is true, even with all the rhythmical signs in the world, not excluding those discovered by Dom Mocquereau there are no two renditions of the same piece of music by different executants, which sound exactly alike, just as there are no two elocutionists who will recite the same piece of poetry or oratory with like feelings and expression, although both are sure to observe all accentuation marks and rhythmical divisions. In his—Esthetic of Music—Busoni says: ' Notation, the writing out of compositions is primarily an ingenious expedient for catching an inspiration, with the purpose of exploiting it later. But notation is to rendition as the portrait is to the living model. It is for the interpreter to resolve the rigidity of the signs into the primitive emotion."

Mr. E. K. Krehbiel, the veteran musical critic of the New York "Tribune," writes apropos of the Gregorian Congress, that it would be folly to assert that it solved all the questions raised in the controversy by the edict of Pope Pius X. He crystallizes some of the questions in the following declaration made by an eminent member of the American Hierarchy published immediately after the issuance of the Motu Proprio on Church Music. He quotes: "There are certain parts of our chants and musical services which require just such voices as those possessed by women, and if they are taken away I fear that the inspiration and effect of the music and singing will be materially diminished. There can be no reason for the exclusion of women from the choirs and I feel that it is my duty to say that I do not desire to see such a move made, and furthermore, that I am opposed to it."

The Gregorian Congress of New York has proved that women voices as part of the liturgical choir are not necessary to make sacred functions devotional and impressive. Mr. Krehbiel himself recognizes it when he says: "there was something beautiful and spiritually uplifting in the singing of the ordinary of the 'Missa De Angelis' at the opening of the recent Congress and lovers of pure music were no doubt cheered by it in the hope that the next generation might see a restoration of the part which, in almost primitive times, the congregation took in the office of the Mass."

From a liturgical standpoint there are no parts of our chants and musical services which require women's voices to be devotional and inspiring, for there are no liturgical offices of the Church that require women officers. Women acolytes would no doubt draw to church functions more male admirers, from a worldly impulse, than mere boys men and priests ever do; but, apparently, it was not the feeling of Our Lord when he entrusted the performance of every little office of His Church to men alone, not even His Blessed Mother excepted, and St. Paul, the great herald of His Master, speaks accordingly when he writes: "Mulier taceat in Ecclesia!" Hence the whole tradition of the Catholic Church from the Apostolic times to our present day is opposed to such a departure. It was only since the advent of Protestantism that women have been admitted to take up the office of singers in Catholic Churches of Protestant countries. It all came about at the time when altar, mass, sacraments and liturgical functions meant nothing more to the faithful than popish superstitions. The liturgics of the sacrificial worship of the Almighty could not but be abolished; countries, however, that have remained Catholic as a whole and in spirit, have never failed to keep intact the tradition of using male voices only since the office of a singer has always been considered as a sacred office.

Nor shall we be satisfied with the modern view that since choirs no longer sing in the sanctuary women can, without breaking the rules of the Church, take an official part in the singing. This would be a very specious and hair-splitting explanation were it not for the fact that the sacredness of an office is not attached to the place where it is performed, but to the performance itself. If such were not the case, a woman could ascend the pulpit and preach to the faithful when the pulpit is placed outside the sanctuary; she could carry the cross in a procession when the latter is held on this side of the communion rail; she could even attend sick calls and anoint the dying since these sacraments are not even performed in church. Everybody sees the ridiculousness of such a contention. Let us remember also that our separated brethren of the Anglican Church have finally understood the religious feature of this tradition of the Church, when they have returned to it by establishing choirs of men and boys in their services.

From an artistic standpoint there are no parts of our chants and services that choirs of men and boys cannot perform to better advantage for the spiritual uplifting of the Christian mind. Church musicians, when experts in vocal art, agree that women's voices are effeminate, sensuous, and operatic, hence unchurchly; that boys' voices are, on the contrary, unsophisticated, unsensual carrying with them a note of sincerity, candor, and simplicity, a purity of accent that most fittingly expresses the prayerful attitude of the faithful. By means of the latter, church functions would but, gain in devotional spirit, in dignity and nobility of purpose, what they lose to a great extent when they are expressed by voices which naturally carry with them the guises of the world. Even male singers of the stage, used to passionate mannerisms affectations and emotions of the operatic art of singing, are apt to mar and obscure the religious meaning of the liturgical text. A Bonci, a Hackett, a McCormack, a Caruso, would be out of place in church choirs, or rather, the liturgical music would be out of the proper channel in their vocal organs used to all the tricks that make music passionate, dramatic and sensual. They themselves would feel ill at ease in trying to give vocal expression to devotional feelings in sacred functions, of which they are often entirely ignorant and nearly always unfamiliar.

I hope I shall say nothing new to Mr. Krehbiel, when, on the other hand, I call his attention to the fact that the traditional melodies of plain song with all the monodic floriture of the golden age of melody are of a very different character than those of the classic and modern style of music; they represent in music what the gothic style for instance, represents in architecture, the most pure, elevated and at the same time, ornate and beautiful art; while the floriture in classicism and modern music represent the religiously senseless and meaningless dramaticism and sensualism. He himself in transcribing the musical example—Tollite Portas—was unable to give it a nota-

tion, or graphic interpretation, fitting the calmness and spiritual vision of the prayer in worship; he used, as he says, somewhat of the graphic devices of grouping notes by slurs and stem connections. His transcription is the product of a mental attitude unable to connect rich melodic designs with dignity in emotion and expression.

Modern musicians are like those painters who know nothing and seemingly wish to know nothing about the masterpieces of Fra Angelico Raphael and the like, for not only do they imagine they know all when they know modern painting, but whenever they try their hand at imitations of the ancient painters, they miss the more important feature of it, its symbolism. They create a body animated with a wrong soul. Church music can be ornate and devotional as gothic art is but it is so in its own way and style It is not the number of stones, but their arrangement in the building, that makes for a different style of architecture. It is not the number of notes in a musical composition that makes for the classic, sacred or modern style, it is the special arrangement of them that gives it a perception, the perception of the style for which it is intended. Modern musicians and art critics do not seem, unfortunately to have a very definite conception of what liturgical music should express and, consequently what it ought to be. They all seem to be under the impression that technique alone or external form is paramount in music. They forget that it is not sufficient for art to be fine, in its outward form, in order to be correct; symbolism, or inward meaning, which is its soul is necessary. Indeed, no matter how perfectly a work of art is wrought in all its details and proportions, it fails in its true scope when it does not convey the idea for which it was created. Religion especially demands that art be something more than a perfectly formed body, she wants it to be a perfect body but animated with a fitting soul, that is, with true and appropriate symbolisms; otherwise it is a blow to all sense of propriety.

Richard Wagner, that giant of instrumental and operatic music, was genius enough to know something about the symbolism of church music, although he never composed a piece of church music proper, when he said of the music, that was sung in Catholic churches in his time namely, the masses of Beethoven, Mozart, Haydn, Cherubini, Hummel and La Hache: "The first step towards the decadence of true sacred music in Catholic churches was the introduction in church functions of orchestral instruments. Their constant use impressed the expression of religious feeling with a trait of sensualism and had a very injurious influence on the part sung. The virtuosity of the instruments brought singers to emulate them; soon the PROFANE TASTE OF THE THEATRE had to enter the Church. Certain phrases of the sacred text as the Christe eleison—and others, were selected as a permanent subject of 'ARIF DA TEATRO' and for the rendition of them singers, trained according to the fashion of the Italian opera were called upon." Goethe expressed the same idea when he inveighed against the "music that was mingling sacred and profane character at the same time." He was wont to call it "impious" music. Hanslik, in turn, flouted the famous Italian Church music in which he said that "the religious spirit of the text is suffocated by the LUSTFUL FLESH of the musical body." But I do not want to touch here on the religious side of the question of Church music. Let priests take care of it. When they will have fully realized that the Masses, I have just mentioned, have nothing sacred about their musical body of art, that, on the contrary, as Hanslik says, their musical flesh is lustful, they will no doubt see to it that they are relegated from the choir loft into oblivion or left to stage or concert performances. I speak to the artist and musical critic, and to him I make it a mere question of art' for there can be no one with even so little knowledge of the sense of propriety in art, who cannot be convinced, on first mention, that secular music as well as its worldly mode of rendition, is entirely out of place in church functions because it is no more art, it is rather the mockery of it. Formerly secular music was patterned after sacred music, now-a-days the reverse has taken place, secular music has invaded the sanctuary of God, the churches Protestant as

well as Catholic. The cause of it is obvious. Secular musicians, completely ignorant of the true characteristics of church music, and of its spirit, as well as of how to render it are now masters of the musical situation in church affairs.

Mr. Krehbiel speaks of difficulties in carrying out the dispositions of the Motu Proprio and mentions especially that arising from lack of means to effect the change. I quote from the "Catholic Choirmaster" of February, 1916: "Among the prominent delegates who attended the first Congress of church music in Cliff Haven N. Y., none had more interesting accounts to give them than the Rev. P. F. Quinnan of Pittston, Pa. Father Quinnan inaugurated the unusual plan of having his congregation sing the ordinary of the High Mass; men, women, children join in the singing of the Chant every Sunday. The good Sisters were largely instrumental in training the children, who serve as leaders for the adults. The congregation is composed of representatives of many nationalities and one might expect this in itself to provide insurmountable difficulties. The results, however, are reported to be most satisfactory, the congregation having taken up the plan with great enthusiasm." So much for a country place.

I have a letter from a priest of the city of Pittsburg. He writes: "Although I have very little time to spare from the regular parish duties I find sufficient time to do a little to promote interest among the parishioners in the music of the Church. Perhaps you are aware that for some time our congregation here has been singing the Gregorian melodies at the parish High Mass on Sundays. Although the work is far from perfect or yet what we desire it to be, still we are making progress. It is really remarkable what one can do in these matters with a little effort. Our people are willing if WE only will make the effort." So much for a city place.

"Si isti cur non ego?"

Leo P. Manzetti.

Baltimore, Md.

Project of Founding a Solesmes Monastery in America

Mrs. Ward's letter to Dom Mocquereau
Westbrook, Oakdale, June 29, 1920

"Your American visit was one of such lively joy. How kind you are to have come so far to give us so much pleasure and to instruct the ignorant. But your stay was too short—much too short—so it will be necessary to return. I shall never be satisfied until we have a Solesmes Abbey in the United States. That will be the next miracle."

Justine Ward's Journal
1921   December 10th.

"Quarr—saw Dom M. about foundation"

1922   April 27th

"Saw Abbot Cozien about American foundation"

October 26th

"Washington discusses Solesmes foundation with Dr. Cormick"

November 23rd

"Washington. Dr. Dyer opened question of Solesmes foundation at the University, Catholic U., with Rector, B. Shahan"

Dom Mocquereau's letters to Mrs. Ward
March 28, 1922, Quarr Abbey

"I read to Rev. Father D. Cozien the passage in your letter, question of the will. . . . American foundation . . . and paleography . . . Your solicitude for Solesmes touches him profoundly . . . for myself, I preferred to be silent about it and to wait for New York and Washington. My! how good is God."

October 23, 1922—Solesmes

"We have noted the anti-clerical discourse by Caillaux: O, we are not safe from it. It is for this reason that we are keeping Quarr. It will be terrible to return there for the expenses of repairs here are enormous. And from this point of view and between us, I believe that the Abbot and the Cellarer appreciate our campaign in America. This could simplify our return to New York next year. In the end we are in the hands of God.—Yesterday a priest told me: 'Ah, if we are obliged to leave France once more, a foundation in America presents itself. We'll only find peace there! . . . Let the Lord take care of it' ". (D.M. makes reference to a statement in the Chamber by a deputy from the Saar.)

November 10, 1922—Solesmes

"Yesterday evening I received a long letter about the Washington voyage. This morning I placed it in the hands of the Most Rev. D. Cozien for him to read the passage concerning the foundation. He has not returned it to me yet."

Further on in the same letter of November 10th, he continues "I had Father Abbot D. Cozien read the passage in your letter about the foundation. He says for the moment we are not ready. This is true, but it is up to you to prepare everything. The first thing to do, is to put together the funds for the purchase of the land and construction of the monastery. From now until then I know very well that the good Lord will activate the hearts and the events. Let us pray much as we said to Dr. Dyer".

November 21, 1922—Solesmes

"As to Dr. Dyer's letter about the foundation, it is perfect, I am happy to meet with him but he says that the first thing to do is to amass funds for the purchase of the land. If you are successful, you and your friends, all will go well with you and, I believe, here also. But you have so much to do. How can you involve yourself in this considerable affair? . . . Oh! It is necessary to pray, to pray that the good Lord will work for you."

December 12, 1922—Solesmes (Cf. p. 17)

Dr. Dyer's letter is interesting: the matter is progressing *slowly*, but it is progressing. I still believe that it will be difficult to accept the site near The Shrine. There is not enough space for a Benedictine monastery (December 12, 1922)—yes, prayer must accomplish almost everything in a matter which goes straight to the Glory of God (Christmas Vigil, 1922).

(Christmas Vigil, 1922)—Sunday, Solesmes

"Foundation—I read and asked the Most Reverend Father Abbot to read what you say on this very interesting subject. Yes, prayer should accomplish everything in a matter that is directed toward the glory of God. I have not yet found in the open boxes here the map of the university. You will do well, I believe, to bring another one of these." (The map has not turned up at Solesmes.)

September 30, 1923—Solesmes (Monday, October 8th, same letter written at different times)

"Benedictine foundation in W. As you say, it is a sign from the good Lord that he does not wish us close to the University. This is how Providence leads us slowly where she wishes."

October 31, 1924 (Cf. p. 18)

I see that you have not given up the idea of a Solesmes foundation in Washington. It will be rather difficult, I believe. It will be even more difficult if only one monk from Solesmes is to organize the courses.

Dom Mocquereau's Letters to Dom Cozien, Abbot of Solesmes.
Pius X Chair of Liturgical Music, August 29, 1922

"I am not forgetting the Washington affair. Today, Mrs. Ward set the matter down very clearly with her attorney and, in a few days, I

shall have at hand the exact text relative to the foundation. Her thinking is always about the same".

September 1, 9 A.M., Westbrook, Oakdale
"Another 3 or 4 days here and I shall go to Washington. I enclose
herein a codicil added very recently to the will of Mrs. JBW. and which
fixes numbers, conditions, times for the foundation. Mrs. J.W. is encouraged in her hope by the conduct of the Dr. Dyer, Superior of the
Baltimore Seminary. This last recently passed through Quarr and truly
wishes a Solesmes Foundation in Washington. He is a very powerful
man at the Catholic University and in the Dioceses of Baltimore. Also,
Mrs. J.W. herself is full of joy and hope."

"In 3 or 4 days we shall go to Baltimore and to Washington with
Dr. Dyer and Msgr. Manzetti. I shall give you the result of that visit
maybe by cable. This will be my last excursion in America and we
shall leave on the 12th."

Codicil to last will and testament . . . dated May 2, 1921
August 30, 1922. Washington, 1326 Quincy Street, September 7th,
Birthday of Our Lady, 1922. (1st Vespers)

"From my room, I see the vast terrain of the University and Mrs.
Ward pointed out to me the hill on which she would be happy to see a
benedictine monastery built. We place under the protection of Our
Lady the excursions and steps we shall take".

September 8th morning. Last night, a good and fruitful drive by
auto through the University property. Delightful region, small valleys,
wooded at the top of a hill surrounded by forests—the solid foundations, abandoned, of a Polish religious house, not enough money could
be found to complete—56 meters long—18 in width—around, superb
forest. About 10 or 15 minutes from the University. We shall gather information. (In the margin: Dr. Dyer told us that "the land was bought
by the Marists. We arrived too late. All the professors are away. We
are saying nothing of Mrs. Ward's projects. Only Miss Mary Macken-
sie, her secretary, is informed with Dr. Dyer of Baltimore. We shall see
the land tomorrow"). (This phrase added in the margin is after the visit
to the region.)

"The 3rd. Evening. This morning, around 10 o'clock a visit to
another site which could be suitable. It is a plateau dominating all the
region, very strong, superb. Information is unclear as to its ownership.
Mrs. Ward believes that this plateau and the woods belong still to the
University. If so, this land would be given to us. Tomorrow Dr. Dyer
will inform us exactly. This morning, he wrote a letter to Mrs. Ward giving strong support to her project. She intends to let herself be guided
by Providence and wishes to entrust everything to Dr. Dyer. I shall continue this chronicle tomorrow after the visit to this important person".

"September 12th. Aboard the Aquitania at sea.—Our voyage by auto from Washington to New York was achieved happily and without fatigue. While passing through Baltimore we saw Dr. Dyer. Here in a few words is his feeling. I must tell you that Mrs. Ward is entirely open toward his hopes. This honest worthy man is very happy about it because he too ardently desires a Solesmian foundation at the University".

a) The foundation should be made near the Church to be built on land which I shall show you on the map (my opinion is that this land io entirely inadequate).

b) A school of music directed by monks is needed . . To my objections, the good Dr. replied that this School could have professors from outside.

c) We must not be hasty because the bishops are not ready... they know nothing, nothing about liturgy . . . nothing surely about music, except two.

d) only prayer remains . . . to let the idea germinate for 3 or 4 years . . .

e) to find the money to build . . . etc. . . . etc . . .

f) This foundation must be arrived at for the good of the Church in America. Vocations will certainly come. The Superior of S. Sulpice and President of the Major Seminary of Baltimore are not afraid to assure this.

There it is, the résumé of his conversation.

WESTBROOK,
OAKDALE, LONG ISLAND

June 29, 1920

Very dear Reverend Father:

How sad to say goodbye to you aboard the Leopoldina! Did you, at least, have a good voyage with your faithful guardian angel? I hope so.

Your visit in America has been so great a joy — how gracious you are to have come from so far to give us such pleasure and to instruct the ignorant! But your stay was too short — so you must return. I shall never be satisfied until we have a Solesmes Abbey in the United States. That will be the next miracle!

The lessons — so marvellous that you gave us in Albany, are unforgettable. But, alas, I did not benefit from them half as much as I should have because I was still tired from the Congress and the operation so that I was not feeling well. But thinking about it and in making countless exercises I believe that I understand better!

I promise myself the pleasure of seeing you again during the winter at Quarr Abbey or, even better, at Solesmes. Around Passion week I shall come to knock on the door with my manuscript under my arm. Already I am aware of many things that could be changed in the first books of the method for children.

I must tell you that I have not yet changed the $300 into English money that you confided to me. The exchange rate is not advantageous and I have been advised to wait for a better time when the exchange rate will be more advantageous. So, I shall wait until a better time.

You are not too tired, I hope, from your voyage? I would be so happy to know that all went well aboard the Leopoldina.

Believe, very Reverend Father, in my devoted good wishes and my sincere thanks.

Justine B. Ward

St. Mary's Seminary
Baltimore, Md.

Mrs. Justine B. Ward,   November 1st 1922.
Westbrook,
Long Island.

Dear Mrs. Ward:—

I have your good letter of October 29th and I am very glad indeed of the attitude of Doctor McCormick in the matter that interests us both so deeply. I am sure that his influence can help in directions that will count.

I do not immediately see my way clear to urge this project with Bishop Shahan, I am going to ask the advice within the next few days of one who I can trust help me to come to a decision.

Perhaps you are aware that at the recent meeting of the Bishops in Washington Right Reverend Bishop Schrembs of Cleveland and Right Reverend Bishop McDevitt of Harrisburg were appointed a committee to prepare a book of Church Offices and Chant somewhat on the order of the Solesmes Liber Usualis. I intend to go to Cleveland for the Celebration of the Diamond Jubilee of the diocese on Tuesday next. I hope to be able to have a talk with Bishop Schrembs and perhaps even to meet there the Right Reverend Bishop of Harrisburg. I will do my best to interest them in our cause.

The thing I am sure, dear Mrs. Ward, that would count with Bishop Shahan more than anything else is the question of means. — I have not heard at all of any other Community of Benedictines proposing to come to the University. I know that there are some priests connected with the University who contemplate forming a Benedictine Community. How much Bishop Shahan is interested in this I do not know. — But I feel confident that if Bishop Shahan could be assured of the means at hand to establish the Solesmes Community, the question would be solved. If the interest of some of your well provided friends could be aroused to help you in this matter other difficulties would disappear.

This you remember, dear Mrs. Ward, was one of the points that I insisted upon at the time you so kindly called upon me with Dom Mocquereau. The other point was prayer. — There is an important third point which did not occur to me at the time of our interview, but which presented itself very strongly before you had gotten far from the Seminary. It is to endeavor in every way possible to promote your own method of musical training. (I am not going to open this matter with Bishop Whitembs!) I have not been able to accomplish what I had hoped to in pushing this point. The beginnings of the actual year are very busy times and then I had to spend almost two weeks in a hospital from which I was released only last Saturday. Thank God I am quite well now and I will not miss any opportunity to further the Ward Methods in our schools, etc.

I thought I should write you immediately, dear Mrs. Ward, in answer to your kind letter. I will write you again as soon as I can come to any definite conclusion as to what steps should be taken with Bishop Shahan or as soon as I may have any appreciable results to report.

Believe me always

Very respectfully and sincerely yours,

E. R. Dyer, Pres't.

ST. MARY'S SEMINARY
BALTIMORE, MD.

November 25th 1922.

Mrs. Justine B. Ward,
1326 Quincy Street,
Brookland, D.C.

Dear Mrs. Ward:—

It was impossible for me to write you
yesterday.

I was most gratified in finding that Right
Reverend Bishop Shahan was willing to entertain and discuss the project of having the Solesmes Monks establish
themselves at the Catholic University in connection with
the Shrine to Our Blessed Mother. His final word to
me was that he is in no way opposed or unfriendly to such
a development, — but that he could not without much fuller
thought and discussion say that he approved it, — that indeed the decision in such a matter depends upon the Board
of Trustees, — and that it should be laid before them
before any open discussion or positive movement is inaugurated in that direction.

He said also however that he could see no in-
convenience in persons who might aid the project financially being approached discreetly to ascertain what they would
be willing to do in case the proposed plan would be approved
by the Trustees of the University.

Keep on praying, dear Mrs. Ward, and having
prayers said.

Very respectfully and sincerely yours,

E.R. Dyer,
Prest.

Codicil to last will and Testament of Justine B. Ward, dated May 2, 1921

(b) I give, devise and bequeath to the Very Reverend Abbot of the French Benedictine Monks of Solesmes at Solesmes, France, the sum of Two hundred and Fifty thousand ($250,000) Dollars, the income of which shall be used in perpetuity for the maintenance of a community of said order at or near the Catholic University of Washington, D. C., provided, however, that this gift shall not take effect unless and until the monastery of said order shall have been established and building or buildings thereof constructed at the location aforesaid, and in case said condition shall not be met within twenty-five years after the date of my death, this gift shall last. The amount of this gift shall be held by my trustees hereinafter named and their successors as part of my residuary estate and shall be administered as all other parts thereof until the condition aforesaid is fulfilled and the principal amount shall forth- with be turned over in accordance with the terms of this gift, but if the conditions shall not be fulfilled within the time limited, then this gift shall be disposed of in accordance with the provisions in- cluded in my residuary estate as though this gift had not been contemplated.

THE PIUS X HALL OF LITURGICAL MUSIC

The new hall of the Pius X institute of Liturgical Music was solemnly blessed by His Eminence Patrick Cardinal Hayes on the sixth of November at four o'clock in the afternoon. The building, which was designed by Delano and Aldrich, is of brick outside and in, with a few pieces of Gothic stone sculpture set in the walls. The street entrance is at 425 West 139th Street, but the hall may be reached also from the garden of the College of the Sacred Heart. The building, which seats 450 students, contains a small but beautiful organ built by Cassavant Frères and designed by Monsieur Joseph Bonnet.

To those who have at heart the reform of Church Music the occasion held a deeper significance than the dedication of a single building. The ceremony embodied to them a recognition of certain fundamental principles and standards for which the Pius X Institute has been at work for the past seven years: the lifting of music out of the realm of mere material gratification into the realm of divine worship, the restoration to the whole people, through a systematized training in the schools, of the art of liturgical song in its highest expression. Religion, the perennial need of the human spirit through the shifting chances of time, inspired the music of the Church which nourishes the highest aspirations of the soul and satisfies the deepest emotions of the heart in its longing to express the inexpressible. The material symbol of this movement was consecrated and placed under the patronage of Saint Gregory the Great by the Cardinal Archbishop of New York, and the impressive ceremony carried those present far from the pressure of things modern and things material, transplanting them into a quasi-mediaeval atmosphere of deep spiritual significance. The austere yet gracious lines of the building itself,

the exquisite singing of the ancient chants by the double choir of children, the gorgeous ceremonial, the insistent stress of the eternal values, all contributed to the impression that here, in the midst of modern New York, were to be found active centers where the things of a higher and better world were being built up as consistently as any of the material skyscrapers which rise over night before our astonished gaze, and that the occasion truly marked what His Eminence called "the crystallization of a work of magnificent and stupendous proportions."

In the ceremony of dedication Cardinal Hayes was accompanied by the Rt. Rev. Bishop Dunn, pastor of the Annunciation Church, who has been in sympathy with the movement for reform in church music for years and has given zealous support and co-operation to the work of the Pius X School. The Cardinal, vested in Pontifical robes, was attended by the Very Rev. Monsignor Donahue, Master of Ceremonies, and by the Rev. Father Bernard, O. S. B., and the Rev. James Corridan, Deacon of Honor, and by the Very Rev. Monsignor Joseph H. McMahon. In the solemn procession through the grounds of the College to the new building were also the Very Rev. Patrick J. McCormick, Dean of the Sisters College of the Catholic University, Washington; the Rev. Thomas J. Campbell, S. J.; the Rev. Michael Shea, of Dunwoodie Seminary; the Rev. Charles M. de Heredia, S. J.; the Rev. Father Verwhilgen, Chaplain of the College of the Sacred Heart, and many other clergymen. The procession, in the early dusk of a November afternoon, sounded a note of true mediaevalism and was a fitting prologue to a religious pageant only found today in the sublime ceremonies of the Catholic Church. The dark habits of the Religious of the Sacred Heart, velvet-clad pages in scarlet from the Annunciation

Parish Church bearing torches, accolites with cross and censor, a vested choir of men (members of the staff of the Pius X School) chanting the psalm "miserere," preceded the Prince of the Church and his attendants to the far end of the garden, where the Pius X Hall is situated. His Eminence stopped to bless the facade and doorway, then proceeded through the aisle to the throne, which had been erected at the right of the stage. He was greeted by the antiphon:

"*Sacerdos et Pontifex et virtutum opifex, pastor bone in populo, sic placuisti Domino.*" From the treasury of the liturgy the Benediction Loci was read by the Cardinal. Simple and short as this ceremony is, it epitomizes the loving care of a Father by Whom the very hairs of the head are numbered. Before the Cardinal's address the choirs sang alternate verses of "*Christus Vincit*" acclamations of the 8th century, and the antiphon appropriate to the occasion: "*Pax aeterna ab Aeterno huic domui, pax perennis Verbum Patris, sit pax huic domui. Pacem pius consolator huic praestet domui.*"

His Eminence, the Cardinal, spoke feelingly of the establishment of a work consecrated solely to the glory of the name of God. He said he found it somewhat difficult to voice the emotion he felt as he was ushered into the presence of the children, and heard the beautiful chant sung by the boys and girls. He referred to the dedication of the Hall as a work of more than ordinary importance, both in a liturgical and a historical sense. Referring to the approaching celebration of the sixteen hundredth anniversary of the dedication of the Cathedral of St. John Lateran in Rome, where St. Gregory the Great "was not ashamed to teach the Chant himself in the great holy Basilica" when the world was in the height of paganism, His Eminence deplored the fact that worldliness had crept into the music of the Church, and expressed the hope that in a few years all our people will know the beauty of the Chant. "The figure of St. Gregory looms up large here this afternoon, and all you, who know his work, realize the important part he played in the Church when upon earth. One of the matters which he considered of primary importance was the chant of Holy Mother Church, and it is one of the most natural things in the world when we sing the praise of God to give it out in beautiful form. But that expression needs guidance. The Church has ever been solicitous for the expression, by chant, through the ages, and so it came to that day when Pius X felt it was time that there should come over the Church and in the Church a reform in regard to Church music. The spirit of worldliness had crept into the very sanctuary. Thus the Holy Father felt it was necessary to lay down a standard. Gregorian music as it is taught here, while not excluding every other form of church music, is the norm. In so far as church music departs from Gregorian, it is getting away from the standard set by the Holy Father. So today you witness the crystallization of a work which has been on its way for some time, and now gives promise of permanency in this building.

In 1917[*]the work began, and for seven years we have had a small band devoted to the great ideal. One of the obstacles that those introducing the work had to surmount was that it might not be favorably received by the people, or even by the bishops and clergy, and possibly I was among them. Many of us looked askance at this venture. Yet what seemed impossible has been accomplished through the zeal and intelligence of a few people, and we have had a reform in church music. Pope Piux X with his other great works instituted this great work, and it has been carried to this height of attainment through the efforts of Mrs. Ward and the Religious of the Sacred Heart. This reform was intended to popularize the Church's prayer. There is no reason why the people should not use it. It is not

*The correct date is 1916. (Ed. Note.)

intended merely for the priest in the sanctuary or for the trained musician. It is intended by Our Beloved Father for all, that they should know how to pray in the chant of the Church." Continuing, His Eminence referred to the development of the work of the Pius X School during the past seven years, and spoke of the fact that 13,000 students had obtained certificates either by attendance at the School or through its extension department. The work has reached out to more than 500,000 children, covers a territory of 45 states, and has extended to Canada and the Philippines. Sixty religious communities have shown sympathy with the movement and have been formed by the Pius X School. As to the quality of the work, His Eminence called attention to the singing that afternoon, stating that wherever it is demonstrated it appeals to teachers, pupils and the public at large, and was a source of congratulation to those who had labored in the Cause. The Cardinal spoke of his joy in coming that day as Archbishop of the diocese to ask the blessing of God upon the building dedicated to a work which had already been so abundantly blessed by Him, and expressed the hope that the work so successfully begun will continue in the same way and go into every school and every religious community, so that after a time it will be possible to have the song of the Church in all parishes sung as Christ would have it. As His Eminence concluded, the Te Deum was intoned and the glorious paean of praise sung by the children, who then led the procession back to the Chapel of the College of the Sacred Heart, where Solemn Benediction was given by the Cardinal.

The children represented twenty parochial schools where the Justine Ward Method has been taught three years or more. Two hundred boys were grouped on the stage, while the girls' choir, who sang antiphonally with the boys, was placed in the gallery. Both choirs were under the direction of Mr. César Borré, of the staff of the Pius X School, and the organ accompaniment was played by Miss Mary Downey, also a member of the staff and a pupil of Mr. Pietro Yon.

Gregorian Chant as it was sung by these children, who have had a solid musical training as a basis upon which to build a knowledge of the liturgy, has attained a degree of perfection that is probably only surpassed by the chanting of the Monks of Solesmes. With an unearthly purity of tone, expressing the words of the liturgy in full understanding of their solemn portent, the Antiphons and hymns were chanted in rhythmic waves of song. The very walls of the building reflect the charm and beauty of the Chant. An atmosphere of austerity and mysticism pervades the Hall, as if the spirit during these last seven years, in its devotion and zeal for God's glory, had been making ready to quicken the mortar and bricks into a living thing. This triumph of architectural genius is an echo of a mediaeval cloister. To the simplicity of the Greek ideal it unites the spirit of a Gothic Cathedral, and the whole is an inspired example of moderation in design and harmony in proportion. Through this building resounded the voices of three hundred children "with a tone so sweet its joy fades not from memory."

Congratulations were received by cable from the Rev. Dom André Mocquereau in the name of Solesmes, and M. Joseph Bonnet in the name of the Institut Gregorien of Paris.

Among those present were Mrs. W. Bayard Cutting, who has contributed generously to the building of the Pius X Hall; Mrs. Nicholas Brady, Mrs. John G. Agar, Mrs. Winthrop Chanler, Mrs. Robert J. Collier, Mrs. Delancey Kane, Mrs. George Bird Grinnell, Mrs. Adrian Iselin, Miss Catherine McCann, Mr. and Mrs. J. Archibald Murray, Mrs. Robert Peabody, Mrs. Nicola Montani, Mr. McDavitt, secretary of the Saint Gregory Society; Mr. Pietro Yon, organist of the Church of Saint Francis Xavier, and Mr. Chester Aldrich, architect of the building.

Pius X School of Liturgical Music
College of the Sacred Heart
New York City

Blessing of the Pius X Hall

by

His Eminence Patrick Cardinal Hayes

Thursday, November sixth
Nineteen hundred and twenty-four

Order of Ceremony

I. Greeting to the Cardinal

Sacerdos et Pontifex et virtutum opifex, pastor bone in populo, sic placuisti Domino.

Priest and High Priest, and Giver of strength, the Good Shepherd of thy people, thus thou hast pleased the Lord.

SUNG BY GIRLS AND BOYS FROM PAROCHIAL SCHOOLS

II. Christus Vincit

SUNG BY GIRLS AND BOYS ALTERNATELY

III. Pax Aeterna

Pax aeterna ab Aeterno huic domui, pax perennis, Verbum Patris, sit pax huic domui. Pacem pius consolator huic praestet domui.

May everlasting peace be to this house from the Eternal Father, perpetual peace from the Word of the Father. May the loving Paraclete accord peace to this house.

SUNG BY CHOIR OF THE PIUS X SCHOOL

IV. Blessing of the Ball by the Cardinal

V. Adjutorium nostrum in nomine Domini.

V. Our help is in the name of the Lord.

R. Qui fecit coelum et terram.

R. Who has made heaven and earth.

V. Domine, exaudi orationem meam.

V. O. Lord, hear my prayer.

R. Et clamor meus ad te veniat.

R. And let my cry come unto Thee.

V. Dominus vobiscum.

V. The Lord be with thee.

R. Et cum spiritu tuo.

R. And with thy spirit.

OREMUS

Benedic Domine, Deus omnipotens, locum istum: ut sit in eo sanitas, castitas, victoria, virtus, humilitas, bonitas, et mansuetudo, plenitudo legis, et gratiarum actio Deo Patri, et Filio, et Spiritui Sancto; et haec benedictio maneat super hunc locum et super habitantes in eo nunc et semper. Amen.

LET US PRAY

Bless O Lord, Almighty God, this place, that within it there may be health, virtue, victory, strength, humility, kindness and meekness, the fulfilling of the law, and gratitude to God the Father, Son and Holy Ghost; and may this blessing remain upon this place and upon those who assemble in it now and forever, Amen.

V. Te Deum

SUNG BY GIRLS AND BOYS ALTERNATELY

Benediction of the Most Blessed Sacrament will be given by His Eminence the Cardinal in the Chapel of the College of the Sacred Heart

The Choir of Girls is from Annunciation Girls' School
and is the Choir of the Pius X School

The Choir of Boys is composed of ten boys from each of
the following parochial schools

ANNUNCIATION	ST. ANTHONY
ASCENSION	ST. BONIFACE
BLESSED SACRAMENT	ST. FRANCIS XAVIER
CATHEDRAL	ST. IGNATIUS
OUR LADY OF ANGELS	ST. JOHN CHRYSOSTOM
OUR LADY OF LOURDES	ST. JOSEPH
OUR LADY OF MERCY	ST. PAUL
OUR SAVIOUR	ST. RITA
ST. ALPHONSUS	ST. THOMAS AQUINAS
ST. ANSLEM	

Words of the Christus Vincit and of the Te Deum will
be found on each chair.

Pius X School of Liturgical Music
College of the Sacred Heart
New York City

Officium Pastorum

A NATIVITY PLAY OF THE XIII CENTURY

(Words and music from Codex No. 904
Bibliotheque Nationale. Paris)

Christmas, 1928

Envoyé par D.Mocquereau à la demande de Justine Ward et joué trois
fois en décembre 1928, le 20 et le 21 pour la Communauté du Sacré-
Coeur, et le 30 pour les religieuses du diocèse (Ward,Mora Vocis,
26 décembre 1928 et 26 décembre 1929 (note de Solesmes).

𝕯𝖗𝖆𝖒𝖆𝖙𝖎𝖘 𝕻𝖊𝖗𝖘𝖔𝖓𝖆𝖊

1. ANGEL who introduces the action

2. SEVEN BOYS representing the Choir of Angels

3. SHEPHERDS

4. ST. JOSEPH

Officium Pastorum

The *Officium Pastorum* was a dramatic development within the liturgy of Christmas. The earliest germ was in the form of a Trope introducing the Introit of the Third Mass of Christmas. Gradually this germ developed into a true drama and was attached to the end of the Office of Matins linking that Office to the Introit and indeed to the entire Midnight Mass and the Lauds which followed it.

The actors of the drama were Canons, priests and choir boys, and the action took place in the Church itself, about the Crib which was generally placed behind the main Altar. Many forms of this liturgical drama exist. The one which we have selected is taken from a Gradual of Rouen, which contains not only the full text, verbal and musical, but also directions for the action, costume, setting, etc.

In reproducing this piece, we have preserved intact the words and music, but, in apportioning the various parts to school children, we have made certain changes in the costumes.

The Office began, as it does today, by the singing of *Matins*, the recitation of the *Geneology of Christ*, and the singing of the *Te Deum*. Instead of beginning immediately the Midnight *Mass*, it was the custom, as early as the XI Century and until the end of the XII, to perform a little drama which linked the Matins to the Mass. At the moment when the Shepherds, (represented by five Canons, wearing white tunics and the amice, and carrying in their right hand the symbolical staff or Shepherd's crook) entered the Choir by the main entrance, a choir boy, dressed also in white and standing upon the *ambo* or pulpit, sang to them the announcement of the great news of the birth of Christ, like the angel in the Gospels.

"Nolite timere. Ecce enim evangelizo vobis gaudium magnum quod erit omni populo, quia natus est nobis hodie Salvator mundi in civitate David, et hoc vobis signum: invenietis infantem pannis involutum et positum in praesepio."

"Fear not, for behold, I bring you tidings of great joy which shall be to all the people, for this day is born to you a Saviour, in the city of David, and this will be a sign unto you: you shall find the Infant wrapped in swaddling clothes and laid in a manger."

Seven other boys, placed in a high gallery of the choir,
dressed also in white, and representing the angelic hosts,
answered in a high voice:

"Gloria in excelsis Deo, et in terra pax hominibus bonae voluntatis."	"Glory to God in the highest, and on earth, peace to men of good will.

At this celestial message the Shepherds advanced in the
Choir singing the following:

Pax in terris nuntiatur *In excelsis gloria* *Caelo terra faederatur* *Mediante gratia*	Peace on earth is announced; In the highest, glory. Heaven and earth are united By mediating grace.
Mediator, homo, Deus *Descendit in propria,* *Ut ascendat homo reus* *Ad admissa gaudia. Eya! Eya!*	The Mediator, man-God, Has descended to His own, That man may ascend and be admitted To his promised joy. Behold! Behold!
Transeamus, videamus *Verbum hoc quod factum est,* *Transeamus ut sciamus* *Quod nuntiatum est.*	Let us go over, let us see That Word which has been made (flesh): Let us go over, let us know That which has been announced.
In Judea Puer vagit, *Puer salus populi,* *Quo bellandum se praesagit* *Verus hospes sacculi.*	In Judea the Child is weeping The Child, Salvation of the people, Who has taken on Himself to wage war Against the ancient enemy.
Accedamus, accedamus *Ad praesepe Domini,* *Et dicamus:* *Laus fecundae Virgini.*	Let us approach, let us approach The Crib of the Lord, And let us express our Praise to the Virgin-mother.

The Shepherds pass through the choir, their staves in
their hands, singing as they approach the Crib of Christ:

"Transeamus usque Bethleem, et videamus hoc Verbum quod factum est, quod fecit Dominus et ostendit nobis."	"Let us go over to Bethlehem and let us see this Word which is come to pass, which the Lord hath shewed to us."

ST. JOSEPH:
"*Quem queritis in praesepe, pastores, dicite?*"

"Whom seek ye? Speak ye Shepherds!"

SHEPHERDS:
"*Salvatorem Christum Dominum, infantem pannis involutum secundum sermonem angelicum.*"

"The Saviour, Christ the Lord! The Infant wrapped in swaddling clothes. According to the angels' word."

(Opening the curtains which hide the Child, and showing the Child with Mary His Mother:)

ST. JOSEPH:
"*Ad est hic parvulus cum Maria matre sua, de quo dudum vaticinando Ysayas dixerat propheta.*"

"Behold the Child with Mary His mother, of whom in times past, Isaias, prophecying, said:"

BOYS: (pointing to the Mother)
"*Ecce Virgo concipiet et pariet filium; et euntes dicite quia natus est.*"

"Behold, the Virgin shall conceive and bear a Child. Go ye forth and announce that He is born."

Then the Shepherds bow down and salute the Virgin, saying:

"*Salve, Virgo singularis,*
Virgo manens Deum paris
Ante saecla generatum
Corde Patris;
Adoremus nunc creatum
Carne matris."

"Hail Virgin most marvellous,
Who, remaining Virgin, bearest God
Begotten before the ages
In the heart of the Father.
Let us adore Him Who took flesh
From the Mother."

"*Nos, Maria, tua prece*
A peccati purga fece;
Nostri cursum incolatus;
Sic dispone
Ut det sua frui natus
Visione."

"O Mary, by your prayers
Set us free from our sins.
And so dispose the course of our life
That we may be made worthy
To enjoy of His birth
The vision."

The Boys and the Shepherds adore the Infant Jesus. Then turning toward the people, they say:

"Alleluia, Alleluia!
Jam vere scimus Christum natum
in terris, de quo canite omnes cum
prophetis dicentes:

"Alleluia! alleluia; Now we know in truth that Christ is born on earth, He of Whom the Prophets sang and we, with them, saying:

INTROIT
Dominus dixit ad me: Filius
meus es tu, ego hodie genui te.
*Ps. Quare fremuerent gentes: et
populi meditati sunt inania?
Gloria Patri.

The Lord said to me: Thou art my Son, this day have I begotten thee. Ps. Why have the Gentiles raged, and the people devised vain things? Glory be to the Father, etc.

The Shepherds direct the chorus during the Mass. They sing the Gloria in Excelsis Deo, the Epistle and the Trope. One of the Shepherds reads the Lesson *Populus gentium.* The Sub-deacon reads the Epistle, two shepherds sing, from the steps of the *ambo* the Gradual *Tecum princip-ium.* Two of the highest rank sing from the pulpit: Alleluia, Dixit Dominus, etc. The Mass finished, the Celebrant turns towards the Shepherds and entones this Antiphon:

"Quem vidistis, pastores? dicite:
annuntiate nobis, in terris quis ap-
paruit?"

"What did you see, O Shepherds? tell me! Announce to us, Who has appeared?"

THE SHEPHERDS ANSWER:
"Natum vidimus, et choros Ange-
lorum collaudantes Dominum,
alleluia, alleluia."

"We saw Him who is born, and the Angelic choir praising God, al-leluia, alleluia!"

Chorus sings the psalm etc. Lauds finished, the Shepherds sing the *Benedicamus Domino.*

* When children are giving the play it may end here.

THE NATIVITY PLAY
WILL BE FOLLOWED BY CAROLS
SUNG BY 250 CHILDREN AND
THE PIUS X CHOIR

SACRED CONCERT

BY

SINGERS *from the* PIUS X SCHOOL *of* LITURGICAL MUSIC

UNDER THE DIRECTION OF

MRS. JUSTINE B. WARD

CONRAD BERNIER, *Organist*

At 4 p. m., Tuesday, November 20, 1928

I—"EXSULTET ORBIS GAUDIIS"   ·   ·   ·   *Gregorian Chant*
        Hymn for feast of the Apostles

II—"LOCUS ISTE" ·   ·   ·   ·   ·   ·   *Gregorian Chant*
        Feast of Dedication of a church

    "ALLELUJA"   ·   ·   ·   ·   ·   ·   *Gregorian Chant*
        Feast of Dedication of a church

III—PRELUDE ·   ·   ·   ·   ·   ·   H. Purcell (1658-1694)

IV—(a) "DE PROFUNDIS"   ·   ·   ·   ·   *Gregorian Chant*
        Offertory for 23rd Sunday after Pentecost

    (b) "DUO SERAPHIM"   ·   ·   ·   ·   *Gregorian Chant*
        Responsory
    (c) *Cantate in initium (Responsory)*   *Ambrosian Chant*

V—TOCCATA PER l'ELEVAZIONE   ·   ·   G. Frescobaldi (1583-1643)

VI—(a) "ILLUMINA OCULOS MEOS"   ·   ·   Palestrina (1526-1594)
    (b) "JESU, REX ADMIRABILIS"   ·   ·   Palestrina (1526-1594)

VII—GRAND-JEU   ·   ·   ·   ·   ·   ·   ·   ·   Du Mage

BENEDICTION OF THE MOST BLESSED SACRAMENT

                Home guidance
        Salus mater   ~~Ave Verum~~   ·   ⎫
                           ~~Salve Regina~~   ·   ⎬   *Gregorian Chant*
                           Tantum Ergo   ·   ⎭

THE NATIONAL SHRINE OF THE
    IMMACULATE CONCEPTION
CATHOLIC UNIVERSITY OF AMERICA

Catholic University of America,

Divinity College,   **Washington, D. C.**

CHAPEL, CALDWELL HALL.

7:30 P. M. Tuesday   November 20th 1928.

Eve of Feast of Presentation of Our Blessed Lady in the Temple.

SACRED CONCERT
by
Singers from the Pius X School of Liturgical Music
under the direction of

Mrs. Justine B. Ward.   Mr. Conrad Bernier, Organist.

I—"TOCCATA" (in five parts)   G. Muffat (1645-1704).

II—(a) "IN ISRAEL" (Antiphon ad Magnificat).   Ambrosian Chant.

(b) "STIRPS JESSE." (Responsory)   Gregorian Chant.

III—"AVE MARIS STELLA"   Gregorian Chant.
Pius X Choir with Organ interludes by: J. Titelouze (1563-1633).
                                            N. De Grigny (1671-1703).

IV—(a) "HOMO QUIDAM"   Gregorian Chant.
(b) "O ESCA VIATORUM"   Ehrico Isaak (1493).   J. S. Bach (1685-1750).
(c) "ILLUMINA OCULOS MEOS"   Palestrina (1526-1594).

V—FANTASY AND FUGUE in G. minor   J. S. Bach (1685-1750).

SOLEMN BENEDICTION OF THE MOST BLESSED SACRAMENT AND RENEWAL
OF THE ACT OF CLERICAL CONSECRATION.

AVE VERUM.
QUAM PULCHRE GRADITUR.
SALVE REGINA.
TANTUM ERGO.
TE DEUM LAUDAMUS.

The congregation is kindly asked to join in the chant for the Benediction.

"Therefore, O God, do we
Thy people, consecrate ourselves to Thee,
Who, Virgin-born for men,
By men art daily Altar-born again."

1326 Quincy Street N. E.
Washington, D. C.

June 28, 1929.

Rt. Rev. G. Cozien O.S.B.
    Solesmes,
        France.

Rt. Rev. and dear Dom Cozien:

Through the generosity of
Mrs. J. B. Ward, the Catholic University
of America is to have a separate building
for its Faculty of Liturgical Music.
Her desire, as well as that of the University,
is that this new building bear the name
of Dom André Mocquereau. For this
reason, I am writing to you, Dom
Mocquereau's Abbot, asking your
permission to use the name of Dom
Mocquereau and asking your to bless our work,
which must at all times be closely
connected with your famous monastery.
                I need not tell you about
the Dom Mocquereau Schola Cantorum
Foundation established by Mrs. Ward. I
know that she corresponds with Solesmes
and that you know about this great
work. Neither time, means, nor work
has been spared by Mrs. Ward to assure
the success of the Liturgical music
movement in our country. Through

this foundation the Catholic University
School (Faculty) of Liturgical music has
been established and will be maintained
for all times at this important centre
of Catholic Education.

This new Faculty will answer
a long felt need at our University.
We follow steadily the teachings of Solesmes
on the chant. The use of Dom Mocquereau's
name will be a constant object lesson
to our pupils and to the Catholic public.

The erection of this building, this
summer, will prevent my going to
Solesmes with our twelve students. I
wish to thank you and your fathers
for the kind hospitality offered me and
our young men.

Hoping to recieve a favourable
answer in regards the use of Dom
Mocquereau's name —, I am,

Yours faithfully in our Lord,
Wm. J. DEs Longchamps.

The Dom Mocquereau
Schola Cantorum Foundation, Inc.

SCHOOL OF SACRED MUSIC TO BE ESTABLISHED AT THE
CATHOLIC UNIVERSITY, WASHINGTON, D. C.

The Dom Mocquereau Schola Cantorum Foundation, Inc., is an educational foundation for the following purposes:

1. Education in Gregorian Chant according to the principles of Solesmes, as set forth by Dom André Mocquereau in his published works, particularly in *Nombre Musical Gregorien,* Volumes I and II, and the series of volumes which make up the *Paleographie Musicale.* The preparation of teachers therein, through normal courses and advanced courses, leading up to the degree of B.A. and M.A., also courses for choirmasters and church organists.

2. Education in Classic Polyphony, especially that of the Roman School of the sixteenth century, culminating with the works of Palestrina and Vittoria.

3. Education in all other subjects dealing with technical and cultural equipment, including sight reading, vocal training, choir conducting, piano and organ playing, harmony, counterpoint, history of music, liturgy and kindred subjects to be taught in so far as they serve to contribute to the principal educational purposes of the foundation.

The Foundation will foster the training of teachers for the elementary grades of the parish schools, as well as for the intermediary grades up into the colleges, the universities and the novitiates of religious orders; thus, it will meet the desire expressed by Pope Pius XI in his latest Apostolic Constitution on liturgy, Gregorian Chant and sacred music. Gregorian Chant is put particularly in the foreground, because it is "the only chant which the Church directly proposes to the faithful as her own,"[1] which "has always been regarded as the supreme model for Sacred Music,"[2] and which Pius XI once more insists should be restored to the people.[3]

Classic Polyphony is given a prominent place, because "it agrees admirably with Gregorian Chant, the supreme model of all sacred music, and hence has been found worthy of a place side by side with Gregorian Chant in the more solemn functions of the Church."[4]

Dom Mocquereau's name has been given to this Foundation because, in the judgment of the founders, he is considered the outstanding figure of modern times in the world of ec-

clesiastical chant, in the same sense that Guido d'Arezzo was the outstanding figure in the Middle Ages.

The name Schola Cantorum was used because this title comes down to us from the fourth century in the time of Pope St. Sylvester I, and has remained the classic term for schools of sacred chant and music throughout the history of the Church.

The Foundation starts out with an endowment of a million dollars, a sum which is quite insufficient to carry out even the immediate program before it, but it is the hope of the directors that the Foundation will serve as a nucleus to which others will contribute, and will thus make it possible for the work to spread on a larger scale.

The first Board of Directors are Mother Georgia Stevens, R. S. C. J., Directress of the Pius X School of Liturgical Music; Rev. Dr. W. J. DesLongchamps, Dean of the School of Liturgical Music of the Catholic University of America, Washington, and Justine B. Ward, Mus.D. Greg. Ch., Dobbs Ferry, N. Y.

In confining its efforts to Chant and Classic Polyphony, the directors desire to affirm their belief that what is most needed at present is a thorough acquaintance with the classical liturgical music which the Church recommends positively. The clergy, choirmasters and the Catholic public need to know and love the true ecclesiastical standard. A new mentality will result as regards sacred music. To-day the type which the Holy See considers most desirable is practically unknown to the majority of Catholics in this country. The Foundation then, in limiting its activities, has no desire to be "more catholic than the Church." It has merely selected out of a larger possible program its own special function, namely, to devote all its energies to the types that the Holy See has declared to be the best. In insisting upon the Chant as the foundation of all ecclesiastical music, and insisting upon it to the exclusion of everything else, save Classic Polyphony, the directors feel that they could do no greater service to the art of music in general. Even modern composers, who are working on truly ecclesiastical lines, will find a better understanding of their motives and ideals as a result of this training.

The first work of the Foundation, and, indeed, its only work until other funds shall come forward to help the spread of its activities, is:

[1] *Pius X, Motu Proprio, Par. II, 3.*
[2] *Ibid.*
[3] *Pius XI Apostolic Constitution, ix.*

[4] *Pius X Motu Proprio, Par. II, 4.*

1. The maintenance of the Pius X School of Liturgical Music in New York;

2. The establishment and maintenance of the new School of Liturgical Music of the Catholic University of America.

The work of the Pius X School is already well known in this country and in Europe.

The School at the Catholic University will continue the work already launched several years ago by the University Schola Cantorum, but it will be on a larger scale and in a more permanent form. The School of Music has the same rank and importance as the School of Theology, The School of Canon Law, etc., etc. The Rector of the University, Mgr. Ryan, deserves the gratitude of all church musicians for the energy and zeal he has shown in the organization of this School and the perfect co-operation he has shown the Foundation. The School will be open to undergraduate and graduate students, to the students at the religious houses which surround the University, and to the students at The Sisters' College of the University.

The School will also conduct all the University offices at the Shrine of the Immaculate Conception. These offices will be made, as far as possible, a model of what the Holy See desires; there will be a liturgical choir, confining itself to the singing of Gregorian Chant and Classic Polyphony. Most of the singers will be priests and seminarians. A choir of boys will take the soprano and alto parts in the polyphonic pieces and will alternate with the men in the Chant. Thus, the School offers the required courses of study and also model renderings.

The Dean of the new School, the Rev. Dr. DesLongchamps, has studied for many years abroad, preparing himself under the world's greatest masters for the important position which he now holds. For three years he was a student at the Papal College of Music in Rome. His summer vacations were spent with the Monks of Solesmes, first at Quarr Abbey and then in France. Later, Dr. DesLongchamps carried on post-graduate work in Vienna and at the Benedictine Monastery of Beuron. He familiarized himself with the work of the more important European colleges and conservatories. In short, Dr. DesLongchamps has had an ideal formation. He will undoubtedly build up a school at the University which will be not only of national but international importance, and Americans will find themselves in the front rank of those countries who have taken positive action to bring about, in an effective manner, the reforms that have been urged upon us so emphatically by three recent Popes, and which Pius XI has just made the subject of his recent Apostolic Constitution.

In speaking of the Foundation, Mrs. Ward said: "The Foundation will, I hope, do two things: First, it will provide a permanent organization for teaching liturgical Chant and Classic Polyphony, with all the branches necessary to lead up to their correct understanding and rendering. Secondly, it will bring together in a single directorate the individuals who have built up two of the most important schools of liturgical Chant and music in this country. These two schools will work in harmony, and will supplement one another in many respects.

"The problem of the immediate future is the formation of teachers. The Pius X School has done an immense work in the last twelve years, toward the formation of the teaching sisterhoods in particular. This work is necessary and fundamental if our children are to be taught in the schools and if the true ideals are to penetrate the novitiates of Religious Orders of women. This alone, however, will not suffice. If we are to accomplish permanent results, it is necessary that the clergy should be helped to obtain a solid education in liturgical Chant (as Pope Pius XI so clearly states), the clergy, both secular and religious. The Catholic University is ideally placed to organize such a movement, because of the large number of its own students, both undergraduate and graduate; also because of the students in the various Religious Houses which surround the University, as well as the students of the Catholic Sisters' College. The priests and seminarians, moreover, will take part in ecclesiastical offices which are truly liturgical in character in the Shrine of the Immaculate Conception.

"The mere fact that the University desires such a school and has shown the most perfect spirit of co-operation with the Dom Mocquereau Schola Cantorum Foundation is the best proof that we are entering upon a new and better era as regards sacred liturgy and chant. The whole subject is one which concerns primarily the clergy and only secondarily the musician. Hitherto, the musician has taken a more active interest in the subject than the clergy. But the action of the University is, to me, the most encouraging thing that has happened since the appearance of the Motu Proprio of Pius X. All those who are interested in sacred music will feel a special debt of gratitude to the Rector, Msg. Ryan, to whom this new school owes its existence. Also in no small degree is the building up of this school due to Dr. DesLongchamps, who started several years ago with a modest 'Schola Cantorm,' which has now blossomed forth into this important undertaking. Dr. DesLongchamps' extreme modesty has kept him in the background and probably will continue to do so, and it is all the more pleasure, therefore, to speak of the very fine work which he has done and will certainly continue to do at the Catholic University."

The Rev. Wm. J. DesLongchamps Appointed Dean of Liturgical Music School in Washington

SCHOOL WILL BE HOUSED IN NEW BUILD-ING—MADE POSSIBLE BY NEW YORK FOUNDATION WHICH HAS $1,000,000 EN-DOWMENT FUND.

The executive committee of the board of trustees of the Catholic University of America has completed arrangements for the establishment of a School of Liturgical Music, the Right Rev. Monsignor James H. Ryan, rector of the university, announced today. (April 5, 1929.)

The school has been made possible by the Dom Mocquereau Schola Cantorum Foundation, a New York corporation, whose sole object is education in Gregorian Chant and Classic Polyphony, and other closely allied branches of music. The Foundation starts with a million-dollar trust fund, the income from which is available immediately. Through this Foundation, the university will give a certain limited number of courses in liturgical music at its coming summer session, and will be ready to give regular instruction at the opening of the next school year.

To Erect New Building

A building for the School of Liturgical Music is to be erected at once, the university board of trustees having set aside for this purpose a site close to the monumental Shrine of the Immaculate Conception, now under construction. Ground will be broken for the new building within the next few weeks, it is expected.

Trustees of the Dom Mocquereau Foundation are the Rev. Dr. William J. DesLongchamps, of the Catholic University of America, who has been named dean of the new school; Mother G. Stevens, R. S. C. J., of the Pius X School of Liturgical Music in New York, and Mrs. J. B. Ward, of New York, who is foundress of the latter school and through whose generosity the Foundation was made possible.

Dr. DesLongchamps has been professor of music at the Catholic University of America for the past four years. He made his preparatory studies in some of the best schools of liturgical music in Europe, namely, at Rome, Vienna, Beuron, and with the Fathers of Solesmes. He is at present engaged in organizing a faculty for the Catholic University School of Music, many members of which will be of international standing in their respective fields.

The School of Liturgical Music will be open to undergraduate students preparing for the degree B. S. in Music. Its aim will be not only to prepare choir leaders and teachers of Church music, but also to train research students in the various departments of this artistic knowledge. The school will offer courses in liturgical music, school music, applied music, theory, harmony, counterpoint, and fugue, and graduate courses leading to higher degrees. The curriculum will follow closely the courses of study now being given at such famous institutions as the Pontifical School of Sacred Music in Rome and the Academy of Church Music in Vienna.

Work of the school will be confined to the field of chant and classical Church music, and will not engage in general musical education. The fundamental purpose will be to build up a better understanding and appreciation of Gregorian Chant and of Classic Polyphony, and all modern vocal Church music composed since Palestrina is expressly excluded from the school's objectives.

In announcing the establishment of the school, Monsignor Ryan said that he considered it most timely, coming, as it does, with the Apostolic Constitution on Liturgy, Gregorian Chant, and Sacred Music of Pope Pius XI, who commands that music be taught in Catholic schools from the earliest stages of instruction.

Monsignor Ryan's Views

"The university," continued the Monsigner, "accepts this gift with gratitude and pledges itself to the perpetuation and development of the ideals which actuate the donors. The School of Liturgical Music will be a noteworthy addition to the educational and artistic life of the City of Washington. Classical Church music is one of our greatest artistic heritages. We hope that from the Catholic University School of Liturgical Music there will go forth, not merely trained students of the best in the liturgical music of the Church, but that there will issue, too, inspiration and aid toward the development in the United States of the best and highest in music of every type. We are concentrating here on liturgical music, because we think that the Catholic University is peculiarly adapted to the study and production of this special type of music. We look forward happily to the effects of this experiment which we are to conduct on music in general. Music-lovers who appreciate the close ties which have always bound together Church and secular music cannot but welcome the establishment of a school with such high classical ideals as we intend to conduct. They will watch, I feel sure, the course of its work with great pleasure and expectancy."—N. C. W. C.

The New Schola Cantorum

W. J. HENDERSON, MUSIC EDITOR OF THE NEW YORK *SUN*, COMMENTS ON THE ESTABLISHMENT OF THE *DOM MOC-QUEREAU SCHOLA CANTORUM FOUN-DATION*, *INC.*

The most important musical news of the week was that Mrs. Justine Ward had acquired a million dollars for the establishment of a schola cantorum at the Catholic University of America in Washington. The purpose of this school will be to teach chant and ecclesiastic polyphony. The new school has been made possible by the creation of the Dom Mocquereau Schola Cantorum Foundation, a New York corporation. Mrs. Ward had already founded the Pope Pius X school in this city, an institution devoted to the cultivation of church music on the lines prescribed in the celebrated "motu proprio" of the Pontiff after whom the school is named.

Music lovers not especially informed about Catholic church music should be told that Dom Mocquereau is the head of the great school of chant at Solesmes and is the foremost authority in the world on the chant of the Roman church, commonly called the Gregorian. The Rev. Dr. William J. DesLongchamps of the Catholic University will be the dean of the new school. He is a distinguished scholar in the music of his church and will have charge of the organization of the faculty.

The importance of this establishment will be its widespread influence as well as its authority in Catholic church music, which needs in this country just such a court of last resort as this institution seems likely to become. The most precious musical heritage of the church is its chant and its polyphonic music as developed by the great masters of the fifteenth and sixteenth centuries. A return to the style of these masters cannot be regarded as a retrogression, because after Palestrina the composers of the church departed from the best models and introduced into their music devices meant to captivate the senses of worshipers rather than to express the devotional spirit of the liturgy.

No medium for the recitation of the ritual better than the plain song has ever been found, while for the grand musical numbers of the mass the a cappella polyphonic style remains unequaled. The use of the orchestra has been attended with danger ever since it began in the days following the invasion of the sanctuary by the delineative theatricalism developed in music by the rise of the opera. Hand in hand with this went the growing fondness for the display of vocal virtuosity. The mass became a field for the exercise of musical invention and the liturgy was buried under the splendors of a musical art, glowing and seductive, but entirely devoid of the austere chastity of the older creation. That the mass will continue to furnish composers with a text for expressions of religious passion cannot be doubted; but with such matters the church has no concern. Its path should assuredly be clear. It will seek to hold the thought of the congregation to the solemn mystery of the service and to do that must rid itself of all musical display.

The Schola Cantorum

The first schools of chant were founded by Pope Sylvester in Rome about 315. Their aim was to spread through the churches a uniform manner of delivering the chants then extant. But the epoch-making Schola was that established by Gregory the Great, who was the sovereign Pontiff from 590 to 604. There are radical differences of opinion as to just how much Gregory actually did in shaping the chant which bears his name, but it seems to be well proved that he did found the school in which the system was taught and the parish school boys trained as choir singers.

That graduates of this school carried its gospel into distant lands cannot be questioned and the study of its history and achievements by the fathers of Solesmes has fixed permanently the facts about its teachings and the correct method of singing its chants. The meretricious style of the seventeenth century, with its theatricalism and its tendency to make a show of the service, was diametrically opposed to all that the Schola Cantorum taught, and in subsequent days the plea was always made that to return to the plain song would deprive the church of some of its most beautiful music. But, as already said, the church is more anxious about the purity, propriety and intelligibility of its service than about the fame of composers.

The chant is of ancient origin and is not the exclusive property of Rome. It belonged to the Hebrews and the Egyptians before it did to the Italians. It belongs today to the Anglican Church as clearly as to the Catholic, and assuredly the Greek Church would not readily renounce its claim. The style of delivery of the chant has been greatly altered by the various changes in the style of the other music introduced into the church repertory, and the new school will doubtless find abundant work in correcting abuses and eliminating evil habits. One of the latter is a tendency to a staccato which is diametrically opposite to the smooth and fluent legato of the chant. However, this is not the time for a long disquisition on the rendering of liturgical music. The foundation established through the efforts of Mrs. Ward deserves a welcome here because of the inestimable benefit it may bring to the musical service.—*New York* "*Sun.*"

A School of Liturgy

Now and then, suddenly, something genuinely important happens in the domain of education. Then one discerns clearly a need that has long existed, a work that clamors to be done. Certainly the establishment of a liturgical music school at the Catholic University of America is just such an epochal event. For years training in ecclesiastical music suffered, despite many intrinsic excellences, from a lack of connection with general clerical and lay education. A man could complete a course of study under first-rate auspices and in a thoroughly religious atmosphere without ever giving so much as a thought to that question of Church music which has engrossed entire generations of earnest observers. In the United States especially the result was indifference to the form of divine worship, willingness to accept even the most decadent melodies, and in some cases a nearly scandalous absence of music in any form. When the work now begun at the Catholic University gets under way, the efficacy of sound standards ought to be felt in even remote places.

The school has been brilliantly established. Mrs. Justine Ward, through whose generosity the foundation of $1,000,000 was made possible, is almost solely responsible for such consciousness of liturgical music as does exist among us. It is rarely, indeed, that a person of her means and talent devotes so much enthusiasm to a humanistic and spiritual cause. Her achievement can be measured, in part, by the faculty which is available for the new school —a group trained in accordance with the best European traditions. It can also be gauged by its value as an example; for, as Monsignor Ryan stated in his address of acceptance, "music lovers who appreciate the close ties which have always bound together Church and secular music cannot but welcome the establishment of a school with such high classical ideals as we intend to conduct."

Life permits deviations from perfection and concessions to necessity. One cannot expect that ordinary parish singing will ever attain the purity and beauty of renditions by age-old monastic choirs. But it is imperative that education be something different from life—that it be courageous in its struggle for perfection and in its defense of standards. Only so can the whole community be kept mindful of the need for the best that heart and soul can do. The school is to be the light set on the hill, for the guidance and encouragement of the valleys. And one may conclude by saying that, in general, the Catholic cause in the United States could profit from nothing so much as from a multiplication of centers for cultivation of the good, the beautiful, the true, for their own sakes.

Despite the vast total of unselfish benevolence in the past, America is not yet as conscious of the stewardship of wealth as it might profitably be. Mrs. Ward's good deed is, therefore, notable not merely because it is charity, but because it has revealed a genuine need, to the removal of which wealth could make an important contribution. That day will be blessed when eyes are turned to the discovery of similar ways in which the civilization of our country may be enriched, strengthened and sublimated in the spirit of Christ the King. Literature and the arts are clearly among the most important of these methods. That neither is able to thrive without subsidy from more practical pursuits is likewise evident—and so the moral may be permitted to make itself.—*The Commonweal.*

THE PLAN

The School of Liturgical Music

THE REALIZATION

The Catholic University of America
Washington, D.C.

Office of the Rector

September 3, 1929.

(Sent to all Ordinaries)

Your Eminence:
Your Grace:
Your Lordship:

With the opening of this scholastic year, the Catholic University School of Liturgical Music will begin to function as a School of the University. This School, with its own faculty and building, will in no way be a financial burden to the University. Its entire budget will be met annually by the Dom Mocquereau Schola Cantorum Foundation, Inc. We feel that this School, so well founded with a splendid faculty, will meet the approval of the Hierarchy of this country.

The faculty is made up of men imbued with a love for Liturgical Music and the Liturgy of the Church; men who are experts in their line of work. For the classes of Gregorian Chant we are to have Dom Maur Sablayrolles, a Benedictine Monk. He comes to teach Chant as it is taught and executed at the famous Monastery of Solesmes, whose monks have done so much for the Liturgy and for the restoration of Gregorian Chant.

In order to do its best work, the School of Liturgical Music must have the full co-operation of the Hierarchy, the heads of seminaries, colleges, and religious institutions, the pastors of our churches, and the sisters of our schools.

With a large body of students, priests, sisters, and lay students, trained for their respective positions, whether as diocesan directors of Liturgy and Liturgical Music, as professors or school teachers in our institutions, or as choir directors or organists, we can hope for far-reaching improvements in the Liturgical life of the Church in this country. We ask your continued interest in the University and especially in the new School of Liturgical Music.

With best wishes and asking your blessing on myself and the University,

Yours sincerely in Christ,

/s/ James H. Ryan

(Monsignor) James H. Ryan   (Rector)

January 5th, 1930

The Right Reverend Monsignor James H. Ryan,
Rector of the Catholic University of America,
Washington, D.C.

Right Reverend and dear Monsignor :—

In accordance with instructions of the Executive Committee of the Board of Directors of The Dom Mocquereau Schola Cantorum Foundation, Inc., I beg to advise you, on behalf of the Foundation, that it feels that the situation which has developed at the University makes it impossible for the Foundation to continue to support the School of Liturgical Music of the University or otherwise to participate in the affairs of such school.

It is with much regret that the Foundation feels obliged to reach this conclusion but it feels so I am sure the University will, that if there is a prospect of continued difficulties and misunderstandings and of continued feeling on the part of the University that the Foundation is, as has so frequently been said trying to run the School of Liturgical Music." It is best that the situation be faced frankly at its inception and that all possibility of further embarrassment to the University and to the Foundation be removed.

It seems due to the University that something be said of the reasons which have led the Foundation to its decision. No attempt will be made to enter into points which are or fairly can be controverted, especially since the Foundation feels there is sufficient in the uncontroverted phases of the matter not only to warrant but clearly to demand that it take the step hereby announced.

As early as the 20th of October, 1929, the University was advised by the President of the Foundation that the Dean of the School of Liturgical Music, Father DesLongchamps, did not hold the Doctorate which he had represented to the Foundation and to the University, and which had accordingly been specified in the announcement of the School, and that therefore and to that extent at least, his appointment had been procured upon a false basis.

The Foundation felt that with this information the University authorities would take prompt action, but no action having been taken up to the 9th day of December the matter was again brought to the attention of the University by the President of the Foundation. On the following day and at the suggestion of the Rector of the University a conference was held between His Grace the Archbishop of Baltimore, Chancellor of the University, the Rector and Vice-Rector of the University and the President of the Foundation. The Chancellor took the most serious view of the imposture and one which coincided precisely with that held by the Foundation, and stated that the Dean should not be permitted to remain but should go that very night or on the following morning at the latest. Surely here, as on the previous occasion, there had been no attempt on the part of the Foundation to do more than to lay the facts before the University authorities in the expectation of action which would protect the University and the Foundation, and the work of both from criticism, and would place everything in the proper light and posture.

There were no immediate results from this conference but about three weeks later the Vice-Rector conferred with the President of the Foundation,— again with no definite results. Meantime Dom Sablayrolles, a guest-Professor at the School, and personal representative of Dom Mocquereau as teacher of Gregorian Chant, whom the University had invited, had become so disturbed over the situation and over the difficulties with which he felt that his work was attended, that it seemed likely that the School would lose his services. Since he is unquestionably one of the great leaders in the work of the restoration of the Chant, and since any failure of his efforts at the School would have a most disastrous effect upon the work of the Foundation, it was decided to make a further effort to impress the seriousness of the situation upon the University authorities in the hope that they would find prompt action possible in accordance with the views of the Chancellor, though the latter, as he has frankly stated, was himself without power in the premises. It was stated by the Chancellor and affirmed by the Rector that the latter had power to suspend the Dean, which power the Foundation hoped he would exercise if the Dean should not tender his resignation. The Rector, however, took the position that he would not ask for the resignation of the Dean nor would he suspend him, but that on the contrary no action would be taken in the matter until the meeting of the Executive Committee of the Board of Trustees on the 24th of the current month unless the Dean should himself resign meantime. The Dean repeatedly expressed his willingness to resign but stated that he would not do so until requested by the Rector.

Thus the Foundation was left in the position of being obliged to submit to the continuance of an imposture, relief from which was readily available, until such time as the Executive Committee might choose to act, and meantime was faced with the loss of Dom Sablayrolles' services, due not merely to the conditions which he felt were militating against the full success of his efforts, but also because it had already brought him to a state of mind and health where he could not safely conduct the work. Under these circumstances a request was made that a short leave of absence be granted to Dom Sablayrolles until the question of the Dean's continuance should have been finally determined and the decision carried into effect. This request was emphatically refused, whereupon Dom Sablayrolles, feeling that he could endure the situation no longer, sought the Rector and Vice-Rector for the purpose of himself laying his situation before them and renewing the request for a short leave of absence. Finding neither available, he left word of his condition with one of his colleagues on the University staff and left, hoping, of course, that an early decision might be reached which would permit of his return.

The attitude of the Foundation has constantly been stated by University authority to be regarded as an attempt to run the School of Liturgical Music or to run the University. The Foundation is unable to concur in this view. On the contrary it feels that when it exposes so serious a situation, it is the duty of the University and not of the Foundation, or any one connected with it, to apply the remedy, and it feels that is has gone to the extreme lengths of patience and endurance in awaiting such action.

It is not clear to the Foundation just how far the imposture has gone; but it is clear that both the Foundation and the University have been imposed upon and that all who have entered the School on the faith of the catalogue thereof have been deceived, as has also the Hierarchy of the United States to which the foundation of the School was especially announced. How far this announcement was made in other countries or to others in authority we are not advised, but to the extent of any such further announcement there was added deception.

If prompt action had been taken upon the exposure of the imposture or upon the pronouncement of the Chancellor, the Foundation might have felt that everything had been done that could be done to remedy the wrong, but to have it said repeatedly that its plea for a remedy of the wrong constituted an interference with the University's prerogatives can lead to no other conclusion than that a continuance of relations is bound to result in further misunderstandings and controversies, harmful alike to the University and the Foundation and to the effort which the latter is making for the restoration of the Chant in accordance with the command of His Holiness Pius X and the amplification thereof by His Holiness Pius XI as set forth in his Constitution <u>Divini Cultus</u>.

It has been said that the Foundation is unreasonable in urging precipitate action. In this view the Foundation cannot concur. In the first place the condition was brought to the attention of the Rector and the Vice-Rector two and a half months ago. It was brought to the attention of the Chancellor nearly a month ago and his sentiments then expressed so agreeably to the feelings of the Foundation and apparently concurred in (and certainly not dissented from) by the Rector and the Vice-Rector, led the Foundation to feel that immediate action would be taken.

A further delay is now proposed and the Foundation's objection to it is characterized as unwarranted interference. If such a grave condition cannot be remedied within three months, and if the request for the prompt exercise of admitted power to remedy it is to be regarded as a wrongful interference by the Foundation, it is clear that the University and the Foundation do not see alike upon matters of principle involving deception of the gravest sort, and if they do not see alike upon a matter of such moment it seems indisputable that upon matters of less grave import likely to arise over many years of attempted cooperation there will be lack of harmony. It therefore seems best from all viewpoints that the relations be terminated and the Foundation has so decided.

Nor upon full consideration does it seem possible that the decision of the Foundation either could or should be affected by any change which might now take place in the attitude of the University authorities. Even supposing the possibility that the pleas of the Foundation should lead to a prompt resignation of the Dean, the difficulties already encountered in effectively presenting the views of the Foundation can lead to but one conclusion, namely, that any present adjustment would be temporary only and that the future would not be secure from any standpoint. Surely if the presentation of so grave a situation is to be charged repeatedly as an unwarranted interference by the Foundation in the affairs of the University, the whole future of the relations of the University and the Foundation rests upon too insecure and too controversial a basis to warrant any hope of successful cooperation.

There remain two matters which may require further consideration. The Foundation has undertaken to construct a building upon the campus to be used by the School of Liturgical Music so long as that School shall be supported by the Foundation. This building is well on toward completion. If the University has, by its conduct, breached the agreement under which such building was to be constructed, the Foundation would seem not only to be relieved from further obligation in that respect but would seem also entitled to compensation for the outlay to date. The Foundation however does not desire now to take this position. The funds for the building were to be donated by the President of the Foundation outside of her specific donation upon which the Foundation was erected. It is therefore probable that some just arrangement can be made for the completion of the building though it can hardly be expected that it will be equipped for use as a School of Liturgical Music in view of the severance of relations between the Foundation and the University.

The second matter which may remain open for consideration and as to which the University is perhaps not at all concerned, but which it seems should nevertheless be mentioned, is the sum of nearly $6,000. which the President of the Foundation paid to the Bishop of Detroit in order to secure what was represented to be an effective release of the Dean for the conduct of the School. We are now authoritatively advised that this release is ineffective since a priest cannot be released from one Diocese until adopted by another. Wherefore, while the consent of the Bishop of Detroit was of course given in the utmost good faith and with the expectation that it would become effective through proper supplementary action, the fact is that the release did not in fact become effective, wherefore, there may have been no actual consideration for the payment made. Father DesLongchamps has stated that he does not want Mrs. Ward to lose by this transaction and that he will himself repay the sum when he is able so to do. It is impossible at the moment to state what should be done in this respect, but since the transaction in some respects bears upon, and was an integral and moving factor in, the whole situation, it seems best to mention it at this time.

Since it has been stated that "every Bishop in the United States" would be advised of the withdrawal of the Foundation in case it should withdraw, the Foundation respectfully requests that in giving such advice, this communication may be included in order that there may be a clear understanding among the Hierarchy as to the position of the Foundation upon the matters referred to.

As stated in the beginning, there are other matters of which complaint has been made and as to which answer has been given. These raise issues which it seems unnecessary to consider at the moment and they are therefore omitted at this time with the hope that, in view of the fact that the matters alluded to so greatly over-shadow all others, it will be found unnecessary to go into any other phase of the matter either with the University or with any other authorities.

Very truly yours,

THE DOM MOCQUEREAU SCHOLA CANTORUM FOUNDATION, INC.,

By _____ _____

President

**The Dom Mocquereau Schola Cantorum
Foundation Inc.**

February 15, 1930

My Most Reverend Father:

You already know the events in Washington that render the ideal interview impossible.

It was agreed that the building erected at my expense for the School of Liturgical Music on the University property would bear the name Dom Mocquereau. You yourself had permitted it, but on one condition, that the teaching of Solesmes would be given to the students of this school.

But, we no longer hope that such a condition will be realized in the future. Besides, already before the break between the "Dom Mocquereau Schola Cantorum Foundation" with the University, we were very skeptical about it, so clearly to the contrary were the proofs before our eyes. The reception given by the Music Faculty and the University authorities to Rev. Father Sablayrolles, the direct and personal representative of Dom Mocquereau, was significant in this regard. In this alone, we were given adequate proof that the University professors would never teach the method of Solesmes in their Courses.

So, now with the break being accomplished, it seems to us, that the name of Dom Mocquereau given to this building, would be an insult to that glorious name and also to that of Solesmes. Do you not think, my most Reverend Father, that it would be prudent that your fatherly concern should intervene and by a letter addressed to the Monsignor Rector, refuse permission to give the name of Dom Mocquereau, for the reasons set forth above, to the building of the School of Music of the Catholic University of America? There is still time to do this since the building had not yet been dedicated, but could be in the very near future.

Please accept, my Most Reverend Father, the homage of my filial and grateful respect.

Justine B. Ward

P.S. The name and address of the Rector follows:
  Rt. Rev. Mrg. James H. Ryan
  Catholic University of America
  Washington, D.C.

The
Dom Mocquereau Schola Cantorum
Foundation, Inc., and the Catholic University
of America at Washington, D. C.

THE DOM MOCQUEREAU SCHOLA CAN-
TORUM FOUNDATION, INC., AND THE
CATHOLIC UNIVERSITY OF AMERICA
AT WASHINGTON, D. C.

Preliminary Statement

Since 1910 I have spent my entire time and all the means at my disposal for the restoration of the Ecclesiastical Chant of the Church according to the Motu Proprio of Pope Pius X. I have specialized in the propagation of Gregorian Chant, the training of teachers, and the formation of the children in the Catholic Schools of America and Europe. For this object I organized the Pius X School of Liturgical Music in New York, in 1916. The text books for this work, written by me, were published at Washington, by the Catholic Education Press, a corporation under the control of the Catholic Sisters' College.

1.—DOM MOCQUEREAU SCHOLA CANTORUM FOUNDATION, INC.

To assure the permanence of my work I organized an educational corporation under the laws of the State of New York, with a capital of $1,000,000; the object of this Foundation being the propagation of Gregorian Chant according to the principles of Dom Mocquereau of Solesmes, of Classic Polyphony, particularly of the school of Palestrina, and such musical training as was required to build up an appreciation of these two subjects.

This corporation was called THE DOM MOCQUEREAU SCHOLA CANTORUM FOUNDATION. It has the right to function in America, Canada, or even in Europe, provided it functions according to the conditions mentioned above.

One of the principal works contemplated was to help the Pius X School of Liturgical Music at the College of the Sacred Heart, in New York. Another was to work with The Catholic University of America toward the establishment of a School of Liturgical Music according to the exact conditions set forth by the Foundation, and which was to follow literally the aims and objects of said Foundation. No capital was given nor was promised at any time to the University nor had the University any rights over the income. The funds were and are the exclusive property of The Dom Mocquereau Schola Cantorum Foundation, Inc.

2.—MISLEADING PUBLICITY

This latter project was still under negotiation when the Rector of the University, Mgr. Ryan, announced to the newspapers that the University had become the beneficiary of a trust fund of a million dollars for the foundation of a School of Liturgical Music at the Catholic University of America. Against this erroneous announcement I protested energetically, but in spite of my protestations such statements continued to be circulated in many newspapers and still continue to circulate. Furthermore, in the Rector's annual report for 1929, page 20, under "Gifts to the University" is listed "One million dollars trust fund from the Dom Mocquereau Schola Cantorum Foundation, Inc." Also page 9, under School of Liturgical Music

Consequently here was a first contradiction of the facts given out by the Rector of the Catholic University.

3. — Reverend William Joseph DesLongchamps

The Reverend William Joseph DesLongchamps had been instructor of Liturgical Chant at the Catholic University at Washington, since 1926. On the official catalogue of the University he was given the title of "Doctor of Music, Rome 1923." This priest made himself the intermediary between the Foundation and the University. He pretended to have obtained his doctorate of music, to have followed the entire course of advanced studies at the Pontifical College of Music at Rome, to have made serious studies at Vienna and at Solesmes.

On the strength of these representations the Foundation recommended him as Dean of the new School of Liturgical Music at the Catholic University of America, and the University accepted him in that capacity. It is evident, however, that the University was in a position to have obtained correct information regarding him and it would even seem as though it would have been their duty to have obtained said information before having taken him originally upon the University faculty.

On the strength of these representations he obtained an important position on the Board of Directors of The Dom Mocquereau Schola Cantorum Foundation, Inc.

These representations have all turned out to be false; consequently the Foundation has asked and

obtained Father DesLongchamps' resignation from
its Board of Directors.

4.—DISCOVERY OF THE FACTS

While I was in Europe during the Summer of 1929
I had some reason to feel doubts on the subject of
Father DesLongchamps' competence and I checked
up carefully on the studies which he had made. The
result of this investigation follows:

ROME. At the Pontifical School of Sacred Music he had studied only the elementary courses
given the choirmasters of Churches; he had re-
ceived in 1923 only the small diploma called the
"Licenza" in Italian, and in Latin *Prolyta*, and
not, as he pretended, a doctorate of music.

VIENNA. His name has not even been inscribed as pupil at the University, which is the
only institution having the right to confer a doctorate; nor was his name inscribed as pupil at the
Conservatory of Music where he had claimed to
have worked under Dr. Schutz.

SOLESMES. The choirmaster of Solesmes
who had been his teacher during a very brief
period at Quarr Abbey in 1921 affirmed that the
Reverend W. J. DesLongchamps was one of the
worst pupils he had ever had, that it was impossible to teach him anything because of his lack of
ear and of talent, and because of the supplementary fact that he would not do any work.

5.—FATHER DESLONGCHAMPS AND HIS DIOCESE

Early in the Winter of 1929 Father DesLongchamps requested and obtained from me the sum of
$10,000 with which he proposed to obtain a release

from all rights which his Bishop (Detroit) had over
him in favor of the Foundation, in order that he
might be free to devote himself wholly to the work of
the Foundation without fear of being called back to
parochial functions in his Diocese.

According to his statement to me and to others,
this reimbursement to the Diocese for the expenses
of his education at the Ecclesiastical Seminary, and
for the four years of studies which he had made in
Europe at the expense of the Diocese would obtain
for him permanent freedom from the authority of his
Bishop and thereafter he would have as Superior
only the Holy Father.

According to his own affirmation, he paid this sum
to the Bishop of Detroit and obtained his liberty.

As to the disposition which he made of this money
I have the assertion of Father DesLongchamps and
the fact that my check of $6,000 was cashed by Father
DesLongchamps personally on May 13, 1929. He
showed me what purported to be a carbon copy of the
release obtained from his Bishop, bearing the seal of
the Chancellor and his signature, in addition to the
signature of the Bishop. I wrote to His Lordship,
the Bishop of Detroit, to ask him to be good enough
to let me know the facts on this subject, but received
no answer to my letter. Thinking the letter might
have miscarried, I sent a duplicate under date of
February 25th, 1930; this letter was registered and
personal delivery required. It was returned to me
unopened and marked "*refused.*"*

---

* A statement just received from the Chancery Office of Detroit, dated
March 19, 1930, certifies that on June 30, 1929, Father DesLongchamps re-
funded the sum of $5,919.31 expended by said Diocese for his education.
No mention is made of any "release."

6.—THE BUILDING

Under the pretensions stated above I undertook to build upon the Campus of the University a structure to house the School of Liturgical Music, for the purposes of the Foundation exclusively, and to remain so as long as such school should be supported by the Foundation. This was before I had discovered the truth about Father DesLongchamps. This building is almost finished; the work has now been stopped because of the action of the University which rendered the work of the Foundation impossible.

7.—RUPTURE OF RELATIONS BETWEEN THE FOUNDATION AND THE UNIVERSITY

Immediately upon my return to America I notified the Rector and the Vice-Rector regarding the falsity of the claims to a doctorate by Father DesLongchamps and told them the facts as regarded his studies in Europe (See paragraph 4). This was on the 20th of October, 1929.

No action having been taken in the matter, on the 9th of December I renewed my insistence to the Rector, telling him that the new School of Music could not continue to function under such circumstances. I also told the Rector the affair regarding the release claimed by Father DesLongchamps from his Diocese. At the suggestion of the Rector a conference was held at Baltimore with the Chancellor of the University, His Grace Archbishop Curley. At this conference were present the Chancellor, the Rector, the Vice-Rector and myself. The Chancellor took the strongest possible position in the matter, that is to say that

Father DesLongchamps should not remain even a single night at the University, or that he should be suspended the following morning at the very latest. His Grace stated that the Rector had the right to suspend him and that such action should be taken immediately. The Rector admitted at that time that such action was in his power. I also informed His Grace of the money obtained by Father DesLong-champs from me in the affair of his Diocese and the release which he claimed to have obtained. His Grace affirmed that this pretended release, if he had obtained it, had no validity. (See Sections 111 to 117 and 143 and 144 of the Canon Law).

On his return to Washington the Rector of the University instead of following the advice of the Chancellor, retained Father DesLongchamps as Professor and Dean of the School of Liturgical Music, in spite of the fact that the latter admitted that he had no doctorate of music and had never had any doctorate; in spite also of the fact that he had been inscribed for years on the official catalogue of the University as "Doctor of Music, Rome, 1923."

From that date, December 11, until the date of the final rupture with the University (January 5, 1930) I continually urged upon the Rector and upon His Grace the Chancellor that appropriate action be taken in the matter, that it would be impossible for the Foundation to take part in maintaining what would be in effect a fraud upon the public and upon the Hierarchy of the United States.

At this point, in view of the continued inaction of the University, I sought legal advice. My attorney brought to my attention and I in turn to the attention of the Rector and the Chancellor the fact that the Foundation could not either legally or morally be a party to such a fraud. We obtained no results.

Our last effort was made at the reopening of the Courses at the School, on the 2nd of January. At this time the Rector stated to my attorney:

1st—That he would not accept the resignation of Father DesLongchamps even if offered.

2nd—That he would accept the resignation if offered by Father DesLongchamps but that he would not *request* it.

3rd—On his side, Father DesLongchamps stated to my attorney that he would offer his resignation at any time, but only if such resignation were *requested* by the Rector.

After patient efforts and having exhausted every possible resource to bring about action, and when once convinced that neither the University authorities nor Father DesLongchamps were willing to recognize the seriousness of the fraud complained of above, nor had any intention of putting an end to it, the Executive Committee of the Foundation called a meeting, passed resolutions and informed the University that because of the conditions named above and other complaints which derived from this first one, all relations were terminated between itself and the Catholic University of America.

8.—Protestation from Rome

Later a letter of protestation against the unjustified use of this doctorate by Father DesLongchamps was sent to the Rector from Rome. The letter stated clearly and officially the studies made by him, and the fact that he had neither taken the courses necessary for a doctorate nor had he obtained a doctorate. The protestation was sent in the name of the faculty of the Pontifical School of Sacred Music and of its Protector, Cardinal Bisletti. After receipt of this letter, at the meeting of the Executive Committee of the University, on the 24th of January, 1930, the resignation of Father DesLongchamps was accepted, or so we are informed by the Rector, Monsignor Ryan.

The acceptance of this resignation has had no practical effect upon the situation, since Father DesLongchamps as late as February 22, 1930,

a) continued to live in the building now serving as home to the School of Liturgical Music, in a position of apparent authority;

b) as far as we can learn he continued to teach in that school;

c) he is announced by a new official pamphlet, published and circulated by the University as late as February 22nd, 1930, under the title of "Doctor of Music," and a number of courses are announced for the Summer School by "Dr. DesLongchamps."

In fact, therefore, the only change brought about by this complaint of Rome and of the Foundation, and by this "resignation" is that the word "Rome" has been suppressed in connection with the doctorate of Father DesLongchamps.

9.—Dom Sablayrolles

In order to demonstrate the fact that the University authorities showed little if any desire to further the cause of Liturgical Music but, on the contrary, put every obstacle in the way of the new school, I must bring forward the treatment given to the eminent guest-professor, the Reverend Dom Maur Sablayrolles, O.S.B.

Upon the urgent and repeated invitation sent by the above mentioned Dean of the School of Liturgical Music, for many months, backed up by telegraphic insistence of the Rector himself and by my own auspices with Dom Mocquereau, that the latter might urge upon Dom Sablayrolles the acceptance of the invitation, the latter came to America early in October 1929. It was he who represented the central doctrine of the work of The Dom Mocquereau Schola Cantorum Foundation, Inc., at the University, and who personally and officially represented Dom Mocquereau himself, after whom the Foundation is named.

On arrival, he was received without ordinary politeness on the part of the Dean, of the Rector or of any other official of the University.

The work of Dom Sablayrolles instead of being helped was impeded by ridiculous and grotesque translations, by an aggressive and contemptuous attitude on the part of the Dean in public, and finally by the complete suppression of all Dom Sablayrolles' courses during the week preceding the Christmas recess, either without notice or with a last moment telephonic message. This was after Father DesLongchamps knew that I had complained of him to the University authorities.

Against this sabotage, Dom Sablayrolles received
no protection from the Rector or from the Vice-Rector, although both were aware of what was going on,
having been informed thereof by me in writing. The
Rector, on the contrary, appeared to take the side of
the Dean, excusing and explaining his action where
such excuse and explanation were totally invalid.

After nearly three months at the University, in
which he received no sign of encouragement from any
official of the University itself, Dom Sablayrolles realized that the work he had come to do for the Ecclesiastical Chant could not succeed under such conditions and he sent in his resignation to the Rector of
the Catholic University. This was immediately after
the final rupture between the Foundation and the
University. Dom Sablayrolles' resignation was accepted on January 24th by the Executive Committee
of the University in a single motion in which they
accepted the two resignations recommended by the
Rector: that of the guilty and the innocent together.

This action toward the representative of Dom
Mocquereau and of the Foundation makes it doubly
evident that the work of the Foundation could never
be carried on successfully at the Catholic University
of America. No professor of eminence could be obtained in future to teach there, nor could the purposes
of the Foundation be carried out by persons lacking
in competence.

In closing, I think it well to add a brief statement
as to how the arrangements with the University came
to be made, in order that a clear conception of the significance of the foregoing facts may be realized.

Brief Historic Summary

From 1913 to 1927 I had contributed to the maintenance of the faculty of music at the Caholic Sisters' College of the University. During this time the Sisters' College alone was making a serious attempt to give instruction in liturgical music in which the Catholic University itself took no part. Consequently the work to which I was contributing did not reach the seminarians or the priests

When in 1927 the Reverend W. J. DesLongchamps came to me with a proposition to inaugurate a Schola Cantorum which would be available to the University as well as to the Sisters' College I received his proposition gladly.

The Schola Cantorum was approved by the Rector (Bishop Shahan), was inaugurated, and I increased my contributions to its support to the sum of approximately $10,000 per year. The greater part of this sum passed directly to Father DesLongchamps and was disbursed by him personally.

The work was approved and encouraged not only by the Rector of the University, Bishop Shahan, but also by the Chancellor, Archbishop Curley.

I was unaware of the fact that the work of the Schola Cantorum had never been formally accepted by the Trustees of the University (if such be actually the case) until I returned from Europe in the Autumn of 1928. At that time the Reverend W. J. DesLongchamps met me at the steamer. He appeared to be almost hysterical and stated that the new Rector-elect, Mgr. James H Ryan had pronounced the Schola Cantorum wholly irregular from the University standpoint and that only one of two policies would be permitted:

a) Immediately to close the Schola Cantorum and bring its activities to an end.

b) For me to found a School of Liturgical Music at the University, subject to all the conditions of the other schools at that institution.

Father DesLongchamps stated that he had induced Mgr. Ryan to take no action until my return from Europe. I answered that I would have to talk with the Rector and find out what this proposition of his would mean.

Shortly thereafter, November 8, 1928, I saw the Rector in the presence of Father DesLongchamps and Miss Lebreton. He stated at that first interview that he would recommend a School of Music to the trustees of the University, but under the following conditions:

a) a building must be provided, costing $150,000.

b) $10,000 as minimum should be provided annually for its maintenance.

c) a fund should be put aside, yielding between $80,000 and $100,000 for the annual support of such a school. He calculated this on a basis of the salaries required, and based these on the Reports of the Rockefeller and Carnegie Foundations.

I replied that such a proposition was totally beyond my means, and if these were the amounts required the entire project would have to be abandoned.

I asked him whether the other schools of the University had all begun on so elaborate a scale. He did not give me a definite answer but said he had not the figures with him.

As I was about to leave, the Rector asked me what my proposition would have been. I told him that I certainly could not go beyond $15,000 a year, as an extreme maximum. He then stated that he would bring up the matter on my basis at the Autumn meeting of the Board of Trustees which was soon to be held, and that if the general project were approved by the Board, we would then have until the Spring meeting to work out the matter in detail. He gave me the impression, however, that so modest a proposal would hardly interest the Trustees. Later, however, I received the information that the Trustees were in favor of this project, and that the details were left to the Rector and the Chancellor to work out with me.

PRELIMINARY NEGOTIATIONS FOR INDEPENDENT COLLEGE OF MUSIC

Father DesLongchamps had, all along, advised me strongly to insist upon an independent College of Music which should manage its own affairs and handle its own funds. As to the latter point he stressed the unfortunate experience of other donors whose funds had been placed directly in the hands of the University. Accordingly, Father DesLongchamps, my attorney and I interviewed the Rector on February 18, 1929, and presented our proposition in the manner outlined above.

COUNTER PROPOSITION OF THE RECTOR

The Rector stated that no more independent Colleges would be permitted but that in lieu of this independence requested by us, the Foundation would be permitted:

a) to nominate the members of the Faculty.

b) to control the expenditure of the funds by whatever officer the Foundation itself should appoint to represent it at the University.

c) that the School should be housed in a temporary building off the Campus, which building would remain the property of the Foundation.

All this was promised not only verbally but in writing, provided the Foundation would agree to abandon its proposition of an independent College and would instead provide for a School of the University itself.

AGREEMENT

The above conditions seemed to give the Foundation the needed assurance and an agreement was reached by an exchange of letters of the following dates:

a) February 18th and February 20th, addressed by my attorney to the Rector.

b) A letter from the Foundation to the Rector, dated March 7th.

c) The Rector's reply dated March 12th.
Copies of each will be found in the appendix, pages 32, 34, 37.

The matter was settled as above only after full and exhaustive conferences with Father DesLongchamps, during which two items were stressed as of primary importance, and which, in view of what has followed, must be mentioned once more in this place:

a) that he had the doctorate of music which was required to qualify him for the position of full Professor and Dean of the new school.

b) that the site on Quincy Street selected for the temporary building off the Campus was not only satisfactory but the best of all the possible sites which had been proposed by him or to him, and that this site was advantageous from the standpoint of attendance by priests and seminarians as well as by the students from the Sisters' College.

REVERSAL OF POSITION

My attorney had hardly left for the West, having completed these preliminary negotiations, when I began to hear, through Father DesLongchamps, criticisms from all sides of the plan adopted.

a) the building would be too far away; the pupils of the University would never come.

b) it would be useless to consider such a site for the Summer School; it was too far from the Campus.

c) Professors were quoted as being unable to understand why so important a school should be situated anywhere but on the Campus.

d) Seminarians, pupils of Father DesLongchamps, were quoted as insisting that their Superiors would never allow them to study in any building off the Campus.

During this period Mgr. Ryan visited me in New York and said: "Father DesLongchamps seems to be afraid that a temporary building may mean a temporary school." I was dumbfounded by this change of attitude on the part of Father DesLongchamps.

On March 24th I was taken extremely ill and threatened with an operation. During this serious illness of mine Father DesLongchamps visited me, bringing the working drawings of the architect for the temporary building on Quincy Street. He stated that

a) the building was going to be cramped for space;

b) would be impractical;

c) that the site was too distant;

d) the influence of the School of Music, on such a site, would remain almost negligible.

e) To function effectively the school would have to be on the Campus.

This attitude was the complete contradiction of the position he had taken in all the conferences which had led to the correspondence and agreements with the Rector.

After having taken the position described above, Father DesLongchamps then added that I myself must make the decision, since I was the one who was making the sacrifice of a financial nature, that he did not want to influence me. Obviously, however, his previous statements had influenced me and had been made with the object of so influencing me. I told him that I must think the matter over, since it was obviously useless to build a structure which he was condemning in advance as meaning failure of the work.

The next day I told Father DesLongchamps that in view of his statements that a building on Quincy street would be useless, I would consider the possibility of putting up a wing of the permanent building on the Campus, provided the Rector would favor such a step. He answered without hesitation: "O, the Rector would be willing. *I have asked him already* and he answered that as we had all agreed to the plan for a temporary building, any proposition for a change of plan must come from Mrs. Ward and not from us."

I drew the attention of Father DesLongchamps to the fact that any change of plan at this late date had many awkward features:

a) Mr. Murphy had completed his working drawings,

b) Negotiations for the purchase of the land at the Quincy street site were all but complete; both Dr. McCormick and Mr. Murphy, the architect, had to be considered.

To this Father DesLongchamps answered: "I know where I can reach Mr. Murphy today. I will telephone and he will come up and talk with you."

He did communicate with Mr. Murphy that very evening in New York City, and the next day, Friday, March 29th, Mr. Murphy came up to my house. I was then too ill to get out of bed, and at my bed-side we made out a plan for a permanent building, one wing of which (the study wing) would be built immediately, while the rest of the structure would be built

later. On the following day Father DesLongchamps
left for Washington to notify Dr. McCormick of the
change regarding the purchase of the Quincy street
site.

Meanwhile I notified my attorney of the change
which affairs were taking. The latter wrote me an
extremely indignant letter, stating that he had been
in the East for nearly six weeks, devoting all his time
to putting through a proposition for a school off the
Campus, as desired by Father DesLongchamps; that
he could not understand how it was that the moment
his back was turned Father DesLongchamps should
come forward with a totally contradictory proposition. He advised me not to give in. Unfortunately
I had already given in before receiving his letter.

On April 5th Father DesLongchamps returned to
New York and I asked him to explain his sudden
change of attitude, or, why he had not expressed
these views when the whole matter was under discussion with my attorney, Mr. Mason. He became very
angry. He objected to the precautions which I had
taken on the advice of my attorney that the whole
matter should be set up legally, and the work be fully
protected, stating that my attorney was treating the
University authorities like thieves! This took place
in the presence of Miss Agnes Lebreton. I was still
very ill and under doctors' care, and no business
matters should have been brought to me at all at that
time.

It was during this period or a little earlier that the
false publicity was given out, as mentioned in paragraph 2.

On April 24th, having somewhat recovered, I went

to Washington and Mr. Murphy brought me the plan for a single wing of the building; this wing had entirely changed from the plan agreed to in New York; instead of being merely a classroom wing of the final building, leaving the auditorium to be constructed later, it contained an immense auditorium in addition to the classrooms. Mr. Murphy stated that Father DesLongchamps had asked for this change and that he had made it supposing it to be my wish. When questioned on this subject Father DesLongchamps answered that the students were so numerous that the big auditorium was absolutely essential even at the very beginning of the work, since a room was required large enough to hold three or four hundred students. *This statement turns out to have been absolutely untrue, since no class in music at the University has as many as one hundred students; most of them are very much smaller.*

Since it would have been a great waste to have constructed a building which ultimately would have two auditoriums, and on the faith of Father DesLongchamps' insistence of the immense numbers who would attend the classes, I decided to consider erecting the whole building on the Campus instead of one wing, in order to give required space at once.

My decision to erect the entire building instead of merely one wing was brought about by misrepresentation on the part of Father DesLongchamps as to the number of pupils who attended class simultaneously.

Mr. Murphy stated that before making final plans for the building the site on the Campus should be settled, that the building might be adapted to such

site. The Rector, Mgr. Ryan, was in the hospital.
Mr. Murphy offered to see the Rector and also the
Chancellor. He did so. On May 4th, Mr. Murphy
brought me a sketch for a music building on the Campus, made according to the general plans agreed to.
The following day Father DesLongchamps came to
visit me and expressed extreme annoyance that Mr.
Murphy should have brought the plan to me before
having shown it to him. In the presence of Miss
Lebreton he expressed his displeasure with great violence, saying: "Either I am the Dean or I am not."

When Father DesLongchamps saw this sketch he
remarked that the money allotted to building a Cloister should be spent for bed-rooms to house the professors. I stated emphatically that I would not agree
to the inclusion of living quarters for the professors
in the music building. He answered that all the buildings on the Campus contained living quarters for the
professors. I replied that even were that so, this
building must be treated differently, because the University was permitting for the first time co-education
on the Campus in this music school and that no possible grounds for criticism should be given. Father
DesLongchamps became violently excited and made
the following remarks: "Either I am Dean or I am
not." "Why does Mr. Murphy bring sketches here
without showing them to me first? Why does he go
to see the Rector and the Archbishop? It was *my*
place to have seen them; there is nothing left for me
to do but to hand in my resignation. If things were
left in *my* hands they would move along without all
these delays and changes."

He was in too hysterical a mood for me to point

out that the only changes which had been made had been at his own instigation.

When he had calmed down a little I told him that he might well be the proper person to see the Rector and ask the latter for the necessary guarantee regarding the use of the music building in perpetuity for the object specified by the Foundation, since naturally, such a guarantee on the part of the University must precede any steps toward the erection of a building on the University grounds. He agreed to see the Rector and then pulled from his pocket a contract already drawn for the erection of a grand organ for the auditorium of the new building. The price of this organ instead of being $8,000 as agreed to, was for the sum of $15,000. I answered that I was not prepared to sign any contract until everything had been settled in an orderly and businesslike fashion as regarded the building itself, with the conditions of the gift clearly specified.

On May 9th Father DesLongchamps telephoned to say that the Rector accepted the building with the conditions of the gift and would give all the necessary guarantees.

On May 10th the Rector wrote, accepting the building, but making reservations which left a possibility open by which the University might take over the building and use it for purposes other than those for which it would be given. This letter did not seem to me a full guarantee.

On its receipt I telephoned to Father DesLongchamps, and told him that I would not be willing to proceed without something which would be fully binding on the part of the University; I said that

I would wait to consult my attorney before proceeding. He showed extreme annoyance at my hesitation but stated, as he had done on a previous occasion, that since it was I who was making the sacrifice the decision must be mine.

I reminded him of the insistence with which he had warned me at the beginning, against the methods used heretofore by the University in dealing with donors and their gifts, that this was one of the fundamental reasons why I had been all along so insistent that everything should be on a legal and solid basis. The question, I stated, was not one of sacrifices on my part but one of providing proper safeguards for the work itself. In view of this I asked him for his present opinion. To this he answered: "To my mind we should pay no attention to the Rector's letter but should go ahead with the building."

I decided to await the coming of Mr. Mason, my attorney.

On the 14th of May Mr. Mason arrived. Meanwhile Father DesLongchamps had telephoned me again and seemed to regret his violence of the previous evening. Upon hearing that Mr. Mason would be in New York on the 14th he stated that he would come to New York to be present at the interview.

He arrived on the 13th in a mood verging on hysteria, accused me of assuming that the University authorities were dishonest, that they were only accepting the building for music with a project of diverting it finally to other purposes and added: "You evidently think that I am a traitor, working with the Rector against you."

Since I had made no such accusations nor had any

such ideas until that time entered my head. I was indignant and told him so. I assured him once more that what I was demanding was normal business procedure and that he ought to desire this as much as I. He then attacked the intentions and actions of my lawyer in a most violent manner.

What astonished me most was:

a) Father DesLongchamps' complete change of attitude; since, at the beginning, it was *he* who had urged precautions and now it was he who was resenting ordinary business procedure.

b) His resentment of my insistence on a contract which should be binding, since this should have been his desire as well as mine.

I could arrive at no understanding with him. Where I talked principles and permanence of the work, he reacted with personalities.

Father DesLongchamps mentioned that he had stated to the Rector that the letter sent by him to me had been unsatisfactory and had "spoiled everything." According to Father DesLongchamps, the Rector answered that if this letter of his did not give the guarantee that I wanted, I should simply destroy that letter and that he would write another; since he was as anxious as I that the contract should be legally binding. In view of what appeared to be so reasonable and just an attitude on the part of the Rector, I was still more at a loss to account for the violence of Father DesLongchamps' attitude when he arrived in New York.

There was some further correspondence but no definite adjustment was made of this matter until my attorney went to Washington during the final days of May. On June 1st he had a conference with Father DesLongchamps alone, who stated that while he preferred a building on the Campus, he was ready to accept a building elsewhere since he considered that "one should not look a gift horse in the mouth." He also stated that with a new administration at the University he considered that we should no longer have any feeling of insecurity about building on the Campus. Thus he explained his complete change of attitude.

The following day, June 2nd, my attorney saw the Rector and drew up a short proposal substituting a building on the campus in lieu of the one on the Quincy Street site containing specific guarantees that the building should serve for the exclusive objects of the Foundation as long as the Foundation continued on its side to support the work. The Rector submitted this to the Vice-Rector, Monsignor Pace, who expressed his agreement and approval. See page 38.

The execution of this agreement was never completed, nor was it ever delivered. On the faith of the proposal, I went ahead with the construction of the building. After the severance of relations between the Foundation and the University, I suspended operations, since the building obviously could never serve the objects of the Foundation. The building was practically complete at that time, and had cost approximately $140,000.

CONCLUSION

The series of events which I have outlined briefly, namely those by which I was led to build upon the

Campus and those which caused the severance of relations between the Foundation and the University,
would suggest the conclusion that there was at no
time a serious interest manifested in the work of a
School of Liturgical Music as such, but that the pre-
vailing desire was merely to obtain a building on the
University Campus. The ideal which I wished to
serve appears to have been exploited with the practical result that the University now has a building
on the Campus, practically free of cost, and which—
now that the School of Liturgical Music is eliminated
from the situation permanently—may be considered
by the University as available to use for its own purposes. In this connection, it must be mentioned that
no proposal has been made by the University to reim-
burse me for the expenditure which, on my side, was
made in good faith.

The purpose of this statement to the Reverend
Trustees of the University is not a desire to reopen
the matter, since the withdrawal of the Foundation
is permanent and its decision, based on the facts
briefly stated above, is irrevocable. It is made because
of my own desire that the Reverend Trustees should
be apprised of what has taken place with the reasons
which caused the withdrawal of the Foundation from
the Catholic University of America. It is not only in
justice to the Foundation that I do this, but also, I
cannot but think, as a matter which affects the true
interests of the University at least as much as it does
my own and those of the Foundation, which made
every possible effort to carry on the work undertaken
at the University, and exhausted every possible resource to effect an adjustment of the intolerable situa-

tion, before coming to the conclusion that it had no
choice but to withdraw, since the conditions actually
existing, and under which alone, it was to be allowed
to function, were such as it could neither morally nor
legally tolerate.

Respectfully submitted:

JUSTINE B. WARD
*President of The Dom Mocquereau
Schola Cantorum Foundation, Inc.*

March 1, 1930

APPENDIX

Appendix No. 1

**Copy of Articles of Incorporation of
The Dom Mocquereau Schola Cantorum Foundation, Inc.**

[COPY]

THE UNIVERSITY OF THE STATE OF NEW YORK

STATE OF NEW YORK } ss.:
COUNTY OF ALBANY

Pursuant to the provisions of Section 11, Article 2 of the Membership Corporations Law, as amended by Chapter 722 of the Laws of 1926, consent is hereby given to the filing of the annexed certificate of incorporation of "THE DOM MOCQUEREAU SCHOLA CANTORUM FOUNDATION, INC." as a membership corporation.

This consent, however, shall in no way be construed as an approval by the Education Department, Board of Regents or Commissioner of Education of the purposes and objects of this corporation, nor shall it be construed as giving the officers and agents of this corporation the right to use the name of the Education Department, Board of Regents or Commissioner of Education in its publications and advertising matter.

{*Seal reading: The University of the State of New York — The State Department of Education. State Coat of Arms (Excelsior) (1784).*}

IN WITNESS WHEREOF, I, Ernest E. Cole, Acting Commissioner of Education of the State of New York, for and on behalf of the State Education Department, do hereunto set my hand and affix the seal of the State Education Department, at the City of Albany, this 27th day of February, 1929.

(Sgd.)   ERNEST E. COLE,
Acting Commissioner of Education.

[COPY]

CERTIFICATE OF INCORPORATION OF
THE DOM MOCQUEREAU SCHOLA CANTORUM FOUNDATION, INC., pursuant to
the Membership Corporations Law of the State of New York.

WE, the undersigned, being desirous of associating ourselves together
for the educational purposes hereinafter more particularly described, pursuant to and in confirmity with the Membership Corporations Law of the
State of New York, do hereby make, sign, acknowledge and file this Certificate of Incorporation in duplicate, to wit:

FIRST: The name of this corporation shall be **THE DOM MOCQUEREAU
SCHOLA CANTORUM FOUNDATION, INC.**

SECOND: The particular purposes for which said Corporation is formed
shall be:

A. Education in, of, and concerning, the Gregorian Chant according to
the principles of Solesmes as set forth by Dom Andre Mocquereau, in his
published works, imprinted in and after 1908, and particularly in Le Nombre
Musical Gregorian, Volumes I and II, and in the series of volumes which
make up the Paleographie Musicale, edited by him from 1889 to date, which
educational purposes shall include cooperation with the clergy in acquiring
and disseminating a knowledge of the Gregorian Chant aforesaid; the
preparation and instruction of teachers therein, including the conduct of
normal courses to that end, which shall include elementary instruction, calculated to prepare children therefor,—the method in these respects being
that contained in the Catholic Education series of Music Text Books by
Justine Ward, of which Volumes I, II, III, and IV have already been
published; cooperation with, and instruction of choirmasters in the Gregorian Chant aforesaid; cooperation with and instruction of church organists
in the Gregorian Chant aforesaid; the maintenance of a staff of competent
professors and instructors for the purposes aforesaid.

B. Education in Classic Polyphony, especially that of the Roman School
of the 16th Century, culminating with (and not subsequent to) the works
of Palestrina and Vittoria.

C. Education in all other subjects dealing with technical and cultural
equipment, whether sight reading, vocal training, choir conducting, piano
and organ playing, harmony, history of music, liturgy and kindred subjects,
shall be included in the purposes of the Corporation so far (and so far only)
as they shall come within and be a part of the educational purposes aforesaid, and also only in so far as they shall clearly help to build up a
better understanding and appreciation of the Gregorian Chant aforesaid
and classic Polyphony, and a better rendering thereof, it being expressly
stipulated that all modern vocal music for the Church, including all composed since the time of Palestrina, is expressly excluded from the objects
and purposes of the Corporation, nor shall any of the funds, efforts or
activities thereof, ever be expended therefor or directed thereunto.

D. To receive, invest, manage, expend and apply funds and property for any of the purposes of the Corporation, with power to expend only the income therefrom, save and except that, unless otherwise limited by the donor, any sum or sums not exceeding one-third of the gross principal of all the original or later-acquired capital funds of the Corporation may be expended for corporate purposes upon the majority vote of all of the directors whenever they shall declare in said vote that in their opinion such capital expenditures, or at least a major part thereof, can and will be recovered and restored to the capital fund within a period of ten years from the date of such expenditure.

E. To accept donations for any of the purposes of the Corporation on such terms as the donors may prescribe and the directors may accept.

F. To lay out any of the funds of the Corporation in trust as the directors may determine, and to receive the income and profits therefrom or to retake the principal thereof, for the purposes of the Corporation.

G. To found, promote or establish a School of Liturgical Music at or near the Catholic University of America at Washington, D. C., either within or without the campus or grounds thereof, for the purpose exclusively of carrying out the educational purposes above specified, and to make the instruction thereof available to students of the said University and of the Catholic Sisters College thereat and to others desiring such instruction; and to maintain, or contribute to the maintenance of such school so founded, promoted or established by it.

H. To contribute to the maintenance of the Pius X School of Liturgical Music at the College of the Sacred Heart, Manhattanville, Borough of Manhattan, New York City, New York.

I. To do and perform all things requisite or necessary or incidental or appertaining to or connected with any of the objects and purposes aforesaid, and not violative of any of the restrictions above imposed, and always within the limits of the educational purposes of the Corporation.

THIRD: This corporation is not organized for pecuniary profit, and none of the objects and purposes aforesaid shall embrace or shall ever operate for the purpose of profit to the Corporation, or to the profit, salary or emolument of any of the members, officers or directors thereof, save and except that reasonable compensation, together with expenses, may be allowed any member, director, officer, agent or employee of the Corporation, by the concurring vote of two-thirds of the directors, or by the by-laws. Any funds or aid given by the Corporation to any other corporation or to any institution whether those above named or others, shall be limited to educational or charitable corporations or institutions, as distinguished from those operated for profit.

FOURTH: No director of the Corporation shall be personally liable for any of its debts, obligations or liabilities, in the absence of bad faith or fraud.

FIFTH: The territory of the principal operations of the said Corporation shall be the United States of America and the Dominion of Canada, but it may operate in any other part of the world.

SIXTH: The office of the Corporation shall be located at "Mora Vocis" in the town of Greenburg, Westchester County, N. Y.

SEVENTH: The number of directors of said Corporation shall be three and the names and residences of those who shall act until the first annual meeting of the Corporation are the Rev. William J. Des Longchamps, residing at 1326 Quincy Street, N. E., Brookland, Washington, D. C., Mother Georgia Stevens, residing at the College of the Sacred Heart, Manhattanville, Borough of Manhattan, New York City, N. Y., and Justine Bayard Ward, residing at "Mora Vocis," Dobbs Ferry, N. Y.

EIGHTH: All of the subscribers to this certificate are of full age; at least two-thirds of them are citizens of the United States, at least one of them is a resident of the State of New York, and of the persons named as directors, at least one is a citizen of the United States and a resident of the State of New York.

IN WITNESS WHEREOF we have made, signed, and acknowledged this Certificate in duplicate this 25th day of February, A. D., 1929.

WILLIAM J. DESLONGCHAMPS,
GEORGIA STEVENS,
JUSTINE BAYARD WARD,
AGNES LEBRETON,
HERBERT D. MASON.

STATE OF NEW YORK,
CITY AND COUNTY OF NEW YORK. }ss.:

On this 25th day of February, 1929, personally appeared before me the Rev. Father William J. Des Longchamps, Mother Georgia Stevens, Justine Bayard Ward, Agnes Lebreton, and Herbert D. Mason, to me severally personally known and known to me to be the individuals described in and who executed the foregoing certificate and they thereupon severally acknowledged to me that they did execute the same.

WALTER J. N. BRANDINBERG,
Notary Public,
New York County. Clerk's No. 628,
Register's No. 0—710,
Commission expires March 30th, 1930.

I, HON. JOSEPH MORSCHAUSER, Justice of the Supreme Court of the State of New York of the Ninth Judicial District, do hereby approve the foregoing Certificate of Incorporation of The Dom Mocquereau Schola Cantorum, Inc., and consent that the same be filed.

Dated White Plains, New York, February 25th, 1929.

JOSEPH MORSCHAUSER,
Justice of the Supreme Court of the State of New York,
Ninth Judicial District.

Appendix No. 2

Copy of Letter of February 18th, 1929, addressed by my attorney
to the Rector

February 18, 1929.

Rt. Rev. Msgr. James H. Ryan, Rector,
Catholic University of America,
Washington, D. C.

Right Reverend and dear Rector:—

In order that we may have a little clearer understanding of the difficulties which seem to confront the Foundation in view of its original purpose of founding an independent and self-supporting College of Music at
the University in accordance with its corporate objects, and in view of
the suggestion that the substitution of a School of Music as an integral part
of the University should be found more desirable from the standpoint of the
latter, I beg to say that as I understand the suggestions which you were
good enough to make at this morning's conference they were:

(1) That the matter must be so handled, both as to building and operation, that no financial burden will fall upon the University. This is the
intention of the Foundation; it being understood, as was discussed this
morning, that the School will receive for the courses to be given to University students and to students of Catholic Sisters College that proportion
of their tuition which the hours of instruction given at the School bear
to the total hours taken by the students;—such proportion to be paid into
the special fund to be created in the hands of the University through its
receipt of payments to be made by the Foundation, and to be disbursed
accordingly. The Foundation also would like it to be understood that in
view of the general support of the School by the Foundation, the University
on its part will make no overhead, administrative or other charges against
the School for such clerical or other services as it may render in connection
with the work of the School.

(2) The Foundation will be expected to supply in monthly install-
ments such amounts as may be required for the operation of the School;
the same to be held by the Auditor or other proper financial authority of
the University in a special fund to be disbursed upon the order of the
Head of the School of Music or such other person connected therewith as
the Foundation may designate;—it being always understood that no further
disbursements will be required from said fund than are permitted by the
amounts received from the Foundation, and the allocation of tuition aforesaid and such incidental fees and earnings as the School may receive from
its operations.

(3) In order to meet the expectation of the Foundation that a separate College might be established for which the Foundation hoped to secure
additional endowment attracted by the special objects of the College, you
were good enough to suggest that a certain amount of autonomy might be

granted to the School which would put the Foundation in much the same position as would have resulted from the founding of a separate College, and that to this end it might be agreed that the Faculty of the School would be appointed from time to time from names presented by the Foundation which names would be submitted to you, to the Senate and finally to the Board of Trustees as in the case of other nominations. I am frank to say that this suggestion seems likely to remove much of the difficulty which might arise from the abandonment of the idea of having an independent College.

(4) So far as concerns representation on the University Senate, the School plan giving such representation, as distinguished from the College plan under which such representation might not follow, appears to have manifest advantages.

(5) It would be essential to the carrying on of the work of the School that women should be permitted to attend undergraduate courses with the men, which you felt might be permitted in view of the special character of the work contemplated.

(6) The work of the School may at times require the employment of women teachers, especially where men of equal desirability, may in the opinion of the Faculty, be unavailable.

(7) It is of vital importance that the School of Music should continue to conduct the choir services at the Shrine of the Immaculate Conception, since conflict between that work and the work of the School, or the turning of that work over to others, would seriously affect the standing of the School.

(8) The salary scale of the School will, in view of the small number available for giving suitable instruction, and in view of the technical character of the work, run above the usual salary scale of the University in many instances. You were good enough to say that, since the Foundation will be supplying the means, the salary scale would be left to its determination.

The above has been dictated rather hastily and you may find that it does not fully cover what was discussed, but if you should find that it does cover the proposals, I shall be glad to try to determine at once whether the plan can be made to fit in with the purposes of the Foundation which I sincerely trust will be the fact.

With much appreciation of your cordial attitude regarding the proposed work of the Foundation, I am,

Sincerely yours,

(Sgd.) H. D. MASON.

Appendix No. 3

Copy of Letter of February 20th, 1929, addressed by my attorney
to the Rector

February 20, 1929.

Rt. Rev. Msgr. James H. Ryan, Rector,
Catholic University of America,
Brookland, D. C.

Right Reverend and dear Rector:

Supplementing my letter to you of the 18th instant, and after we have
conferred with His Grace, the Chancellor, I beg to state for your convenience the additional points which I understand are desired to be covered, namely:

(1) The matriculation and graduation fees charged by the University
are not to be shared by the School of Liturgical Music.

(2) The School of Liturgical Music shall have charge of and shall
conduct the Liturgical music of the University including the music of the
Shrine of the Immaculate Conception.

(3) The School will provide instruction in the Liturgy through the
appointment of a suitable teacher thereof.

(4) First and advanced degrees will be granted to students of the
School upon recommendation of the Dean as in the case of other Schools
of the University and credit will be allowed to students of the University
for work taken in other Schools.

Thanking you again for your encouraging interest in and support of
the proposals and trusting that the foregoing will be found to cover the
additional points which you wished to have included before sending Mrs.
Ward a letter of acceptance upon which the Foundation can proceed with
its plans in the hope of making work available for the coming Summer
Session, I am,

Sincerely yours,
(Signed) HERBERT D. MASON.

Appendix No. 4

Copy of a Letter from the Foundation to the Rector,
dated March 7th, 1929

Washington, D. C.,
March 7, 1929.

Rt. Rev. Msgr James H. Ryan, Rector,
Catholic University of America,
Washington, D. C.

Right Reverend and dear Rector:—

The proposals of The Dom Mocquereau Schola Cantorum, Inc., for
founding a School of Liturgical Music at the Catholic University of

America for the teaching of Chant, Classical Polyphony and Liturgy in accordance with its purposes, having been passed by the Senate we now desire to present them to you for submission to the Executive Committee of the Board of Trustees of the University for consideration by that Committee. For convenience in referring to the proposals we number them as follows:

1. The School is to become an integral part of the University.

2. The School is to be financed and supported, as to buildings, equipment and instruction, so as not to impose any expense upon the University except the incidental expense hereinafter mentioned.

3. The Foundation will build, or will provide for the building, of a temporary building upon Lots 1 and 2 of Square 3968, Brookland, Washington, D. C., upon acquiring title thereto in the course of the negotiations now pending. It is understood that this is merely a temporary structure and that it, together with the said land, shall be the property of the Foundation. A larger and permanent building for the School is expected to be located upon the Campus and to be erected under such terms as the Trustees of the University shall then approve, it being understood that meantime some suitable site will be reserved for the purpose, the same to be near the Shrine of the Immaculate Conception, if the Trustees shall find that possible.

4. In addition to the funds to be provided by the Foundation, which will be turned over to the Auditor, or other proper financial authority of the University, and held by him in a special fund to be disbursed upon the order of the Dean of the School, or such other person connected therewith as the Foundation may designate, the University shall pay into such funds that proportion of the tuition of students of the University and of the Catholic Sisters' College which the hours of instruction given at the School shall bear to the total hours taken by the student. It is understood that matriculation and graduation fees and other non-tuition fees or charges and any other special fees or charges received or made by either the School or by the University shall not be shared by the other. It is also understood that the University undertakes no obligation to expend any funds for or on behalf of the School other than those created by donations made by the Foundation and such other donations as may be received for that purpose, together with the allocation of tuition and the other charges of the School above specified. It is also understood that the University will make no overhead, administrative or other charges against the School for such clerical or other services as it may render in connection with the work thereof.

5. You will recall that it was the expectation of the Foundation that a separate college might be established for which the Foundation hoped to secure additional endowment attracted by the special objects of the college, but that this plan was abandoned at your suggestion, as well as in view of the apparent advantages of having a School of Liturgical Music

which should become an integral part of the University. In order to meet this changed condition you were good enough to suggest, and we understand the Senate has approved, a proposal that the faculty of the School shall be appointed from time to time from names presented by the Foundation, which names shall be submitted to you or the other University authorities in accordance with the usual custom in view of the nature of the appointments to be made. This we feel will enable us to retain a status which will enable us to attract further endowment much as we could in the case of a separate college.

6. The School is to have representation on the University Senate as in the case of other Schools of the University.

7. The School is to be permitted to receive men and women undergraduates and graduates.

8. In view of the special character of the work of the School it is to be permitted to employ women teachers when the faculty shall deem it desirable so to do.

9. The School undertakes and shall conduct all of the Liturgical music of the University, as well as all of the Liturgical music of the academic functions of the Shrine of the Immaculate Conception, since conflict with the work of the School in this respect, or the turning of that work over to others might seriously affect its standing.

10. The Dean of the School will in due course submit its budget to the proper University authorities and will expect the privilege of consulting with them from time to time upon such administrative matters as they may arise.

11. The tuition charges at the School shall conform to the charges made by the other schools of the University.

12. The School will provide instruction in the Liturgy through the appointment of a suitable teacher thereof, and will in general carry out the plan and program embraced in the curriculum already submitted to the Senate.

13. First and advanced degrees will be granted to students of the School upon recommendation of the Dean as in the case of other schools of the University, and credit will be allowed to students of the University for work taken in the School as in the case of work taken in other schools.

With much appreciation of the cordial cooperation which our proposal has received, we are,

Faithfully yours,

The Dom Mocquereau Schola Cantorum, Inc.

(Sgd.) By: JUSTINE B. WARD,

President.

Appendix No. 5

Copy of the Rector's reply dated March 12, 1929

March 12, 1929.

Mrs. Justine B. Ward,
President, The Dom Mocquereau Schola Cantorum, Inc.,
Mora Vocis,
Dobbs Ferry, New York.

Dear Mrs. Ward:

At the meeting of the Executive Committee of the Board of Trustees of the University held yesterday, the offer which you made to the University of establishing a School of Liturgical Music here was submitted.

The Chairman of the Committee, Archbishop Curley, went over every detail of the plan. The Committee unanimously voted that this offer of yours should be accepted, and it empowered the Archbishop and me to go ahead and see that the plan was carried out according to the lines laid down in the memorandum which you presented.

Our lawyer suggested, however, that one point should be added to the agreement, namely, that the School of Liturgical Music should not duplicate courses actually given at the University. I do not think there will be any difficulty with either you or Mr. Mason agreeing to this added point.

Under the circumstances, therefore, I would say that you could go ahead now with your architect and any other plans that you have. If you think that the School will be ready to give instruction during the Summer Session, I would like to have Father DesLongchamps come in and talk over the matter of the curriculum, etc. I also think that it might be well to make, at least through the Catholic press, some sort of announcement of the establishment of this School. It might also be well to get up a special brochure which could be sent to our colleges, religious communities, and other possible interested parties, so that we would be sure to have a student body on hand next September. May I say that I think we should get out this course of studies about as soon as it can possibly be done.

I wish to thank you again for the great courtesy which you exhibited during this series of negotiations. I know that you feel the same as I do about the matter, that it is well to have everything settled before we begin the actual work of the School.

The Executive Committee asked me likewise to express to you its appreciation of your offer and to assure you of its co-operation in the development of the School of Liturgical Music. The members seem to have great hopes for its possibilities and all of them expressed the view that they would like to see it become the best school of its type in the world.

With best wishes,

Yours very sincerely,

JAMES H. RYAN,
Rector.

Appendix No. 6

Copy of Form of Agreement in regard to the building for the Schola Cantorum on the campus of The Catholic University of America.
(Never properly executed)

THIS AGREEMENT made in duplicate this third day of June, 1929, between Justine B. Ward and The Dom Mocquereau Schola Cantorum Foundation, Inc., first parties, and The Catholic University of America, second party, WITNESSETH:

1. The first parties agree to construct a building upon the campus of the second party, in lieu of the temporary building on Quincy Street, Brookland, D. C., heretofore contemplated, the said building to become the property of the second party.

2. The second party agrees to permit the construction of said building and that it shall at all times be devoted exclusively to the teaching of Liturgical Chant and Liturgical Music in accordance with the object, purposes, and principles specified in the Articles of Incorporation of said Foundation, so long as said Foundation shall conduct and support the School of Liturgical Music of the University therein, in accordance with the agreements heretofore entered into by the parties hereto, which agreements are hereby formally ratified and approved as though fully set forth herein, provided, however, that if the Foundation shall at any time cease on its part to carry out its obligations to support said School of Liturgical Music, then, and in that event the second party shall be entitled to the use of the said building and the Foundation shall no longer be entitled to the use thereof.

3. The plans for said building are to be approved by a committee appointed by the Board of Trustees, and the Dean of the School of Liturgical Music shall supervise the construction thereof consulting with the Rector, or in his absence, with the Vice-Rector.

Witness the signatures of the parties:

JUSTINE B. WARD.

THE DOM MOCQUEREAU SCHOLA CANTORUM FOUNDATION, INC.
By JUSTINE B. WARD, President.

ATTEST:
NEVER ATTESTED,
Secretary.

THE CATHOLIC UNIVERSITY OF AMERICA
By MICHAEL J. CURLEY,
President of the Board of Trustees,
and JAMES H. RYAN,
Rector of the University.

NEVER ATTESTED,
Assistant Secretary.

The foregoing agreement was duly approved by the Executive Committee of the Board of Trustees of The Catholic University of America on the

...................day of........................, 1929.

NEVER ATTESTED,
Secretary.

Dom Mocquereau and the Founder of the Pius X School

To the Editor of THE CATHOLIC CHOIRMASTER:

I note in the excellent article of the Rev. Stephen R. Fogarty, O.S.A., in the December number of THE CATHOLIC CHOIRMASTER the following assertion:

"None were more deserving of the commendation given to them by Dom Mocquereau than the founder and faculty of the Pius X School."

May I ask the following questions, since many readers may be puzzled as I have been in this matter:

1. Who was the founder of the Pius X School of Liturgical Music?

2. What was the nature of the commendation given by Dom Mocquereau to the founder of this school?

3. What was the date at which this commendation was given?

4. What commendation was addressed to the School and its Faculty by Dom Mocquereau apart from and independently of its founder?

5. At what date did the Pius X School break loose from its founder and from the principles represented by its earlier work?

6. At what date did the Pius X School cease to teach the Ward Method?

7. Where and from whom did the present members of the Pius X School Faculty receive their training in Gregorian Chant and in the principles of Solesmes?

8. Have any of these teachers made serious studies at Solesmes with Dom Mocquereau himself or with Dom Gajard, his successor?

I shall be extremely grateful for any light that can be thrown upon these points, either by Father Fogarty or by your able editorial staff.

Yours in search of light,

BROTHER A. S. S.

Rome, Italy.

[Ed.—The questions have been referred to the proper authorities for reply.]

Questions and Answers

DOM MOCQUEREAU AND THE FOUNDER OF THE PIUS X SCHOOL

To the Editor:

DEAR SIR:

You have kindly referred to me the questions which appeared in the last number of THE CATHOLIC CHOIRMASTER under the title, DOM MOC-QUEREAU AND THE FOUNDER OF THE PIUS X SCHOOL. I believe that I can throw some light upon the matter.

QUESTION 1: "Who was the founder of the Pius X School of Liturgical Music?"

The answer can be found in The New Catholic Dictionary, Vatican Edition, Page 766, as follows:

"Pius X School of Liturgical Music. Founded in 1916, and established at the College of the Sacred Heart, at Manhattanville, New York City, by Justine Ward with the help of the late Rev. J. B. Young, S.J."

I originally founded and endowed a Chair of Music which developed into a "School" with a specific program agreed to in advance by the College authorities, and, on the strength of this agreement, I erected a building called "The Pius X Hall" on the grounds of the College. The work was to be based on my series of text books and on the official editions of the liturgical chant with the rhythmic signs of Solesmes. For a number of years the School carried out the terms of the agreement effectively. During that time, scholars of the first rank visited and taught at the School. Gradually, the work deviated from the original plan, with the result that in June, 1931, I severed my relations with the Pius X School.

QUESTION 2: "What was the nature of the commendation given by Dom Mocquereau to the founder of this school?"

Answer: Dom Mocquereau commended my text book "Music Fourth Year—Gregorian Chant" in an introduction which he wrote for that volume, in which, among other things, he said, "Your book on Gregorian Chant reflects truly and luminously the most exact doctrines of Solesmes. . . Your own intelligent, cordial and artistic reception of our doctrines produced both in your mind and in my own a result which was far beyond my expectations. We have rendered one another a mutual service." (Music Fourth Year. Introduction, Page VIII). This was in 1921. Again in 1920, after hearing the singing of a group of pupils, whom I had brought to Solesmes to submit their work to his criticism, Dom Mocquereau wrote me a letter praising the rhythmic interpretation of the chant as rendered by this selected group of pupils.

QUESTION 3: "What was the date at which this commendation was given?"

Answer: 1921 for the text book and 1928 for the pupils.

QUESTION 4: "What commendation was addressed to the School and its Faculty by Dom Mocquereau apart from and independently of its founder?"

Answer: No commendation was ever addressed to the School or to any member of its faculty by Dom Mocquereau apart from or independently of its founder. Dom Mocquereau looked upon the School as a practical expression of my views—which were his own. He did not live to see the School break away from its founder, since he died in January, 1930, more than a year before the final rupture of relations.

QUESTION 5: "At what date did the Pius X School break loose from its founder and from the principles represented by its earlier work?"

Answer: In June, 1931.

QUESTION 6: "At what date did the Pius X School cease to teach the Ward Method?"

Answer: In June, 1931, the School ceased to teach Ward Method officially, though for several years previous to that date the character of the work had deviated considerably by means of unauthorized changes and publications which altered its character, and which, in my judgment, weakened it both pedagogically and liturgically.

QUESTION 7: "Where and from whom did the present members of the Pius X School Faculty receive their training in Gregorian Chant and in the principles of Solesmes?"

Answer: In New York City. I myself taught them the elementary principles with emphasis laid on the presentation of the chant to school children. Few, if any, of the faculty had carried their Gregorian studies beyond the elementary stage.

Mr. Bragers had the benefit of a month's study of Gregorian accompaniment under Dom Desro-quettes at Quarr Abbey on the Isle of Wight, sent there by me. I believe that Mr. Bragers and a few of the other teachers followed the fifteen-hour course given by Dom Mocquereau in 1922, and the brief courses in Gregorian theory and Gregorian musical forms given by the Abbot Dom Ferretti during his visits to the Pius X School during several summer sessions.

QUESTION 8: "Have any of these teachers made serious studies at Solesmes with Dom Mocquereau himself or with Dom Gajard, his successor?"

Answer: No member of the faculty from this School has ever studied at Solesmes either under Dom Mocquereau or under Dom Gajard.

Hoping that these answers will clear up the points in question, I remain,

Yours very sincerely,

(Signed) JUSTINE B. WARD.

New York, June 2, 1936.

ARCHBISHOP'S HOUSE
452 Madison Avenue
New York.

December 6, 1923.

Rt. Rev. Mgr. Charles A. O'Hern, D.D., Rector,
    Collegio Americano del Nord,
        Via dell' Umilta 30,
            Roma, Italy.

My dear Monsignor:-

        This will serve to present
MRS. JUSTINE B. WARD, who is journeying to the
Eternal City, in the hope of having the inestimable privilege of being received in audience by
our Holy Father, Pope Pius XI.

    MRS. WARD is a resident of this city and
diocese, and an exemplary Catholic. She has
given extraordinary service for the advancement
of the Gregorian Chant, and is responsible for
the Pope Pius X Institute of Liturgical Music.

    I bespeak for this good lady every possible
courtesy and consideration.

    With a blessing, I am,

        Sincerely Yours in Christ,

            PATRICK J. HAYES
            Archbishop of New York.

Copia (Janvier 1924)

Errata in the English Terminology of the Nombre Musical Grégorien

1. TITLE Retain the French title: LE NOMBRE MUSICAL GREGORIEN together with a sub-title: GREGORIAN RHYTHM

Its Theory and Practice
by

Dom André Mocquereau
Monk of Solesmes

2. CONTENTS

IV The Rhythmic Beat. The term "beat" suggests a marked stroke, this is translated into French by the term "Temps Frappé". I do not say that this term "beat" is not used often in solfège and in dictionaries of modern music as a translation of the word "Temps" (employed by Dom Mocquereau). But I say that it is precisely because the phenomenon rendered correctly by this word in most secular music, less correctly in truly artistic music does not at all render it correctly when we arrive at Gregorian music. And if the chosen term estranges the reader from the thought of the author it is not sufficient to turn to the dictionary to justify its use.

Conclusion: Substitute for the term "beat" the term "pulse".

Dom Mocquereau	Translation
IV Le Temps rhythmique	The Rhythmic pulse
1. Le Temps simple	The simple pulse or Simple Time
2. Le Temps composé	Composite time

Here, also, there is a difference between Temps composé of Dom Mocquereau and the word COMPOUND used by Standbrook. The word compound in English means a union of diverse elements in an ensemble where the elements are no longer distinguished, where all are merged into the ensemble. I do not believe that the word "composé" of Dom Mocquereau means this complete fusion of the elements, but rather a synthesis. The word "composé" in Dom Mocquereau's sense, is better translated by the word "composite".

So, instead of Compound Beat it is necessary to read: Composite Time.

V. 3. Examples of Simple Rhythms, binary and ternary.

Here the words binary and ternary translate well the words "binaires et ternaires" of the author. Perhaps, then, they should be retained. However, in English these words give quite another musical idea than what is wished. The words "binary" and "ternary" in English give the idea of a DIVISION of a primary unity in fractions.

Binary: in fractions of two, then of four, then, sixteen, etc.
Ternary: in fractions of three, nine, twenty-seven, etc.
Terms otherwise used in biology and always in the sense of division by geometrical degrees.

This phenomenon is indeed what occurs in modern music. When the word binary or ternary is used it represents what is taking place: the unity of the measure, or of a given note which is divided in two equal parts, which, in their turn are divided into four, and these four, in their turn, into sixteen, etc. The same for the "ternary". These words then represent admirably what takes place in modern music, but contradict the fundamental rule of Gregorian music explained by Dom Mocquereau in the Paléographie Musical and in the Nombre Musical: that the unity of the simple time cannot be divided. So we have 1 plus 1: 2. binary time in Gregorian Chant, and not a half-note (semi-breve) divided in two, in four, in sixteen, etc., phenomenon of modern music. It is for this reason that I would have wished to avoid these words binary and ternary. Rev. Dr. Shields advised me well to avoid them because it was his thought that all the books used in the university courses should agree, or at least not contradict each other. And as my books are the base of the University music courses and we wish to make the Nombre Musical the summit: all this for the Music Doctorate, you will understand my wish to avoid an open contradiction — not only between the courses on scientific subjects which are required for the B.A., even more for the Doctorate, but also between elementary and the more advanced music. I do not know if I explain myself well. I return to the terms BINARY and TERNARY I would like to avoid them and replace them by the terms DUPLEX and TRIPLEX, or by other terms that do not have the unhappy connotations of geometric subdivisions. But if the author insists on the words BINARY and TERNARY, I shall conform to her wish, all the while requesting an explanation for these terms that will make the reader understand that the sense given to these words is different from their ordinary meaning.

Thus: all of V 3 D should be changed if you agree with me, explained if you do not.

VII   2. Compound Rhythmic Forms. Same remark: should be "composite."

IX   4. Compound gestures. Again it should be Composite gesture. I should not know how to make a "compound" gesture, nor how to explain it to my students.

XI   2. Here Dom Mocquereau's divisions are changed according to this system:

Dom Moquereau	Stanbrook
Rythme Incise	Rhythm-Incise
Rythme Membre	Rhythm-Sections and Periods
Rythme Phrase	....
Grand Rythme	The Composition as a whole

Dom Mocquereau will determine for himself if these changes are acceptable.

As for me, I believe that there will be great confusion, and especially I do not find that "composition as a whole" conveys the idea of the Grand rythme.

In America (in my books as in the translations of Dom Mocquereau's course), the literal translation of the author's terms is understood and we are used to them. A change might well cause some disturbances. If however Dom Mocquereau likes them, the Stanbrook terms could be retained but with a clear explanation.

PART TWO

I B and C. Plainsong as a translation of Gregorian Chant is not found. The word Gregorian Chant is the translation of the term used by Dom Mocquereau. Plainsong rather translates the French word "Plainchant", which is not the one used by the author, and which carries a very different meaning. I shall not go into details for in this you have already expressed to me your thought.

Same correction wherever the word is used.

III 1 B. The terms clefs and clef signatures do not translate the title of the author which is: Lettres-clefs. "Clef signatures" in English means the flats and sharps which are written next to the clef in modern music, and which do not exist in Gregorian Chant. The thought of the author might well be translated by the words: Clefs derived from letters.

There are other less important errors, however, and which could be identified, but it seems important to me to control first the most necessary things — if we cannot agree on these it is useless to lose time in identifying the less important.

INTRODUCTION

Page XIV   Stanbrook translates Dom Mocquereau Page 18 this:

Dom Mocquereau	Stanbrook
"Le Chant Gregorien, lui, n'a pas de mesure, mais il a du rythme."	Now in Plainsong of course there is no time, but there is rhythm.

to say that there is no time in Gregorian Chant is to contradict all your teaching. What ought to be said is:

"Now in Gregorian Chant there are no regular measures, but there is rhythm".

There are other remarks to make, but less important. I have only read critically to the end of the introduction.

There is much that is good, even very good, in this translation. But the errors identified, and other less important ones, ought to be corrected before the translation can be accepted for my work in America.

A LECTURE BY MRS. WARD AT THE GREGORIAN INSTITUTE

Revue Grégorien 1924, P. 160

Last May 17th, Mrs. Ward, eminent foundress and directress of the Pius Tenth Institute of New York, wished to give a lecture at the Gregorian Institute of Paris, which had the honor of counting her as a member of its committee. She recalled her work in America, presented her method and its results. She took the trouble to beg indulgence for her "poor French" which was not at all granted. It was scarcely necessary. She speaks our language with ease and a very pure accent.

Mrs. Ward then recalled how her Gregorian work began.

There was at the University of Washington, where he occupied a chair in Philosophy, the Doctor Shields who dreamed of renewing the pedagogical methods of primary grade instruction in the Catholic schools. Profoundly intellectual and original, he was convinced that music ought to hold a very high place in the intellectual, moral and religious formation of the child.

A child is not a reasoning being. To reach him one must speak less to his intelligence than to his heart. He is indifferent to abstract truth. But having recourse to images, sound, rhythm, especially dancing, you will quickly grab his attention, conquer his sympathy. Of him it can be said that he approaches truth with his whole soul, heart and body. Music especially gives life to that which we teach him. Through it the dead letter of the book is brought to life. It takes on a sacred character, somewhat supernatural, which corresponds to an instinctive need of the wonderful and the divine that is in the heart of the child.

Doctor Shields then established a pedagogical program for teaching nuns in which music played a major role. He himself, practicing what he preached, had the little ones sing their catechism before he explained it to them.

It was here that Mrs. Ward found her vocation. In fact, the Reverend (Shields) asked her to assist him in his work and to write some melodies for his little ones. Excited by the priest's pedagogical ideas, she became his collaboratice and composed a series of manuals to realize his plan.

But the work was to take an unexpected development and direction when Mrs. Ward and Doctor Shields together became aware of the NOMBRE MUSICALE, of the rhythmic theories and chironometric method of Dom Mocquereau. They found what that had been looking for. Henceforth, Mrs. Ward saw not only the musical formation of the child as a means of education, but also as a preparation for the study and performance of Gregorian Chant. And through Gregorian Chant the authentic means of making a child to come to love the prayer of the Church, to attach him to her liturgy and cult. By way of fashioning the souls of the students through music, while forming their hearing capacity and their voices, the little singers, boys and girls, were being prepared by the Church, to grow up and become the congregation that Pius X wished to see taking active part in the divine service and praying in beauty.

Teachers and students then involved themselves in the study of plain chant. When it appeared that they had arrived at a given point of development, Mrs. Ward invited Dom Mocquereau to come to New York to preside over a Gregorian Congress. Dom Mocquereau was not at all satisfied and said so with his customary frankness, inviting Mrs. Ward in her turn to cross the ocean to come to Quarr Abbey for instruction. "A bit of a surprise, I admit," said Mrs. Ward, "I accepted the invitation. I heard the monks sing and I understood! . . . I understood that plain-chant is not improvised, and that one must have studied it for a long time, especially listening to and performing it. I had composed a Gregorian method which was ready for the printer. I threw it in the waste-basket. The teacher became a student — attentive and enchanted.

"What especially struck me in the solesmian performance was the suppleness of the rhythm, the elegance of the melodic curves. But how to make little children feel this? Beating time is too physical and otherwise how to render perceptible the passages of rhythmical expansions required by the horizontal bars, or required by the amplitude of certain melismas and intervals; how to translate those notes of stress in the salicus and the quilisma, or how to mark the acceleration toward the melodic accent or simply toward the verbal accent? By the hand designing in the air the rise and fall and the fullness of the curve, by these luminous gestures which Dom Mocquereau imagined and which are the "chironomy". For the child, however, this is perhaps not enough. The large undulating gestures of the hand and the arm will be accompanied by a lifting of the whole body to the toe-tips, as if the whole person with the voice was about to fly. Better still, you will control the vocal behavior of the children's voices, you will give them a lightness and grace by equipping yourselves with a net veil whose undulations this time readily seen, and without weight, trace the undulations of the melody. But why stop? The children themselves will take the veil and all the class with the teacher will trace in the air, the same rhythmic designs, the same diaphonous curves, winged, graceful, and which preclude all idea of heaviness. The flight of the voices will follow the flight of the white scarves. The Gregorian line will have achieved all of its fullness, suppleness, all its purity."

This is how Mrs. Ward developed among beginners Dom Mocquereau's chironomy — little beginners or grown-ups, for the lecturer said that spiritually many priests took the veil in our classes.

It goes without saying that the veils are gradually abandoned for the simple hand and arm gesture, and finally, there is no longer any gesture. The singer, even the little one, soon feels the inner rhythm instinctively and follows it in his inner being.

Dom Mocquereau was invited to return to America. This time, said Mrs. Ward, "we were happy because he was pleased."

"Thus, after five years of groping and studies, we had at last the true method. It remained to organize the teaching. Up to then our lessons reached scarcely anyone outside the nuns and the students of the Sacred Heart of New York. But soon, thanks to a nun, a good musician, and very gifted for teaching, the courses were taken by such a great number of students, priests, sisters, choirmasters, and organists, that the Pius Tenth Institute found itself all of a sudden established. It was baptised in 1924, and at that same time, the construction of a hall was achieved there in New York, large enough to accommodate hundreds of listeners"".*

And Mrs. Ward turned to the organisation of the courses of her Institute. The purpose was to form teachers. Notice the word. It was not a question of amateurs, but of teachers, pedagogues, people who came to learn, to learn how to teach, and to teach children from the earliest age.

"The program included a first year of study, given over completely to solfège, ear training, voice, taste, music pedagogy (a group of children was brought in so as to work on the spot), and at the end of the year the student-teachers pass an examination and receive a diploma which permits them to teach children. But their teaching is submitted to the control of a teacher from the Pius Tenth Institute, who, one day a week, at least each fifteen days, inspects the courses and examines the students.

"At the end of the second or third year, second and third examination more difficult, and the diploma candidates are judged less for what they know than for what they have made their students learn. Do not forget that it is not a question of the formation of virtuosos, but good teachers. And what is expected of the children? Some difficult enough things: an impeccable solfège, little music compositions, some improvised phrases. One sings, the other replies, a third writes on the board the melody thought up by his two comrades. The children of the candidate teachers of the third year ought to be able to read and sing in all keys, with all the accidentals of flats and sharps, any melody whatsoever. They should be able to write at the board, and in any key, what you sing to them. They are required even to recognize all the chords, whether with augmented or diminished intervals. Well trained voices are required, the habit of not reading note-by-note, but of noticing, like a musician, the entire phrase before beginning to sing.

"And it is only in this way, after this long and detailed preparation, that professors and students approach the study of plain-chant, which is presented to them not as something inferior which is rendered for no good purpose, but as the summit, like the most noble and most beautiful chant, like the great prayer of the Church, like sacred chant. All

*The hall was built in 1924. (Ed. note.)

the technical difficulties having been conquered, for us the chant is spell-binding. Very quickly the children seize upon the divine melodies, they are happy to sing in the church, nothing is so amusing on Sunday, before the office, seated on the steps of the church, book on their knees, head between the hands, and repeating interiorly, without singing, the hymns or the alleluias of the day. The parents, very proud of their progeny, retrace their steps to the church for the pleasure of hearing their little ones sing. It was thus that a good priest noticed one day that his entire parish had been transformed by the work of an obscure little nun. No more disorder or tense relations among the school children. Some quiet children who were seen after class occupied with writing music on the edge of the sidewalks, while giving lessons and explanations to their parents who were smiling and who themselves began to sing. When he went for his evening walk, the pastor was astonished to hear Kyrie's and Gloria's from behind closed doors. His church was filled a bit more each Sunday. All the children went there and soon the parents followed. The music, the plain-chant, more so than the lyre of Orpheus, had subjugated heedless heads and rebellious hearts.

"And that is how today after six years of effort we number five thousand diplomaed teachers from the Pius Tenth Institute who are teaching a million children."

"Perhaps," Mrs. Ward said at the beginning of her lecture, "perhaps you will find something to take with you from our experience and in our methods. That would be a joy for me as it is for me to say my thanks to my teacher, Dom Mocquereau, and to his dear country, France".

Ah, yes. There are some great lessons to learn here for us French. What place does music have in our schools? who is concerned with vocal formation? who is convinced of the educational value of music? who thinks of preparing among the children the parishioner who will one day sing in church, who will love his church because he knows her and knows all the chants? who judges plain-chant worthy of study and preparation? Alas! three times alas! (rari nantes!) But I am thinking about it. The Benedictine fathers would succeed in their propaganda, without a doubt, if they were to make a sport of plain-chant with public games.

5 mars 1927

Mon Révérend Père,

Le souci de la vérité et la question d'honneur vis à vis de mes élèves me forcent à vous demander une réponse catégorique sur le sujet du *Rythme Ondulant* enseigné dans mon livre *Gregorian Chant.*

Voudriez-vous, donc avoir la bonté de relire au Chapitre VI les pages 90–91–91, et me dire:

1 — Si cette doctrine est de vous ou de moi?
2 — Si vous me l'avez enseignée à Quarr Abbey en 1921–22?
3 — Si elle est toujours vôtre doctrine, ou si vous avez cru bon de la changer ou de la modifier?

Je vous demanderais aussi de bien vouloir regarder la chironomie du *Gloria Ambrosian* (p. 113–114), des répons de la Messe (p. 124–5–6), *l'Ave Regina Caelorum* (p. 209) et le *Regina caeli* (p. 210), pour ne prendre que quelques exemples typiques de l'application de vos principes (ou de ce qu'ici j'ai supposé l'être) et de me dire si cette chironomie est la vôtre ou la mienne?

Je n'offre pas ces exemples comme modèles du côte dessin, mais je demande simplement si la doctrine est la vôtre?

Il m'est impossible de continuer mon enseignement sans vôtre réponse écrite, mon Père, et je vous prie de ne pas me laisser trop longtemps dans cette incertitude.

J'attends vôtre réponse et vous prie d'agréer, mon Père, mon profond respect.

                                        Justine B. Ward

In order to avoid any equivocation between what has been taught in the
past and what will follow, I propose to make a clear distinction between

THE UNDULATING THESIS
AND
THE UNDULATING ARSIS

The Undulating Thesis would be what up to now we have called the Undulation.

The UNDULATING THESIS would have three forms:

1.   Undulating Thesis: melody on one pitch.

In this, it is clearly the tonic accent of the word that lifts the
Undulation since there is no melody.

2.   The UNDULATING THESIS: descending melody.

Here, it is sometimes the tonic accent alone (súper ómnes), or the
melody and accent.

Question: Should examples be added where the melody alone without
textual accent lifts the Undulation?

3.   The UNDULATING THESIS: rising melody.

Here, it is the accent that lifts the Undulation.

Question: Should examples be added where the melody alone lifts
the Undulation in rising melodies?

4.   The UNDULATING THESIS: ascending and descending melody.

Here, it is sometimes the accent, sometimes the melody and the accent
that cause the Undulations.

Question: Should examples be added where the melody alone gives rise to the Undulations without an accent present?

The UNDULATING ARSIS These Arsis would replace at will those linked in succession in: The rising melody.
The melody on one pitch?

The Undulating Arsis would be designed above the arsic note, and not below (as a Thesis would be).

It would be seen - however very lightly - that the arsic curve caused by the tonic accent of the text and by the rising melody, (or by one of these phenomena without the other?).

UNDULATING ARSIS

ARSIS LINKED IN SUCCESSION

UNDULATING ARSIS according to the form given in Chapter XIII of "Le Nombre Musical" and which seems to me to express poorly Father Mocquereau's gesture and arsic character of the Undulations.

The more the chironomic gesture resembles the great rhythm and the great melody, the more perfect it is. Dom Mocquereau.

These designs are very faulty. A lighter and surer hand is needed. It is only the form of the Undulations that I would like to propose.

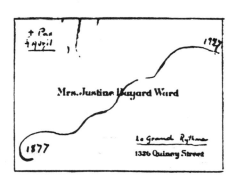

ABBAYE SAINT PIERRE DE SOLESMES
SABLE-SUR-SARTHE (SARTHE)

Ce 12 Mars, 1927
  En la Fête de St. Grégoire le Grand

      Déclaration —

    J'apprends que des personnes mal informées affirment que

certaines pages du Gregorian Chant de Madame J.B.Ward s'éloignent

des doctrines rythmiques et chironomiques de l'école de Solesmes.

Je tiens à protester sans retard contre cette assertion ridicule.

Tout ce que j'ai dit dans l'Introduction du Grégorian Chant, en 1921,

au sujet de la conformité parfaite de l'enseignement Solesmien

et Américain, théorique et pratique, je le maintiens absolument.

Les années écoulées depuis 1921 n'ont fait que confirmer et

resserrer l'entente complète des deux Ecoles : Solesmes et

l'Institut Pie X de New York

    En foi de quoi, je signe

              F. André Mocquereau

              M.B.

+ Pax   7 Mars 1928

IRVINGTON 1676   MORA VOCIS
                                        DOBBS FERRY, NEW YORK

Mon Révérend Père -

    Je ne puis m'empêcher
de vous dire l'immense joie
que m'a causé la lecture
de l'article fait par vous
sur le Nombre Musical, qui
m'a absolument ravie.
C'était si difficile, pour
ne pas dire impossible,
de donner une idée vraie
de la grandeur de l'oeuvre
du Père Mocquereau contenue

dans les deux volumes, mais
ce miracle vous l'avez
vraiment fait, avec ——
la belle vue d'ensemble
de l'oeuvre elle-même, et
avec tant de coeur touchant
le cher vénérable auteur.

Que ce petit mot tout
court, mon Père, vous
porte mes félicitations
les plus profondes avec
l'expression de mon
respectueux souvenir

Justine B. Ward

$\mathcal{PAX}$

**ABBAYE
SAINT-PIERRE
DE SOLESMES**

SABLÉ-SUR-SARTHE. (SARTHE)

22 Aout, 1928

Bien chère Madame,

Le 22 Aout 1928, est une date qui ne peut passer inaperçue: nous devons tous, vous en Amérique, nous à Solesmes, en conserver le souvenir: c'est la première fois que les mélodies grégoriennes ont été executées en Europe dans un office liturgique, par des voix venues d'Amérique, de New York, de l'Ecole Pie X. Je tiens à vous donner toute ma pensée sur cette exécution musicale, bien humble en apparence, mais préparée depuis longtemps par des études sérieuses, et remplie des promesses les plus précieuses pour l'avenir.

Bien humble en effet; car une petite église de village en est le théatre; mais il s'agit de la paroisse de Solesmes située à quelques pas de l'Abbaye des Benedictins de Solesmes.

Bien humble encore; car sept jeunes filles américaines, inconnues, sans renom, vont simplement chanter la Messe de <u>Requiem</u> pour une de leurs compagnes, notre hôte l'année dernière, décédée il y a quelques mois. Mais ces sept jeunes filles ont fait leur éducation musicale et grégorienne à l'Ecole Pie X; elles ont été formées tout d'abord à New York par des professeurs accordés par le Rme. Dom Delatte,
Abbé de Solesmes (alors à Quarr Abbey), ensuite par Madame J.B. Ward et la Révérende Mère Stevens, religieuse du Sacré Coeur. Aujourd'hui, devenues professeurs elles-mêmes, ces enfants viennent à Solesmes, non pour faire admirer leur talent, mais pour soumettre timidement à leur ancien professeur, ainsi qu'il sied à leur âge, les résultats obtenus par un travail assidu de plus de dix années. Dans quelques jours, elles doivent se présenter au Congrès d'Utrecht pour y plaider par leurs chants la cause de l'art grégorien; elles n'osent faire cette démarche décisive sans les encouragements et l'approbation de Solesmes. Et, en tout ceci, bien chère Madame, elles ne font que vous obéir.

Qu'en sera-t-il de cette Messe de Requiem? Dans le village la curiosité est éveillée: nos hôtes, nos étrangers, venus eux mêmes à Solesmes pour étudier le chant grégorien, veulent assister à cet office, et tous s'y trouvent.

Bien chère Madame, vous savez le résultat; mais je tiens à le consigner par écrit, afin que les félicitations de tous les assistants soient pour vous, leur chef, et pour toutes vos enfants, une récompense du zèle constant déployé pendant dix ans au moins à l'application intelligente, artistique et chrétianne de <u>Motu Proprio</u> de Pie X: il faut que cette attestation reste dans vos archives pour l'histoire de votre école et l'encouragement des élèves d' l'avenir.

J'en reviens à l'exécution. D'abord la seule attitude simple, recueillie, de ces enfants dispose en leur faveur et révèle qu'elles sont pénetrées du rôle qui leur est assigné pendant la Sainte Messe: rien de théatral, aucune recherche de pose, de personnalité, de vanité. Dès les premières notes — pas d'accompagnement, bien entendu — toute l'assistance est sous le charme: la formation des voix est exquise; pureté, justesse des sons, discrétion dans les nuances, souplesse et délicatesse du rythme Solesmien qui gouverne et enveloppe toute la mélodie, direction chironomique, vraiment tout est parfait, et cela depuis l'Introit Requiem jusqu'aux dernières notes du Répons Libera me! De tout cet ensemble, il résulte un parfum de piété, un atmosphère de calme, de paix, de distinction artistique qui plonge les âmes dans la prière et le recueillement. Ainsi chantent les Anges en face de la Très Sainte Trinité. Quoi d'étonnant, après tout! Ces enfants, depuis qu'elles sont ici, communient tous les jours; on m'assure que plusieurs ont fait leur chemin de Croix dans notre église abbatiale; aussi réunissent-elles les conditions essentielles, vocales et spirituelles, qui, autour de l'autel, caractérisent les vrais chantres de la louange divine: belles voix, belles âmes!

Après cela, je n'ai rien à ajouter: à quoi bon des louanges, des félicitations. Pas plus que vous, bien chère Madame, elles n'en désirent; elles sont venues à Solesmes pour savoir si elles sont dans la bonne voie, si elles peuvent se présenter au Congrès d'Utrecht, comme des élèves bien authentiques de l'Ecole de Solesmes.

Eh bien oui, elles peuvent se présenter, en Hollande et partout, avec toute confiance, elles peuvent affronter les épreuves les plus difficiles, je puis assurer d'avance que l'Ecole Pie X de New York et l'Ecole de Solesmes seront fières de leurs succès.

Un dernier mot! Je ne crains pas de le dire: si, par impossible, le rythme grégorien venait à se perdre à Solesmes, ou en Europe, on pourrait en ce moment aller le chercher de l'autre coté de l'Océan, à New York, à l'Ecole Pie X, et à l'Université Catholique de Washington où le Révérend Des Longchamps l'implante solidement avec le plus grand succès parmi le jeune clergé, venu de tous les Etats Unis.

Dieu soit loué mille fois!

Il me reste un devoir à remplir: je dois adresser des remerciements profonds à vous, Madame, fondatrice et directrice de l'Ecole Pie X, et à tous ceux et celles qui ont concouru par leur enseignement à une application pratique si parfaitement réussie du Motu proprio sur la musique sacrée du grand Pontife. Un tel exemple est digne de servir de modèle à toutes les Ecoles ambitieuses de réaliser le même programme. Un remerciement très spécial est dû à vos sept élèves qui nous ont révélé tout ce qu'on peut attendre d'elles et de leurs compagnes. Je tiens ici à consigner leurs noms: ils rappelleront à celles qui leur succéderont la campagne glorieuse et fructueuse de 1928 en France et en Hollande.

Miss Margaret Hurley	21 ans.
" Marion Robinson	20 "
" Julia Sampson	20 "
" Margaret Sullivan (sic)	19 "
" Mary Carroll	18 "
" Catherine Carroll	18 "
" Antoinette De Nigris (sic)	17 "

Hommage, remerciement,

[signature] André Mocquereau
m. b.

P.S. Depuis cette lettre, vos enfants se sont fait entendre au parloir de l'Abbaye de Sainte Cécile, devant nos religieuses bénédictines. Celles-ci ont été ravies! Je sais que la perfection du chant de vos élèves a excité vivement leur émulation. Les moniales reconnaissent leur infériorité, elles ambitionnent maintenant d'arriver à cette même perfection! Tel est le bien que peut faire, sur des âmes bien disposées, un seule audition! Sainte Cécile, du haut du ciel, a présidé à cette réunion.

[signature] A. M.
m. b.

in po dark

IRVINGTON 1878

MORA VOCIS
DOBBS FERRY, NEW YORK

22 Janvier 1930

Mon Révérend Père -

Devant l'angoisse qui vient de nous unir dans un commun deuil, les paroles sont bien inutiles. Vous comprenez que le monde a perdu pour moi tout ce qui était le plus beau, le plus idéal, le plus saint. Je ne puis dire qu'un fiat sans réserve en offrant en union avec Solesmes et avec vous l'encens du sacrifice le plus grand de tous.

Quand au reste, le cher Père Mocquereau mérite si bien sa joie éternelle

après ses longues années de lutte et d'œuvres pour la louange divine qu'un rayon de sa joie vient jusqu'à nous pour nous consoler. Nous croyons à Mora Vocis que le chant des Séraphins sera plus exquis, mieux rythmé depuis l'arrivée du Père Mocquereau.

Permettez-moi, mon Père, de garder pour une prochaine lettre tout ce que j'aurais à vous dire sur Washington, comme aussi ma reconnaissance pour votre si bonne lettre du 3 Janvier. Pour le moment il suffit de vous dire que la rupture est définitive.

---

22 Janv. 30

La vérité sera connue à Rome au moment propice. Le R.P. Sallayrolles reste ici avec nous à Mora Vocis. Sa présence a été une grande force pour nous dans notre douleur. Le jour des obsèques du Père M. c'est lui qui a dirigé le Requiem chanté pour tous les professeurs et élèves de Pie X pour le maître qui était tout pour eux - c'était chanté avec les cœurs et avec les âmes.

Pensez, mon Père. Dom Sallayrolles est arrivé à l'Héminité sans une parole bienveillante d'avance possible; il y a travaillé avec dévouement pendant trois mois sans un mot d'encouragement, il est parti sans un mot de remerciement - des uns ou des

autres. Et je parle non seulement de Rome et des autorités, mais aussi des "apôtres" qui eux, avaient été reçus avec tant de bonté et de délicatesse en France, à Solesmes. C'est tout vous dire.

Pour le moment, et pour l'avenir, mon Père, nous vous assurons, tous les trois, de notre union profonde avec vous pour le triomphe des principes du Père Mocquereau et pour la beauté du chant de louange. Dans cette union sera votre force.

Veuillez, mon Père, accepter ma sympathie dans votre souffrance et mes vœux de courage pour la lourde charge qui est vôtre, avec mes prières -

Justine Ward

App. No. 44   321

February 20, 1930

To the Right Reverend Dom Cozien

Your Lordship:

We, the Directors, professors and Schola
Cantorum, of the Pius X School of Liturgical Music, in this
moment of mutual sorrow want to express our profound
sympathy in this irreparable loss. Dom Mocquereau seems
more present than ever to us all. On Monday, January 20th,
we had the supreme consolation of singing the Mass as a
body in the Convent of the Sacred Heart, Manhattanville, in
union with Solesmes. The Mass was directed by Dom
Sablayrolle and the Chapel was filled with the Schola,
teachers and also the children of the Parish School who
joined in singing the Kyrie, Sanctus and Agnus Dei. It
brought us all very closely together and I feel must have
touched the great heart of Dom Mocquereau.

Mrs. Ward was kind enough to read the
wonderful letters from Solesmes to the members of the
staff and the Schola and together we have been united
perhaps more deeply than ever with Solesmes by our prayers.
We want to take this occasion to renew our profound thanks
for allowing Dom Mocquereau to come to America twice. It
is those unforgettable visits that brought the Chant into
our lives in such a living way. We still see his figure
in the Chapel where he directed the Mass and many still

2

PIUS X SCHOOL OF LITURGICAL MUSIC
COLLEGE OF THE SACRED HEART
133rd Street and Convent Avenue
New York

speak of his conducting the vast concourses of children and people in St. Patrick's Cathedral. Hundreds were able to come directly under the sway of his teaching and the visits to America indirectly touched thousands of lives. It has been the privilege of so many of the School to visit Solesmes and the religious courtesy that has been shown them during these visits unites us in a very personal way in the sorrow that is now yours and ours. Dom Mocquereau will be the force, I am sure, to cement the little School of Pius X with Solesmes, as he was during his life, and may we say how earnestly we hope that we shall more and more labor hand in hand in carrying on Dom Mocquereau's great work. How deeply we appreciate this support and help, it would be impossible to express, and I hope that down through the ages the great Abbey of Solesmes will extend its spirit to the Pius X School and its followers.

To Dom Gajard we want to unite ourselves in a very special way as the successor of Dom Mocquereau and to pledge to him our full co-operation. It is unnecessary to say this but our heart demands this expression.

Dom Mocquereau's memory is so vivid here that he seems more a living presence than ever and he will, I am sure, help us even more now that "we are no longer

3

PIUS X SCHOOL OF LITURGICAL MUSIC
COLLEGE OF THE SACRED HEART
133rd Street and Convent Avenue
New York

replaced by the ocean," as you said in your letters to
Mrs. Ward.

Begging for Your Lordship's blessing,
and with profound respect, we are, in union of prayer

Very devotedly and gratefully yours,

Justine B. Ward   *G. Stevens*
                            r.c.j.

Members of the Staff.

Achille P. Bragers	Audrey Freeman
Norbert L. Heagney	Anna Louise Bavoss.
Leo H. Bartinique	Genevieve Lambert Gilgan
Edmund M. Holden	Marie Ohashi
Frank Crawford Page	Agnes Bensique
Margaret L. Hurley	Edith Recktenwald
Julia F. Sampson	Elsie Freeman
Josephine M. Shine	Marguerite Flannigan
Peggy Sullivan	Helen Howe
Mary B. Saunders	Agatha Macken
Catherine A. Carroll	Margaret M. Gleeson
Margaret M. McShane	Rosemary Petralia

4

PIUS X SCHOOL OF LITURGICAL MUSIC
COLLEGE OF THE SACRED HEART
133rd Street and Convent Avenue
New York

Members of the Staff—continued

Margaret Fulton
Marie Lawson
Margaret Hackett
Josephine Keane

Nettie De Nigris
Mercedes Emerson
Margaret Leddy
Anna P. O'Donoghue

Schola Cantorum

Evelyn Leddy
Genevieve McGloin
Helen McArdle
Mary Dunn
Catherine Hannigan
Kathryn McGuire
Rita Clark
Anne Cullen
Mildred Leddy
Dorothy McArdle
Catherine Carroll
Mary Reilly
Ruth Dubarsky
Julia Blake
Madeleine Callahan

Mary Cullen
Rita Barrett
Mary Galligan
Mary O'Shea
Margaret Sullivan
Elizabeth O'Toole
Pilar Vicente
Mary McGowan
Catherine Flynn
Alice Bettmann
Dolores Connaughton
Mary Pembroke
Grace O'Neill

3, RUE LÉON-LEGLUDIC

SABLÉ (SARTHE)

le 8 août 1935

August 8, 1935

My Reverend Father:

I am very happy to have the two new "Monographs". Your idea was magnificent to give these two articles a more permanent form. It seems to me that the one on the "Rhythmic Editions" could do a lot of good in being translated into foreign languages. What do you think? Especially if — once the public is convinced — they find a way of satisfying — everywhere — their enthusiasm for these signs! Let us hope that the day is coming when we shall all sing with the same rhythms from one end of the universe to the other!

With all my profound thanks, my Reverend Father, believe in the expression of my respectful devotion.

Justine B. Ward

"METHODE WARD"
DE MUSIQUE ET DE CHANT LITURGIQUE
A L'USAGE DES ENFANTS DES ECOLES

Paris, le 8 Avril 1935

———

M

*Le Comité d'introduction en France de la " MÉTHODE WARD " a l'honneur
de vous inviter :*

I

SALLE D'HORTICULTURE, 84, Rue de Grenelle, Paris
Le Samedi 27 Avril 1935, à 15 heures

A LA DÉMONSTRATION - AUDITION

pour la première fois en France, de la " MÉTHODE WARD " de musique et chant
liturgique, destinée aux enfants des classes élémentaires, qui sera présentée,

sous le haut patronage

de son Eminence le Cardinal VERDIER, *Archevêque de Paris*

de son Excellence M. LOUDON, *Ministre plénipotentiaire de Hollande*

et sous la présidence effective

du Révérendissime Père Dom COZIEN, *Abbé des Bénédictins de Solesmes*

par un groupe d'élèves de l'école primaire de garçons de HORN (Hollande)
sous la direction de leurs instituteurs

En présence de Madame Justine WARD

II

EGLISE St-DOMINIQUE, 20. Rue de la Tombe-Issoire, Paris

Le Dimanche 28 Avril 1935, à 10 heures

A LA GRAND'MESSE PAROISSIALE DE QUASIMODO

T. S. V. P.

Le propre et l'ordinaire de cet office seront chantés en grégorien par
les mêmes élèves de l'école primaire de Horn.

ENTRÉE LIBRE ET GRATUITE A L'ÉGLISE
(MÉTRO SAINT-JACQUES OU DENFERT-ROCHEREAU)

N.-B. - Entrée à la Salle d'Horticulture participation aux frais : 5 francs

Les cartes pourront être prises le jour de l'audition à la Salle d'Horticulture,
ou retenues d'avance :
  à la même salle, 84, Rue de Grenelle (VII⁰),
  à l'Œuvre des Orphelins-Apprentis-d'Auteuil, Succursale : 5, Rue Férou (VI⁰),
  chez MM. Desclée et Cⁱᵉ, 30, Rue Saint-Sulpice, Paris VIᵉ. *Editeurs de l'Edition
française de la " MÉTHODE WARD ".*

New Papal Honors Conferred on Justine B. Ward

Mrs. Ward, who is a sister of the late Senator Bronson Cutting of New Mexico, has been highly honored for her contributions to the advancement of musical education. In recognition of her work, she has been awarded the honorary degree doctor of music, by the Pontifical Institute of Sacred Music at Rome. She is the only woman who has received a degree from this Papal university. She has also been awarded the gold cross *Pro Ecclesia et Pontifice* by the Holy Father, and has been decorated by the Italian Government with the gold medal for distinguished service in education. She was awarded the Cross of the Order of Malta on the feast of St. Gregory this year.

She is the author of a system of musical education for school children now internationally known, which she originally set out to devise at the request of the professors of the Department of Education of the Catholic University of America, as part of a general revision of methods for the primary grades. Her method has had an extensive spread in Europe, especially in Italy, Holland and France, where courses for teacher training are organized by local educational authorities.

Mrs. Ward said that in America the courses in her method for teachers are given at the Sisters' College of the Catholic University during the academic year and at the summer session of the university. Webster College, St. Louis, has also organized teachers' courses in her method, which will offer facilities for teacher training in the Middle West. These are the only institutions in America providing teacher training in the method.

[Les ___ sont de Mrs Ward]
et aussi les notes repassées au noir

The Accompaniment of Gregorian Chant

By Roland Boisvert, Mus. Doc. *

NO ONE today would think of accompanying Gregorian Chant with a chord for each note. Dom Delpech, organist of the Abbey of Solesmes many years ago, was one of the first to break away from the accepted custom of his day. It is true that the Medicean did lend itself to such a treatment. But this is not the case with the Vatican Edition, and in particular, with the Rhythmic Signs added to the Official Edition. After years of research and experimental harmonizations, while no definite solution has been reached, our written accompaniments are greatly improved. There was no instrumental accompaniment at all until the 11th century, possibly because the Church wanted to break away from the use of instruments so much in vogue with the Pagans.

MANY believe that a suitable accompaniment is impossible and their many arguments for taking that stand are too important to set aside unanswered. They rightly claim that the Gregorian melody carries within itself all means of expression and that a harmonic garment cannot add anything essential, it being unison melody. The best accompaniment exposes the all important melody to various kinds of embarrassments of a rhythmic and modal nature. Often the melody itself is so bare that the elements it furnishes are not sufficient to the harmonizer. In modern music, a melody contains within itself its own general harmony and we know only too well, that this will vary with each composer. Gregorian Chant is impersonal, absolute melody, a melody of one dimension, its extent is purely horizontal and is not the slave of regular recurring strong and weak beats. When we accompany Gregorian Chant we add a new and dangerous dimension.

The opponents of Gregorian Accompaniment also claim that it is not indispensable; that it compromises the melodies because the average accompaniment is nothing more than an aimless succession of awkward chords.

RECENT important research on the subject by Dr. L. Söhner, of Germany, proves that he is definitely against any sort of accompaniment. He arrived at this conclusion after a minute analysis of all written accompaniments. It is true Gregorian Chant is essentially a vocal art. To be a work of art an accompaniment must do more than support the voices and add a little timbre. It is hardly possible that it can ever be part of a work to the extent that the accompaniments are inseparable from the Songs by Schumann or Schubert. A well-trained Choir does not need the support of an accompaniment in Polyphony; why then should it be required during the singing of Chant? The organ will not prevent singers from singing out of tune unless it is made more prominent. Loud playing will not cure the ill. The untrained often sing off-pitch; this even happens to trained singers under certain conditions. It is incorrect to state that voices generally have a tendency to flatten. Accompaniments written too low often cause this, in children's voices in particular. In case of habitual flat singing it is by far better to raise the pitch than to lower it. This will force the singers to use a lighter register. The rendition of Gregorian Chant demands such fluidity that it is hardly possible with the use of the so-called big tone.

HOLY Mother Church, while imposing Gregorian Chant upon the faithful, permits the use of the organ as an accompaniment (barring a few instances clearly indicated in the rubrics). **The place of Gregorian accompaniments is officially recognized,** mind you, **not tolerated.** We are then free to make use of it, if we wish. It is being accompanied in most cases, even at Solesmes. While this may be regrettable, it is, nevertheless, true. With all Occidentals the inherent need of harmony is instinctive. Many singers refuse to sing without accompaniment. For Congregational Singing it is almost indispensable. There is no need to be more concerned about this matter than Holy Mother Church is. We cannot be total strangers to our own times.

A GOOD accompaniment can hide the defects of inexperienced singers, but it is regrettable to note that most of these accompaniments are unfit for use. Many of them were written some 25 years ago. At

* Dr. Boisvert is now in Solesmes continuing his research work with the Solesmes Monks.

that time the research in rhythm or modality was not sufficiently advanced to formulate a good system of accompaniment. Neither can we depend upon our organ virtuosi, most of whom are deplorable Gregorian Accompanists. Bad accompanists do as much to discredit Chant as do the indifferent renditions of the venerable melodies. If we were as particular about them as we are about modern music, the Gregorian melodies would have everything to gain. The accompaniments of Singenberger, Wagner, Griesbacher, Matthias, and those given in the Roman Hymnal, are all anti-rhythmic, and cannot be used by the followers of Solesmes. It would be better to play the melody alone. Some place chords on word accents, others use dominant sevenths, perfect cadences, chromatics, etc. Still others place chords invariably on the first note of neumes. While this may be correct in many cases, we must keep in mind that **neumes are derived from grammatical accents and have melodic rather than rhythmic significance**. The great danger in all accompaniments is the tendency to exaggerate. The parts other than the Soprano are secondary and must necessarily be so.

ANOTHER difficulty is of a modern nature. It is impossible to judge the music of our day by the text books on Harmony. So it is with the Gregorian Chants. They cannot be judged by the Greek Modes. Very little music has come to us from the Greeks. We only have a few fragments and these do not enlighten us very much. The frequency of the B flat as an essential note is not taken into account by the theory of the Greek Modes. It was all well and good in the Middle Ages to explain its existence by the presence of the notorious **"Diabolus in Musica,"** but we know that numberless B flats are not concerned with the famous interval. While there is similarity between the Greek modes and the modality of Gregorian Chant, it is not so pronounced as is generally believed. In the melodies themselves and through their careful analysis we find the correct answer.

THE system of the "Three Tonalities" was first noticed by Dom Desrocquettes. Later it was systematized by Henri Potiron in Monographie No. 9. This study proves beyond a doubt, that composers were little concerned about Greek Modes. It is hoped that this Monographie and other studies by the same author will be translated. Last

Summer, Mons. Potiron read an important communication at the International Congress of Sacred Music held in Paris. The paper was entitled "The Modal Equivalences in Gregorian Chant." We hope to make this the subject of a special article at a later date.

AS WE all know, the followers of the Solesmes School generally place chords on ictuses. The greater rhythm of a piece should decide on which ictuses the chords should be placed. Elementary rhythm is often more emphasized in written accompaniments than in improvized accompaniments. This is due to the fact that when writing there is a danger to concern one's self with minute details, all of which may result in the overloading of the accompaniment. Certain types of modal cadences should not be used indifferently for both feminine and masculine cadences. The accompaniment of the future, we believe, will concern itself more about important tonic accents. Too many followers of Solesmes are ictus-minded and have never mastered the various treatments of the word accents according to that school. In syllabic chant in particular, the word accent is an important factor. By disregarding it we expose the Solesmes School to undeserved criticism. Without a doubt the tonic accent is independent of the rhythmic movement of the piece. Nevertheless certain tonic accents (important ones, even on the up-beat) can sometimes receive a chord which will serve as a resolution of the preceding one. Abuse of this procedure would of course over-burden the accompaniment. Then too, the accompaniment should vary with the chyronomie of the conductor.

THE use of dissonances and discords is another point that concerns all interested in the subject. While some ultramoderns may like them the faithful in general will be disturbed by their constant use. That some writers inject them in their accompaniments without rhyme or reason, merely to please their own musical tastes, there can be no doubt. The austere melodies of the church should retain their limpidity even when garbed with an harmonic garment. Some recent writers suggest that it would be well to keep the alto part away from the soprano,—say a fourth, as a general rule. This is not always possible, but they claim that at least harmonic intervals of seconds in particular should be avoided between the soprano and alto parts. The melody would then stand out in clearer fashion. Another improvement they claim would be to write the bass with as few skips as possible. The Gregorian Accompaniment can be either three- or four-part. Much depends on the instrument, the acoustics, size of the choir, etc. The same piece should be treated according to the particular circumstance. Three-part is undoubtedly lighter than four.

The average accompaniment is a mixture of both. We find numberless unisons, many of which are the result of temporary embarrassment and the use of this procedure seems to be the simplest way out. Some of these unisons are legitimate. What becomes of the missing voice, no one knows. How can its absence be explained? The constant aimless mixture of these three- or four-part chords is annoying to say the least. Some writers employ one or the other. In parts reserved for the Cantors the accompaniment should be lighter, preferably written in three parts. The recent accompaniments by Aug. Le Guennant, Director of The Gregorian Institute of Paris, seem to be the first to put that point into practice. For large choruses the organist can fill in the intermediate parts.

FEW accompaniments are dependable, even those presumably written according to the Solesmes theories. Their best disciples sometimes slip up on these finer points. The Desclée catalogue of Plain Chant Publications contains some 70 pages. Several publications listed therein are not the work of the Solesmes Monks and they cannot be held responsible for them. These may be the works of some well-intentioned, but sometimes none-too-well-informed persons, who lack the facilities of Solesmes Abbey. Apparent discrepancies confuse people who, in turn, blame Solesmes. Their chief mistakes are of two kinds, both are committed unintentionally. The first consists in the applying of a certain rule for placing ictuses, a rule generally ignored by writers of Accompaniments (excepting the recent accompaniments of Mons. Le Guennant, Potiron, and Abbe Pothier). Here is the rule:

A VIRGA or isolated punctum preceding a group or neume of at least three notes receives the ictus in the place of the first note of the neume, especially if this virga or punctum coincides with a syllable. If the virga or punctum precedes a long note the ictus is placed on the long note. For many years the Schola at Solesmes unconsciously

observed this rule and even naturally lengthened the note in question. After a close examination of the manuscripts, there was no doubt that the rhythmic alighting point was on the punctum. Dom Mocquereau placed quite a few ictuses in such cases, but the greater number remained unmarked. He was forced, as we know, to reduce the number of ictuses for reasons too well known to repeat here. His opponents who accused him of inventions then, now claim he should have been more prodigal with them. It was later noticed that the interpretation of this above mentioned group is similar to that of the quilisma group. In the new edition of the Chants for Holy Week (which is the work of the Second Vatican Commission), it was found more practical to place only the horizontal episema in the above cases, it being very difficult for typographical reasons to place both episemas over or under the same note. This note, like the note preceding the quilisma, is an ideal place to place a chord. Solesmes teaches that the placing of ictuses on the first note of a neume should only be used as a last resort. Let us not forget that they are derived from grammatical accents and have no rhythmic significance whatsoever.

WHILE this rule may not seem to be of great importance, still, all directors and accompanists should know it, and how to apply it. It will not be found in antiquated books on the Solesmes Theories nor in the preface to the Liber Usualis. (Many of the finer points of the Solesmes teachings cannot be found in books.) A typical example of the above case is in the intonation of the Absolve of the Requiem Mass. On page four of Dom Desrocquettes' Accompaniment of the Requiem Mass, the chord is at the right place on the note preceding the neume, under the syllable sol. In Bragers' Kyriale, page 142, same example, the chord is on the syllable Ab of Absolve—(Wrong). In the accompaniment of this Mass by Dom Desrocquettes, we find that he has treated it according to the above rule. His pupil, Mr. Bragers, fails to do so in the same case, and places the chord on the first note of the neume. We advise our readers to try both ways and decide for themselves which is the more musical. Upon further investigation we note that Dom Desrocquettes failed to observe the same rule seven times in his accompaniment of the Agnus of Mass No. 2. So does Mr. Bragers in his Kyriale and Accompaniment of the Forty Hours (in the Graduale). In Dom

15) we find seven wrongly placed chords in the Agnus of Mass No. 2. In the first of these the second ictus and chord should be on the syllable "gnus," and not on the first note of the neume. The six other cases are similar. Another traditional Solesmes interpretation missed by both is that of the *Hosanna* after the Benedictus of Mass No. 9 (cum Jubilo). There should be three ternary groups in place of the three binary. Dom Mocquereau himself made this correction in the Chapter several times so it is no invention of Dom Gajard as some might say. Dom Mocquereau recommended three ternary groupings in place of the stiff three binary groups commonly used. No doubt the ictuses should have been placed there, but that was impossible thirty years ago. When in doubt about ictuses in the Office, consult the Antiphonale Monasticum. No one is obliged to follow Solesmes in these details or in fact any detail at all. But those who claim to follow that School should endeavor to keep in step with it.

THE second type of mistake is that of the salicus. We all know the traditional interpretation, but many ask, when is there a salicus? Many only notice the standard type, a punctum and podatus, under which is to be found the vertical episema. But Solesmes gives another rule (not to be found in obsolete books). We notice in the Accompaniment of the Requiem Mass by Rev. Carlo Rossini that there are no horizontal episemas under the salicuses in the Introit and Libera. By this omission it is entirely possible for singers and organists to convey a totally false impression of the proper rhythmic interpretation.

ACCORDING to Solesmes, three conditions are required for a salicus:
1. At least three notes (there may be as many as six).
2. The last two must form a podatus.
3. The first note of this podatus must bear the vertical episema.

Many fail to notice salicuses of more than three notes. Dom Desrocquettes, for instance, in his accompaniment to the Ave Maria (Offertory), dated 1934, fails to place the horizontal sign on the two salicuses in the word ventris, while Mr. Potiron in an accompaniment of the same piece, dating several years before, treated it correctly, according to the above rule. With the three conditions required for the salicus, it, of course, means that there is no such thing as a second form of the salicus (like in the intonation of the "Gaudeamus,") but the interpretation of this mis-termed salicus is similar to that of the normal salicus. That there are other salicuses there is no doubt, but the imperfect grouping of the Vatican makes it impossible to observe them.

ANOTHER point that confuses singers is that certain publications printed by Desclée like "Plain Song for Schools" in two volumes, we find that some ictuses are not under the same notes as in the editions compiled by the Monks. There is a possibility of several solutions in certain cases in syllabic chant, but to change the place of the marked ictuses, whether voluntary or not, is regrettable. In Volume One of the "Plain Song for Schools" the intonation of the Antiphon Ave Maria, the ictus is placed on the syllable A. In the Liber No. 801 and in the Antiphonale Monasticum, the ictus is under the syllable ve. The Domine Salvum further in the book gives the opposite of the first example. We know only too well that Solesmes always places ictuses at the same place in the same melodic formulas, and that is the case for the above example. The same thing applies for "Attende Domine." In the second volume certain Hymns like Salve Festa Dies, and others, the same error is committed. We like to think that possibly these were copied from some antiquated book, but nevertheless there is no excuse for it. The least we can do is to respect the Solesmes signs.

THE only text-books in the English language according to Solesmes Rhythmic System are those by Potiron and Bragers. The latter book being a resume of the former (Dom Desrocquettes being a pupil of Mr. Potiron and Mr. Bragers a pupil of Dom Desrocquettes). Strange to note that the Bragers text-book resembles Mr. Potiron's Old Method of 1912 in its general get-up more than the newer edition of 1925. The accompaniment of the Kyriale, though signed by both Dom Desrocquettes and Mr. Potiron, is the work of the former. One has but to compare the accompaniments of Potiron published some thirteen or more years ago by H. Herelle and those now being published by Desclée with those in the Kyriale by Dom Desrocquettes. While the modal theory is the same the writing is not the same.

x Pourquoi, parce qu'ils n'indiquent plus le rythme

HIS system of accompaniment is not officially recognized at Solesmes. We must admit that they are sympathetic to it and to their modal theories in particular. Solesmes does not use written accompaniments. Other accompaniments like those of Aug. Le Guennant in particular (the recent ones) are regarded very highly. In other words, the door is wide open for research in this matter. For a time, Dom Mocquereau was partial to the accompaniments of G. Bas, and rightly so. He later endorsed those of Dom Desrocquettes, but his enthusiasm was short lived, due to the protests coming from divers quarters shortly after the publication of the Kyriale.

FOUR months before his death he confided to the writer of these lines that new accompaniments were being prepared by a certain organ virtuoso. In these accompaniments the soprano part (or Chant Melody) was to be omitted entirely. This procedure would, no doubt, serve to lighten the accompaniment, but, it is certain, it would not be very useful to the average modest choir. So far, nothing has appeared from the pen of this virtuoso organist. Dom Gajard has not given his blessing to any particular accompaniment. The return to the ancient dominants in the Antiphonale Monasticum and in other publications to follow later would make it very unwise for the Solesmes Monks to commit themselves to any system, as they may not hold good once the melodies have been restored to their primitive versions.

SINCE the Monks left Quarr Abbey some fifteen years ago, all research work has been undertaken only at Solesmes, not in the Isle of Wight. All directions come from Solesmes. Solesmes does not have any official representatives in the United States. Dom Gajard does give courses in The Institut Gregorian which is part of the famous Institut Catholique of Paris. (This is the only school under the personal control of Solesmes.) Round table conferences are held in the Summer months at Solesmes. Students and Scholars come from many parts of the world, and all agree that the accompaniment as used there does not hinder the singing nor does it seem obtrusive.

TOO many followers of the Gregorian Restoration have been hero-worshipers. Some became greatly attached to Dom Pothier and insisted that nothing further could be done. We are not of those who believe that the last word was spoken with the passing of Dom Mocquereau. The victims of these attachments do not understand how this restoration is being carried out. While a certain Monk may sign his name to some work it does not necessarily follow that he is the sole author of the work in question. The foundations for the work of restoration have been carefully laid; improvements are constantly made; they clarify this or that point and a frequent check-up is necessary to keep step with the findings. When one has carefully examined the Paleographic (Library) one realizes that the work of restoration has only begun.

WILL the accompaniments of our day suffer the same destiny of those written twenty-five years ago? It is possible. So far, the prediction of Rameau in his famous "Traite d'harmonie" of 1722 (page 147) remains true. "Musicians deprived of æsthetic taste will uselessly struggle to find suitable harmonies to the Gregorian melodies."

The Catholic Choirmaster

An Important Communication
from Solesmes

DOM J. GAJARD DEFINES SOLESMES' POSITION

✝

ABBAYE SAINT PIERRE DE SOLESMES
PAR SABLE-SUR-SARTHE (SARTHE)

May 9, 1938.

To Mr. Nicola Montani,
Editor of The Catholic Choirmaster:
Dear Sir:

The last issue of The Catholic Choirmaster (March, 1938) contained an article on *The Accompaniment of Gregorian Chant* by Mr. Boisvert which is open to criticism. Mr. Boisvert was moved, no doubt, by the best of intentions and a desire to serve the cause of Solesmes with which, I feel sure, he is sincerely in sympathy. But he failed to realize that the question of rhythm is not only delicate but complex and requires extreme precision, and an article written with excellent intentions but which lacks these qualities is bound to slip into loose statements and even positive error. Thus Mr. Boisvert, having failed to bring to his subject the required precision, has fallen into the error of hasty conclusions and affirmations which either exaggerate or completely misrepresent the teachings of Solesmes.

As Choirmaster of Solesmes and, as such, responsible for our Method, I feel authorized to bring the required precision on the following points regarding which I do not wish any misunderstanding to arise. Indeed this seems all the more necessary in view of the editorial footnote added to the article which states that "Dr. Boisvert is now at Solesmes

continuing his research work with the Solesmes monks," a statement which might easily create the impression that the article had been inspired by us, or that it possessed some official or semi-official character—which would be absolutely contrary to the truth.

In what follows, I will confine my remarks to questions of *rhythm,* leaving aside that which regards mere accompaniment, except where the latter is intimately bound up with the rhythmic principles themselves.

(a) It would indeed be unfortunate were an impression to be created, or even a mere supposition, that there could ever be the slightest divergence between the doctrines taught by Dom Mocquereau and those taught by me. All that I know, I have learned from Dom Mocquereau; I am, and wish to remain merely his pupil. To this fact all my published articles and my conferences give testimony as well as the singing of the monastic choir at Solesmes.

(b) It is entirely false to pretend that "the work of restoration has only just begun" both as regards Paleography and Rhythm. It was Dom Mocquereau himself who not only laid the foundations for the work of research on all these points, but who established and organized on a scientific basis the general principles which govern the reading and interpretation of the manuscripts. That Dom Mocquereau never pretended to "have said the last word" is self-evident;

---

* *Dr. Boisvert's rejoinder to this Communication and to the comment of Mr. Achille Bragers (included in this number), may be expected in the next issue of* The Catholic Choirmaster. —(Ed.).

and we who are continuing and developing his work along the lines of his own system and direction are conscious that our task is to delve ever more deeply and to verify with ever stronger proof the reality of the conclusions at which he had arrived.

(c) It would be equally unfortunate should an impression be created that the technical books for practical teaching published by Solesmes are "obsolete" or even incomplete. *The Nombre Musical* and the *Paléographie Musicale* remain today what they have been always—the base and foundation of our teaching, both theoretical and practical. While it is evidently true as regards all musical training that an oral initiation is clearer and more effective than one which is acquired exclusively from the printed page, it does not follow from this self-evident fact that "many of the finer points of the Solesmes teaching cannot be found in books!" Let it be understood clearly once for all that the oral teaching at Solesmes consists in the unfolding, the explanation of the doctrines handed down by Dom Mocquereau in their strict and most exact sense by means of commentaries and illustrated by examples, that the truths contained in Dom Mocquereau's written works and notably in his *Nombre Musical* may be understood and assimilated.

(d) It is paradoxical to state that "The only textbooks in the English language according to the Solesmes Rhythmic System are those by Potiron and Bragers!" No doubt Mr. Boisvert intended to refer to textbooks on *accompaniment,* for as regards rhythm itself he must certainly be acquainted with the works of Mrs. Ward, of Bishop Schrembs and the translation of the method of Dom Suñol, to say nothing of the translation of the *Nombre Musical* itself, of which the first part is already

available and the whole of the first volume will soon be completed in the English language.

(e) It is dangerous to state, without making the necessary explanations, that "Solesmes teaches the placing of ictuses on the first note of a neum should only be used as a last resort." While it is true that a neum may have an ictus on its second note, a fact clearly indicated in the manuscripts (*pressus* and others), and that there are signs of length in the manuscripts which attract the ictus irresistibly and more powerfully than the first note of the neum in its *material form* as it appears today in the printed editions of the Chant (the Vatican edition included)—yet it would be rash and extremely dangerous to assert as a general rule that the form of the neums and the grouping of the notes therein has no rhythmic value *per se* and that these forms are without influence as regards the interpretation of Gregorian Chant. Such a conclusion would be inexact.

(f) While it is true that where a virga or punctum—isolated—precedes a neum of three or more notes, this virga or punctum is frequently a *long note* in the manuscripts and by that very fact it attracts the ictus. But this can only be true where the single note and the neum that follows it are united on a *single syllable.* Where, on the contrary, an isolated note has a distinct syllable apart from the neum which follows, then—whether the syllable be accented or not but by reason of its position—the punctum or virga will be on the "up-beat" and the ictus will fall on the first note of the neum that follows. This is obviously an elementary principle of rhythm.

(g) While it is possible that Monastic version of the *Antiphonale* might occasionally throw some light on the interpretation of a given passage, it must be borne in mind that the Monastic version differs even melodically from the Vatican edition and that its use is reserved exclusively to the Benedictine monks, for whom alone it has been approved by Rome.

(h) To insinuate that Dom Mocquereau ever disapproved the accompaniments of Dom Desrocquettes is misleading. The truth is that Dom Mocquereau concentrated his attention upon the rhythmic question as distinct from the harmonic or modal treatment advanced by musicians. For this reason, he refused to take a definite stand on the modal theories of these composers of accompaniments. But, without expressing an opinion for or against any of these systems and regardless of whom might be the composer of the accompaniment, Dom Mocquereau always sustained the work of Dom Desrocquettes precisely because of his fidelity in following the rules of rhythm.

(i) It is incorrect to state that chords should be placed on tonic accents; on the contrary, chords should be placed on the *ictus*—otherwise there will be syncopation. On the other hand, it must be borne in mind that it is not desirable that each and every ictus should be underlined by a chord; the principal ones should be selected and these should be brought out in proportion to their importance in the whole architectural scheme of the phrase, of its greater rhythm.

(j) In rare and altogether exceptional cases, in view of giving to a tonic accent a particularly expressive relief, one may place a chord on such an accent occurring on the "up-beat," but only on condition *sine qua non* that such a chord should resolve into another chord immediately following it on the ictus of the note that comes after this accent, otherwise there would clearly be a syncopation.

These are the principal points which I felt it necessary to clarify, for the sake of precision and that there might be no misunderstanding as regards the actual teaching of Solesmes. Indeed, I welcome the opportunity thus offered to affirm once again the fact that the doctrines of Solesmes are today what they always have been and that our work is animated by a spirit of logical continuity. It is always the teaching of Dom Mocquereau that we follow with ever increasing certitude as our publications themselves reveal. The tradition established by Dom Mocquereau continues to affirm itself effectively and increasingly not only as regards the singing of the liturgical chant at Solesmes, but also in the continuity of the scientific studies as organized by him at the *Paléographie Musicale*. Any contrary rumors that may have been circulated are utterly unfounded and are manifestly false. Today, more than ever, it is true that the two expressions "Method of Solesmes," "Method of Dom Mocquereau"—are equivalent and synonymous.

Believe me, dear Sir.

Yours very sincerely,

Fr. Joseph Gajard, O.S.B.
Choirmaster of Solesmes
Director of The Paléographie Musicale

3, RUE LÉON LEGLUDIC
SABLÉ SARTHE

Le 6 Mai 1941

Mon Révérend Père -

Ce petit mot doit vous porter mes adieux. Hélas mon départ pour l'Amérique est pour demain et le temps me manque matériellement pour aller jusqu'à Solesmes.

Inutile de vous dire que je reste toujours uni de cœur et de conviction profonde avec Solesmes et que pendant mon exil je continuerai de travailler de mon mieux pour que son Chant soit mieux connu et goûté.

Avec l'espoir que cet exil ne sera pas trop long et que je pourrai bientôt retrouver la France et Solesmes.

Veuillez agréer, mon Père, l'expression de mes sentiments dévoués.

Justine B. Ward

P.S. Nous préférons que ce départ ne soit pas connu à Sablé - pour le moment.

NOTICE REGARDING THE GREAT ORGAN OF SOLESMES ABBEY

Le Lutrin, 1946, P. 49

Until 1930, the organ at Solesmes was a modest instrument of 22 ranks on two keyboards and pedal. Restored in 1870 by Debierre, Nantes, and in 1896 by Cavaillé-Coll, the organ deteriorated significantly during the twenty years of exile in England (1901-1921). Upon returning, a complete restoration was called for; this was made possible by the generous intervention of the directors of the Dom Mocquereau Schola Cantorum Foundation, Inc. Wishing to offer the Abbey "an articulate and living sign of their admiration for Dom Mocquereau", they decided "with joyous enthusiasm" to endow the Church of Saint Pierre de Solesmes "with an instrument that was worthy through its perfection of detail and sonority, of the divine melodies restored by the Master". (Letter of Mrs. Justine Ward, dated September 14, 1930.)

It was thus that a plan could be drawn up; it was entrusted to the builder Victor Gonzales who, because of his restoration of the Great Organ of Saint-Eustache, Paris, placed himself at the head of the French organ building profession.

The task lasted almost two years; the new instrument was solemnly blessed by Father Abbot at the close of Christmas Matins (1932) and was immediately pressed into service, preluding the Introit of the Midnight Mass. Here is its design:

GREAT ORGAN OF THE ABBEY CHURCH OF SOLESMES
Electro-pneumatic System
Three Manuals of 61 notes—32-note Pedal
49 ranks

PEDAL

1.	Soubasse	32	7.	Bourdon	8
2.	Flûte	16	8.	Flûte	4
3.	Violoncelle	16	9.	Bombarde	16
4.	Soubasse	16	10.	Trompette	8
5.	Flûte	8	11.	Clairon	4
6.	Violoncelle	8			

GREAT ORGAN (I)

12.	Montre	16	19.	Flûte à cheminée	4
13.	Bourdon	16	20.	Quinte	$2^2/_3$
14.	Montre	8	21.	Doublette	2
15.	Flûte harmonique	8	22.	Plein jeu	4 ranks
16.	Salicional	8	23.	Trompette	8
17.	Bourdon	8	24.	Clairon	4
18.	Prestant	4			

POSITIVE (II)

25.	Montre	8	29.	Doublette	2
26.	Bourdon	8	30.	Tierce	$1^3/_5$
27.	Flûte	4	31.	Plein jeu	4 ranks
28.	Nazard	$2^2/_3$	32.	Trompette	8

SWELL (III)

33. Quintaton	16		42. Plein jeu	4 ranks
34. Diapason	8		43. Bombarde	16
35. Flûte traversière	8		44. Trompette	8
36. Bourdon	8		45. Clairon	4
37. Gambe	8		46. Hautbois	8
38. Voix celeste	8		47. Cromone	8
39. Flûte	4		48. Voix humaine	8
40. Nazard	2²/₃		49. Tremblant	
41. Octavin	2			

On the manuals: Pedal couplers, cancels, lower octave couplers, upper octave couplers, upper octave pedal couplers to Swell, 16 and 32 cancels, pedal coupler cancels

7 fixed combinations
4 free combinations for each keyboard

On the Pedals: Pedal couplers, Expression pedal III, Expression pedal II, Crescendo pedal.

4 free combinations for pedal
5 general combinations

This is not the place to discuss any further the characteristics of the instrument, its qualities and also — alas! — its defects, for there is no absolutely perfect human endeavor. What will perhaps be of interest to the readers of this notice, is that the organ of Solesmes is played.

The design which was just read, shows well enough that all music for the organ old and new, can be played on it. But it is necessary to give an explanation right away. Here Gregorian melody reigns supreme, and rightly so, for nothing will replace or equal in beauty and quality, the sung prayer of the Church. The use of the organ is then entirely determined by this priority. No chant is suppressed (Offertory) or shared between the organ and choir (Kyrie, Gloria, Sanctus, etc.) and the intervals of silence which the organ fills are very short, even on feast days. However, there is still a nice enough part for the organist: to prelude the Office, to insert between the chants music that seems to prolong them and to express their sentiment; and by way of conclusion, to recapitulate the feast of the day as if to invoke its mystery, of joy, sorrow or glory.

As a result it seems that what is always best is for the organist to improvise! And in theory, this is exact. But in practice, improvising for the liturgy is an art so difficult, one that requires such a combination of natural and supernatural talents, that very few musicians, even priests or religious, can pride themselves on always achieving such a high ideal. It is wise to accept a more modest but safer solution: to search in the immense repertory of the high ages of organ for the most beautiful works, musically speaking, and which, at the same time, adapt themselves best to the atmosphere of the liturgical function being celebrated in the choir.

This research was undertaken here in the light of the principle that Pope Pius X expressed in clearly defined terms in his Motu Proprio: "A composition, by its charm, structure and inspiration, is more worthy to be played in Church, the more closely it approaches the Gregorian melody, model of all sacred music". This formula could lead to very long developments being so germinal in a musical, in an aesthetic and in a spiritual sense. It will suffice to give by example, three programs for feasts to show how this principle applies.

I) At Christmas, during the so-called Office, find a way of inserting the versets of Jean Titelouze, Nicolas de Grigny and Samuel Scheidt, on the Hymn for Lauds: A solis ortu cardine; the two chorales by Bach on the same theme transfored into the chorale: Christum wir sollen loben schon; the versets of Scheidt on the Hymn of Saint Ambrose: Veni, Redemptor gentium; and the chorales of Pachelbel, Buxtehude, Nicolas Bruhns, J.S. Bach on: Nun Komm der Heiden Heiland (same melody); the 15 first chorales in Bach's Orgelbüchlein, etc. . . .

II) At Easter, the versets, chorales and fantasias of Scheidt, Pachelbel, Bach, on Christ lag in Todesbanden (melody of the Latin sequence Victimae paschali laudes); the great Agnus Dei of Bach: Christe, du Lamm Gottes; the hymn of Scheidt, De resurrectione Christi, etc.

III) At Pentecost, the pieces on the Veni, Creator by Cabezon, Titelouze, Nicholas de Grigny, Scheidt, etc.; the chorales of Pachelbel, Buxtehude, Bach, Komm Gott Schöpfer Heiliger Geist (on the same theme but slightly changed).

Outside the so-called liturgical office, it would seem that several great works of the Masters would find their natural place, in view of the fact that they affirm secret relationships with the feast of the day. For example, the Pastorale or the Prelude and Fugue in A major of Bach at Christmas; the Prelude, Fugue and Chaconne of Buxtehude in C Major, or the Prelude and Fugue in D Major of Bach, at Easter; the Fantaisie and Fugue in g minor, at Pentecost, etc., etc.

There is a whole world of "correspondence" to discover.

Before terminating, an inevitable objection has to be responded to in few words: "But are modern works to be excluded from your service?" No, not because they are modern — as if the sonorous discoveries of our age were to be systematically condemned! — It is not a question of juxtaposing the old versus the new. It is simply a choice resulting from a careful study of organ music and its rapport with liturgical chant. It is a fact that almost always classical works interpret better than modern works the conditions which Pius X signaled above for true church music. Nevertheless, considerable attempts have been made and sometimes it is the harmonic system adopted, sometimes the rhythm, or finally and especially the "spirit", which is too much in contrast with the natural resonance, the calm rhythm, the deeply meditative quality of the Gregorian melody. Religious works, even "pious" works have been written in our times, but if they attain the level of "true art", they only rarely possess the qualities of "holiness" and "universality" which the Church requires also of "her music", of all music that is properly liturgical. But should a contemporary musician finally realize all these essential conditions, his works will be included with joy into our divine office.

Rev. Antony Bonnet
Monk of Solesmes

Pour Dom Gajard

𝔗𝔥𝔢 ℭ𝔞𝔱𝔥𝔬𝔩𝔦𝔠 𝔘𝔫𝔦𝔳𝔢𝔯𝔰𝔦𝔱𝔶

𝔬𝔣 𝔄𝔪𝔢𝔯𝔦𝔠𝔞

SOLEMN SERVICE OF THE VESPERS

in Commemoration of the
Solemnity of Saint Joseph

Presented by the

MUSIC DEPARTMENT

of the

CATHOLIC SISTERS' COLLEGE

———

Preceded by a Program of
ORGAN MUSIC

Wednesday, May 15, 1946   National Shrine of the
7:30 P. M   Immaculate Conception

ORGAN RECITAL

Prelude, Fugue, Chaconue_____ _____ Buxtehude
Ave Maris Stella _____ Titelouze
Sarabande grave_____Couperin le Grand
Chorale-Prelude "Ye Watchers"_____ Bach
Romance sans paroles_____ Bernier
Choral No. 3 in A minor_____Franck

CONRAD BERNIER
Organist of the University

VESPERS SERVICE

I.   Ant: Jacob autem Ps: Dixit Dominus
II. Ant: Missus est Ps: Confitebor
III. Ant: Ascendit autem Joseph Ps: Beatus vir
IV. Ant: Et venerunt Ps: Laudate pueri
V.   Ant: Et ipse Jesus Ps: Laudate Dominum
     Hymn: Te Joseph celebrent
     Antiphon: Fili, quid fecisti
     Cant: Magnificat
     Ant; Regina cheli

Celebrant: His Excellency, The Most Reverend Arsene Turquetil, O.M.I.

Benediction of the Most Blessed Sacrament

———•———

O Sacrum Convivium
Virgo Parens
Oremus Pro Pontifice
Tantum ergo
Alleluia: Laudate Dominum
Choir under the direction of the
Reverend Father Alexis C. Wygers, SS.CC., S.T.L., B. Mus.

Recessional: "Grand jeu"_____ du Mage

Post Office Box 267
Stockbridge, Massachusetts

July 23, 1948

Dear Reverend Father,

Thank you immensely for your letter of July 16th. I understand your anxieties and your desire for precision. As far as I am able, for I speak only for myself and not for the University, I will explain to you what the project includes — to which I am very attached, needless to tell you, for it seems to me to be the ideal moment to place the Catholic University absolutely and publicly on the side of Solesmes. All the members of the Hierarchy of the United States form the Directorship of this University that gives Pontifical diplomas and which serves us a model for the affiliated colleges. Thus the influence of this University is extensive (this aside from the question of merit). This is my thought on the project itself. If you could make this sacrifice (and it would certainly be that and not a pleasure!) I think that it would the right moment to do it. At the moment we have a Rector who is supportive and a Dean of the Sisters' College who is also supportive and ready to help us in the spreading of liturgical Chant. They do not know, neither one nor the other, about the disputes and diverse theories which have rocked Europe and which from time to time penetrate onto this continent. We can easily impose upon them — some "interests" are always behind the scene, like the children of darkness, to make use of the things of iniquity better than the children of light. So much for the over-all project.

Now to reply to your questions in detail:

1. Time: six weeks (a little less by a few days.)
            End of June to mid-August.

2. Frequency: 45 hours of teaching (the "hours" are 50 minutes!)
            One lecture per day (not counting Sunday or Saturday.)
            It would be 5 times per week for your main course.

3. How many Courses: a) One — as minimum.
                        b) Two -- possible, at most,
                                    (depending on you.)

            On this point I would like to talk with the authorities and find out what they are thinking. I am only giving you what I am thinking.

4. Precise goal:
            a) For the public: Advanced Course in Gregorian Chant according to the bases of the Solesmian doctrine.
            b) For us: Deepen the true doctrine and practice of Solesmes; eliminate the known or unknown resistances that are currently circulating.

5. <u>Doctrine emphasized to what point?</u>

    a) It can be assumed at the beginning that the students have a knowledge of fundamentals, that is:
Clef — Notation — Modes — Time (can place the ictus) — Rhythm — but not the nuances of the great rhythm, and not the true phrase in all its nuances.

    You could then suppose that the students present are those who are familiar with my Music Fourth Year — Gregorian Chant. This for the ordinary students.

    We hope to attract especially some unusual students for your courses — the big question whether we shall succeed. We would like to attract those who think themselves "masters". They are the ones who are most in need of your course. These persons (if they come) might perhaps pose questions that will force you to discuss deeper matters which the students mentioned in the category above would not need. In case there is a certain number of these persons, it would be preferable to assemble them apart from the others for a half hour — so as not to arrest the flow of the general course. But here is something that you can make a judgment about when you are here.

    So, for the course, <u>you could begin where I left off:</u>

    a) by passing over rather quickly what the students are supposed to know — and doing this by performance which will give you the occasion to criticize and correct.

    b) To begin the advanced Course in Gregorian Chant.

    To give you an idea as to what has been done (for better of worse) up to now: This advanced course should touch on the Modes, fixed formulae, etc., on Aesthetics, and the structure of the various forms of the pieces; and the study of <u>performance</u> of the Propers of certain Masses, the most often used in the parishes. It seems to me that that is about what constitutes the content of the Advanced Course.

    c) The Course should finish with a written exam. M. Woollen could explain to you the rather bizarre system in use in all the educational institutions in our country: it is a system called "credits" of which each course carries a given number — and at the end, the diplomas (master, doctor, etc.) are based on the accumulation of these <u>credits</u>. Thus, to each regular course are attached so many credits — obtained by the student who passes his examination. Your course, according to this system, will carry some "credits" — how many I do not know. But this to tell you that this is a system already established. So the matter must be fixed in advance for which the students are expected to pass a written exam.

Apart from this point, which requires matter on which a clearly defined exam can be based at the end of the course, — I am completely in accord with you to reduce as much as possible the theoretical baggage in order to concentrate on performance.

There will be a double advantage in doing this: the difference in language does not exist in music, there will be a large number of lessons where the role of the translator will be reduced practically to zero. It will be the students who do the work. For they are in great need of it.

Here is what could be done (and naturally I express my idea about which it will remain to consult with the University authorities if you approve).

1. The advanced Course in Gregorian Chant about which there was a question up to now, This will be the Course carrying the "Credits".

2. A supplementary course (or half course) based on performance, in which all the students — even those in the Elementary Gregorian Course, could come together to sing under your direction the rather easy pieces of the Gregorian repertory which you would choose. In this supplementary course, you could, if you wish, have some of the students conduct while correcting their chironomy. If these are lessons which are not into the "credit" system, whatever seems practical from the point of view of performance could be done.

3. For your course, it will probably be the "Liber Usualis" that will serve as a text book for the students? For the beginner's Course it would be the Kyriale.

THE GREAT QUESTION OF TRANSLATION AND OF AN ADVANCED WRITTEN OR SPONTANEOUS PLAN

I believe, dear Father, that it is always preferable to do something spontaneous. Readings do not hold the attention of students.

But, the completely spontaneous is impossible because of the difference of language; also because of the final exam which ought to touch on the matter of the courses.

It seems to me that the most practical thing is to write out certain points: what in general terms the lesson will contain. Woollen will examine these points ahead of time with you, if necessary, to find the exact English equivalents of those words which are more or less technical.

Then, in front of the students, you will speak spontaneously, but on the subject agreed upon with Woollen, and by making pauses as at the mediant. During these pauses (which eventually become rhythmical) you think only of your next phrase and you do not listen to what Woollen is doing, who explains in English what you have just said in French. Really it moves along quite well in this fashion. On the condition that the translator knows the matter well and is quick. After a while what happens (and you will notice it from these figures) is that the students will understand you before the translation — and at that moment — when it will arrive — you can do as in Rome by asking help from the translator only when you are not understood. But, if we announce a course in French over here, there will be very few students who will believe themselves capable of following it.

The moment of waiting for the translator is embarrassing only at the start before the routine is set. After that, everything will move along as on wheels. This is the way it was in Dom Ferretti's courses.

Another thought, before ending this letter already too long. At the time we made large wall charts containing the principal points of Very Reverend Dom Ferretti's courses. We could do the same for you if you wish. Moreover, there are modern inventions which might perhaps serve our needs better. There is nothing that helps more than an example. But the students who are studying cannot give the perfect example. Your role, then, is confined to that of critic. If you could include in your teaching some perfect examples, this will help the understanding of the theory that you will set forth. Here, then, is what I propose. If you approve, you could discuss the details with Woollen. There exists a small instrument that reproduces exactly the chants on a metal wire. If the example does not please us, it can be erased and we use the same wire to make another. I will send you an instrument, you make as many wires as seem useful to you. This could be done during a rehearsal at Solesmes. Woollen knows this instrument — he will explain things to you. You will have these metal reels with you which can be played here on an instrument like the one you will have at Solesmes. The result obtained in this fashion is less perfect than a recording on a very good disc made by a very good company, but it is as good if not better than the discs made in a mediocre fashion. While travelling you need only take with you these very small reels, and your students in the course will hear the real Solesmes to give them a perfect example. Think of this, dear Father, and give me your opinion. The next person we know who travels from here toward you, could carry the instrument and the directions for its use which ought to be simple for many people (without special competence) to make use of it readily. One of the other monks could operate the machine — you will have to think only of the chant. When arriving here, it will be the same thing. Someone will be put in charge of the "wire recorder".

In finishing, I must tell you that Regina Laudis entreats you if you come to America. Mrs. Fauconnier wanted to give some lessons to the nuns but they prefer to wait for your arrival.

Finally, dear Father, we have time. I am sure that all can be arranged without difficulty. What I have said in this letter, is by way of responding as clearly as possible to your questions. There is always the possibility of agreeing on this or that point. So, do not take literally everything that I have said here. I know that the Rector has already written to Reverend Father Abbot to invite you. Here then is the reason for my haste in writing to you.

Please believe, my Reverend Father, in my devoted good wishes.

J.B.W.

General Introduction

<u>SOLESMES</u>

and the

<u>GREGORIAN CHANT</u>

The Monks of Solesmes are chiefly responsible for the scientific restoration of the music we call <u>Gregorian Chant</u>, of its melodies and of its rhythm. They are celebrated at once for their science and for their art. Nowhere else in the world can this liturgical musical prayer be heard in such perfection. Solesmes provides a model that all Gregorianists imitate. The importance of these recordings made in the monastic church is inestimable.

The Gregorian melodies are very ancient, composed between the fourth and seventh centuries to texts taken, for the most part, from the Bible. They are called "Gregorian" after St. Gregory the Great (592-604) who, in art, is represented as writing them out under the dictation of the Holy Ghost in the form of a dove, who sits on his shoulder whispering in his ear. As a matter of fact, St. Gregory was not the composer of all these melodies but their reviser and codifier. Indeed many of them were composed after his death.

Gregorian Chant is purely melodic. No harmony nor polyphony adorns its unfettered flow. It is also purely vocal. Its richness consists in the freedom of its rhythm and the variety of its Modes. Instead of two (Major and Minor) it uses eight which give it a subtlety and eloquence that compensates for its lack of harmony. Its forms are multiple, some similar to modern forms (as for instance the Rondo form, found in the Responsories), others are no less interesting, if unfamiliar.

The golden epoch of Gregorian Chant ended in the 11th Century. After that, decadence set in and with the popularity of polyphony, the Chant was treated as a poor relation. Its ruin was completed by incorrect printed editions.

Not until the middle of the 19th Century was its restoration attempted by the French Benedictine monks of the Abbey of Solesmes. It is, thanks to their research, that we can hear today the ancient chants sung as they were conceived by their composers and as our ancestors in the Christian centuries sang that wonderful music.

Three names stand out in this restoration. Dom Guéranger, first Abbot of Solesmes who ordered the work of research to be undertaken by his monks for use in their own monastery; Dom Pothier, who began the work, cutting a trail through the impenetrable forest, and Dom André Mocquereau, a musician of mark, who completed the work and, as it were, built a highway over which all can pass, turning theory into practical form. Under his direction the choir of Solesmes attracted world-wide attention of musicians from all nations. The present Director, Dom Joseph Gajard, was the close collaborator of Dom Mocquereau, now his successor and under his guidance the choir has attained a marvelous fluidity and eloquence.

For those who imagine that the history of music begins with Palestrina or Bach, a surprise is in store, and, no doubt a delight, as these melodic masterpieces reveal their perfection when sung by these monks who are artists in the realm of music as in the realm of prayer. This is the music that the Pope (Pius X) called the model of all sacred music. Its official restoration, now embodied in the Vatican edition, is based on the researches of the monks of Solesmes.

Liturgical Music Award-1948

SHORTLY after the presentation of the Catholic Choirmaster Liturgical Music Award on March 30 by The Most Rev. Archbishop Patrick J. O'Boyle of Washington, D.C. the following letter was received by our President the Rev. John C. Selner, S.S.

Dear Father Selner,

How can I express in words my sense of deep gratitude in receiving the honor of this precious award from The Society of Saint Gregory of America? My gratitude is all the greater because I realize that the thought of the members of that Society as well as my own·includes my collaborators, those whose persevering zeal has created that surge of renewal from the roots, a whole generation of little children brought by their efforts to a knowledge and love of the liturgical music of the Church.

This award given by the outstanding group of Catholic musicians of our country will be an encouragement and a stimulant, not to me alone, but to those legions of devoted teachers—mostly Religious—who are sowing good seed in Universities, Colleges, High schools and, above all, in the grade schools, translating a dream, and ideal into a living reality. They are deserving of your reward and it is in their name as well as in my own that I accept it and thank you from the bottom of my heart. Were I to name them all, this letter would read like the pages of the Catholic Directory. I will spare you the enumeration, but all are in my thoughts today as I know they are in yours.

The fact that the Society of St. Gregory stoops benevolently to give the stamp of its approval to this humble groundwork is symbolic of the closer union that we hope to see flourish between the efforts of clergy, choirmasters and school teachers, a collaboration upon which the success of each group depends. When these pull at cross purposes, the efforts of all may fail. Together, they must of necessity succeed. The parish priest finds his church music problem already solved through his school. The choirmaster is provided with an unending supply of trained boys' voices, little singers who can read music and thus spare him the drudgery of teaching the A.B.C. of intervals and rhythm to the choristers. The school teachers know that their work is not in vain since they bring their pupils to the foot of the Altar. The children appreciate their class work in music, knowing they can offer it to God. They learn to love the liturgy by experience which is the only way to learn or to love anything. Finally, how much time is saved in the Seminary when candidates for the Priesthood enter with a fundamental knowledge of music and of chant and do not have to waste the precious time in the Seminary learning, as adults, primary grade principles.

It is good to see so many Priests today embodying these ideals in practice, giving fresh courage to the humble workers in the vineyard, for this task is one that can be guided effectively only by consecrated hands. We lay people, like St. John the Baptist, must now diminish and, like Simeon, cheerfully sing our *nunc dimittis*.

This occasion, so full of joy and gratitude, is not without a cloud of sorrow as we remember that good and noble man who received this award a year ago and has since then left us to receive a still higher recompense. May we all serve the Master as faithfully as he in our respective fields of action.

I thank you, dear Father Selner, and through you all the members of the Society of St. Gregory, for their kindness in conferring upon me this great honor. I pledge to the cause we all have at heart, the restoration of true Sacred Music to the Church, every bit of energy that I possess as the only way in which I can express my gratitude.

Faithfully yours,
JUSTINE B. WARD

— ■ — ■ — ■ —

Centennial Celebration at Solesmes of
Dom Mocquereau's Birth and Baptism
(*Revue Grégorien* 1949, p. 167)

The May-June issue of the REVUE GRÉGORIEN announced the
centenary of the birth and baptism of Dom Mocquereau. The anniversary
could not pass unnoticed at Solesmes. It seemed entirely right, according
to our well-known custom, to celebrate it with as much discretion as
possible in the intimacy of the monastic family. June 6th, Monday of
Pentecost, Reverend Father Abbot dedicated in the room reserved for
Paléography, thus in the interior of the cloister, a plaque which was at
the same time a commemorative souvenir and an instruction for those
who are called to continue the work of the master, in the various works
that obedience assigns to them: study of the manuscripts, works of
transcription and restoration, adaptation of new texts to old melodies,
etc. In a brief allocution Reverend Father Abbot moreover signaled the
essential character of Dom Mocquereau's work and stated precisely what
was the source of the inspiration of this true son of Dom Guéranger. We
shall reproduce these brief but substantive words which reveal the secret
of this great monk's prodigious success in the restoration of Gregorian
Chant.

"We are gathered together in the intimacy of the family, to remember
the anniversary—one hundredth—of Dom Mocquereau's birth and baptism. Born on June 6, 1849, in La Tessoualle, near Cholet, he was baptised
on the same day in the parish church.

"The grace of Baptism,—where God lays down in anticipation all
potentiality, of which he holds the secret,—is certainly at the source of the
direction which he gave to his work and of the spirit that moved him; the
grace of the Profession, second Baptism, set him in the school of the
Church in which prayer was his life, and in the school of Saint Benedict,
whose Rule, understood, loved, and practiced, was his strength and
security: for the musical work which distinguished and honored him, and
with competence of first rank, he achieved it without putting aside the
normal conditions of the monastic life, by simply fulfilling his vocation as
monk with all his heart.

"Those among us who knew him know that he put in it not only his
whole heart, but all the ardor, the flame, and even a Vendean combativity,
a rare tenacity over-riding suffering, contradictions, (wherever they
might come from) proceeding without detour straight to the end, for love
of truth alone, even careful to bow before the slightest aspect of that
truth, melodic or rhythmic, as a man of tradition which he always was.

"His program? Here it is, henceforth engraved in marble in this room
where the work he began continues:

"RESEARCH THE THOUGHT OF OUR FATHERS, BOW-
ING BEFORE THEIR AUTHENTIC INTERPRETATION,
HUMBLY SUBMITTING OUR ARTISTIC JUDGMENT TO
THEIRS: THIS DEMANDS AT THE SAME TIME THE
LOVE THAT WE MUST HAVE FOR THE ENTIRE TRADI-
TION, WHETHER MELODIC OR RHYTHMIC, AND THE
RESPECT FOR A FORM OF ART THAT IS PERFECT OF
ITS KIND"

Paléographie Musicale, Vol. X.

"We thought it was good to set it in this way: it is a tribute to his memory, it is an authoritative lesson, a continuing teaching for those who come after him, faithful to his spirit, under the direction of Father Dom Gajard.

"It is in following him that they will contribute in their turn, to maintain first here at home, and then to spread to the exterior world, for the good of the Church, that which Dom Mocquereau called the ideal of Christian prayer, and which they will transmit to the generations to come, the heritage received, enriched by their own labor, and also by their sharers, if any exist.

"We are happy, moreover, to acknowledge that the spirit that animates these research and restoration labors is what it should be: a spirit of prayer, always with the purpose of recalling the saying of Saint Benedict: 'That in divine praise our soul be fully in accord with our voice: ut mens nostra concordet voci nostrae.'

"I close in sending the expression of our profound thanks to the "Dom Mocquereau Foundation", who, through its directors, Misses Justine Ward and Miss Agnès Lebreton, associate themselves with our homage, in spirit, in prayer and in generosity . . . : and at the hour which will be our time for Vespers, a Mass will be celebrated at Sisters College in the University of Washington, for the intention of the united family: unanimes, uno ore, honorificemus Deum et Patrem Domini Nostri Jesu Christi."

It was proper to terminate this brief ceremony by singing a Gregorian piece. The antiphon Si quis diligit me, which was sung as the Magnificat antiphon on Monday of Pentecost, was doubly appropriate. The day of Dom Mocquereau's birth was also the day of his baptism; for the text chosen was in truth an affirmation of the taking possession of the soul by the Divine Trinity: et ad eum veniemus, et mansionem apud eum faciemus, an affirmation whose melody admirably underscored tenderness and intimacy.

An "exposition" brought together in the main Scriptorium of the Abbey, various souvenirs of Dom Mocquereau: personal souvenirs, pontifical honors and various tributes to his reputation throughout the world. Around the Nombre Musical were grouped the first volumes of the Paléographie and other publications of the master, as well as various French or foreign Méthodes, inspired by his teaching. The list, quite long, of Institutes and Schools which, in various countries, propagate or follow the Solesmes method made even more evident the progression of Dom Mocquereau's influence in the domain of Gregorian Chant. Let us mention in this matter a quite recent proof of this growing influence: Dom Gajard has just left for America, where he is invited to participate in the first Inter-American Congress of Sacred Music, which will hold its courses in Mexico, at Guadalajara, Morella, Léon, Queretaro, and Mexico, during next November. This Congress will treat of various problems related to the liturgy and Sacred Music, in the spirit of the Motu Proprio and other papal documents; a special place will be reserved for Gregorian Chant and the Solesmes Method.

We were not the only ones to celebrate the centenary of the restorer of Gregorian Chant. Also, we thank all who intimately or with more solemnity, have associated themselves with our family. All, like the recent jubilarian celebrations at the Gregorian Institute of Paris, are an encouragement for us. They are also a great joy, to think that the Church's sung prayer is being spread among Christian people for the glory of God and for the benefit of souls.

```
APOSTOLIC  DELEGATION                        WASHINGTON
                                             27 JANUARY, 1954
```

My dear Mrs. Ward,

        On this most happy occasion of your Golden Jubilee
as a member of the Catholic Church, it affords me extreme
pleasure to inform you that our Most Holy Father, Pope
Pius XII, has graciously deigned to bestow upon you his
special Apostolic Benediction to be shared by every one
who joins with you in celebrating this memorable Anniversary.

        This Benediction is granted by His Holiness as a
token of his paternal affection and as a pledge of divine
favors for the years which lie ahead. It must conspicuous
works of charity and religion perfomed during these fifty
years, in addition to the significant stimulus you have
given to Sacred Music in accordance with the wishes of
Blessed Pius X, thus contributing to Divine Worship in the
House of God. The remembrance of these achievements should
fill you with joy, for many have benefited from them in
the charity of Christ.

        To the August Message of the Vicar of Christ
I desire to add my own personal congratulations and good
wishes for God's choicest blessing upon you.

        With sentiments of esteem and renewed felicitations,
I remain

                              Sincerely yours in Christ

                              A.G. Cicognani

                              Archbishop of Laodicea
                              Apostolic Delegate

Mrs. Justine Bayard Ward
2500 30th Street, N.W.
Washington, D. C.
```
```

2500-30TH STREET, N.W.
WASHINGTON 8. D.C.

21 Dec
1965

Cher Père Dom Gajard —

Merci infiniment pour votre lettre qui nous assure de Notre fidèle pensée et [...] qui montons la Via Crucis aussi bien que nous le pouvons. Tout est offert — Je pense

-2-

que l'Église a besoin de victimes en ces temps si tristes.

Dans les paroisses des États Unis c'est une hémorragie d'ordures musicaux. Même la [...] du [...] et [...] La musiquette est encore pire (si c'est possible) —

Nous sommes sauvés par la chapelle privée où demeure Notre Seigneur et où un bon Monsigneur de la D[...] + pratiquant

Nous apportons le Saint Communion tous les matins et célèbres la messe tous les dimanches. Nous aurons les 3 messes de Noël — en Latin — mais sans chant. Nos disques tournerons pour nous consoler un peu.

Nous vous envoyons pour tout Solesmes nos profonds vœux pour Noël et le nouvel An.

Vot devouée
[signature]

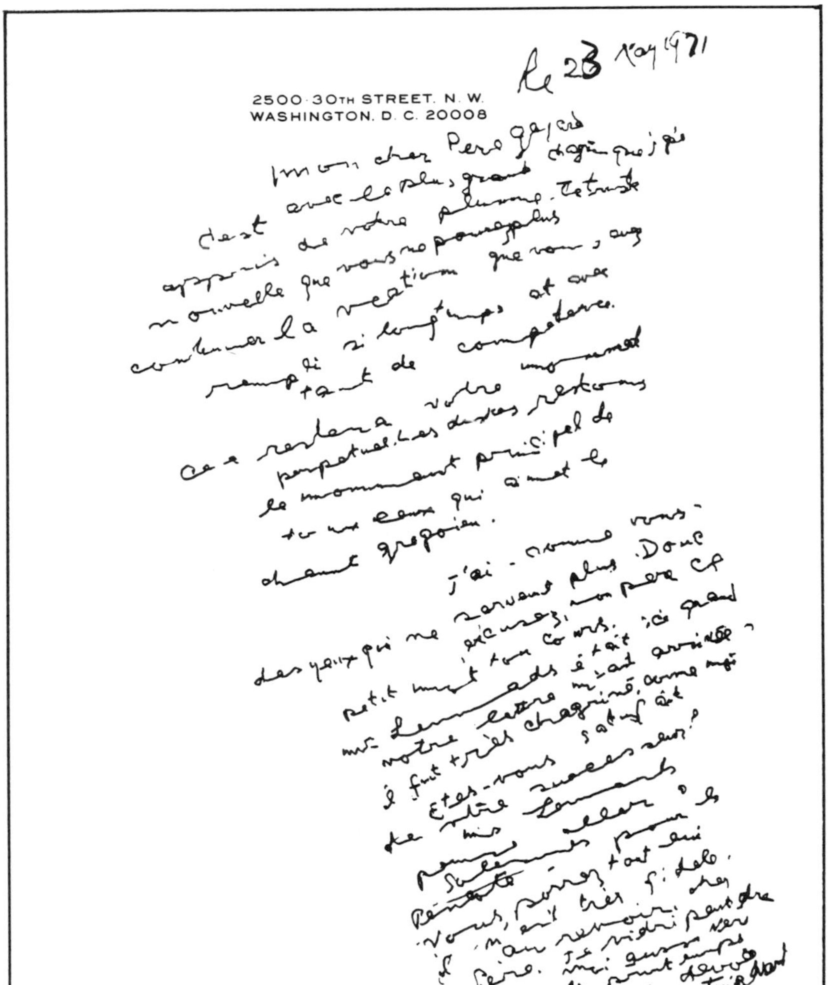

2500·30TH STREET. N. W.
WASHINGTON. D. C. 20008

le 23 May 1971

Mon cher Père Gajard

[handwritten letter in French cursive, largely illegible]

Votre tout dévoué
Justine Ward

Father J. B. Young, S. J.

By Justine B. Ward

When a great movement spreads throughout the length and breadth of a continent few stop to consider the hidden forces which have provided the motive power. Yet the field ripe for the harvest assumes the seed, assumes the chemical changes wrought below the surface of the soil, which convert the rays of the sun and the dew from heaven into that new matter from which our harvest springs.

In the liturgical restoration which we see today we have among us a hidden force. The Rev. J. B. Young, S. J., has been an ardent champion of true liturgical music for the past forty-five years. Through his own deliberate choice he has remained hidden, at least to a great extent, yet if today this renovation is a living thing and a practical thing, it is due largely to the quiet, but persistent, effort of this secret worker.

Father Young is an Alsatian by birth. In Strassbourg, as a child, his imagination and piety were fed on the liturgy of the Church, his taste formed according to the official chant, his heart fired by the flame of pure beauty to give himself as a holocaust to the religious life. His taste drew him toward the Benedictine order, toward a life of prayer in song and of scholarly research, but an inner conviction led him to sacrifice this attrait and enter the Society of Jesus. To finish his studies in the Society he was sent to America, where his health broke down and his superiors, knowing of his musical talent and wishing to give him what they considered to be a light task, appointed him Choirmaster in the Church of St. Francis Xavier, in New York city.

The music in parish churches was then at its lowest ebb. To attempt anything in keeping with the true ideals and standards of the Church would have

REV. J. B. YOUNG, S. J.

been not only a herculean task, but would have been far ahead of what the parish was prepared to understand and accept. Twenty-five years were to elapse before the regulations of Pope Pius X were to be given to the world. These were the days of the choir of warbling ladies or of "mixed" choirs of men and women in the "organ loft"; the days when the standard aimed at was a slavish imitation of cheap opera. Liturgical music was unknown. Under these circumstances, musicians will understand the greater sacrifice which Father Young was called upon to make when he undertook to organize a parish choir. To abandon music was one thing; to do daily violence to his standard of perfection was the supreme holocaust to which, under obedience, he gave himself. To the daily agony of compromise between a clear ideal and the shifting human equation, to this Father Young devoted himself for nearly forty-five years, never moving too fast for the parish needs, yet keeping as close to his ideal as he dared: this has been the exterior work of Father Young, a work which for many years has made the Church of St. Francis Xavier famous for the dignity and beauty of its music.

This, however, was not the greatest contribution which Father Young was destined to make to the restoration of Church music in America. When organizing his choir he decided to form a group of boys to take the place of the women. At that time a distinguished Italian teacher of singing was visiting New York. Father Young arranged for some lessons in vocal placing for his boy choir. After a few of these lessons, Father Young penetrated deeply into the principles which underlay this system of vocal training and devised a series of simple exercises within the reach of little children, which would produce, unfailingly, but by simpler means, the tone quality obtained by this great teacher. These exercises, which have been developed and perfected by Father Young through the intervening years, are those which have since been incorporated with Father Young's permission into the Catholic Education Series of primary textbooks, which are now forming the voices of our school children from coast to coast of this continent.

Father Young's ambition was not merely to form a good choir for a single church, but to do so according to a plan which might become a practical model for all parishes. He soon realized that the great difficulty of the choirmaster lay in finding suitable material. It was hard to obtain singers, even among grown men, who could read music at sight and whose voices were properly formed. The boys offered a still greater problem, for about as soon as a group of singers was trained the mutation of the boys' voices took place and the whole process had to be begun again with a new group. It was then that Father Young began to formulate a simple and effective musical training for parochial schools, which could give

to all the children a correct vocal production and a solid foundation in sight reading. With this elementary musical formation in the school the parish choirmaster would be able to count on a steady stream of boys who would be ready to enter the choir as they graduated from the fourth grade, and prepared to receive the additional training which only a musician could give. Moreover, the less gifted boys and all the girls would thus be ready to sing as part of the congregation and, in time, the future priests, the future choirmasters and organists would be drawn from these children formed from childhood to a knowledge and love of that music which the Church has incorporated as an intrinsic part of her teaching function.

With this idea, Father Young set about preparing an outline for a course in music suitable for parish schools, after careful experiments in his own school. He based the course on the principles of Chevé, using numbers to represent the tones of the scale, but he added many valuable features as a result of his own experience, and demonstrated that it was possible to prepare the children by the age of 10 or 11 years to enter the choir with well-trained voices and able to read at sight all music suitable for use in Church.

The outstanding problems became those of finding capable teachers to carry out the work in the grades and of finding schools willing to give sufficient time to the study of a subject which was then considered, not as a fundamental element in education, but, at best, as a superficial ornament, or, at worst, as a silly fad. And here Father Young was brought to a standstill.

The time was not yet ripe, but Father Young could afford to wait. He set in motion the secret forces and prayed ardently and consistently for a Pope who would do for the restoration of true Church music what Leo XIII had done for the renewal of sound philosophy. When Cardinal Sarto, Patriarch of Venice and well-known champion of sound Church music, entered the Consistory of 1903 he was raised to the Chair of Saint Peter, where his first official utterance as Pope Pius X was the famous Motu Proprio on Sacred Music, in which, gathering together the rulings of his predecessors, he gave them to the world as an official code of sacred music.

The publication of the Motu Proprio was followed by a brief period of spasmodic effort. Pathetic attempts were made to build bricks without straw. Congregational singing was attempted where no individual worshiper knew how to sing; women were removed from choirs where no boys or men had been prepared to replace them. Gregorian Chant was substituted for operatic arias where nobody understood the laws of Gregorian rhythm or tonality. The reaction was as swift as it was inevitable: even where there had been good will, the sense of failure produced discouragement and a relapse into complete inaction. The spark had blazed up for a moment and, finding nothing upon which to feed, has flashed and died.

Yet the ashes were still alive and a slow fire was simmering beneath the surface of the soil. Other hidden forces were at work. The Benedictine Monks of Solesmes were engaged in wresting their secrets from the ancient manuscripts and publishing works which gave new life to the dry bones of Gregorian Chant as it was then known. Books, official books, were being published by the Vatican with the authority of the Holy See; books with rhythmic commentaries by the Monks of Solesmes gave the needed guidance to singer and choirmaster. Thus the period of hesitation and inaction was almost providential, for it gave time to lay a sounder basis on which to build up a practical and effective response to the directions of Pope Pius X.

Father Young was among the first to adopt the new official books, to have his choir sing the proper of the Mass from these books, and to make his choir ring true to the desired type. Yet he had never been over-sanguine as to the permanent good to be accomplished by centering the reform movement in choirs. Choirs depended upon the personality of the director and of singers formed in a foreign mold. When the artificial pressure of the choirmaster's influence should be removed by absence or death, his years of work would disappear as though carved in sand. To be sound and lasting, the restoration must begin in the schools and form a completely new spirit. Then, according to Father Young, the directions of the Motu Proprio could and would be obeyed.

In 1910 aid came from an unexpected source. The Department of Education of the Catholic University of America had undertaken to reconstruct the curriculum for the elementary Catholic schools; in this reconstructed curriculum music was to play an important part; it was openly declared to be an essential element in the development of intellect and in the formation of character. As music was to be correlated with the other elements in the curriculum, those aspects of music were to be developed which would enable the children to appreciate and take an active part in the liturgical singing. The teaching of music was to be begun in the first grade and to continue part of the texture of the child's unfolding mind and heart until maturity. It was to be graded and taught with the same care and skill as the other studies.

The musical part of this plan had to be worked out in detail, and the Very Reverend Dr. T. E. Shields asked the co-operation of one of Father Young's pupils, who thus had the privilege of becoming a link between the two great men, using the vocal exercises of Father Young and the broad general plan of his original course for parish schools, combined with the psychological principles and pedagogical methods of Dr.

Shields. The work for the grades was published as rapidly as possible, and from that time the movement began to spread, the Sisters' College providing the first important center for the formation of competent teachers. The elementary series of textbook was made the basic study in the courses required for a Doctor's Degree in Music at the college, which lent prestige to the course.

In 1917[*] the movement received a fresh impulse and a powerful one in the foundation of the Pius X Institute of Liturgical Music in New York, at the College of the Sacred Heart. Once again this series of textbooks was made the base of all the studies, which were directed to forming teachers for the parish and convent schools and with a view to bringing about the restoration of Liturgical Music through the new generation. Normal courses were organized for teachers, both religious and secular, and here Father Young was able to keep in close touch with the developing movement and give his personal attention to the vocal work in which he remained the supreme master.

In the years which followed Father Young had the consolation of seeing his dream come true: The whole United States and large sections of Canada began to ring with the song of little children, taught by members of the various Religious Orders. In 1920 he heard 10,000 school children take part in the Gregorian Masses, which were sung on three consecutive days at the International Gregorian Congress, held at Saint Patrick's Cathedral in New York City. He witnessed the growth of the work, the issuing of each textbook, leading directly to the study of the liturgical chant, prepared under the guidance of the one whom Father Young declared to be "the greatest authority in the world on Gregorian Chant"—Dom Andre Mocquereau of Solesmes. From the Pius X Institute and its extension courses he saw 13,000 students go out into the field; he saw the work established in forty-five states of the Union, in 632 cities, in nearly

[*]The correct date is 1916. (Ed. Note.)

100 dioceses; he realized that more than 500,000 children were taking part in the liturgical revival throughout the length and breadth of the land. He witnessed the supreme day when this work of which he had dreamed, for which he had prayed and suffered, was at last brought to the attention of His Holiness Pope Pius XI (March 14, 1924) and received the approval and blessing of the Vicar of Christ. Then, on that exact date and hour Father Young received in his body the counter shock. He was stricken down suddenly and taken to the hospital. From that time he has been incapable of any further active work. His choir has fallen into other hands. But his real life work continues and he continues to set in motion forces that are irresistible, hidden but potent.

Incidentally Father Young has proved himself a prophet, with perhaps the fate of a prophet, for his choir which represented the active work of forty-five years, having fallen into other hands, has in six months been stripped of every vestige of that character which Father Young had imprinted upon it; whereas the movement in the schools which he helped indirectly, for which he prayed and suffered, continues to form a whole generation to a love of the liturgical chant. Developing with almost miraculous rapidity it has won the support of the principal Religious Orders, of the Hierarchy and many priests, and the approval of the Pope. Myriads of little boys and girls in constantly increasing numbers are singing the praises of God in the parish churches to the inspired strains of the ancient chants.

Turning from the dream to the dreamer, there is no incense which we may offer him save that of a new and stronger hold on the eternal truths which his life throws into bold relief: a more realistic faith in the power of the invisible and the triumph of the intangible; for peering far into the future the faithful seer, who knew how to wait, has conquered, building—no, not better than he knew—but faster.

Le Nombre Musical Gregorien--II

By Dom Andre Mocquereau

A REVIEW BY JUSTINE WARD

THE reason why a work of genius can seldom be loved immediately is because of the very fact that the creator is extraordinary. Among his contemporaries, few resemble him. It is his creation, the work of art itself, which must fertilize those rare minds capable of understanding it and cause them to increase and multiply. . . . Thus, an artist who wants his work to take its normal course must cast it where it will find sufficient depth, in the full and far-off future." (Marcel Proust.)

The monumental work of Dom Mocquereau is a striking example of this truth. Twenty years ago the first volume appeared. It struck and rebounded against a public which was utterly unprepared for its deep and subtle teaching. But the decades slipped by, and the work itself generated a public, not numerous perhaps, but distinguished in quality, which is rapidly increasing and multiplying. The second volume will find greater depth for its roots.

The long interval is explained by Dom Mocquereau in his introduction with his usual modesty. Time was required to delve more deeply into the rhythmic truths embodied in the ancient manuscripts, to confer with critics and listen to their difficulties and objections, to submit his theories to the severe test of daily application in the monastic choir. All this is no doubt true and guarantees the maturity of the work before us. But beyond these reasons, the reader will be struck by the need of time in which the first volume could generate a mentality capable of loving the second, and today, as we open this new volume and turn its 850 pages of text, we are amazed, not at the twenty years' delay, but at the possibility of its having created its public in so short a time.

The artistic truths set forth in these two volumes are in reality a by-product. The work of Dom Mocquereau was undertaken under obedience and with the single object of elucidating the ancient music which is the voice of the Church's prayer. Dom Guéranger, the first abbot of Solesmes, found that the restoration of the Benedictine life in France involved the restoration of Liturgical life in all its aspects, and among them the chant of Saint Gregory. The editions then in use were not only incomplete, but incorrect in melodic text, unscientific as to rhythm. The study of the ancient manuscripts was undertaken before the time of Dom Mocquereau, but it was he who placed this study on a thoroughly sound and scholarly basis, the results of which have been made available to students in the Paleographie Musicale, now in its fourteenth volume, and the methods used by him and the truths thus discovered having been the main factor in giving us the official edition of the chant in use today, the Vatican version, in its bare substance or accompanied by the rhythmic signs of Solesmes as an aid to correct interpretation.

These highly technical studies organized and directed by Dom Mocquereau over a period of nearly fifty years would have failed of their full object had they lacked the penetrating light of genius. For to say that Dom Mocquereau is a scholar is but a half-truth. He is an example of that rare combination of profound scholarship and flaming artistry which is given us but seldom in this imperfect world.

The certitudes of a creative artist are the fruit of an intuitive process which seems at variance with the process of science. Based on facts, indeed, the conclusion of the artist is reached, not by logic alone, but by logic reinforced by trained intuition. The certitude reached by this process is fully convincing to the artist himself. The trouble arises when he wants his discovery to reach other minds and form them. It is then that his perception must be recast, and an equivalent found which will reach the mentality lacking the sixth sense of the artist.

It is here that Le Nombre Musical has triumphed. It is one of the rare books which have translated those truths perceived instinctively by a great artist into terms which can convince the intelligent but non-intuitive reader and gradually move him toward an appreciation of high and subtle things. This was but one of the difficulties which confronted the author. Dom Mocquereau's researches led him to conclusions regarding the nature of rhythm which a lesser genius would have resisted because they were in direct opposition to the musical dogmas of the Victorian era. Dom Mocquereau, himself a musician, was undaunted by this fact. Indeed, had his discoveries and theories been submitted to the really fine musicians of the epoch, had they been passed upon by a Debussy, a Ravel, a Respighi, or by a Paderewski, a Casals, an Ysaye, the bitter water of contradiction might have been sweetened by understanding. But his work, from its very nature, was judged, not by the great musicians of the day, but by the small fry of the musical world. It was weighed and measured by the standards of those half-educated, routine men of the choir loft whom lack of talent debarred from the concert stage, who had never lifted up their eyes to the higher things of contemporary art, much less dreamed of the art of the past or of the future. Thus, this fine flower of genius was ridiculed, its author taunted. "The bee and the wasp suck the same flowers," writes Joubert, "but they do not extract the same honey." Le Nombre Musical fell among wasps. For years it was the object of stinging sarcasm from those whose notions of rhythm were bounded on the north by jazz, on the south by Gounod, on the east by Puccini and on the west by a faint outline of Haydn and Mozart in their more obvious aspects. True criticism was as rare as it was precious. When it came it was welcomed, for it forced the author to dig down to bed rock in his analytical processes. To the wasps he paid no heed, and it is one of the striking features of this new volume that it never descends to the plucking of an easy victory over a mean or petty adversary, but remains throughout on a high, constructive plane. If the criticism of other schools of thought be dealt with, it is always met in the broad field of general principles, in the open light of assertions with their proof, and never in the stuffy arena of controversy.

The result is a book on rhythm which is, first of all, an authoritative guide to students on Gregorian chant. Furthermore, it is a book which will be found immensely suggestive by the general musician. The first volume contained, in germinal form, those principles which were to be unfolded fully in the second. It explained the nature of rhythm in itself, as conceived in classical times, that is to say, as the art of movement independently of dynamics; rhythm, then, as it was understood and practiced in medieval times, this part being illustrated with a wealth of example that could not fail to be conclusive to an artist worthy of the book before him. In the second volume, the detailed application of these principles to the musical setting of the Latin text reveals the nature of the Latin accent itself during the golden epoch of Gregorian chant, as a melodic and not a stress phenomenon. Accent and rhythm unfold before our eyes as parallel and not identical forces.

Finally the author develops with a genius all his own the art of representation by gesture of the movement of the ancient melodies, the conductor's art, which he calls "chironomie." This part of the book will prove both useful and fascinating to the average student.

The work of Dom Mocquereau has one characteristic in common with other works which are destined to endure. His principles are transferable to the highly cultured and to the utterly simple. The teaching which offers a world of suggestion to scholars and artists has become the delight of little children. It is only to the group between these two extremes, the group which mistakes the fashion of a day for the universal standards of art, that this work will remain anathema. But in "the full and far-off future" the difficulties of this group, indeed the group itself, will no doubt appear as the shadow of a dream against the enduring monument created by the gentle and modest monk, whose genius was subject to the ordered movement of his monastic life, wherein scholarship and art are gathered up in the greater rhythm of a science which leads to the one and enduring Truth.—*The Commonweal.*

The Last Days of Dom Mocquereau

(FROM VARIOUS LETTERS RECEIVED FROM SOLESMES)

DOM MOCQUEREAU was 82 years old. Apart from a slight unealthness of the heart, increasing with the years, he was in perfect health, in full exercise of his vast science and the ripeness of his art. He continued at work until the end, setting all things in order that there might be no sharp interruption of the work which he had built up so laboriously and on so solid a base. The *Paleographie Musicale*, the *Revue Gregorienne*, the editing of the books of Chant for the Sacred Congregation of Rites, the preparation of the Monastic Antiphonale—all these activities were placed in the hands of those who are to succeed him and in whom he had full confidence.

He had finished the second volume of *Le Nombre Musical Gregorien* in 1927, and had celebrated, during the same year, his monastic jubilee. On December 28th, 1929, he celebrated his sacerdotal jubilee. "We have just celebrated the jubilee of Father Mocquereau on the Feast of the Holy Innocents. The Pope sent him a telegram of congratulation and benediction. He received congratulations from everywhere—as the supreme master of Chant, of Rhythm, of Chironomy, of Melody —and all this does not agitate him—he remains himself—tho lion." To the blessing from the Holy Father he answered: "Cette bénédiction est pour moi la joie suprême de mes derniers jours et, en quelque sorte, un gage de mon salut éternal! Que Votre Sainteté soit à jamais bénie de cette grâce immense: *in pace in idipsum dórmiam et requiéscam.*"

The words were prophetic. He had only two more weeks to live, and he passed in peace, with a simple elan from this world to life eternal—from sleep to vision.

On the 12th of January, Dom Mocquereau felt ill during the recreation. On the 13th he celebrated Mass in spite of violent pains in the heart. The doctor was summoned and treated him with such good results that during the following days he appeared to be out of danger. A telegram, however, was sent on

THE LAST PHOTOGRAPH OF
DOM ANDRE MOCQUEREAU, O.S.B.

the 15th to one of his American pupils telling of his illness and asking for prayers. The improvement was so great on the 16th and 17th, that on the latter date Dom Mocquereau himself telegraphed, signing his own name, to say that the doctor found him greatly improved and that the past night had been excellent.

"He had begun to get up out of bed on Wednesday with difficulty but unaided. The evenings were excellent. We found him just as usual—absolutely *himself*. Yesterday, Friday, everything was *perfect*. I went to see him at six o'clock in the evening and found him giving directions to Père X to answer a Religious of the Sacred Heart in America: 'Tell her to write to Mrs. Ward and to Dom Sablayrolles.' We talked after that, as usual, of all the things which were close to his heart.

. . . Only last night Dom Mocquereau said to me: 'It would have been better not to have telegraphed (to America) on Wednesday. . . .' "

Early the next morning, January 18th, the infirmarian went to prepare Dom Mocquereau's cell and to bring him Holy Communion. "He knocked. There was no answer. The lamp was lighted. He entered and found the dear Father in his bed as though asleep, still quite warm. Nothing betrayed the slightest movement, the least pain. . . . He had been heard moving at four in the morning and then must have gone to sleep again—and, from sleep, had passed to the clear vision of God. His face has kept its beautiful calm expression—he seems to be sleeping."

On the morning of the 18th the news of the death of this great and holy monk was cabled to America. The following letter was written the morning of his death:

"Telegrams will tell you the fatal news. When this letter reaches you Dom Mocquereau already will have slipped under the earth. He has just been found dead in his bed. I was returning from the celebration of Mass when I met his infirmarian who stopped as though hesitant, then, in a whisper said 'He is dead.' As he continued on his way toward the Church I went rapidly up to the poor Father's room. He was very pale but so calm, his eyes closed and his left arm rested tranquilly on the blanket. There was no trace of contraction or of movement. An ethereal departure, a flight as discreet as the close of a melody. He who had always taught us a light ending to the phrases had laid down his life as he had taught us to lay down our voices, in a final *ictus* light as a snow-flake touching the earth, but his ictus had alighted in heaven.

"I had seen Dom Mocquereau yesterday at noon. He said: 'The doctor found a great improvement. I have sent a telegram (to America) which I signed myself to reassure them.' I almost began to regret having alarmed you in vain . . . Dom Mocquereau had come out victorious from other crises of the sort, and we used to say, laughing: 'Lions only die when they choose to.' But this time the symptoms were particularly grave and I had been struck by his increasing weakness during the preceding days. That is why I thought you should be warned. Alas, I was but too correct.

"The first to reach his bedside this morning, I stayed a few moments with him. I took his hand as you would have done—it was supple—and I gave him your last shake-hand. I touched his cheek with a caress. It still retained the warmth of life. He must have died at about five o'clock. . . .

"What a void here and what a stir in the whole Catholic world! Dom Mocquereau is the glory of Solesmes. For many people, Solesmes *was* Dom Mocquereau. How many were bound to him by invisible threads? He will have had the joy on earth, not of having invented beauty, but of having recognized the beauty of the Church's Chants, of having given back to them their true expression. An idea of genius, developed, illumined, fathomed, exalted by an entire life. And toward the end of his life he knew the joy, perhaps still keener, of seeing his thought reflected in a faithful mirror. *Adjutorium simile sibi.*"

"He rests now between the two Churches— of Our Lady and of Saint Peter until the great day of the Resurrection. . . . You have been told how he ended his beautiful monastic life and how, literally, he fell asleep in the Lord. We kept him two days in his cell surrounded with psalmody and with prayers; truly at rest, grown young again, with an expression of calm and joy: his head leaning slightly to the right, his hands holding his Rosary and his Crucifix,—beautiful and pacifying. I helped to dress him for the last time in his monastic cowl which clothes him for eternity, and to place him in the simple monastic coffin. . . . On Sunday we chanted the Office for the Dead; our sorrowful hearts more than our voices sang softly, but with a great élan. . . .

"The night was full of stars: a profound calm and fullness of silence. Near the dead it is splendid. Rarely did I feel it so keenly as last night during the time I was with Dom Mocquereau, kneeling beside him. At such times the dead teach us beautiful lessons. For this one it was the great rest after the élan of an entire life: and the quality of the one was the guarantee of the other.

"This morning we had the office of the burial. The entrance to the Choir during the *Subvenite* was really royal. The voices were perfect, our hearts at the tip of our lips: monks really love one another in spite of what Voltaire may have thought! It was the Rme P. Abbé who celebrated. Monsignor Rousseau assisted with the delegate of the Bishop of

Le Mans and of the Bishop of Chartres. In the Church were the faithful friends of Solesmes and of its old monk. . . . You know the funeral rites in monasteries. All are alike, yet they differ. The singing of In Paradisum is different for the one or for the other. . . . A grey sky covered all this liturgy, so beautiful, so full of hope. *Requiescat in spe.*

"Saturday evening *La Croix* of Paris already had announced this death which strikes Solesmes with an irreparable blow. Sunday at its noon announcement, Radio Paris gave out a change of program for its concert of sacred music. Due to this death, the Choir of Marc de Ranse would sing the Gregorian 'O vos omnes' in honor of the great Master who had left us, and whose loss throws the whole world of sacred music into mourning.

"All this is in the realm of created things. To us there remains the great and strong soul of this monk whom we dearly love. . . . He always sought God by prayer as much as by science. . . . What he leaves us is his spirit and his work.

"Our mourning is two-sided; sadness is its earthly side, perfection, the side of heaven. The wrong side tortures. Not so the right side. Dom Mocquereau surely is not saddened to have cast aside his earthly envelope, grown old, burdensome and hard to manage. Young once more, he hears at last the Chants of his dreams: light ictus, gentle endings, ethereal accents, faultless chironomy—the angels give him full satisfaction. Perhaps they are showing him something new, and he will enjoy going back to school that he may add fresh chapters to his Nombre Musical."

[*Editor's Note.*—This, and the following article, are printed through the courtesy of Mrs. Justine B. Ward.]

(Translated from "La Croix," Paris, January 30, 1930)

On Sunday, January 19th, Radio-Paris announced, *urbi et orbi,* the death of Dom Mocquereau, which had been published by *La Croix* the previous day, and instantly—touching detail—a Schola which had announced a polyphonic recital intoned a Gregorian number in honor of the dead Master. The radio has its moments of tender and poetical efficacy.

The disappearance of Dom Mocquereau will be felt deeply throughout the Catholic world. Dying at the age of eighty-two, he had taught, formed and enthused for fifty years innumerable disciples, either directly or

PHOTO OF DOM MOCQUEREAU TAKEN IN NEW YORK, JULY, 1922

by correspondence, both in Europe and in America. His whole life, like that of his master Dom Pothier, was spent in the service of a single idea, the restoration of the Gregorian melodies. Predecessors, no doubt, he had, but to their teaching he owed less than to his own genius. Eminent as a 'cellist, and —had he wished it—with a brilliant career before him in the world, the first time he came to Solesmes and heard the Gregorian melodies as sung by the monks, there flashed across his spirit an affinity between the art which he had practiced hitherto and the Gregorian melodies with their flexibility, suppleness, legato, and "*fondu*" essential to their true expression. Only the long swinging strokes of a bow across a string could convey an idea of such legato. And it was this first impression which, consciously or not, inspired his inveterate labor, his immense research; and which—when he passed from pupil to master—appeared, living and vibrant, in the formation he gave to the Choir of Solesmes: "Fluidity, softness, grace, no shocks nor blows," he repeated always, "let everything be unified, soddered, linked. Begin gently, finish softly, preparing the cadence by a rallentando. Light accents, soft ictus, rhythmic regularity yet no mere spelling out of each note; gather up and unite the long neums as though with a single stroke of the bow."

He himself, when directing a choir, was careful to avoid anything that might suggest a hammered rendering. He never beat the rhythm but outlined it with a gesture most delicate and graceful, the gesture of a 'cellist. And thus he came to invent his chironomy.

How simple all this appears, and one would think that the life of this monk, this recluse, devoted to an art which softens customs, should have been a most simple life, calm and peaceful. Error! It was a continual struggle, a warfare. He fought for his *Paleographie* which he founded against adverse winds and tides; he fought for the regularity of the rhythm, for the binary and ternary groups, for the accent on the up-beat; he fought for an ictus which could be weak or strong according to circumstance and not necessarily stressed; he fought for the rhythmic signs to facilitate the reading of rhythm and make an ensemble rendering possible, etc. . . . And, as a fighter, he was ardent and rugged.

Born on the confines of Vendee near Cholet, where he sold little handkerchiefs, and having "*fait la guerre*" of 1870 as a Sergeant, his natural reactions were not unlike those of Clemenceau. The latter was known as "the Tiger." In his own Community, Dom Mocquereau was called "the Lion." What blows he received, what thrusts he gave! He began his articles always by establishing himself in the realm of charity, assuring the reader that he would not attack persons, nor say a word which could hurt the feelings of anyone in the least degree. This declaration once made and in perfect good faith, he proceeded to annihilate you with "directs to the heart," with "uppercuts to the chin." And when you bled profusely, he assured you that you had not stolen what you had received but that you should really thank him. If, however, he treated you roughly, it was with such intense conviction, such sincerity, such simplicity that you felt disarmed, —better yet— you were already half convinced.

His artistic sense was so unerring, based, moreover, on incessant study of the manuscripts, that it left him under no possibility of indecision or doubt. He had made his own the maxim "he who is not with me is against me, he who sows not with me scatters his seed to the winds," and humanity, for him was divided into two very simple groups: those who are for and those who are against Solesmes—the sheep and the goats.

Photo of Teachers and Students: Gregorian Summer School, Appuldurcombe, Isle of Wight (Eng. 1906)
(No. 1) Dom Mocquereau; (2) Dom Eudine; (3) Rev. James A. Boylan (Overbrook, Pa.);
(4) Nicola A. Montani (Philadelphia)

Apart from his polemical writings, he is the author of a vast number of *Monographies Gregoriennes,* little masterpieces of science and of taste, which he published in the *Tribune de Saint Gervais,* the *Revue Gregorienne,* in the *Paleographie Musicale,* etc.

His great work was *Le Nombre Musical Gregorien* published with a lapse of twenty years between the first and second volume, which, even recently, has received a supplementary and final perfecting touch on chironomy.

At the age of eighty-two, he still worked, celebrated Mass daily at 6.30 o'clock, assisted regularly at High Mass and at Vespers in a little corner of the choir. The doctor proposed that he should lay down his pen and his sword. But no. Hardly had he emerged from the heart attack that had nearly carried him off on the 13th of January than he began to dictate a letter of advice to a Religious in Cincinnati. The 18th, he was found dead in his bed.

Sed defunctus adhuc loquitur. He speaks, still, by his works, he speaks through his disciples, those of Europe and those of America, of whom, recently, he said that "they had understood him so well; and that if by some impossible chance, the Gregorian rhythm should be lost in the Old World, it would be found intact and pure, in the New." He speaks especially through the heritage left to his brethren of Solesmes, through his spirit which lives on among them.

This was clearly felt on the day of his funeral when the Schola of Solesmes, massed in a horseshoe around his open coffin, sang the admirable Offertory of the Mass for the Dead. Dom Mocquereau was there, reclining, his beautiful face, petrified by death, was turned toward the singers. He moved no longer, he no longer traced the chironomy,—but the rhythm moved by itself and the voices gave out that softness, that *fondu,* those accents which had been taught them by the Master, with that *something more* which sprang direct from all those hearts so painfully wounded. Still more moving was to be the Chant of the *Libera.* The scene was majestic, unforgettable, when all the monks came down from their stalls and formed an immense circle around the body. The two halves of the circle overlapped, soddered as in a double padlock, from

the Cross of Gold carried by the sub-deacon on the one side to the celebrant at the other,— the Abbot, in black cope and white mitre. And the Chant mounted, the candles glimmered, while the holy water, the fire and the incense passed around the dear remains,— admirable symbols of respect, of hope and of love which transfigure death into the semblance of a feast around a cradle!

The Monks were not weeping. They knew that their brother had heard even at the threshold of eternity, the antiphon of the First Mode: *Euge serve bone et fidelis, intra in gaudium Domini tui!* For Dom Mocquereau was not merely a great artist, he was a holy monk. He—the impetuous, the violent—had known how to bend his whole life to the most scrupulous monastic observance, his fire to the most filial obedience. When the love of God required it, the Lion had become a Lamb, and thus he gave a full example of fidelity to his two-fold ideal: the ideal of a monk and of an artist.

A life that was *single,* valiant, full,—a great and beautiful life.

MARCEL-JOSEPH COCHET.

A SNAP-SHOT TAKEN OF DOM MOCQUEREAU IN
THE ISLE OF WIGHT, AUGUST, 1906
(BY C. SHERWOOD)

DEATH OF THE
RIGHT REVEREND ABBOT DOM FERRETTI, O.S.B.
President of the Pontifical Institute of Sacred Music

On Monday, May 23rd, 1938, the most illustrious and gifted leader in the realm of Sacred Music ended his laborious career as rapidly, cheerfully and unostentatiously as he had lived and worked.

Dom Ferretti had left Rome in the morning in the best of health and spirits on the train for Budapest where he was to attend the Eucharistic Congress. As the train neared the station of Bologna, the Abbot pronounced the last words of the Rogation litanies and his companion noticed a change come over his face. "Is there anything I can do for you, most Reverend Father?" he asked. There was no answer, and his companion had but time enough to give him the final absolution. In five minutes the Abbot was dead. He was in his seventy-second year.

The Abbot Dom Ferretti will long be remembered in the United States by those pupils who had the privilege of following his courses in New York City during the summers of 1925, 1927 and 1928. They will not soon forget his powers of clear presentation and analysis, those lectures at once so scholarly, so entertaining and so full of life, to the point that the translator's task became almost superfluous, so vividly did the Abbot convey his thought not in words only but by gesture, by intonation and almost by mimicry, which, supplemented by charts and blackboard, made us forget that he spoke a language that was not our own. His profound science enabled him to prove each point advanced with overwhelming evidence, yet this wisdom was tempered with the salt of humour and—with the soul of an artist—he made his pupils love the truths so clearly revealed.

The immense work done by the Abbot Ferretti in the cause of Sacred Chant and Music can hardly yet be estimated. Gifted in a special manner for the work he was to carry out he was scholarly, prudent, experienced. Born in Subiaco, near the Sacro Specco of St. Benedict, his vocation developed when he was yet but a boy. At the age of eighteen, he had already made his monastic profession. Named professor of Philosophy, in teaching he formed habits of logical thought and clear presentation, habits which made him one of the most brilliant and beloved professors in Rome in later life. Elected Abbot of Torrecchiara near Parma at the early age of thirty-four, he held that office for more than twenty years *"sapiente e prudente"*.

Called to Rome by Pope Pius X to teach Gregorian Chant, Liturgy and Paleography in the newly created School of Sacred Music founded at Rome by Father Angelo di Santi, S.J., he responded with alacrity, while—for five years, his monastery remained without an Abbot, hoping in vain for the return of Dom Ferretti. But, at the death of Father di Santi, the Abbot Ferretti was appointed by the Pope to the life position of President of the School.

Under Dom Ferretti's direction (1922-1938) the school grew in importance both academically and materially. Under Benedict XV, the school was given a new and dignified headquarters; under Pius XI, it was given a new constitution and raised to the rank of a Papal University, with the name of "Institute" replacing the former name of "school". The academic standards which had been, at first, a bit casual, were raised and broadened by the new president. "I am determined that our institute shall not turn out charlatans. Few in number but solidly formed—that is what I am aiming at," he used to say.

Besides directing the Institute, Dom Ferretti taught regularly, maintaining his regular courses in Paleography, History of Gregorian Chant, Esthetics, or Gregorian Musical Form, and in the Higher Theory which included a study of the Greek systems and the musical theorists of the Middle Ages, a subject upon which he was considered the greatest living authority.

In addition to these courses which were open to the regularly inscribed pupils of the Institute, Dom Ferretti gave public courses once a week which were largely attended by the students from the various Roman Seminaries and Religious Orders.

Thus, during the sixteen years of his administration, the authority and standing of the Institute made giant strides both in Catholic circles and even outside the Church among musicologists in general, a fact which can be illustrated by the recent election of the Abbot Ferretti to the Royal Academy of Italy, followed, later, by an invitation to conduct a series of lectures on Gregorian Chant and ancient music at the Royal Academy of Santa Cecilia for the benefit of post-graduate students of music in that institute.

In addition to his work as director and teacher in the Pontifical Institute of Music, Dom Ferretti held a post of the utmost importance to the Church, as Consultor to the Sacred Congregation of Rites. All matters affecting liturgy and chant were referred to him. Through his hands and on his sole responsibility were issued the new publications bearing the imprimatur of the Vatican. Much of the actual work was carried out in the laboratories of Solesmes, but after this preparation, it was the Abbot Ferretti who controlled and endorsed the work in the name of the Sacred Congregation of Rites. It was thus that many of the new Propers were prepared and thus, notably, appeared the new versions of the Christmas and Holy Week offices.

And, as though these responsibilities were not yet enough for his strong shoulders, his own Congregation elected him Procurator General. Again and again he tried to resign one or the other of these charges, but was always re-elected despite his disinclination for office.

After the death of Monsignor Manari several years ago, the minute detail of administration of the school which had been carried by this able collaborator, fell entirely upon Dom Ferretti himself, already overburdened and advancing in years. It was too much for his strength. He never complained but carried the burden gallantly to the end, and to the end remained one of the most brilliant and beloved professors in Rome. He was never satisfied with his work. Each year his courses were renewed, enriched and vivified. He always wanted to dig down to the ultimate sources. Until everything had been controlled, examined, compared, he considered that he was still in the region of intelligent hypothesis. Thus, when once he announced a conclusion, a demonstrated fact,

one could be certain that the last word had been said.

A strong character but extremely kind and possessing a veritable genius for friendship, he held the highest positions in the gift of the Church with extreme modesty and simplicity. On official occasions, the Abbot Ferretti was dignified with a certain charm and elegance, but on unofficial occasions he was the simplest of men. There was nothing pompous about him and he detested pose or sham. Despite his busy life, he was always ready to lift the burdens of others, promptly, cheerfully and most efficiently. How many of his friends will find a void which can never be filled both in their work and in their heart!

When and how did this busy man rest? His brief vacations during the summer months were spent almost entirely at Solesmes. Resting? Far from it. He was never so busy as during his vacation, which represented a change of work. At Solesmes, he delved into the library of ancient manuscripts, comparing them with the photographs which he had collected himself in the libraries of Italy and other countries. It was during his vacation that he wrote the greater part of his *Estetica Gregoriana*, perhaps the most important work since the *Nombre Musical* of Dom Mocquereau. His real interest was research. The manuscripts were his friends, each one having, in his eyes, an individuality, speaking to his ears a familiar language. He dreamed of a day—never, alas, to dawn—when he might retire from active work and follow his true inclination. But the summers, at least, were his, and *ours* since the first volume of his *Estetica* has been published in Italian and, recently, in French, translated by Dom Agaesse, monk of Solesmes, his friend. The second volume is but partially completed, but it is to be hoped that it may be given to the public later by the care of some of his pupils.

The announcement of Dom Ferretti's death has left the church musicians of the world in consternation. Who will succeed him in each of the difficult and delicate functions which he filled so eminently and with such exceptional gifts of intelligence and vision? Not one of his closest associates can even suggest a name. For there are certain men of rare qualities whose place can never be filled. That place remains forever occupied by a memory. Another man will certainly follow him in time and in function, perhaps half a dozen will be required, but no one will replace him. His gifts were of a unique quality. Before our misfortune we can but pronounce our *fiat* of faith.

The Abbot Ferretti was buried in the cemetery of his old monastery at Parma on the 28th of May in the presence of the Abbots and Bishops of his own congregation; the Abbot General from Subiaco, Dom Caronti; of the Abbot Primate from Rome and the Abbot of the new Pontifical monastery of S. Girolamo; the Bishop of Assisi, his master of Novices during the time he was Abbot; Mgr. Respighi, Papal Master of Ceremonies; the professors of the Pontifical Institute of Sacred Music—Maestro Refice, Maestro Casimiri and the others, besides countless prelates and monks. The Office for the dead was chanted, then the Requiem Mass, followed by the five absolutions due a Prelate. In a short discourse, the Abbot Caronti spoke of his great services to the Church and of his exceptional qualities as a man: "Men of high intellectual gifts," he said, "are often lacking in heart. With him, there was a perfect equilibrium between heart and intellect: he had the heart of a Father, almost that of a Mother."

Among the crowds that lined the streets of the little town, the funeral procession wound its way to the last resting place of the Abbot Ferretti where, only the week before, a new vault had been prepared by the monks of Parma, little thinking that the first to be laid to rest would be their first Abbot, Dom Ferretti. R. I. P.

J. B. W.

SOLESMES AND THE WAR

We are indebted to the LITURGICAL ARTS magazine for permission to print the following letter of Mrs. Justine Ward revealing one aspect of the conditions brought about by the present world conflict.

———

"It occurred to me that the following account of events at Solesmes, during the war and after the armistice, would be of interest

When war was declared in September, 1939, most of the young and middle-aged monks were mobilized, including several who had fought in the last war, as they were reserve officers in the army and navy. At the same time, the greater part of the monastery was requisitioned as a military hospital and those among the monks who were left were crowded into the old building that remains from the time of Dom Guéranger. The guest parlors were turned into cells for the monks and brothers. Even so, when the mobilized men came back on leave, the monastery was crowded to capacity. They all returned for Holy Week, 1940. It was the last time they were to meet. Already the shadow of death was hanging very low, but in spite of this, perhaps because of this, the singing of those great Offices was more beautiful than ever before. The men returned from an open-air life which put a certain vigor into the voices, and though the perfection that comes from daily singing in common may have been less remarkable than in other years, the tragic intensity of the voices was unspeakably moving. Yet we still dreamed of victory in those days!

After the tragic days of May, when Holland and Belgium were invaded, and where most of our men were engaged in the Battle of Flanders, many disappeared. Nothing more was heard of them for a long time. Finally, it became known— first as a rumor, then with certitude— that three had given their lives for their country: Dom Moulinet, the *Grand Chantre* (a very grave loss to the monastery), Dom Turpault, killed on the beach at Dunkerque, and a lay brother. Several more had been seriously wounded and were hospitalized in Holland; seventeen others were (and still are) prisoners in Germany; among these last are the Prior and sub-Prior. Also the organist, Dom Bonet.

When the invasion of France had almost reached our region, it was thought that the lines could hold on the other side of the Loire. The Abbot determined to send the novices and many of the monks to a place of safety, he himself remaining at Solesmes with the aged and infirm. By that time, it had become impossible to procure any normal means of transportation, as the trains were reserved for the movement of troops; the automobiles had been requisitioned long ago, and even horse-drawn vehicles were rare. Consequently the monks left on foot, on bicycles, or in the care of friends who might dispose of some means of locomotion. Not more than eight or ten were left at Solesmes. Those who left on foot or on bicycles met with many a dramatic adventure, but there were no casualties, thank God. Some were mistaken for "parachute troops," as the ecclesiastical garb had been worn (it was claimed) by the Germans when they descended in Holland. The wildest rumors were circulating everywhere yet no one imagined that France was already conquered. The news was scarce and often contradictory. No instructions were given to the civilian population. The result was that all joined the throng of refugees that had begun to flow from Holland and Belgium in May, had continued from the north of France, and from regions getting ever nearer to our own. And the current swept on.

Paris had been occupied on the fourteenth. The monks left Solesmes on June 15. On the seventeenth Sablé was bombarded. Some people were killed, but Solesmes was spared. A few days later, the Germans, having crossed the Loire, and having nothing further before them but plain sailing, advanced far into the very heart of France and no further resistance being possible, Marshal Pétain requested an armistice.

After the armistice. From the time the armistice was granted, the return of the monks began, some by demobilization, others by a return from across the Loire. Solesmes turned out to be in the part of France that was "occupied" by the Germans. No one knew, at that time, just how the army of occupation would treat the civil—and particularly the religious—

population. As a matter of fact, they have behaved correctly as a general rule, and when abuses occurred due to individuals, complaints could be carried to the *Commandatur* and redress was always obtainable. Moreover, the part of the monastery that had been taken over as a hospital by the French army was not requisitioned by the German army of occupation, and the monks are now occupying the whole building.

While the dead, the wounded, and the prisoners have left sad vacancies, these are more than filled by the "guests" from other monasteries now scattered among the houses of their Benedictine brethren. Among these are some of the monks from the great Luxembourg monastery of Clairvaux. At the time of the invasion, these monks were notified that they would have two hours in which to leave and turn the building over to the Germans. They could only take with them a small valise apiece. The magnificent library of seventy thousand books had to be abandoned. The patronal Feast of Saint Maur was selected for the notification and expulsion. Other monasteries (in Belgium particularly) were also forced to leave in like manner. These monks are now scattered here and there wherever they can find a hospitable Benedictine roof. The French monks of San Girolamo, the Papal monastery in Rome founded for the revision of the Vulgate, are also among the exiles, though these left Rome at the time of the declaration of war and not by order of the Germans.

As regards the French monasteries and other religious houses in France, the German army of occupation has treated them with perfect correctness so far. How long this will last no once can foresee, but when I left France on May 8, all was serene at Solesmes. The monks are suffering, as are all other French men and women, from the scarcity of food. Every square inch of soil is planted with potatoes and other foodstuffs. Solesmes is situated in a good farming region, and may manage better than some others.

So far, the monks have managed to exist, and as they are hardened to a fare which ordinary mortals would consider light, the Offices are sung with the usual perfection, marred slightly by the number of "guests" who have not yet been broken in to the perfection of style of the monks of Solesmes. The great library is intact, the work of the paleography continues—for how long, God only knows. Moreover, communications have been reopened between France and Belgium, so that printer's proofs can pass between Solesmes and its publisher, Messrs. Desclée & Cie, at Tournai.

We can all pray for the day when normal conditions will return to this sadly battered world and the work of the Benedictines in every country can continue for the benefit of mankind."

Yours truly,

JUSTINE B. WARD

Solesmes and a Centenary

JUSTINE WARD

Through the long, soft English twilight, a nightingale intoned. Then, like an orchestra of clarinets, the chorus took up the theme and developed it in free and soaring rhythm. The whole countryside echoed liquid arpeggios in innocent rivalry of the bells of Quarr Abbey calling us to Compline. Hastening through the wooded lane, enchanted by the birds, we resisted their fascination and entered the abbey church.

"*Jube, Domne, benedicere*" a gentle voice intoned, and the chorus replied: "*Noctem quietam*" . . . yet, from without, a more insistent chorus poured through the open windows their vibrant tones in desperate competition, covering the soft voices of the monks with a multi-colored veil of masterly song.

The monks of Solesmes were in exile. They had been driven out of France some twenty years earlier for the crime of belonging to a Religious Congregation, and had settled on the beautiful Isle of Wight. They built a monastery on the site of a tenth-century Benedictine ruin at Quarr. The new building was constructed of warm, golden-red brick and was a bit Oriental in conception. It stood on rich land sloping gently down to the shore of the Solent, among great oaks and elms, rolling lawns and pasture lands covered with grazing cattle. The milk, the butter and the eggs of Quarr Abbey were famous in the neighborhood and the poet-monk in charge of the feathered flock was affectionately known on the Island as "The Chicken Father."

Of course, the Gregorian chant, for which the abbey was distinguished above all others, attracted a few specialists in music and liturgy. In general, however, there were few strangers, fewer guests, to disturb the intimacy of the Offices. Yes, those days of exile had their charm. The church was not too large. The acoustics were warm and sensitive. Those simple interior brick walls were not only resonant,

Dom Mocquereau

but in their freedom from all so-called decoration, provided a sympathetic surface where the sunlight could play melodies of its own rays flowing in happy designs from high windows, or touching the altar tenderly in the manner of a primitive painter. The voices of the monks filled the church simply, naturally, without strain or effort. The first impression, indeed, was one of quiet, holy stillness that the chant, far from interrupting, reinforced. It was a silence that could be heard.

My first impression had been one of astonishment. I had read all Dom Mocquereau's books on rhythm and had seen him direct groups of singers with the subtle magic of his "chironomie." This was when he came to New York in 1920 to preside at the International Congress of Gregorian Chant. He was an old man, then, with deep, kindly, mystical eyes that could flash with indignation when things did not go as he wished. After the Congress, he had said to me: "One thing worries me greatly." "What is that?" I asked. "That you know nothing." "Nothing? Then will you teach me?" He consented and that is why I had come to Quarr Abbey—to learn.

I arrived, expecting something more rich, more dramatic; I expected more striking contrasts in rhythm and nuances. This was because I came as a worldly, secular musician, rather than as a worshipper.

"*Il faut perdre ce petit air artiste*," Dom Mocquereau used to remark. As the weeks and months rolled by, what had seemed at first a bit colorless, a bit over-restrained, went through a gradual transformation. I began to discern a magical tissue of subtle and exquisite nuances. What simplicity! What delicacy! My own soul was in process of a higher education. I was becoming attuned to the sound of music which spoke of God alone. Here were sounds too sincere to be dramatized, too true for "effects" or artifices. Hardly touching the senses, they penetrated the soul. I swung to the opposite extreme, and renounced artistic standards. What could it matter, I persuaded myself, if the great cantor intoned *flat?* That great, strutting cantor who was reputed to take a single breath as he dipped his finger in the holy water font on entering the church, and the next breath as he made his exit several hours later. What could it ᴗ ᴗ indeed, if he intoned flat? I had ᴗ st, whether it might not ᴗ s while to take anothe⸱ sing true to pitch. worldly thoughts! ᴗ deaf, and did not kr⸱ did. Dom Mocque⸱ and critical musici⸱ each false intonat⸱ breath: "*Faux, en*⸱ nothing he could⸱ that best of all⸱ cure. Patience th⸱ note the perfect⸱ keep in step wit⸱ Watch the gestu⸱

movements about the altar: a noble pageant, disciplined but without a shade of militarism. At the *Gloria Patri* notice how the monks bend down, all together as naturally as a wheat field touched by a slight breeze. Watch how the kiss of peace in the Mass passes from monk to monk with the gracious charm of a sacred ballet conceived by a Fra Angelico and executed by saints in glorified bodies. Of course these were not the recommendations of Dom Mocquereau, to whom all these things had become mere routine, but the impressions of his student who had not yet cast off the worldly atmosphere of the artist's point of view.

Day by day, this liturgical splendor unfolded itself before the eyes of the few who assisted, almost as intruders. This beauty concerned them only indirectly. One alone was the object of this consecrated magnificence, this perfection of song and gesture. He who had created beauty could be adored only through the full beauty of truth, only through the *Opus Dei*, the *Work of God*, to which these monks had dedicated their lives. The sense of that Invisible Presence animated each note, each phrase, each movement, while clouds of incense rose in spiral designs and, mixing themselves with the sunbeams, entwining their mutual rhythms, executed an aerial dance that flooded the church with rays of perfume and patterns of light.

I thought the while: how many of our rich churches at home are stingy with incense; we see within them no clouds, no fumes; we smell no odor of sanctity, whereas the poorest little Catholic chapel in Europe testifies to its belief in the Real Presence by the first breath one takes on entering its doors. One feels sure of being in the home or the Blessed Sacrament, and kneels, happily conscious of the privilege.

It was the Centenary of the birth of André Mocquereau that brought all these memories of Solesmes surging and crowding and elbowing each other out of the way. Dom Mocquereau in the garden armed with an extra hankerchief with which to wipe off the bench: "O, *ces petits oiseaux, ces petits oiseaux!*" and with indulgent reproach eliminating their crimes. Dom Mocquereau receiving an exercise he had set me and handing it back uncorrected because my syllables had not been aligned exactly under the note or neum to which each one corresponded. Dom Mocquereau, weighing a musical phrase with his hands to decide whether it was arsic or thetic in character and then caressing it as with a sculptor's touch. Dom Mocquereau watching my own awkward efforts and remarking: "This may be a strange thing for an old monk to say to a young woman, but you are certainly not graceful!" Alas, at that time, grace was the least of my preoccupations. Yet Dom Mocquereau was right, for rhythm is ordered movement and all order is full of grace. Rhythm, indeed, should spread its life of grace even to the gesture that indicates its flow.

SOLESMES AND DOM MOCQUEREAU

But to return to the Centenary. Of course the reader will realize that Solesmes is Dom Mocquereau and Dom Mocquereau, Solesmes. It is for the Chant of the Church that Solesmes is known, and, while other monks have worked for its restoration, it is the genius of Dom Mocquereau, his perseverance, his insight, his courage in battle against enemies within and without, that has won the final victory, the musical peace that reigns today in the monastic world.

It is a shock of a sort when events that have been familiar, flexible, changing from day to day and intimately connected with our own life, suddenly take on the rigidity of historical events. Can it be that Dom Mocquereau, if still alive, would be a hundred years old?

It will be recorded in history that on June 6, 1849, a boy was born in a little village near Cholet in Brittany, was baptized that same day and given the name of André. His father carried on a small trade in linen, producing those *"petits mouchoirs de Cholet"* that are celebrated in folk lore. The boy must have received a serious musical education for we find him, as a young man, playing the cello part in the quartets of Mozart, Haydn, Schubert, and Beethoven with a group of his companions. This same cello, now with broken strings, was the most touching object exhibited at Solesmes on the day of the Centenary.

The musical studies of young André Mocquereau were interrupted by the war of 1870 when the young officer was mobilized. Wounded while fighting in Belgium, he lay on a pile of straw near the door of a barn. There he was noticed by two charitable Belgian ladies, who took pity upon him and nursed him back to health in their home. He was, then, a dashing young officer with large, flashing black eyes, bristling, black moustaches, worn still, standing out from each side of his mouth according to the fashion of the day. Soon the cello joined the family group. It may, perhaps, have spoken more ardent messages to the charming sisters than was intended. Yet, grateful as he was for their care, the young officer left for France and bade farewell to the kindly sisters immediately after his demobilization. He had plans of his own which involved neither marriage nor a professional musician's career.

He had decided to give his life to God. Music was to be cast out of his life absolutely. He applied at the monastery of St. Pierre de Solesmes where he was received as a postulant and became a monk in embryo. The monastic vocation to him meant the complete abandonment of music, the art that had been his delight hitherto. He renounced it forever, sincerely, completely. He knew, of course, that he would chant the Offices with the other monks, but he did not consider chant to be music. It was a dull, drab, necessary evil, to be endured though disliked.

The experiments for restoring the Chant were still mere gropings in the dark. Some manuscripts had been copied in libraries by two monks assigned to this task by the first Abbot of Solesmes, Dom Gueranger, the elder of whom had died during the process. The younger, Dom Joseph Pothier, had published a volume entitled, *Les Mélodies Grégoriennes*, embodying some of their joint conclusions. Here was an intuition of truth, a trail blazed through the tangled jungle, which Dom Mocquereau was later to convert into a great highway. At this time, Dom Pothier was choirmaster at Solesmes. The rude, untrained voices of the monastic choir failed to charm the young postulant. He would have laughed at the idea that he was destined to devote his life to the defense of his master, Dom Pothier, in a formidable work of Gregorian research, the *Paléographie Musicale*. He still found the Chant boring, rude, colorless, and uncouth.

MOCQUEREAU CONVERTED TO THE CHANT

In the quiet of his cell, Dom Mocquereau was preparing an Offertory for the feast of a martyr, "*Posuisti Domine in capite ejus coronam de lapide pretioso.*" He hummed the melody softly. Fascinated, astonished, he exclaimed, "Why this is music, real music, beautiful music." He reached for his cello, tuned it and played the melody, very legato. That was the moment of his conversion. The Offertory *Posuisti* was the blinding light which, as in the conversion of St. Paul, reversed the direction of his entire life. From a hater of Gregorian chant, Dom Mocquereau became its most distinguished apostle.

While still a novice, Dom Mocquereau was charged with the direction of the *schola*. The abbot realized that in this young monk, he had a musician of talent and training. Then began the unfolding of a world of unsuspected beauty. The Chant at the Abbey of Solesmes attracted musicians from Paris and from even further afield. The crowds came to listen to a "novelty," a "musical curiosity"—and they stayed to pray. Writers raved. And, naturally, opposition was aroused, organized, fanned with fury by financial interests involved in the existing editions. Year after year, offense and defense filled reams of paper.

"Opposition has always been precious to me," Dom Mocquereau used to say in after years, "it forced me to dig down to rock bottom and to leave nothing to possibility or even probability. Without the opposition, I might never have done all that work."

Fortunately, Dom Mocquereau was endowed with that rare combination of patience and scientific integrity as well as with artistic insight. Nothing was too minute, too apparently insignificant to be cast aside as trivial; all details were codified for study; study, however, carried on by a man of intuition and musical genius. Without this combination of virtues, the final triumph would have been impossible, victory over obstacles from without and even from within. Yet, patiently he continued to unravel the snarled threads, clearing away rubbish that hid the true character of the Gregorian rhythm, that mysterious force, so difficult to define, yet instinctively felt by every artist. Out of the complexity, he developed a theory that was marvelous in its clarity and logic, so simple, indeed, that little children could grasp it and sing the praises of God devoutly. Not only was Gregorian chant revealed, but music in general profitted by the light thrown on the subject of rhythm by this monk of genius.

While the battle still raged in the realm of Gregorian rhythm, we began to hear whispers, at Quarr Abbey, of a return to France. The laws against Religious Congregations were still in force; technically, the monks were still criminals, but it was becoming rather awkward for the French government to enforce these laws. During the first World War, those exiled French monks had volunteered to return to their country and fight in the army. From Quarr Abbey, the "Chicken Father" had been the first to depart. Others followed. Some did not return. The government could not exile those dead bodies left on the field of battle, nor the living souls who had survived and had been decorated for exceptional bravery with the *Croix de Guerre*. So the monks began to leak back into France by groups of two and three at a time.

I remember visiting the Abbey of Solesmes before the return of the monks. The property had been confiscated, and the building used as a hospital during the war. It was filthy, full of rubbish, the grounds were overgrown with thorns and thistles. The entire monastery property was squeezed into an oblong space between a road and a river. It lacked the charm of the generous lands of Quarr. The church was long, high, and narrow, with some fifteenth-century sculpture, but the whole place gave the impression of an untidy wilderness, without, and suffocation, within. Yet it was "home" to the older monks.

Soon the monks began to tidy up that mess. The "Chicken Father," turning his hand from feathers to fruit, created an orchard: planted, pruned, watered, grafted. His grapes grew as fat as prunes, his apples, as large as melons. The brambles disappeared as though by magic; tidy avenues and gardens took their place. Even the narrow, cold, white church seemed better proportioned when the voices of the monks filled it with beauty of sound and when clouds of incense rose in spirals as of old. The paleographical work redoubled in force and extent. Vocations poured into the monastery. Young fresh voices gave velvet to the choir. A new cantor replaced the old, (soon, alas to be slain in the next World War). The Offices resumed their splendor. Visitors, like flies, overcrowded the tiny village of Solesmes and spread into the neighboring town of Sablé.

The return to his native land was one of the final joys to be given Dom Mocquereau, with that deeper satisfaction that his work had triumphed over so many years of opposition. His last days were full of serenity. He who had been known in his community as "The Lion," had become a very gentle lamb in those years that preceded 1929, when he was destined to undertake a longer voyage than that of the return to France. He had worked long and hard for God's honor. Like St. Paul, he had fought the good fight and now it remained for him merely to receive the promised reward, the *coronam de lapide pretioso.*

(By permission of the author and *The Benedictine Review.*)

Studies and Conferences

Questions, the discussion of which is for the information of the general reader of the Department of Studies and Conferences, are answered in the order in which they reach us. The Editor cannot engage to reply to inquiries by private letter.

TWENTY-FIVE YEARS.

AUTHORITY AND OBEDIENCE.

A quarter of a century ago the Holy See laid down certain memorable rules regarding Sacred Music. To these instructions, says the Papal document, " as to a juridical code of sacred music, we will with the fullness of our Apostolic authority, that the force of law be given; and we do, by our present handwriting, impose its scrupulous observance on all."

To whom does this law apply? The Instruction seems to make this plain in its opening paragraph when it states: " Among the cares of the pastoral office, not only of this Supreme Chair . . . but of *every local church,* a leading one is without question that of maintaining and promoting the decorum of the House of God ". The rules of Sacred Music follow.

In conclusion, as though to avoid all obscurity on this point, the encyclical names those whose special duty it is to carry out the instructions, namely: " choirmasters, singers, members of the clergy, superiors of seminaries, ecclesiastical institutions and religious communities, parish priests, rectors of churches, canons of collegiate churches and cathedrals, and *above all,* the diocesan Ordinaries." The reason is added: " that the authority of the Church (which herself has repeatedly proposed these rules and now inculcates them) may not fall into contempt ".

The Pope would appear therefore, to have legislated for every local church. He would appear to have imposed the duty of observing these rules " above all " upon the Ordinary (though not exclusively) — and also upon every parish priest, as well as upon every individual choirmaster and singer. The language of the Instruction would certainly bear such an interpretation, and as it stands, the subject has caused many a genuine scruple of conscience to those directors of music who believe that they are included in that "*all*" upon whom the strict observance is imposed.

On the other hand, if the Instruction had been intended to be no more than a gentle piece of Fatherly advice from the Pope, which was not binding upon any diocese outside of Rome, nor upon any individual church unless the local Ordinary should decide to enforce it, then the language of the *Motu Proprio* was strangely deceptive.

The instructions themselves contained little that was new. They did but sum up and codify the past rulings of the Church from the early fourteenth century, when worldly music first crept into the churches, through the sixteenth, seventeenth, eighteenth and nineteenth centuries, each one of which contributed its peculiar forms of worldliness which in turn had to be weeded out. The *Motu Proprio* makes this purpose clear: "that all *vagueness* may be eliminated from the *interpretation* of matters *which have already been commanded*", it says.

These commands were not onerous nor difficult to obey. Often they were merely negative: commands to omit the doing of certain things, such as the performance of frivolous, or theatrical music in church; such as arias by solo singers; such as the undue repetition or distortion of the text. This negative side of the reform could well have been obeyed to the letter from the first day, for it is within the power of each one of us to keep silent.

Other rules were of a positive nature. They set standards by which the *character* of a musical composition could be judged (whether holy or the reverse); the *form* which would suitably clothe the liturgical text; the relation of music to words; the function of instruments other than the human voice. These positive rules might have been considered difficult, perplexing, had we been obliged to create suitable music according to the standards demanded by the Pope. As a matter of fact, however, suitable music existed already, and in abundance. To obey, we were only required to study existing masterpieces.

Indeed the strange, the staggering thing for a Catholic is this: that we ever should have wandered so far from the

obvious standard of respect due the House of God as to have
required correction upon such elementary matters. Yet, as
we approach the quarter-century mark, who will dare to say
that these mild and just instructions have been " scrupulously
obeyed *by all* " ?

Since we must admit our non-conformity, let us try to find
the reason. This question is proposed not in a spirit of carp-
ing criticism, nor of discouragement, but in an honest desire
for constructive suggestions from the readers of THE ECCLESI-
ASTICAL REVIEW.

Some advance indeed has been made in the past twenty-
five years. The official books of the Church are in our hands.
The scientific researches of scholars and artists have opened
the secrets of the ancient melodies to those who are willing to
study. We are no longer groping in the dark. Schools of
sacred music have been established, both at home and abroad.
We are far already from the first moment of panic when—in
this country at least—there were few if any choirmasters or
singers who had a knowledge of true sacred music; when even
the clergy lacked musical instruction and were unable to dis-
criminate between the various types of emotional appeal in the
realm of sound. To-day these conditions no longer hold.
Competent choirmasters are available. Schools of liturgical
music exist where inexperienced musicians may receive adequate training. Most significant of all perhaps, a widespread
movement is sweeping this country for the formation of our
Catholic school children in the official music of the Church.
Thus, the false standard will be eliminated by substitution of
the true. The teaching Sisterhoods have fostered this constructive side of the reform, and, at great personal sacrifice,
these devoted women have given up their summer vacation to
attend normal courses in sacred chant and music. They have
added this subject to the already crowded curriculum in their
class rooms, with a consequent increase of piety among the
children committed to their care.

All this means a real advance. Competent directors of
music are obtainable, and an army of little singers are ready to
be called upon for choir service.

With this hopeful advance, what is it which still prevents
the full triumph of the reforms demanded by Pius X? I will

not attempt to answer this delicate question, but will set down briefly some of the lessons which have been given me by competent persons. I do so with the hope of arousing an open discussion of their merits.

The first excuse is that the *Motu Proprio* has " no teeth "— by which is meant that no penalties are inflicted upon those who disobey.

To the mind of a layman, this seems a strange reason for disobedience. Are we to obey the Holy See solely through fear of punishment? Is such a standard to apply to all other matters of ecclesiastical ruling or merely to music? If so, what becomes of the laws which we obey through love and loyalty? If I obey the rule which requires me to assist at Holy Mass on Sundays, is it through fear of being drawn and quartered in case of disobedience? If I abstain from flesh meat on Fridays, is it through fear of a heavy fine? If I contribute to the support of the parish according to my means, may I now omit this duty until such time as " teeth " are put into the regulations? And what are these teeth to be? " Pain of excommunication, suspension from office, loss of revenue from functions," were the penalties imposed by Pope Alexander VII for non-observance of his regulations for Church Music in the year 1657, to which in the case of disobedient choirmasters was added " corporal punishment " to be administered by the Cardinal Vicar of Rome. Are these the " teeth " that we require to-day? In 1856, the Cardinal Vicar of Rome imposed heavy fines on disobedient choirmasters and organists, still heavier fines on rectors of churches: " to which other punishments may be added ". Are we holding back to-day until the fear of corporal punishment or of financial loss shall stimulate our loyalty and devotion to the Vicar of Christ?

The second argument for disobedience is *custom*. " We have always sung as at present; these tunes have been sung by our fathers before us, and we like them; we have always played the organ during Advent and Lent; we have always listened to the singing of arias by a solo voice, usually female; we have always omitted the Proper of the Day at High Mass;—all these things and others of like nature are a custom of long standing, and we will not tolerate any newfangled notions in this church."

This brings us to a question which is still obscure to the lay mind; to what extent does *custom* justify an *evil* practice? If I have a habit of long standing of omitting Sunday Mass, or my Easter duty, will custom be a valid excuse against the mending of my ways? This question of custom is a most puzzling one to the lay mind for this reason: If an evil custom may be maintained in defiance of the formal ruling of the Holy See, then what is the use of the Church's laws? Obviously (or at at least so it would seem) the Church legislates in order to put an end to certain abuses. Her purpose is to call, not the just, but sinners to amendment. Yet if these sinners may claim *custom* as a valid defence against amendment, the legislation will apply only to those who need no reform, their customs always having been exemplary.

A third argument for disobedience is that " the people like it," meaning the type of music which is forbidden by the Holy See. Personally I doubt the truth of this assertion. I believe that the average worshipper goes to Mass desiring to come under the influence of something unworldly, something in a different vein from the ordinary appeal of his secular life. If he desires diversion he seeks and finds it elsewhere. For his parish church to offer him sentimental or tawdry music in place of sacred music, is to place a smoke screen between his soul and the Holy Sacrifice. Indeed, to the layman this sentimental music is not merely a distraction but often a grave temptation; such music is not merely negative in its effects upon the layman (as conceivably it might be to the clergy), but is full of evil associations which drag down his soul.

Assuming however for the sake of argument, that the people *do* prefer the forbidden type of music, the question arises: is this preference on the part of the congregation to become the ruling factor in a matter upon which the Vicar of Christ has made a formal ruling with the fullness of the Apostolic authority? If the taste of the congregation is to be supreme in such matters, why should it not be supreme, also, in other matters of liturgy and rubrics? Why should sacred music alone be the prey of mob fancy—sacred music which, " being a complementary part of the solemn liturgy, participates in the general scope of the liturgy " ? (*Motu Proprio.*)

Should the people once grasp the fact that their likes and dislikes can outweigh the formal rulings of the Church, the consequences might be far-reaching. John Doe might well dislike to send his children to a parochial school: and he might argue that his duty in this regard is far less binding than the laws regarding sacred music, having never been the subject of a papal encyclical. Is he henceforth to follow his liking in the matter and place his children in a non-Catholic school? Mrs Doe, who likes to sing an aria during Mass, might develop a liking for a blue and yellow chasuble, instead of the colors prescribed by the rubrics. Will the pastor, who indulges the lady's musical idiosyncrasies, bow before her preferences in the realm of color? Conceivably the odor of incense might cease to appeal to the modern nostril; will the pastor hastily substitute for the fumes of incense, the beguiling scent of Houbigant's *Quelques Fleures* or Coty's *Rose Jacqueminot*? I doubt it. Yet by what logic does he hold fast to the rubrics which regulate matters of color and smell while capitulating on those which regulate sound? Indeed my comparison does not go far enough, for there is nothing intrinsically degrading about a chasuble of blue and yellow; the perfumes of the great Paris houses remain (even like the incense) a sweet odor rising to heaven; whereas the music which we are forced to listen to is intrinsically *evil, degrading,* and, to quote the *Motu Proprio,* it " puts into the hand of the Lord the scourges wherewith of old the Divine Redeemer drove the unworthy profaners from the temple ", or to use the strong words of Pope John XXII in his Encyclical on Sacred Music given at Avignon in 1324, "instead of promoting devotion they (the modern composers of the day) prevent it by creating a sensuous and indecent atmosphere. Hence it was not without reason that Boetius said ' a person who is intrinsically sensuous will delight in hearing these indecent melodies and one who listens to them frequently will be weakened thereby and lose his virility of soul.' "[1]

Finally I come to the argument based on the "impossibility" of carrying out the papal rulings, either because of poverty, or for some other reason. For the sake of argument, let us

---

[1] ". . . lascivus animus, vel lascivioribus delectatur modis vel eosdem saepe audiens emollitur et frangitur."

assume that there are places where it is genuinely impossible to obey the positive side of the Pope's Instruction. There may be such places, there may be such conditions, although it is generally true that where there is a will there is a way. I met a missionary a few years ago whose parish was spread over a Central American jungle. So far from civilization was he placed that he had to travel three hundred miles to make his Easter confession. As sole companion, he had one lay Brother; as parishioners, the native Indians, as means of loco-motion, a self-built boat in which he traveled along the coast to reach the various little native parishes, separated by hundreds of miles of impassable swamps and jungle. Here, we might say, was a genuine case of " impossibility ". The Pope, in making his ruling, had not in mind a solitary missionary bringing the faith to uncivilized tribes. Yet this argument never occurred to that priest. He followed the rules in their integrity. At each native village, he sang the Mass; his lay Brother sang the Proper of the Day; the native Indians sang the Ordinary, and in pure Gregorian Chant " the supreme type and norm of all sacred music," as the Instruction states. Now it is evident that in singing the Proper of the Day with a solo voice, there was infringement of the letter of the law; here, evidently, there was a real impossibility of doing otherwise. But as far as it was humanly possible, that Missionary obeyed.

Few of our parishes are in a situation where obedience would be more difficult than in the wilds of the jungle. But for the sake of argument, once more, let us assume in all charity that some of our parishes face conditions more difficult than those faced by that holy missionary; let us assume that our local parishioners are more ignorant and helpless than those poor Indians, our clergy more overburdened than was the missionary with his single lay assistant. Even so, there are at least *some* points of obedience which might be enforced. I mean the negative side of the rulings.

No one is so helpless nor so ignorant as to be incapable of refraining from singing a sentimental solo in church; no pastor is so overburdened with work that he could not prevent such songs from being sung; no organist is so violently impelled to play the organ during the forbidden seasons of Advent and Lent, during the singing of the Requiem Mass, the

Preface, the Responses, and the Pater Noster, that he or she is unable to master the temptation. This minimum of obedience, then, is not beyond the most mediocre talent. Good will alone would suffice.

The next degree of obedience would be to refrain from the singing of frivolous and theatrical music. This too might appear easy, for from a technical standpoint the forbidden music is far more difficult than the grave and serious type required by the Church. Yet, in many a parish the omission of frivolous music would involve complete silence; because the amateur singers upon whom a country parish is dependent, are unfamiliar with any other. The question of " possibility " becomes in that case, " shall we sing the type of music forbidden by the Church or shall we keep silent "? The answer given in his diocese to such a question by one of our courageous bishops was this: " You can save your souls by assisting at a low Mass, but you cannot save them by disobedience to the Holy See. Hence, let there be no music until it can be according to the Rubrics." The reform was brought about with amazing celerity and the " impossibility " melted into thin air.

Even in difficult cases, however, a little interest on the part of the pastor could solve the matter. Among the amateurs who have served country parishes in choir and at the organ, there is usually at least one who could be sent to a school of liturgical music to receive an elementary education, and return to impress upon the parish the seal of musical sanctity. The affair would require a small expenditure, but slight in proportion to the result. And in any parish there is money for the things that are considered important. The janitor is paid, and the sacristan, the carpenters and the plumbers; all these who contribute to the material welfare of the parish. Why then hesitate to invest an insignificant sum in contributing, to the spiritual welfare of that parish?

JUSTINE B. WARD.

New York City.

DOM ANDRE MOCQUEREAU OF SOLESMES

ON the 18th of January there went to his reward a great artist, a profound scholar, a gentle and holy monk whose hidden life has changed the accents of divine worship from end to end of the Catholic world, from the great basilicas of Rome to the humblest village church according to the measure of their co-operation in the desire of the Holy See. This death, then, concerns us all, since each one of us shares in the fruits of this life.

The history of Dom Mocquereau reads like a page of the *Légende Dorée*, yet, unlike the legend, the romance of his life contains nothing fabulous or uncertain. His youth was full of music: Haydn, Mozart and Beethoven filled his heart. As a cellist, he had already made a reputation among musicians when the Franco-Prussian war broke out. He enlisted, a typical young musician, with flashing eyes and bristling mustache, and for him the harmonies of the string quartet were replaced by the blast of the cannon, until the war ended. With the peace of nations, a greater peace dawned in the heart of André Mocquereau, and he sought in the novitiate of the Benedictines of France, at the monastery of Saint Pierre de Solesmes, that *Pax* which was thereafter to be his life.

In the generosity of his vocation he had determined to make a holocaust of his love for music, in pledge of which he gave away his cello. Little did he think that a vocation within a vocation awaited him, with music as its objective. For, by one of those strange though not infrequent paradoxes of the religious life, the natural talent and temperament of a man, when once fully renounced, takes on a supernatural quality and attains a new power which bears fruit for the Church and for the world. The supernatural then becomes the flower of the natural and not its contradiction. This is what happened to Dom Mocquereau. Before he had even finished his novitiate, he was thrown into the forefront of a musical mission which, for half a century, was destined to stir the entire Catholic Church, a mission which the Holy See was to notice, to encourage, and which finally the Church was to take over as her own. This mission was the restoration of the Gregorian melodies to their original purity and beauty.

Dom Guèranger, the first abbot of Solesmes, in his effort to restore the full traditions of the Roman liturgy in France, felt the need of a correct version of the ancient melodies—the medium through which the liturgical prayers found daily expression in the worship of his monastic family. His mind was not set on a world movement, but on greater perfection in the *Opus Dei* of the monastery. Accordingly he set two of his monks to work on the manuscripts then available to seek out the original form of the melodies and their primitive rhythm. Dom Jausions, the elder of the two, died in the midst of his task. The younger, Dom Joseph Pothier, was left alone to present the result of their joint labors and to edit the monastic books. These books were offered, not as the expression of ultimate truth, based as they were on limited data, but as the beginning of better things to come. Dom Pothier had shown an instinct which had revealed certain fundamental truths but he lacked that plodding perseverance so essential if truth is to be established on a solid basis of science. He was, to quote a contemporary critic and historian "a scholar less inclined, apparently, to don his accoutrements daily for the extension of his possessions than to enjoy the peaceful occupation of a fixed and clearly defined estate . . . As a man of science, he had only sketched an outline, admirable in its way, of the movement which has been, or will be, erected by his pupils."

The man who blazes a trail is rarely the one who builds a railroad along the same route. The outline sketched by Dom Pothier was a good one, but its author was not the man to fill it in. As for the application of his theories to the singing of the monastic choir, Dom Pothier was successful in proportion to his limitations as a musician. To assist him in this phase of his task the abbot gave him Dom André Mocquereau, who, though still a novice, was placed in charge of the *schola* and, later, of the whole monastic choir in order that the chants might be sung according to the principles of Dom Pothier but with the exquisite art that a true musician could bring to such interpretation. Thus it came about that the young man who had renounced music for-

ever was to produce a sensation in the world of musicians, for so
beautiful became the chanting of the monks under his direction
that the fame thereof spread far and wide. Artists and scholars
the world over began to flock to Solesmes to study the correct
rendering of the Chant. From Paris came the *Schola Cantorum*
with its staff of musical artists. The Catholic Institute brought
Dom Mocquereau to Paris to lecture on the Gregorian melodies
before the great musicians of the day, to whom he revealed, by
words and by sung examples, a new and fascinating art. "The
ingenious and profound distinction which he makes" wrote one
of them, "between *Latin* music (Plain Chant which has adopted
the principles of Latin prose) and *Romance* music which has
borrowed its measure, its rhythm and its cadences from the words
and cadences of the Romance languages, these views are original,
well defined and suggestive, and will soon give a new basis to the
history of musical art."

Dom Mocquereau possessed that rare combination of gifts
which made it impossible for him to rest on an incomplete achievement. His objective was to recapture a lost art: the chants of Saint
Gregory the Great. A brilliant hypothesis based on limited data
could not serve. He wanted scientific conclusions based on objective
evidence of an exhaustive character. He took as his motto the rule
laid down by Dom Guèranger: "When manuscripts of different
periods and places agree on a version, it can be affirmed that the
Gregorian text has been rediscovered." To Dom Mocquereau this
meant the comparative study of all the best manuscripts from the
earliest years (of the ninth century) down through the centuries,
the comparison of the manuscripts of the various countries of
Europe, the deciphering of different types of musical writing, both
before and after the invention of the staff—all this as preliminary
to tabulating and comparing the data once obtained. It was a herculean task.

A group of monks was put to work under Dom Mocquereau's direction. He it was who taught them how to interrogate
the thousands of manuscripts according to a uniform plan, how
to weigh and measure the evidence. He it was, also, who added

to the dry dust of statistics that magical thing which is over and above scholarship, the instinct for truth of a great artist.

As early as 1889 he began to publish the *Paléographie Musicale* to prove by documentary evidence the unity of tradition in the manuscripts. "The editors" wrote Jules Combarieu at the time, "have had the capital idea (for which the world cannot be too grateful) of applying to the study of the Gregorian melodies the principles of the historic method as they are used by the Ecole des Chartres and Collège de France in their most arduous labors. In order to restore the Gregorian tradition in all its purity and to defend this tradition against scepticism, they have become grammarians, scholars and philologists, palaeographers and photographers . . . and in this way they have provided the open minded reader with an abundance of exact demonstrations which allow him to check their teaching down to the smallest detail. They have published in phototypical facsimiles about three hundred passages in manuscript proving that the unity of the liturgical chant was preserved for a thousand years from its origin. They have applied the principles of comparative grammar to the study of these documents; they have analysed them in an artistic and literary spirit so as to make their original beauty felt and appreciated, and so as to lay down the laws of their construction. Such a work marks an advance in French science while restoring to the Church in accurate form one of her most brilliant traditions; it enriches mediaeval investigation with a whole category of documents hitherto too much neglected by palaeographers, adds a new department to philosophy and opens to the general history of music a future which promises to be fertile in results."[1]

This was but the beginning of the studies which have since culminated in the official version of the Gregorian melodies as now restored to the Church by Pope Pius X. Many years of study, of comparison, of analysis were to follow before the melodies themselves at last stood revealed in their truth and their eternal beauty, with all the subtleties of their rhythm, and the secret principles which controlled the laws of Gregorian musical composition.

---

[1] J. Combarieu, **Etudes de philologie musicale.** Paris, Picard. 1897.

The rest is modern history. The incorrect and mutilated version of the melodies which was in general use had been given by the Holy See a thirty years' exclusive privilege. These thirty years were drawing to a close. Pope Leo XIII had already greatly encouraged the studies which were being carried on at Solesmes. His successor, Pope Pius X, carried through the reform, and after the publication of his *Motu Proprio* on Sacred Music, he appointed a Commision to prepare an official edition of the Gregorian melodies which was to be based on the most ancient and authentic documents and which thereafter was to be used by the universal Church. Into the hands of this commission Solesmes turned over the fruits of those long years of research.

This commission, like so many others, had the misfortune to be composed of human beings. Preconceptions and habits of long standing are responsible for the imperfections of our present *Kyriale*, *Graduale*, and *Antiphonale* from the standpoint of strict scholarship. Yet whatever their minor imperfections, these books in their ensemble stand as a revelation of the beauty of this art which is the voice of the Church herself, this voice which was silenced, or worse yet, deformed, for so many centuries, and which miraculously sounds once more with its eternal freshness in this our own day. This language, new to us, because so ancient, is the same in which the early Christians expressed their faith, their praise, their petitions, and their love.

To speak of Dom Mocquereau as a scholar only, would be to do him an injustice. His first work, necessarily, was in the field of research. The correct tradition once restored, his mind turned—not to the privileged few who might study as he had done himself—but to the little ones. These melodies were to be sung, not by experts but by inexperienced singers, by little children. How to prevent incorrect renderings, became his problem. These melodies which had been restored at the price of so much labor, would disappear once more unless the details of their rhythm could be so clearly indicated on the printed page that even the most ignorant would find it difficult to go astray. He undertook, then, the work of editor, a work for which his intimate knowledge of the manuscripts had fitted him, and the editions of the chants with the addition of the rhythmic signs of Solesmes are now in use in almost every center of serious study where Gregorian chant is really sung. The Pontifical College of Music led the way, the Roman houses of study followed, and even the myriads of school children in our own United States have found that with this help it is possible to restore congregational singing with a uniform rendering of the divine melodies of the Church.

In the *Nombre Musical Grégorien*, we see Dom Mocquereau the artist. Rarely has a musician tried to analyse what every great musician feels and makes others feel. Nowhere that I know of has the analysis of musical beauty been carried so far as in this sublime work where artist speaks to artist of those things which are almost beyond the power of words to express.

With this great accomplishment in so many lines it would seem as though Dom Mocquereau's life would have passed without a shadow. Indeed the search for truth and beauty would become, as it were, its own reward were it not for the shadow behind all such things. For the discovery of truth involves the destruction of error. Thus, Dom Mocquereau became a sign to be contradicted and remained so until nearly the end of his life. For a time he stood alone with every man's hand against him. He stood firm, kept his peace, and waited. Meanwhile he worked, strengthened his position, continued to study. "The opposition was of great service to me," he said; "it forced me to go to the root of things."

Today the storms of controversy have calmed down. Or if they stir up an occasional flutter here and there, it is with details that they are concerned. The fundamental principles are established and solidly so. The scholarship of the monks of Solesmes, the data to them available, are being used directly by the Church, for to their care has been confided the preparation of the musical books which are still to be published by the Church—the music of Matins, the Processionale, the Responsoriale, etc. The work of Solesmes is then forwarded to the Sacred Congregation of Rites which passes upon and approves the work before it is given officially to the Catholics of the world. Fortunately, Dom Mocquereau leaves behind him expert successors formed to his own image and likeness who will continue his traditions both in the singing and in the publications of Solesmes. He leaves devoted pupils in every country of the world, in universities, colleges, religious orders, seminaries, and even among little children. For at least in America, it is chiefly among these little ones that the Gregorian Chant is spreading. When Dom Mocquereau came to this country for the first time in 1920 to direct the Congress of Gregorian chant at St. Patrick's Cathedral in New York, he was amazed to hear the Mass, Vespers, and Compline sung each day of the triduum by no less than ten thousand little children. Dom Mocquereau has ever since then shown a special love for America because of those children, and he even co-operated in the writing of a text book for these young American singers. Again he came to America in 1922, this time to teach at the Pius X school of Liturgical Music.

To those who knew Dom Mosquereau only through his published works, through his reputation as a scholar and a genius, it was a genuine surprise to meet him in real life. Humble, gentle, as candid as a child, he had reached that wondrous simplicity of the saints which is as truly the mark of genius as it is of holiness. He held nothing back of the riches that were his. If he accepted a pupil at all, he gave him treasure of purest gold. Who could forget who had ever seen that great man outlining with a gesture of infinite eloquence and grace (that *chironomie* of his own invention) the melodies which he sang in a voice which quavered a little but remained true to the end of his life,—softly because he was old, and sweetly because he was holy?

To his pupils, Dom Mocquereau was accessible, simple, kind, but always frank. "You know nothing," he remarked on his first trip to America, expecting as a matter of course the answer which he himself would have given under like circumstances: "If I know nothing, then I will take the trouble to study, and will not stop short of a full grasp of the subject." *"Haussez-vous"* he wrote in a posthumous article which has just been published in the Revue Gregorienne, "Lift yourselves—your spirit, your heart and your taste to the full ideal which soars in every work of art, in its melody and its text." This alone satisfied Dom Mocquereau

for his pupils as for himself. Begin again, do better, arrive at last
at perfection, and when you get there, you will find there is still
something beyond, which you would never have found unless you
had attained that early idea of perfection. *"Haussez-vous."* It
sums up his influence and his life, and will remain with his pupils.
For *"Le sommet de l'art est atteint au moment même ou il est
oublié; la mélodie est imprégnée, trempée de prière, de supplica
tion de joie, de jubilation.*

'True scholarship, like true art, is akin to sanctity. The same
faculties of the soul come into play. I am not speaking of what
too often passes for scholarship or for art where vain contact
with statistics dries up the heart or mere technique fritters the
soul. But I speak of the process and motivation in a life completely given to the search for truth, where the slightest deviation
is intolerable, where no pains are too great, no details insignificant, where personal preconceptions must be set aside, where prejudice becomes betrayal, and compromise, a lie. Science and art,
taken in this sense, use the same facilities of the soul which function in the ascent toward God. Here art and science, in God and
for God, become a true form of sanctity if not its highest manifestation.

To place the name of Dom Mocquereau side by side with
that of Saint Gregory the Great, of Saint Ambrose, of Pius X,
would be to anticipate the judgment of history. Yet what did
Saint Gregory do for sacred music? He collected, codified, edited
and spread abroad the melodies which he had inherited from the
past. What did Pius X do? He ordered the restoration to the
faithful of their lost musical heritage. But who was it that gazed
into the past from a distance infinitely greater than that over
which Saint Gregory looked? Who was it that sought and found?
Dom Mocquereau followed the steps of St. Gregory, but it was
a *tour de force* indeed to collect, codify, and publish what no
longer existed by any oral tradition, which was hidden from the
world in writings which no one knew how to read, which was
separated from even the earliest writings by at least two centuries. This is what Dom Mocquereau did, by what might appear
a sort of musical alchemy, were we still poring over the pages of

the *Légende Dorée*. But no. He sought persistently, and he found. He recognized beauty under its disguise. Its face, distorted for centuries by its passion, contained nothing lovely, nothing desirable. He wiped it as with the veil of Veronica, and behold, that face was the face of beauty.

From a distance Dom Mocquereau recaptured that beauty. It was a distance of time and a distance of spirit. Ancient traditions of music had faded away to make room for arts founded on secular ideals, on secular rhythms. It was from this immense distance, exterior and interior, that Dom Mocquereau perceived afar that peculiar, characteristic loveliness which belongs to the prayer of the Church, and his name, side by side with that of Saint Gregory, will be held in benediction by those who believe that beauty need not be divorced from truth, but that in beauty will be found the true mirror of sanctity.

Dom Mocquereau lived, worked, and directed the vast activities he had set in motion until the age of 82. When the appointed time came near, he left the earth with a swift, silent arsis. Ill for a few days, but discreetly so as to cause no undue alarm, he literally fell asleep in the Lord quite early in the morning. The infirmarian went to his cell to prepare it and to bring him holy Communion. He knocked and received no answer; he entered and found the light burning and Dom Mocquereau as though sleeping. There was no sign of struggle or of pain. "He had finished his life like the close of a melody: lightly, softly." Thus wrote an eye witness. "He who had always taught us to lay down our voices in a final *ictus* which falls light as a snow-flake touching the earth,—his ictus alighted in heaven . . . Dom Mocquereau is the glory of Solesmes. For many people Solesmes *was* Dom Mocquereau. How many were bound to him by invisible threads! . . . He had the joy on earth, not of having invented beauty but of having recognized the beauty of the Church's chants, of having given back to them their true expression. An idea of genius developed, illumined, fathomed, exalted by an entire life!"

JUSTINE B. WARD

Dobb's Ferry, N. Y.

Liturgical Scholar Led in Restoration of the Gregorian Chant

Dom Andre Mocquereau died on the 18th of January, 1930, at the age of 82. He was a Benedictine Monk of the Congregation of France, and died at his monastery, St. Pierre de Solesmes, Sable-sur-Sarthe, which he had entered fifty-two years before as a novice. He worked until the last days of his life with the same lucidity and brilliance as when a young monk.

His principal work for the Church was embodied in the 14 volumes of the Paleographie Musicale, which, through tabulation and comparative study of the fundamental manuscripts of the Chant throughout the various centuries and countries of Europe from the ninth century on, led to the recapturing of the ancient traditional rhythm—now officially restored to the Church by Pius X. His two volumes, *Le Nombre Musical Gregorien*, of which the second volume has been published in 1927, are the finest and most authoritative study of the interpretation of the Chant.

He visited America twice; the first time, in 1920, to direct the Congress at St. Patrick's Cathedral, New York City. The second time to give a course in Gregorian Chant at the Summer Session of the Pius X School of Liturgical Music, in 1922.

He had passed his Jubilee as a monk two years ago, and his Jubilee as a priest on the 28th, December, 1929, with a telegram from the Holy Father Pope Pius XI of felicitations.

Dom Mocquereau, an eminent liturgical scholar, was credited with a large part in the world-wide restoration of Gregorian chant, which has been formally adopted by the Catholic Church and published in its official editions. He was the principal author of fourteen volumes of the Paleographie Musicale and the Nombre Musical Gregorien.

Dom Mocquereau was a Frenchman, born at La Tessonalle, near Cholet, France. He studied music at Paris and was only a boy when he played the 'cello in Dancla's chamber music concerts. In 1875 he joined the order of the Benedictines of Solesmes. He lived and worked at the ancient Abbey of Solesmes, founded in 1010, until the expulsion of the monks from France in 1901. Then he moved to the Isle of Wight, and returned to France in 1922.

(Continued on page 35)

The Gregorian Commission in Session at Appuldurcombe, (Isle of Wight, Eng. 1904)

(1) Dom Mocquereau; (2) Dom Pothier; (3) Rev. Angelo di Santi; (4) Mo. Giulio Bas

Soon after taking holy orders, he became interested in Gregorian music, to which he devoted the remainder of his life. In 1889 there appeared the first of his series of photographic reproductions of medieval manuscripts, with accompanying explanatory monographs, which is known as the Paleographie Musicale. In 1904 Pope Pius X decreed that all subsequent reprints of Gregorian music in the Editio Vaticana must conform to the versions of the ancient manuscripts so happily restored by those recent studies. Dom Mocquereau also wrote "L'Art Gregorian" and other works on his favorite subject.

The following is culled from an inspiring article, "The Response to the Call of Pope Pius X," by Blanche M. Kelley:

"The original abbey of Solesmes near Sablé, France, was founded early in the eleventh century, but was suppressed during the Revolution. The property then passed into private ownership, where it remained until 1833, when the great Dom Prosper Guéranger there restored the Benedictine Order, and eventually made it the mother-house of the French Congregation of which he was the founder. It has been four times dissolved by the French Government, the final expulsion having taken place under the Associations Law in 1903, when the monks went to the Isle of Wight where they have built a new abbey at Quarr, on what was formerly monastic property. Here is lived the ideal Benedictine life, with the liturgy as its centre, the *opus Dei* carried out in its perfection, and here is sustained that reputation for monastic erudition which had already been achieved by the community in its French home. Dom Mocquereau belongs to a line of savants which began with Dom Guéranger himself and includes such names as Dom, afterwards Cardinal, Pitra, Dom Pothier, Dom Cabrol, Dom Ferotin, Dom Cagin and Dom Delatte."

"Dom Pothier was one of two monks entrusted by Dom Guéranger with the task of collating the liturgical manuscripts of various countries and periods for the purpose of securing the correct Gregorian text. This task was later carried to its full perfection by Dom Mocquereau and a staff of monks under his direction. When Pope Pius X undertook the preparation of an official edition of the liturgical chant of the Church he based this edition upon the researches carried out by the Monks of Solesmes. Dom Mocquereau's contribution to Gregorian scholarship will live down the ages. Apart from his personal researches, he has edited the monumental work known as the Paleographie Musicale in which the true rhythm of the ancient manuscripts is illustrated by photographic reproductions of manuscripts from all the important European libraries and monasteries. The rhythmic principles which are brought out in this work are contrary to many of the rules which musicians of the last few centuries have held as axiomatic, but from whose shackles modern musicians are rapidly freeing themselves. Rhythm to Dom Mocquereau is the art of motion in accordance with the Platonic definition, or the art of beautiful movement described by Saint Augustine, and the underlying rules of rhythm have been developed by him in their most minute details with the genius of a great musician combined with the patient scholarship of one who will spare no trouble to get back to original sources. Moreover, an analytic temperament enabled him to explain with luminous clarity and simplicity in the Nombre Musical Gregorien the underlying principles of those truths which, as an artist, he sensed."

SOLESMES, ABBEY OF, or Abbaye Saint-Pierre, in the village of Solesmes (Sarthe), France, was founded in c.1000 by Geoffroy de Sablé as a priory of the Benedictines dependent on the abbey of La Couture. In the 12th century it was given a relic of the •crown of thorns, which is still an object of great veneration. The priory was destroyed during the Hundred Years' War by the English (1425) but was soon reconstructed. During the Renaissance the 11th-century church was rebuilt and adorned with magnificent statues, called "the saints of Solesmes." The monastery was placed in • commendation (1556–1773), and aggregated to the Benedictine Congregation of St. Maurus, or •Maurists (1664). During the French Revolution it was suppressed and put up for sale, and the monks dispersed (1791). Prosper •Guéranger, then a curate in Sablé, purchased the property (1833) and reestablished Benedictine life. Pope Gregory XVI raised it to the status of an abbey (1837), named Dom Guéranger as first abbot (1837–75), and made it head of the new Benedictine Congregation of France, known also as the

The Abbey of Saint-Pierre (Solesmes), France

Congregation of Saint-Pierre de Solesmes. Under Guéranger Solesmes became a famed center of religious renewal. The French government expelled the monks in 1880 and again from 1882 to 1896. Dom Paul Delatte, abbot (1890–1920) succeeding Dom Charles Couturier, regained possession of the abbey and began large-scale construction until the laws against religious (1901) sent the monks into exile to •Quarr Abbey on the Isle of Wight. Dom Germain Cozien, fourth abbot (1920–59) led the community back to Solesmes (1922). The monastery has gained world renown for its role in the •liturgical movement and the restoration of Gregorian chant (see SOLESMES, MUSIC OF). In addition to Guéranger it has produced such well-known scholars as •Cabrol. •Ferotin. •Leclercq. •Mocquereau. •Pitra. •Pothier. and •Quentin. Among the most notable publications of the monks have been editions of the writings of St. Gertrude. St. Mechtild, William of Saint-Thierry, St. John of the Cross, John of St. Thomas, Bérulle, and the English mystics. Current projects include the publication of the works of Pseudo-Dionysius the Areopagite, and papal documents (*Collection Les Enseignements Pontificaux*), and a series of phonographic records of Gregorian chants. In 1964 the Abbey of Solesmes had 90 monks.

Bibliography: Cottineau 2:3055–57. Kapsner Ben Bibl 2.5253–99 P. GUÉRANGER. *Essai historique sur l'Abbaye de Solesmes* (Le Mans 1846). H. QUENTIN, *Nouce histor-*

ique sur L'Abbaye de Solesmes (Tours 1924). Benedictines of Solesmes. *Le Monastère Saint-Pierre de Solesmes* (Solesmes 1955): *Les Saints de Solesmes* (Paris 1951). A. SAVATON, *Dom Paul Delatte, Abbe de Solesmes* (Paris 1954). J. HOURLIER, *Les Églises de Solesmes* (Paris 1951). P. SCHMITZ, LexThK³9:864.

[L. ROBERT]

SOLESMES, MUSIC OF

The musical reform of the abbey of •Solesmes in the 19th century was but the complement of the liturgical reform accomplished by Prosper •Guéranger, first abbot of Solesmes. Guéranger himself laid down the principles for a return to the traditional •Gregorian chant (in a state of decadence for several centuries) by formulating two rules (1) When the MSS of many churches are in agreement on the same reading, one may accept that reading as the authentic version. (2) In such a comparison one must put more faith in MSS written in staffless neums, because they contained the original version in all its purity. At the same time, Guéranger reformed the execution of Gregorian chant at Solesmes, even though he had only poor editions to work with. He abandoned the general practice of hammering out the chant and gave back to it a relaxed and natural flow, an accentuation and a rhythm that restored its beauty and its value as prayer. Canon Mathurin Gontier of Le Mans described this execution of the chant as an oratorical rhythm, which is essentially free (*Méthode raisonée de plain-chant*, Paris 1859).

First Scientific Attempts. Guéranger charged two of his monks. Paul Jausions (1834–70) and Joseph •Pothier (1835–1923), with the preparation of a new edition of the chant books. After copying and studying the old MSS, they produced a *Directorium chori* (1864) for use at Solesmes. This book used a notation without rhythmical value but one retaining the traditional grouping of the notes. In 1880, 5 years after the death of Guéranger, Pothier published *Les Mélodies grégoriennes d'après la tradition*, which gave the key to the neums, describing and explaining them with precision. The laws of oratorical rhythm were better defined and more solidly established, and the role and nature of the Latin accent brought to light. The book was highly praised at the Congress of Arezzo in 1882. In 1883 he published the *Liber gradualis*, which earned him the title of "restorer of the Gregorian melodies." The melodies of the Mass were here reconstructed according to the ancient MSS available to the editor. The *Antiphonale* for the Divine Office appeared in 1891 (see CHANT BOOKS, PRINTED EDITIONS OF)

The Paléographie Musicale. The Gradual of Pothier was bitterly attacked by those who held to the truncated and altered Ratisbon edition. In its defense Dom André •Mocquereau undertook the publication of some of the primary MS sources of Gregorian chant in the *Paléographie musicale* (1888). In the second and third volumes he traced a typical chant piece in more than 200 antiphonaries of different origins, dating from the 9th to the 17th century, to prove that the ancient melodies had actually been rediscovered and that there had been a universal tradition in the Church. Certain studies of Mocquereau (in PalMus) on the Latin tonic accent and the *cursus* in relation to the Gregorian melody awakened new interest in the rules of composition of Gregorian chant and revealed the grave mutilations in the editions in use in his time. All this research laid the groundwork for the reform urged by Pope St. Pius X in 1903 and 1904. Mocquereau also took part in the work of the Vatican commission for revising the Gregorian chant of the liturgical books. To this end he had his monks prepare comparative tables of each melody from about 30 MSS of varying origins in which the versions of each neum were written in columns. Although this research was not used for the first books of the Vatican edition, it was the basis for the books prepared by Solesmes monks from 1913 on. It was at this time that Mocquereau established the paleographical studio at Solesmes with its hundreds of photocopies of MSS.

Rhythmic Studies. By way of clarifying the rhythm of Gregorian chant, Mocquereau managed to establish a rhythmical synthesis, the principles of which he published in 1901 (PalMul 7) and later in a more didactic fashion in *Le Nombre musical grégorien* (2 v. 1908–27). He defined the rhythm no longer as oratorical (a term he considered too imprecise) but strictly musical, at the same time both free and precise. In 1903 he had produced the *Liber usualis* with special rhythmical signs; following that, he reproduced with like markings all the books of the Vatican edition. In 1911 he collaborated in founding the *Revue grégorienne* for spreading his rhythmic principles.

Later Research and Critical Editions. Dom Joseph Gajard (1885–   ) succeeded Mocquereau as director of the paleographical studio of Solesmes and of the *Paléographie musicale*. He edited the *Officium majoris hebdomadae* (1922) for the Vatican edition and all later books of the Vatican edition. In 1934 he published the *Antiphonale monasticum* and in 1949 the monastic *Agendis mortuorum*, bringing new research to bear on the melodic restoration (e.g., restoring certain recitations on "b" in the third and the fourth modes). He wrote several articles for the *Revue grégorienne* and in 1954 founded the *Études grégoriennes*, which was exclusively scientific in intent. In 1957, under his direction, Solesmes began the large and ambitious scientific project of publishing a truly critical edition of the Roman Gradual. Further studies in musical paleography by Dom E. Cardine, professor at the Pontifical Institute of Sacred Music at Rome, have aided in making the principles of Gregorian rhythm more explicit and have sought scientific evidence for free rhythm against the ever-increasing popularity of mensuralist theories (see "Is Gregorian Chant Measured Music?" Solesmes 1964). Solesmes has taken an active part in controversies on old Roman chant and its relation to Gregorian chant.

Bibliography: N. ROUSSEAU, *L'École grégorienne de Solesmes, 1833–1910* (Rome 1910). P. COMBE, "Bibliographie de Dom André Mocquereau," *Études grégoriennes* 2 (1957) 189–203; "La Réforme du chant et des livres de chant grégorien à l'abbaye de Solesmes, 1833–1883," *ibid.* 6 (1963) 185–234. E. MONETA-CAGLIO, "Dom André Mocquereau e la restaurazione del canto gregoriano," *Musica Sacra* 84–87 (Milan 1960–63), *passim.* W. LIPPHARDT, MusGG 12:835–839.

&P. COMBE]

BIOGRAPHICAL SKETCHES

Dom Prosper Guéranger. Born in Sablé, April 4, 1805. Restorer of Benedictine life in the ancient Priory of Solesmes in 1833. Died at Solesmes, January 30, 1875. The restoration of Gregorian Chant which was achieved after his death is a consequence of the liturgical restoration of which he was the prime mover. Moreover, he is the one who set down the principles of the Gregorian restoration: return to the pure neums of the manuscripts, confrontation with the manuscripts of the different Churches. It was he who assigned the first workers of this reformation, Dom Paul Jausions and Dom Joseph Potier, whose first labors he followed closely. It was he surely who reformed the chant at Solesmes, by restoring its rhythm which had become totally neglected.

Dom Joseph Gajard. Born in Sonzay (Indre and Loire), June 25, 1885, professed at Solesmes, August 15, 1911. He became Dom Mocquereau's assistant in 1911. He thus had a part in the publication of the 2° volume of the *Nombre Musical Grégorien* and some Vatican books after 1913. In 1946, he was named Director of the *Revue Grégorien* (founded in 1911), in which he published many practical articles, and in 1954, of the *Études Grégoriennes* of a more scientific content, founded the same year. At last, he directed the *Paléographic Musicale*, founded by Dom Mocquereau and conducted all the recordings of Gregorian Chant until his death on April 25, 1972, Voix de son Maitre in 1930 (Victor), and Decca from 1951 on.

MOCQUEREAU, ANDRÉ, founder of the Solesmes system of Gregorian chant: b. Tessoualle (Maine-et-Loire). France, June 6, 1849; d. Solesmes, Jan. 18, 1930. His musical education was nurtured in an atmosphere of strict classical formalism and directed and developed by Charles Dancla, with whom he studied cello at the Paris Conservatory. He entered the Benedictine Abbey of Solesmes (1875), was professed April 9, 1877, and ordained Dec. 28, 1879. As director of the paleographic scriptorium and choir master, he soon determined the community's commitment to the restoration of the pristine purity of chant. Working closely with Dom Pothier for 13 years, but later in opposition to Pothier's theory of "free oratorio rhythm," Mocquereau developed the Solesmes system, basing it on the theory of "free musical rhythm." This system, first proposed in PalMus v.7, was expansively developed in the *Le nombre musical* (1908–27). Under the title of *Paléographie musicale grégorienne,* Mocquereau launched the publication of over 15 volumes of photographic reproductions of medieval MSS with important historical studies. These laid the foundation for the reform of chant prescribed in the 1903 motu proprio of Pius X. Mocquereau's system is incorporated in the modern publications of the Solesmes editions by the addition of certain rhythmic signs. He defended his system by many scholarly publications, often controversial, in the

André Mocquereau

Tribune de Saint Gervais, the *Rassegna gregoriana,* and the *Revue grégorienne.*

Bibliography: P. COMBE, *Études grégoriennes* 2 (1957) 189, for a list of Mocquereau's writings; "Les Préliminaires de la réforme grégorienne de S. Pie X," in *Études grégoriennes* 7 (in preparation). M. BLANC *L'Enseignement musical de Solesmes et la prière chrétienne* (Paris 1953).

PIUS X SCHOOL OF LITURGICAL MUSIC
COLLEGE OF THE SACRED HEART
Its Growth and Development
+ + +

Threefold recognition has come recently to the Pius X School of Liturgical Music, College of the Sacred Heart, New York City,—on two occasions through the medium of the Girls' Choir, and in the third instance to the foundress of the School herself from the source most appreciated by the Catholic world. Mrs. Justine Ward, who was in Rome during the first two weeks of March, was received in private audience by His Holiness, Pope Pius XI. The Holy Father, who is keenly alive to all that pertains to the education and welfare of his children, is deeply interested in the unique system of musical instruction devised by Mrs. Ward some years ago and now nation-wide in its results. Looking forward a few years he sees the children of today as the parents, the guardians, the teachers of tomorrow, and he realizes in a particular way what their knowledge of music and their ability to interpret it will mean in the services of the Church. The restoration of Gregorian Chant, as the fitting expression of the divine praises is Mrs. Ward's life work, and her truly inspired method of teaching music is a means to that end. The

Holy Father blessed Mrs. Ward, her work and all who cooperate with her. A cablegram from Mrs. Ward to Mother Stevens, Director of the Pius X School, conveyed words of encouragement from Pope Pius XI, with his heartfelt blessing upon the work that is being done in America in the interests of liturgical music.

Endorsement by foremost musicians is no small meed of praise for the Justine Ward Method. Eminent artists who have heard children trained according to the Justine Ward Method sing at sight, and have seen them write original melodies—such peers in the musical world as Sembrich, Alma Gluck, Zimbalist, Bodansky, Dirk Foch, Alexander Lambert, Nicola Montani—give unqualified praise to this method, and are unanimous in stating that it has no equal in the field of musical instruction. Among those who may criticize technically and artistically, the dictum of the great Sembrich must be recognized as having the dual value of that of artist and teacher. Her visit on February 6th, 1924, to the Annunciation Girls' School, 130th Street and Convent Avenue, New York City, was a revelation to her of the musical accomplishments of children ranging from six to fifteen years of age. A staff of expert teachers under the supervision of Mother G. Stevens has been training these classes for six years. Obviously, some have been studying for several years, while there is the other extreme of little ones whose musical education began last September when they entered school for the first time. Madame Sembrich confessed she was amazed by their purity of tone, perfect pitch, admirable ear-training and creative work. In the third and fourth grades she was further convinced of the value of the Ward Method training by the singing of difficult intervals, complicated rhythms, and the original melody writing of seven and eight year old children. But the complete conquest was made by the girls of the eighth grade and high school classes. These children are proficient in the comprehension and interpretation of music, they have entered into the intricacies of counterpoint and harmony; no interval is beyond them, no chromatics too difficult for them to sing in chironomy and rhythmic expression they give evidence of the excellent training they have had in musical rhythmic principles. Madame Sembrich commented with enthusiasm on their impeccable intonation, their rendering of Gregorian Chant and of modern music, their delightful singing at sight of a three-part chorus. She said after hearing intervals sung, "I am amazed at what these children have accomplished through their remarkably thorough

knowledge of counterpoint and harmony. The admirable training of the ear as developed by this method cannot be too greatly emphasized. If only all students and artists could have this essential foundation to rely on, in whatever branch of music they undertake, what time and labor it would save students as well as their teachers, who strive to teach them to learn to hear, in order that they may become musical."

At the request of Mother Stevens, Madame Sembrich sang a fragment of an operatic aria from which the girls were to develop an original composition. A beautiful two-part melody was produced from this theme and written on the blackboard by two children as quickly as they could have written English,—one writing the development of the theme, and the other adding a second part.

The Justine Ward Method has won a valuable ally in this renowned musician famous on three continents as the foremost exponent of vocal art, and one of the world's greatest artists. Madame Sembrich pronounces the Method a phenomenal means of securing intelligent and artistic response in music. In turn the children were buoyant with the pleasure of singing for so distinguished a personage.

A third triumph was won for this remarkable and rapidly growing movement when the Girls' Choir of the Pius X School of Liturgical Music contributed to the programme arranged by the Calvert Associates on March 9th, 1924, in celebration of the anniversary of the founding of Maryland. The Century Theatre, transformed at present into the interior of a Gothic cathedral for the presentation of "The Miracle," was an ideal setting for the purpose. Appearing also on the programme were the names of Madame Lucrezia Bori of the Metropolitan Opera Company, Monsieur Dezso D'Astalffy, organist of the Hungarian Royal Academy, and the new Paulist Choir under the direction of Mr. Nicola Montani. The singing of the children from the Pius X School was a singular demonstration of the beauty of Gregorian Chant, the traditional music of the Catholic Church. The choir was conducted by Mr. Theodore Heinroth with Mr. Achille Bragers at the organ, supervisors from the Pius X School. The children sang a hymn to Our Lady, a *Kyrie, Sanctus,* and the sublimely beautiful *Ave Maria* of Cesar Franck with remarkable sweetness of tone, purity of diction, and with an ease and assurance that are rarely found in older organizations. No doubt remained with those who heard the Girls' Choir but that Gregorian Chant sung by trained voices is truly the reflection of the Divine harmony that exists in the natural order created by a beneficient Providence.

MARY MANLY, B.A.

The People's Plainsong

Istituto di San Gregorio

(Reprinted from THE LONDON TIMES, February 9, 1929)

When Pius X. issued his famous *Motu Proprio* on Church Music in 1903, many people in Italy must have read it with misgiving for it meant the end of Italian operatic influence over sacred music. Pius X. in taste, as in many other things, was far ahead of his time. His strict regulations were very difficult for Italians to obey, partly because the public had grown unaccustomed to any but the operatic type of music, and also because, owing to the division of Church and State, the revenues of the Church were so low as to make the upkeep of a choir very often an impossible luxury. Various attempts at reform were made especially by the Società di Santa Cecilia, the Pontifical school in Rome, and in several northern dioceses, but until quite recently little has been done to help the people of the country parishes. For them music consisted in the *stornelli* they sang in the fields, the snatches of opera that every Italian knows, and the few hymns and litanies and perhaps a Mass that they had learnt by ear as children and sung ever since.

A new school of liturgical music has now been founded, the Istituto di San Gregorio, which is as much needed as any of the famous singing schools of Italy. The name recalls the first of their number, that established by Gregory the Great, to which Europe owed her medieval musical culture. The new institute has a limited field, but it can do a great work, for its mission is to give back to the people the liturgical art they have lost, and to make it part of their lives. It has already been wonderfully successful in Serravalle in Casentino, which hitherto has been its headquarters.

Seravalle is a scattered village of about a thousand people, and a few years ago the old church was falling down. It was imperative to build a new one and Signor Egisto Fabbri, an artist of great generosity and practical idealism, offered to design and carry out the new building. Thus on a spur of hill between La Verna and Camaldoli arose the fine church of the Spirito Santo. That, however, was not enough for Signor Fabbri. He had once heard the choir of the Pius

X. Institute in New York, and determined that a choir for the Serravalle church should be trained on the same system. In 1925 he brought over his first teacher, Miss Mary McElligott, who has not only proved herself to be a splendid mistress, but to have the courage and spirit of a missionary. The people of Serravalle are poor mountaineers, and they come in to the lessons after their day's work, tired and often having walked a long distance in any weather. They come because it gives them real pleasure, not because they are paid to do so. Three years ago they knew nothing of music. They now can read at sight and sing extremely well anything from the *Liber Usualis* and some polyphonic pieces.

They have been taught by the Justine Ward Method, which is used at the Pius X. Institute and in many schools in England and Holland. Mrs. Ward was one of the founders of the Pius X. Institute, and studied for several years at the famous Benedictine Abbey of Solesmes under Dom Mocquereau. It was at Solesmes that Dom Gueranger in the last century began the far-reaching liturgical revival which has led on to this new impulse in all matters relating to sacred music. Mrs. Ward has brought the learning and art of Dom Mocquereau and his fellow monks within the reach of the most ignorant, and her method, which is intended primarily for children, is a work of genius.

The children learn unconsciously both theoretically and practically. First of all they are made to sing on the syllable "Nu," pronounced as in Italian, which ensures the soft, light tone indispensable for plainsong. Then come the intervals, scales, modes, modulations, musical dictation, and improvisation, in fact a complete system of *solfège*, and the children are amazingly quick to catch any idea and quite unselfconscious. Their power of improvisation is especially remarkable. Someone of the audiences is asked to give them a theme, and they develop it with the greatest ease in one or more parts.

Mrs. Ward had a particularly happy idea for the teaching of rhythm. Although the method can be used in teaching any kind of music, it is planned especially with regard to Gregorian Chant, and from the beginning the children are given the notion of the *arsis* and *thesis* on which depends the subtle and beautiful plainsong rhythm. First of all the rise and fall of any given melody is drawn on the blackboard; then, as the children sing, they rise on their toes, making graceful swaying movements with their hands and arms. Thus the whole body responds to the rhythm; the children are made to feel the inevitable succession of *arsis* and *thesis*, to feel each delicate phrase, each light touch of an *ictus*. Nothing in plainsong must be heavy lest it should lose the soaring quality which is so beautiful; moreover, its interpretation depends above all upon right understanding. This understanding is what one feels strongly in the singing of the Serravalle people. The educational and cultural value of such a training is obvious and it touches people who so far have been beyond the reach of the regular schools of music.

The Serravalle singers have now received an invitation to Rome this spring to sing a Mass that the Pope will celebrate, and they have lately given some successful demonstrations in Florence. Signor Ernesto Consolo and other Italian musicians are most appreciative, and are using their influence in favor of the Justine Ward method being adopted in the public schools. A branch of the Istituto di San Gregorio will shortly be opened in Florence under the directions of Miss McElligott and two excellent assistants who have joined her from New York. Here Italian teachers will be trained and a summer course will also be held for the same object at Serravalle. The first steep step has been taken; now the moment has come for the work to spread, and it is to be hoped that soon many thousands of Italian children will learn to know and love this great Italian art.

The recall to plainsong is not an attempt to enforce the use of medieval melodies, for Gregorian music is one of those perfect arts which never age. Its restoration to its rightful place in the service of the Church brings a new element of beauty into the lives of many people and this is what the Istituto di San Gregorio is here to do.

Plain Chant Award Made at Capital

As the result of a competition held among the students of chant in the Schola Cantorum of the Catholic University of America here, a priest and ten seminarians, representing seven dioceses and a religious order, have been selected to go to Solesmes, France, to study under Dom Andre Mocquereau, the world famous teacher of liturgical music.

Those selected for this trip are the Rev. John P. Kelly, of the Diocese of Scranton; Charles Bermingham, of the Diocese of Brooklyn; Thomas Dennehy, of the Diocese of Hartford; Vincent Kavanagh, of the Diocese of Helena; Ralph Kelley, of the Diocese of Hartford; Joseph McAllister, of the Archdiocese of Baltimore; James McAndrews, of the Diocese of Scranton; Brother Joseph Diers, S. D. S.; William Morris, of the Archdiocese of New York; Leo Schumacker, of the Diocese of Sioux City, and Joseph White, of the Archdiocese of Baltimore.

Before sailing for France, on August 3d, these winners and the Rev. Michael Larkin, S. M., of the Marist Seminary, Washington, D. C., another student of chant, will take a summer course at the Pius X School of Liturgical Music in New York.

Justine Bayard Ward, *Doctor of Humane Letters*

. . . Annhurst is proud today to honor a most gracious lady, an outstanding artist "a rare treasure . . . one clothed with strength and dignity" (Prov. 31) Justine Bayard Ward who has been graciously and meaningfully called "the valiant lady of the Chant". She was born in 1879 in New Jersey. She belongs to a distinguished family, renowned as lovers of music, and Justine herself became an accomplished musician at an early age. In 1904 she was converted to Catholicism and shortly thereafter, stirred by the appeal of Pius X for better music in the Church, she decided to make the great Pope's "Motu Proprio" the inspiration of her life. In order to further the musical training of the children of our Catholic schools, she devised a method which became known as the Ward Method, first taught in America and now taught in many European countries—particularly, France, Holland, England, Belgium as well as in Australia and the Far East. Her Gregorian technique, acquired at Solesmes in France where she remained for a period of ten years, made it possible for her to have a profound influence in matters pertaining to the musical education of Catholic children and their active participation in the sung liturgy. Thus, by carrying out the wishes of a pope now a saint, she has brought the spiritual and esthetic glory of music into the lives of many. Accordingly, in just recognition of her devoted services, we at Annhurst gladly proclaim Justine Bayard Ward fully entitled to our highest academic reward.

Citation accompanying the conferral of a doctoral degree *honoris causa* on Justine Ward, May 15, 1966, at the convocation celebrating the 25th Anniversary of the founding of Annhurst College, Connecticut. The degree was presented *in absentia*. One month later, on June 16, a committee from the college made a formal presentation of the degree to Mrs. Ward in her Washington home, "Interlude".

DR. JUSTINE WARD

WARD METHOD OF MUSIC
888-17TH STREET, N.W.
WASHINGTON, D. C. 20006

TELEPHONE 337-2622

To the Ward Method Teachers

My dear Colleagues:

Because of my profound affection for France, the dissolution, decided by the Dom Mocquereau Foundation, of the Institute that bears my name, was sad and painful.

But it was inevitable. The Ward Institute had deviated from its purpose.

It must be known that it depended on an American Foundation whose center of operations it occupied at 80 Boulevard Pasteur and which paid the salaries of the teachers as well as the expenses associated with class inspections. The functioning of the Ward Institute was the responsibility of the Dom Mocquereau Foundation. As a result, the Ward Institute should function according to the fiscal laws of the United States in that which pertained to commercial activities. Such activities were forbidden.

Contrary to these laws, the Director of the Ward Institute organized a business on the very property of the Foundation, thus placing in danger the fiscal relations of the Foundation with the Treasury Department of America. In spite of warnings which she received, she obstinately continued these illegitimate activities. She had to be divested of her responsibilities.

It was not the intention of the Foundation to dissolve the Ward Institute but simply to place it under a disinterested and noncommercial directorship, but this was impossible because of the legal conditions which managed this institute. In order to change the personnel it was necessary to dissolve the Institute.

After the dissolution, the Director and her assistant pretended that they had been treated brutally by my representative. This is not true. They were treated with courtesy and great concern; paid almost a quarter above what was their due (calculated according to the French code). Use of the Foundation's property was forbidden to them because of the illegal usage they had made of it.

The Ward Institute — International Center of the Ward Method — is today in Washington, D.C. at 888 - 17th Street, N.W. It is there that I hope to continue our professional relations and to receive every request for financial aid according to need.

Please accept, my dear Confrères, the expression of my sincere and devoted good wishes.

Justine B. Ward.

HISTORICAL ACCOUNT OF THE WARD METHOD

1910   The Department of Education of The Catholic University of America, Washington, D.C., commissions Mrs. Justine Ward to compose a music pedagogy for the Catholic schools of the United States.

1913   The first book for six-year olds published. Teacher-training courses given at Sisters College of CUA.

1916   From this time on, the growing number of students cannot be accommodated in Washington. Thus the Pius Xth School is founded in New York.

1920   At a three-day International Congress of Gregorian Chant, St. Patrick's Cathedral, New York, is filled to overflowing with children trained in the Ward Method, singing Gregorian Chant. The children sing the Ordinary of the Mass each day under the direction of Dom André Mocquereau.

Some Features of the Method

In the beginning, Mrs. Ward made use of number notation according to the well known systems of French authors Galin, Pais, Chevé. This notation was well adapted to the children of six years of age whom she wished to win over to the love of music. But Mrs. Ward departed radically from these authors by making an ingenious transition from numbers to staff by using the ancient C clef to indicate the place of DOH (Ut). She proposed a complete method for placing and developing the child's voice, spanning even the time of voice-change. She trained the ear by logical exercises, taught an understanding and appreciation of rhythm through captivating gestures, as well as designing melodic relationships by gestures. Original pedagogical discoveries abounded rendering music as a game for children, at the same time preserving its artistic value. The Ward Method enjoyed a great success in the country of its origin: its principal function was the training of teachers. Mrs. Ward devoted herself to this task in Washington and New York.

1921   Mrs. Ward travels abroad, first to Quarr Abbey on the Isle of Wight, to study Gregorian Chant under Dom Mocquereau.

1923   Then to the Abbey of Solesmes, France.

The Ward Method in Europe

1927   Holland is the first country to use the Ward Method. The teachers, having taken the courses at the Pius Xth School, begin to use it in their schools. Dr. Joseph Lennards, Roermond, is the leader of this movement in Holland.

1928   The Ward Institute of Roermond is founded by the St. Gregory Society, after the successful demonstrations in Utrecht made by a class of young students from New York under Mrs. Ward's direction. (See photo p. 125.)

1925   Ward Method teaching begins in Italy. (Cf. Appendix No. 71.)

1925   Justine Ward decorated by the Pope with the Crux *Pro-Ecclesia et Pontifice*. Presentation made in Pius Tenth Hall by Abbot Paolo Ferretti, O.S.B.

1926   The Pontifical Institute of Sacred Music honors Mrs. Ward with a Music Doctorate.

1930   A whole village—Serevalle d'Arezzo—sings in the presence of His Holiness, Pius XIth and Mrs. Montessori. Dr. Montessori promises a collaboration between herself and Mrs. Ward but dies before the plan can be realized. Groups of children also sing before Mussolini.

1936   France becomes the third foreign country to use the Ward Method. Mrs. Ward, with the help of Joseph Lennards of Holland, gives summer courses in Sablé-sur-Sarthe for some religious orders. These courses continue every year until the start of the war. This tragedy puts a temporary end to every educational and musical effort.

Period of Reconstruction

1949   At the close of the War, Mister Auguste Le Guennant, Director of the Gregorian Institute of Paris, indicates an interest to create a Ward Department in the curriculum of the Gregorian Institute. He invites Joseph Lennards to give a course in Paris. Among his students in the course he chooses Miss Odette Hertz to make a short trip to the United States to come to know Mrs. Ward and to consider the opening of the Ward Department of the Gregorian Institute. (This Institute was aided generously by Mrs. Ward and by the Dom Mocquereau Foundation because of the common ideal they shared.) Miss Hertz also goes to St. Louis to observe the Method in the classrooms. She stays for a short period in Washington with Mrs. Ward who instructs her further in the basic musical and pedagogical principles of the Ward Method.

1950   The Ward Method enjoys success in the French schools. Students abound and this is why Miss Hertz feels the desire for greater independence of action. For this purpose she founds the Ward Institute which inherits the activities begun by the Gregorian Institute.

A word must be said here about the Dom Mocquereau Foundation since this American foundation was the financial support of the Ward Institute and also to a lesser degree, the Gregorian Institute.

The Dom Mocquereau Foundation was created to perpetuate the principles of the Master and to make these come to life especially among school children and seminarians, whether in the United States or abroad. This foundation was tax-exempt as long as its subventions were effective in realizing its educational and charitable end and in no way engaging in supporting business ventures.

1957   Ward Institute outgrows its rather limited quarters in the Gregorian Institute and moves to new headquarters at 80 Boulevard Pasteur in an apartment belonging to the Dom Mocquereau Foundation of America.

Over the next ten years the Ward Method enjoys phenomenal success in France with courses offered in Switzerland. Pilgrimages of thousands of school children are organized to sing Gregorian Chants at Lourdes, Lisieux, Mont St. Michel, Sacré Coeur, etc.

1967   All activities of the Ward Institute of Paris cease because of the involvement of the director in publishing and selling teaching materials for a profit in the headquarters of the Institute at 80 Boulevard Pasteur, a private business venture strictly forbidden by the franchise given to the Dom Mocquereau Foundation by the United States Government. (Cf. Appendix No. 73.)

1969   The International Center of the Ward Method set up in Washington, D.C., at 888 - 17th Street, N.W. The teaching of the Method is offered at The Catholic University of America. Newly established Ward Centers in England, Ireland, Portugal, and Switzerland, indicate interest in receiving accreditation for courses given in the Ward Method.

1975   Mrs. Justine Ward dies in her home "Interlude", in Washington, D.C., at the age of 96.

Center for Ward Method Studies established at The Catholic University School of Music, Washington, D.C.

1986   Ward Centers continue to be active also in Bulle, Switzerland; Le Mans, France; Lisbon, Portugal; and Helmond, Holland.

APPENDIX III - INDEX OF NAMES
Pages 1–135 inclusive